PIETIST AND WESLEYAN STUDIES
Editors: David Bundy and J. Steven O'Malley

This monograph series will publish volumes in two areas of scholarly research: Pietism and Methodism (broadly understood). The focus will be Pietism, its history and development, and the influence of this socioreligous tradition in modern culture, especially within the Wesleyan religous traditions.

Consideration will be given to scholarly works on classical and neo-Pietism, on English and American Methodism, as well as on the social and ecclesiastical institutions shaped by Pietism (e.g., Evangelicals, United Brethren, and the traditions and the Pietist traditions among the Lutherans, Reformed, and Anabaptists). Works focusing on leaders within the Pietist and Wesleyan traditions will be included in the series, as well as occasional translations and/or editions of Pietist texts. It is anticipated that the monographs will emphasize theological developments, but with close attention to the interaction of Pietism with other cultural forces and to the sociocultural identity of the Pietist and Wesleyan movements.

1. Gregory S. Clapper, *John Wesley on Religous Affections.* 1989.
2. Peter Erb, *Gottfried Arnold.* 1989.
3. Henry Knight III, *The Presence of God in the Christian Life: John Wesley and the Means of Grace.* 1992.
4. Frank D. Macchia, *Spirituality and Social Liberation: The Message of the Blumhardts in the Light of Wuerttemburg Pietism.* 1993.
5. Richard B. Steele, *"Gracious Affection" and "True Virtue" according to Jonathan Edwards and John Wesley.* 1994.
6. Stephen L. Longnecker, *Piety and Tolerance: Pennsylvania German Religion, 1700-1850.* 1994.
7. J. Steven O'Malley, *Early German-American Evangelicalism: Pietist Sources on Discipleship and Sanctification.* 1995.
8. R. David Rightmire, *Salvationist Samurai: Gunpei Yamamuro and the Rise of the Salvation Army in Japan.* 1997.
9. Simon Ross Valentine, *John Bennet and the Origins of Methodism and the Evangelical Revival in England.* 1997.
10. Tore Meistad, *Martin Luther and John Wesley on the Sermon on the Mount.* 1999.
11. Robert C. Monk, *John Wesley: His Puritan Heritage. 2nd edition* 1999.

John Wesley

His Puritan Heritage

2nd edition

Robert C. Monk

Pietist and Wesleyan Studies, No. 11

The Scarecrow Press, Inc.
Lanham, Maryland, and London
1999

SCARECROW PRESS, INC.

Published in the United States of America
by Scarecrow Press, Inc.
4720 Boston Way
Lanham, Maryland 20706

4 Pleydell Gardens, Folkstone
Kent CT20 2DN, England

British Library Cataloguing in Publication Information Available

Library of Congress-in-Publication Data

Monk, Robert C.
John Wesley : his Puritan heritage / Robert C. Monk. — 2nd ed.
p. cm. — (Pietist and Wesleyan studies : 11)
Includes bibliographical references and index.
ISBN 0-8108-3637-8 (alk. paper)
1. Wesley, John, 1703-1791. 2. Puritans—Influence. 3. Methodist Church—Doctrines—History I. Title. II. Series: Pietist and Wesleyan Studies : no. 11.
BX8495.W5M6 1999
287'.092—dc21 99-13626
CIP

∞™ The paper used in this publication meets the minimum requirements of American National Standard for Information Sciences—Permanence of Paper for Printed Library Materials, ANSI/NISO Z39.48—1992.
Manufactured in the United States of America.

In Memory of
Olin and Mary Monk
Exemplary Methodists

Contents

Editor's Foreword

Three decades have passed since a seminal study appeared exploring the roots of John Wesley's theology. That study helped to ignite an explosion of interest in the Wesleys that continues to the present day. It is now our privilege to present this work to the public in a revised form that takes into consideration advances in scholarship that have occurred in the intervening years. Robert Monk's study of John Wesley's Puritan heritage remains the preeminent work that deals with this significant facet of Wesley's theological lineage. While retaining the important research that had appeared in the first edition, this revised edition also includes an expanded treatment of Wesley's use of key Puritan thinkers, such as Richard Baxter and John Goodwin, as well as a more intensive analysis of the ways in which Wesley's ministry to the poor displayed continuities with his Puritan heritage.

A renewed awareness of this legacy may also serve to provide balance to the extensive attention that has been given in recent years to patristic influences upon John Wesley. In view of the important connections between English Puritan and Continental (Dutch and Rhineland German) Reformed thought, Monk's work should also help us in probing the Continental influences upon Wesley's thought—a feature that advances a basic purpose of this series, which is to facilitate conversation between Pietist and Wesleyan studies.

J. Steven O'Malley, Co-Editor
The Pietist and Wesleyan Studies Series

Acknowledgments

When this study was first published in the mid-1960s, American Methodist scholars had only begun to rediscover the breadth and depth of John and Charles Wesley's unique contributions to Christian theology and the life of the church. English Methodist scholarship led us into broader study, but *The Bicentennial Edition of John Wesley's Works*, the creation of the Charles Wesley Society, and the Wesley Studies Group of the American Academy of Religion were only fond dreams in the minds of a few. Perhaps no one anticipated the explosion of interest in the Wesleys or the plethora of studies, including some one hundred dissertations, that would emerge in the intervening decades.

Similarly, I could not have anticipated that this study would be useful to as many as it seems to have been, a phenomenon for which I am immensely grateful. When I was encouraged by Rex Matthews and Richard Heitzenrater to renew the study through a second edition of the work, I also did not understand the challenge involved. I have found both daunting and exhilarating the task of reviewing, and attempting to incorporate, information and insights published in the intervening decades. Certainly, no attempt has been made here to be inclusive of this continually expanding Wesley scholarship, but I hope that my debt to those who have augmented our knowledge through these years is evident in this new edition of the work.

The original research published in the first edition remains the foundation of the study. Greater attention has been given in this edition to the considerable dependence of John Wesley on the insights and work of Richard Baxter and John Goodwin. Significant additions include expanded treatment of the Puritans' and Wesley's teachings and experiments as they applied the gospel insights to the world around them—particularly their treatment of, and involvement with, the poor.

No acknowledgment could recognize and thank all who contributed to this study, but neither should the study be republished without mention of those who made the work possible. As noted in the first edition, Professor Horton Davies guided my original work and taught me the joy of research, whereas Professor Gordon Harland first whetted my interest in Wesley's relationship to the Puritans. My debt to Professor Albert Outler as teacher, mentor, helpful critic and friend through most of my academic career must also be noted.

The services of Rex Matthews and Richard Heitzenrater in bringing this edition to publication have already been mentioned. My faculty colleagues Walter Hofheinz, Joseph Stamey, and Doris Miller patiently suggested many clarifications and improvements of the manuscript. Richard Heitzenrater and Mrs. Pat Shackelford helped bring the original manuscript into digital form. Library staff members of Princeton University, Perkins School of Theology, the Methodist Library at Drew University, Dr. Williams' Library in London, and John Ryland's Library of the University of Manchester, all contributed most helpfully to the research.

My measureless debt to my wife, Carolyn, for sustaining me through her care, encouragement, and assistance cannot be calculated but is again gratefully acknowledged.

Robert C. Monk
McMurry University
May 1998

1

John Wesley and the Puritan Ethos

The resemblance between John Wesley's teachings and practices and those characteristic of the seventeenth-century English Puritans has been recognized since Wesley's own ministry. Among Wesley's contemporaries Bishop Warburton identified the "true character of Methodism" with the "old Precisians, Puritans, and Independents." Samuel Johnson and Horace Walpole similarly suggested such identification.[1] Accusations that eighteenth-century Methodism was another form of Nonconformity were often heard during Wesley's ministry. Late in his life, after he had become comfortable with the term "Methodist," an admirer demonstrated that, though Wesley presumed the name had not been used before his own day, it had in fact been applied to certain of the seventeenth-century Nonconformists.[2] Clearly, in the eyes of many of his contemporaries, Wesley revived the spirit and practice of Puritanism. Wesley ordinarily turned aside such comments as irrelevant, for they were often a means of casting aspersions on Methodism, or, as in the case of Bishop Warburton, they were irrelevant to the issue Wesley was pursuing or commenting upon.[3]

Wesley's unwillingness to accept inappropriate identification should not, however, blind us to his recognition and use of Puritan insight, practice, and instruction where it might supplement and clarify his own teachings and patterns. Wesley was engaged in his public ministry before he fully appreciated what resources Puritan teachings and writings offered, particularly as these sources explained the Christian life. Having identified instructive Puritan treatises and teachers, Wesley did not hesitate to appropriate what was useful to his own movement. Such selection from Puritanism was, of course, only one example of Wesley's often recognized theological and practical eclecticism. From widely diverse religious traditions, Wesley borrowed whatever treatises, organizational patterns, worship aids, or instructions concerning daily living that might contribute to Methodist instruction. Such borrowing was usually done without regard to the theological or denominational labels these materials might bear. Wesley tempered this openness to ideas and material from any source by his continual refinement and modification of all material he selected. By the time these items were in Methodist hands, they reflected Wesley's distinctive theological understandings, emphases, and practical daily instructions. As we shall see, this pattern of modifying material appropriated from others certainly adds to the complexity of any examination of Wesley's distinctive theology and practical instructions.

Early nineteenth-century studies of Wesley and Methodism concentrated on biography, refinement of doctrinal standards, and emphasis on Methodist rules of personal and social conduct. By the latter part of the century, Wesley studies shifted toward a wider consideration of Wesley's distinctive theology and practices. Among many specialized studies in the current century, scholars have given particular attention to the sources from which Wesley drew his theology and practice—investigating Wesley's use of materials from Roman Catholic, Moravian, Anglican, patristic, Puritan, and Lutheran sources. Studies of Wesley's appropriations from these traditions continue to draw attention and to be used widely.

Examination of each of the major traditions upon which Wesley was dependent will not, however, explain the theology or practice of Wesley. His practice of carefully melding each contribution with his particular theological principles and practical instruction guaranteed that they would be understood and used in his own distinctive pattern. Nevertheless, one can hardly hope to understand Wesley without reflecting on his relationship to these traditions and their contributions to his thought and practice. Recent bibliographies on Wesley and Methodist studies helpfully chronicle a profusion of articles and books that examine Wesley's relationship to the several traditions he used most extensively.[4]

Wesley's Puritan Connections

This book examines Wesley's relationship to the broad range of Puritan mentors and his use of Puritan emphases, teachings, and practices. It reviews Wesley's appropriation of Puritan theological instruction where it usefully served his concerns and focuses on the striking similarity between Puritan and Wesleyan interest in the Christian gospel's practical application to a believer's daily life. In order to examine the nature of Wesley's relationship to the Puritans, be it that of similarity, affinity, or dependence, investigation is herein made of Wesley's use, recommendation, and abridgment of Puritan literature. Relying on primary source materials, this study explores the theological foundations on which the Christian life rests and the specific teachings, practices, and emphases that connect Wesley to the Puritan divines. This methodology reveals areas in which Wesley himself related his own understanding of the Christian life to that of the Puritans, rather than depending in any large measure upon the outward manifestations where similarities seem evident but actual relationship may be tenuous. Examination of notable correlations between Wesley and the Puritans gives one insight into the interconnection of two of England's most representative religious movements. Yet, just as Wesley correctly rejects the accusation that he has reinstated Puritanism as he formed the eighteenth-century Methodist societies, this discussion recognizes the inherent limitations of any study examining "relationships." Such an inquiry can establish Wesley's significant appreciation for and use of Puritan insights, teachings, and practices. It can suggest those areas where significant influence seems to be present. It can occasionally show direct appropriation of some materials and practices. However, one must recognize that these are only partial reconstructions within a most complex religious movement.

When the limited nature of the study is recognized and added to the difficulty of analyzing Wesley's own unique personality and charisma, the study can claim at best to further illuminate one important facet of John Wesley's multifarious theology and practice. Clearly, on the basis of such a study, no claim can be made that Wesley was a reinvigorated seventeenth-century "Puritan," nor that Methodism was an eighteenth-century form of English Puritanism. He and his movement recombined many divergent Christian emphases and traditions and should not be understood simply to incorporate the views or positions of any other group, even when the contributions of one tradition to the Wesleyan community are significant enough to merit close and careful study.

What's in a Name? The Meaning of a Word—"Puritan"

Before examining aspects of the Puritan ethos that Wesley found helpful in his own ministry, we must identify what portion of a multifaceted Puritan tradition Wesley found useful. The positive and negative labels we humans create to categorize our neighbors often tell us as much about ourselves as they tell others about those to whom we attach the labels. We should not be surprised to learn, then, that in the sixteenth and seventeenth centuries the use of the word "Puritan" among Englishmen could be either complimentary or derogatory, and that the source and the way the word was used defined its character at the moment. The term might suggest "purifying" of church polity and governance, "purity" of religious and theological opinions, "pure" moral teachings, or "purity" in the daily practice of Christian living, among other possibilities.[5] Whether one sought to establish such reforms or resisted their establishment usually determined a person's positive or negative evaluation of a "Puritan." Consequently, in the English culture the label came to refer to persons, often representing different social classes and issues, who had a great variety of opinions, motivations, and interests in modifying individual and societal belief and behavior.

Puritan attitudes and understandings of church polity were so varied as to make it difficult for them to form one cohesive company. Some with Puritan sympathies remained loyal to the Established Church; some, designated Separatists, sought only local church autonomy; Independents separated from the Established Church but joined together in an association of local churches; and Presbyterians sought to institute a social and ecclestiastical organization patterned after Calvin's Geneva—theocracy. Numerous clergy with a multiplicity of Puritan opinions concerning church polity, doctrine, and practice nonetheless agreed that they could not support the patterns and practices of the Church of England that emerged following Charles II's restoration in 1660. Therefore, many found themselves forced out of the church in 1662 when Parliament passed an Act of Uniformity. This act, imposed after the restoration of Charles II, required that all Church of England clergy accept "all and everything contained and prescribed" in the revised Book of Common Prayer, reestablishing a single standard of belief and worship within the church.[6] Geoffrey Nuttall has described these clergymen as

> all spiritually nearer to one another than is any of them to the Roman Catholic Church or to the Laudian party within the Church of England. They have their own internal differences . . . but in a large sense they have much in common, and for this faith and experience which they share . . . there is no other name than Puritan.[7]

Laypersons who shared their beliefs also soon found themselves "outside" the church.

In the course of the succeeding centuries the term "Puritan" has become widely used for so many different purposes that some attempt must be made to identify how it will be used in this book. The most common reference to Puritans in late-sixteenth-century England denoted those who sought to continue the Protestant

Reformation by establishing what they understood to be "pure" forms of doctrine, worship, church polity, and exemplary Christian living within the English church. The political implications and consequences of these endeavors identified seventeenth-century Puritans with the struggle for liberty and constitutional rights. Although such concerns are significant for this study, the Puritans' religious interests are most relevant, particularly their desire to purify and renew Christian thought and life. Puritans of varying ecclesiological persuasions were united in their conviction that Christianity, based on a vibrant faith, involved humanity in an experiential relationship with the God revealed in Christ wherein all human existence was to be patterned after Christ's teaching and example. For them religious authority found its base in the Scriptures, which became the primary rule and guide for thought and action. The usual and conventional English dependence on Scripture *supplemented* by church tradition and reason became suspect—particularly dependence on tradition. As John Wilkinson points out, their theological concentration was on the "sovereignty and righteousness of God and the all-pervading character of human sinfulness" buttressed by a deep concern for salvation. Their ethical idealism grew out of these convictions, since no human action was understood to be free from moral demands and consequences. These attitudes combined to produce an emphasis on a serious, circumspect, and disciplined daily life.[8] Their insights into the bases of such Christian living, and their instruction concerning it, were the things that specifically attracted John Wesley's attention.

Studies Relating Wesley to Puritanism

Although, as we have seen, the similarity between Methodism and Puritanism was recognized in Wesley's own day, only in the nineteenth century did particular attention to this resemblance begin to be appear in historical and specialized theological studies. For J. R. Green, attention to the Christian life provided the connection between the movements. In his *Short History of the English People* Green credited the Wesleyan movement with having "wrought out . . . the work of religious reform" that the Puritans had attempted, but failed to accomplish, the century before.[9] Leslie Stephen, finding the connection in their moral and ascetic austerities, called Methodism a "new Puritanism" but one that was really "a faint reflection of the grander Puritanism of the seventeenth century."[10] J. H. Overton, though recognizing these similarities, also noted some of the theological interests common to the traditions, such as their contention "for the immediate and particular influence of the

Holy Spirit, for the total degeneracy of man, for the vicarious nature of the Atonement."[11] Such recognition became more prominent in this century beginning with the work of Élie Halévy, who understood the Evangelical revival under Wesley to be the revival of the Puritan religious consciousness that, with its accompanying practice, formed part of the very character of the English people.[12] J. Scott Lidgett's essay in *A New History of Methodism* (1909) asserted that the mission of Methodism was to "make the universal Christianity witnessed to by the Established Church real and the real Christianity of the Nonconformists universal."[13] George Cell identified the ascetic temper of Wesley's ethic of life with Puritanism.[14] By midcentury such identification had become widely accepted. Stressing the motivation, or spirit, of the movement, Horton Davies credited Wesley and Methodism with reviving the "evangelical passion and experiential religion" of Puritanism.[15] Albert Outler recognized a most significant relationship by suggesting that Wesley "borrowed" his doctrine of Christian life from the Puritans.[16] Such examples illustrate the widespread recognition among scholars during the past century of significant relationship between the work of Wesley and that of the Puritan divines.

This general recognition of Wesley's connection to certain aspects of the Puritan ethos has been further validated by suggestive investigations into specific areas of contact between Wesley and the Puritans. An essay by George Eayrs entitled "Links between the Ejected Clergy of 1662, the Wesleys, and Methodism," although primarily a survey of Wesley's Nonconformist ancestry, demonstrates Wesley's appreciation for the Puritan tradition and comments on Wesley's church policy as it relates to Puritan ideas.[17] Duncan Coomer, in "The Influence of Puritanism and Dissent on Methodism," enumerates several areas of direct connection. He traces similarity in teachings regarding the Christian life, Wesley's use of Puritan authors in *A Christian Library,* and his borrowing from this tradition of the covenant service that became a popular Methodist service.[18] A more comprehensive monograph is John Newton's *Methodism and the Puritans.*[19] Newton reviews the Puritan writers in Wesley's *A Christian Library* and outlines his indebtedness to the Puritans in the areas of "Theology, Liturgy, Pastoralia, Family Piety, and Ethics." In addition, he suggests that Puritanism substantially influenced many of Wesley's lieutenants. Newton notes in this work that Susanna Wesley's creation of an essentially "Puritan household" contributed to John Wesley's early appreciation of the disciplined life and, perhaps, an unconscious respect for the Puritan ethos. Newton further elaborates Susanna's influence in *Susanna Wesley and the Puritan Tradition in Methodism.* Here he suggests that one can "discern continuity within a given stream of Christian life [the Puritan stream and that of Methodism]" and, therefore, can trace Wesley's relationship to Puritanism through Susanna. Susanna can be seen, then, as one who found no inconsistency being at one and the same time a "Puritan, an Anglican, and a Methodist, . . . who embodies all three types of churchmanship."[20]

Specific connection between the traditions has been demonstrated in several extensive investigations into Wesley's liturgical indebtedness to the Puritan tradition. John Bishop's analysis of Methodist worship, *Methodist Worship in Relation to Free Church Worship*, draws together information concerning Wesley's appropriation for Methodism of Puritan forms and modes of worship.[21] Horton Davies outlines Wesley's dependence upon Puritan liturgical practices in his chapter, "The Methodist Union of Formal and Free Worship," in *Worship and Theology in England*.[22] Investigation of the covenant service by Frederick Hunter and Frank Baker shows that the covenant is a direct incorporation into Methodism of a Puritan form, though used in a special way by Wesley.[23] Frederick Hunter suggests that Wesley's modifications in The Book of Common Prayer for American Methodists carried out the suggested changes offered by the Presbyterians at the Savoy Conference in 1661. He further contends that Wesley consciously followed the summary of these suggestions as found in Edmund Calamy's *Abridgment of Mr. Baxter's History of His Life and Times*.[24] A. Kingsley Lloyd shows that, in at least some of his hymns, Charles Wesley was directly dependent upon the biblical expositions of Matthew Henry. For example, "A Charge to Keep I Have" is a direct paraphrase of Henry.[25] The influence of Isaac Watts on John and Charles Wesley's repeated ventures into hymnody, *A Collection of Hymns for the Use of the People Called Methodist*, is noted by Franz Hilderbrandt and Oliver Beckerlegge in their commentary and notes to the recent annotated edition of that work. They suggest that in "basing his hymns on scripture John Wesley, and later his brother Charles, was in a sense carrying further the work initiated by Watts."[26] Gordon Wakefield also comments on the general relationship between Wesley and the Puritans in this important area.[27]

Although these investigations clearly indicate a real dependence by Wesley upon the Puritan tradition in terms of liturgical innovations, none of them sufficiently addresses Wesley's use of two principal Puritan practices—extemporaneous preaching and "free" prayers. Obviously, in the eyes of his contemporaries, these practices must have also identified him with the Puritan tradition.

F. C. Pritchard in *Methodist Secondary Education* places Wesley's organization and curriculum of Kingswood School in the heritage of the Dissenting academies and shows the close similarity of these respective educational institutions.[28] Although such similarity certainly does not demonstrate dependence, Wesley exhibits his familiarity with and respect for Dissenting academies when, in preparing *A Christian Library*, he consults Phillip Doddridge, a leading Dissenting educator.

Collectively, these studies confirm Wesley's familiarity with and appreciation for many Puritan emphases and practices. I turn now to an overview of Wesley's Puritan forefathers.

Wesley's Puritan Ancestry

Wesley's familial link with the Puritans was investigated at length by nineteenth-century biographers and is still a topic of interest and research.[29] The connections were substantial and show rather extensive historical linkages between Puritanism and John and Charles Wesley's immediate family.

The Puritan family lineage of the two brothers included two of their great-grandfathers. Bartholomew Westley, grandfather of Samuel Wesley, and John White, grandfather of Susanna Wesley, were Puritans active during the period of the Commonwealth.

Biographical information for Bartholomew Westley is sketchy, but it is known that he was the third son of Sir Herbert Westley of Wesleigh, County Devon, and Elizabeth Wellesley, a member of the Irish branch of the family.[30] Although little is known of Bartholomew's early life, Edmund Calamy notes that he received a university education studying both theology and "physic."[31] Listed as the rector of the parishes of Charmouth and Catherston in Dorset County in 1650, he evidently had been called to Charmouth by the congregation after the removal of the rector in 1640.[32] When he moved to the parish at Allington is not known, but he was rector there when the Act of Uniformity was enforced in 1662.[33] Bartholomew Westley, along with some eighteen hundred clerical colleagues who held Puritan sympathies, could not accept these requirements and so was ejected from his church and living on St. Bartholomew's Day, August 24, 1662, joining the ranks of the Nonconformists. Forced by the Five Mile Act to abandon his parish and not return, Bartholomew supported himself and his family by practicing medicine.[34] He continued to preach occasionally but never resumed an active ministry before his death in 1670.

Bartholomew's son, John Westley, was known more widely in Puritan circles than his father. Born in 1636, he attended New Inn Hall, Oxford, during John Owen's vice chancellorship of the university. Other renowned Puritans were in Oxford at the time as fellows and students, for example, Thomas Goodwin, Stephen Charnock, John Howe, Philip Henry, and Joseph Alleine.[35] Young

John Westley received special attention from John Owen and achieved distinction among his peers as a diligent student of Oriental languages in the course of attaining his B.A. and M.A. degrees. On leaving the university, he associated himself with a "gathered church" at Melcombe Regis, preaching in the area and serving as a seaport chaplain. He accepted the call of the combined parish of Winterbourne Whitchurch, Dorset, as a minister on probation, and, after receiving the approval of the Triers, he was awarded the living by the Trustees in 1658.[36] During this period he also organized a private school to supplement his income. In 1661 charges were brought against him for his unwillingness to use the prayer book. Calamy, using Westley's diary, recorded an account of the resulting interview with Bishop Gilbert Ironsides. This exchange reveals that he had not been episcopally ordained and, indeed, felt that his call and commission to preach by the gathered congregation at Melcombe was quite sufficient.[37] He explained his refusal to accept ordination by commenting that he was called to the "work" of the ministry but not to the "office," which some interpreters have understood to be an anticipation of John Wesley's distinction between lay helpers and the ordained clergy.[38] However, since Westley accepted the full responsibility of the parish as well as the living at Winterbourne Whitchurch, this supposition is questionable. Westley's strongest defense of his ministry was, nonetheless, on the basis of the "fruits" of his work evident in those persons converted "to the power of Godliness" or "the reality of religion" under his preaching at "Radipole, Melcombe, Turnworth, Whitchurch, and at sea." Similar arguments concerning the fruits of a ministry were to be used by his grandson, John Wesley, as justification for the work of the Methodists. Although John Westley swore allegiance and loyalty to Charles II upon the king's restoration, he, like his father, could not accept the requirements of the Act of Uniformity and was ejected from Winterbourne Whitchurch in 1662. Forced to wander for some time before finding permanent residence, he affiliated himself with the ministry of Joseph Alleine and others preaching to several semiclandestine Presbyterian, Baptist, and Independent congregations. Given the use of a house by a friend in Preston, he ministered to several congregations in the area, for which action he served at least four short prison terms. At his death in 1670 he was the pastor of a "gathered church" in Poole. To judge from his interview with Bishop Ironsides and his subsequent action, Westley was an Independent in his understanding of church order. In any case, he was a respected Puritan whose convictions did not allow him the comfort and security of service in the post-Restoration Church of England.[39]

Samuel Wesley, John Westley's son, was only a child at the time of his father's death, having been born in the year of his father's ejectment. Although the family suffered from the restrictions placed on Nonconformity, Samuel was given a thorough education in several London Dissenting academies. Forsaking Nonconformity in his teens, he entered Exeter College, Oxford, as a servitor and upon graduating in 1688 was ordained in the Church of England.[40] That year Samuel Wesley married Susanna Annesley, the bearer of a renowned Puritan heritage.

John White, Susanna's maternal grandfather and a Puritan from his youth, extensively served the Puritan cause as a barrister before his election to Parliament in 1640. In the Long Parliament, the Puritan-dominated Interregnum parliament (1640-1660) that governed following the Puritan revolution, his position as chairman of the "Committee for Scandalous Ministers" gave him an active role in the examination and ejection of many Anglican clergymen. Active among those seeking to remove episcopacy as the form of church government, he also participated in the organization of the Massachusetts colony; he may have drafted its charter.[41]

Samuel Annesley, Susanna's father, was "one of the most eminent of the later Puritan Nonconformists."[42] Edmund Calamy in his *The Nonconformist's Memorial* comments that "he [Annesley] was so early under serious impressions, that he declared he knew not the time when he was not converted."[43] Earning his B.A. and M.A. degrees at Queen's College, Oxford, in 1644, he was honored with a Doctor of Laws degree in 1648. Episcopally ordained a deacon, Annesley received Presbyterian ordination in 1644. He began his career as a naval chaplain and followed that service by accepting his first parish at Cliff, Kent. Receiving the London parish of St. John the Evangelist in 1652, he became vicar of St. Giles, Cripplegate, also in that city, in 1658, from which position he was ejected when he refused to conform in 1662. Forced into retirement, he continued to preach and, with others, established a meetinghouse at Little St. Helens that quickly became a center of London Nonconformity. Descended from minor nobility and enjoying sufficient private income beyond that needed simply to sustain his family, he supported and educated several young Nonconformists. It was at Little St. Helens in 1694 that Annesley and others conducted the first public Presbyterian ordination since the 1662 Act of Uniformity had prohibited such services.[44] Susanna Annesley, the twenty-fifth child of Dr. Annesley, was born in 1669. The Annesley home was an exemplary Puritan household where demanding educational standards accompanied disciplined devotional and moral training. Because this home served as a center of Nonconformity, the children were exposed to intense theological discussion and debate. In this setting Susanna gained such an appreciation and knowledge of Scripture and theology that, in Frank Baker's phrase, she later "proved a valuable source of theological reference for her sons."[45] At an early age she appears to have been familiar with the distinctions and arguments between the Established Church and Nonconformity and sometime before her marriage in 1688 she made her decision to leave Nonconformity and join the Church of England.

Whatever reasons led Samuel and Susanna Wesley to abandon the ranks of Nonconformity and join the Church of England, the move initiated significant shifts in their thought as well as practice. Samuel Wesley, embracing the Anglican emphasis on the theology and liturgical patterns of the early church, became a staunch supporter of a "high church" interpretation of the sacraments. Susanna appears to have also adopted many Anglican theological emphases and never questioned her decision to join the Church of England.

However, to change one's religious affiliation out of honest conviction does not mean necessarily to abandon or reject completely one's heritage and background. Although Samuel Wesley could write a devastating critique of Dissenting academies, he carried with him into the Church of England many of the virtues of Puritan training and education. Martin Schmidt suggests that Samuel Wesley's great interest in biblical scholarship and instruction was greatly dependent on the legacy of his Puritan background.[46] Like the Puritans, Samuel Wesley displayed a love for the Scriptures that culminated in his major scholarly endeavors being biblical expositions. Maldwyn Edwards points out that, by precept and example, he set a pattern of disciplined daily scholarship that greatly influenced his sons.[47] In a statement from his deathbed he affirmed another Puritan emphasis: "The inward witness, son, the inward witness; that is the proof, the strongest proof of Christianity."[48] It is this same inward witness that is professed in his son John's doctrine of assurance. Unlike many of his contemporaries, Samuel had not relinquished his conviction and confidence in a vital personal religious experience as central to Christian faith and life—a conviction to which he would have been thoroughly exposed in his Puritan home. Samuel, perhaps unconsciously, passed along to his children the vestiges of Puritan influence and emphasis evident in his own life.

Susanna's contribution to this legacy is at least as great as Samuel's and perhaps exceeds it. A. W. Harrison comments: "The Epworth parsonage had a High Church atmosphere, yet it was essentially a Puritan home."[49] John Newton, attempting to document this statement and convinced that Susanna was the formative figure of the home, asserts that the Puritan piety and training of her own childhood molded the character of her household. "Her careful ordered timetable, her regular times set apart for meditation and self-examination before God, her keeping of a spiritual journal or day-book, her observance of the strict Puritan Sabbath—these were all part of her 'method' of life, to use the Puritan key-word."[50] Her pastoral care over the souls of her children to bring each to a "personal appropriation of God's grace" also reflects Puritan patterns.[51] To these can be added Puritan emphases affirmed in her theological advice to her sons and finally her total Christian personality.[52] Newton's statements perhaps do not give adequate attention to the accent on discipline and piety found among many seventeenth- and eighteenth-century Anglican pastors not necessarily connected to Puritanism. He rather exclusively locates these characteristics as arising among the Puritans. Nevertheless, the general character of the home, with its emphasis on genuine piety, biblical training, and rigid discipline that left no time for "light" diversions, is strikingly similar to Puritan prototypes.

Whatever Puritan influence may be noted in the Epworth household and parental heritage, we cannot be sure how much of it was unconscious so far as Samuel and Susanna were concerned. Frank Baker suggests that because they were both converts from Dissent, "it is not surprising that they did not fill their children's heads with stirring tales of their predominantly Puritan forefathers."[53] Baker's caution is well taken. It keeps one from assuming extensive discussion of Puritan thought and patterns in the household. Newton's declination of the Puritan influences in the household can hardly be denied, but they were likely more subtle than explicit.

Clearly, John Wesley's conscious and genuine appreciation of the Puritans and their teachings emerges after Aldersgate. Only in later life did he begin to express an interest in his Puritan ancestry. Intrigued by the idea that one of Charles's sons might become a minister, he wrote: "It is highly probable one of the three will stand before the Lord. But, so far as I can learn, such a thing has scarce been for these three thousand years before, as a son, father, grandfather, *atavus*, *tritavus*, preaching the gospel, nay, and the genuine gospel in a line."[54] His recognition here of forebears who had been Puritan divines is clear.

His appreciation of Puritan teaching and practice of the "genuine gospel" exemplify his continual and constant criterion for identification of any Christian leader—one who expressed the genuine gospel in both teachings and life itself. This standard of measure continually guided Wesley in his appropriation of the many resources he used from Christian forebears of widely differing theological and polity persuasions. Such is also the standard that will most effectively guide us in our examination of Wesley's extensive involvement with the Puritan ethos.

Notes

1. J. H. Overton, *The Evangelical Revival in the Eighteenth Century* (London: Longmans, Green, 1886), 171-73, cites these and several other examples of this type of identification.

2. See Curnock's note on the subject in *The Journal of the Rev. John Wesley, A.M.*, ed. Nehemiah Curnock (London: Epworth Press, 1909), 5:42 n. Cited hereafter as *Journal*. See also Luke Tyerman, *The Life and Times of the Rev. John Wesley, A.M.* (New York: Harper & Brothers, 1872), 1:67. Richard Heitzenrater's discussion of the term "Methodist" insightfully traces the use of the word through English church history, *Mirror and Memory* (Nashville: Abingdon Press, 1989), 13-32.

3. John Wesley, *The Letters of the Rev. John Wesley, A.M.*, ed. John Telford (London: Epworth Press, 1931), 4:353. Hereafter cited as *Letters*.

4. As the field of Wesley studies has expanded, a number of bibliographies have emerged that reference the varied sources of Wesley's theological and practical instruction. Useful and readily available bibliographical articles include Frank Baker, "Unfolding John Wesley: A Survey of Twenty Years' Studies in Wesley's Thought," *Quarterly Review* 1 (1980): 44-58; Frederick A. Norwood, "Methodist Historical Studies 1930-1959 (Part I)," *Church History* 28 (December 1959): 391-417; Frederick A. Norwood, "Wesleyan and Methodist Historical Studies, 1960-1970: A Bibliographical Article," *Church History* 40 (June 1971): 182-99; J. Gordon Melton, "An Annotated Bibliography of Publications about the Life and Work of John Wesley," *Methodist History* 7 (July 1969): 61-66; Lawrence D. McIntosh, "The Place of John Wesley in the Christian Tradition," in *The Place of John Wesley in the Christian Tradition*, ed. Kenneth E. Rowe (Metuchen, N.J.: Scarecrow Press, 1980), 134-59; Richard P. Heitzenrater, "John Wesley and the Historian's Task," in *Mirror and Memory* (Nashville: Abingdon Press, 1989), 205-13.

5. Christopher Hill, *Society and Puritanism in Pre-Revolutionary England* (New York: Schocken Books, 1964), 20. Hill enumerates many uses of the term "puritan" in this chapter. See also J. Brauer, "Reflections on the Nature of English Puritanism," *Church History* 23 (1954): 101.

6. John Wesley's opinion of this act is clearly stated in his "Thoughts upon Liberty": "So, by this glorious Act, thousands of men, guilty of no crime, nothing contrary either to justice, mercy or truth, were stripped of all they had, of their houses, lands, revenues, and driven to seek where they could, or beg, their bread. For what? Because they did not dare to worship God according to other men's consciences! So they and their families were, at one stroke, turned out of house and home . . . because they could not assent and consent to that manner of worship which their worthy governors prescribed." *The Works of the Reverend John Wesley*, ed. Thomas Jackson (London: Wesleyan Conference Office, 1872), 11:39. Hereafter cited as *Works* (Jackson).

7. Geoffrey F. Nuttall, *The Holy Spirit in Puritan Faith and Experience* (Oxford: Basil Blackwell, 1947), 9.

8. John T. Wilkinson, "The Mind of the Puritan," *London Quarterly*

and Holborn Review 187 (1962): 35-38. This Journal hereafter cited as *LQHR*.

9. J. R. Green, *Short History of the English People* (New York: Harper and Brothers, 1898), 604, 739.

10. Leslie Stephen, *History of English Thought in the Eighteenth Century* (London: Smith, Elder, 1881), 2:433.

11. J. H. Overton, *Evangelical Revival in the Eighteenth Century*, 44-45.

12. Élie Halévy, "La Naissance du Methodisme en Angleterre," *La Revue De Paris* 4 (1906): 521-22.

13. J. Scott Lidgett, "Fundamental Unity," in *A New History of Methodism*, ed. W. J. Townsend, H. B. Workman, and George Eayr (London: Hodder and Stoughton, 1909), 2:438.

14. George C. Cell, *The Rediscovery of John Wesley* (New York: Henry Holt, 1935), vii.

15. Horton Davies, *The English Free Churches* (London: Oxford University Press, 1952), 141.

16. Albert Outler, "Towards a Re-Appraisal of John Wesley as a Theologian," *The Perkins School of Theology Journal* 14 (1961): 7.

17. George Eayrs, "Links between the Ejected Clergy of 1662, the Wesleys, and Methodism," in *The Ejectment of 1662 and the Free Churches*, ed. Alexander Maclaren (London: National Council of Evangelical Free Churches, n.d.), 99-119.

18. Duncan Coomer, "The Influence of Puritanism and Dissent on Methodism," *LQHR* 175 (1950): 346-50.

19. John A. Newton, *Methodism and the Puritans* (London: Dr. William's Trust, 1964), 4.

20. John A. Newton, *Susanna Wesley and the Puritan Tradition in Methodism* (London: Epworth Press, 1968), 17.

21. John Bishop, *Methodist Worship in Relation to Free Church Worship* (London: Epworth Press, 1950).

22. Horton Davies, *Worship and Theology in England: From Watts and Wesley to Maurice, 1690-1850* (Princeton: Princeton University Press, 1961), 184ff.

23. Frederick Hunter, "The Origins of Wesley's Covenant Service," *Wesley Historical Society Proceedings* 22 (1940): 126-30. Proceedings hereafter cited as *WHSP*. Frank Baker, "The Beginnings of the Methodist Covenant Service," *LQHR* 180 (1955): 215-20.

24. Frederick Hunter, "Sources of Wesley's Revision of the Prayer Book in 1784-88," *WHSP* 23 (1941-42): 123-33. Other Wesley scholars, particularly Wesley Swift, J. E. Rattenbury, and Paul R. Blankenship, question the emphasis Hunter gives to Calamy's influence on Wesley, but there is little question that the revisions are those suggested by the Presbyterians, whether or not Wesley was dependent upon Calamy for these suggestions. See Wesley Swift, "Methodism and the Prayer Book" *WHSP* 27 (1949-50): 33-41, and "The Sunday Service of the Methodists," *WHSP* 29 (1953-54): 12-20; J. E. Rattenbury, "Note on Article on 'Sources of Wesley's Revision of the Prayer Book of 1784-88,'" *WHSP* 23 (1941-42): 173-75; Paul R. Blankenship, "The Significance of John Wesley's Abridgement of the Thirty-Nine Articles as seen from His Deletions," *Methodist History* (August 1989): 35-47.

25. A. K. Lloyd, "Charles Wesley's Debt to Matthew Henry," *LQHR* 171 (1946): 330-37. See also *The Bicentennial Edition of The Works of John Wesley*, ed. Frank Baker and Richard Heitzenrater (Nashville: Abingdon Press, 1984–), 7:473 n. Hereafter cited as *Works*.

26. *A Collection of Hymns for the Use of the People Called Methodists*, ed. Franz Hilderbrandt and Oliver Beckerlegge, in *Works*, 7:23. See also the introduction and repeated notes.

27. Gordon Wakefield, *Puritan Devotion: Its Place in the Development of Christian Piety* (London: Epworth Press, 1957), 1-144, passim.

28. F. C. Pritchard, *Methodist Secondary Education* (London: Epworth Press, 1949), 59-73. A. G. Ives provides insight into the creation, disciplined character, and curriculum of Kingswood School under Wesley's leadership (*Kingswood School in Wesley's Day and Since* [London: Epworth Press, 1970]).

29. See John Whitehead, *The Life of the Rev. John Wesley, A.M.*, 2 vols. (London: Printed by Stephen Couchman, 1793); Adam Clarke, *Memoirs of the Wesley Family* (London: Printed by J. and T. Clarke, 1823); George Stevenson, *Memorials of the Wesley Family* (London: S. W. Partridge, 1876); and William Beal, *The Fathers of the Wesley Family* (London: J. Mason, 1833). For a more recent treatment see Frank Baker, "Wesley's Puritan Ancestry," *LQHR* 187 (1962): 180-86.

30. Stevenson, *Memorials of the Wesley Family*, xiff. Stevenson's tracing of the various branches of the Wesley family demonstrates a variety of spellings for the name of this early English family: Wellesley, Westley, and Wesley.

31. Edmund Calamy, *The Nonconformist's Memorial*, ed. Samuel Palmer (London: Printed for W. Harris, 1775), 1:442.

32. Beal, *Fathers*, 26-27.

33. Beal, *Fathers*, 22ff., argues that Bartholomew Westley was ejected from Charmouth rather than Allington, but Baker, "Wesley's Puritan Ancestry," points out that deed records indicate that he was at Allington.

34. The Act of Uniformity was followed by the Five Mile Act, prohibiting those who would not conform from residing within five miles of an incorporated town or any parish they had formerly served.

35. Luke Tyerman, *The Life and Times of the Rev. Samuel Wesley, A.M.* (London: Simpkin, Marshall, 1866), 34.

36. Upon the elimination of the traditional episcopal examinations during the Commonwealth, a system of "Triers and Trustees" had been set up to examine, license, and appoint ministers for service in the church.

37. Calamy, *NonConformist's Memorial*, 1:478ff.; Tyerman, *Life and Times of the Rev. Samuel Wesley A.M.*, 34ff.

38. Clarke, *Memoirs of the Wesley Family*, 36-37; Tyerman, *Life and Times of the Rev. Samuel Wesley, A.M.*, 43.

39. Calamy, *The Nonconformist's Memorial*, 1:478-86; cf. Frank Baker, "Wesley's Puritan Ancestry," 182-83.

40. It was evidently at Oxford that Samuel dropped the "t" from the name, understanding "Wesley" to be the ancient and correct spelling.

41. *Dictionary of National Biography*, ed. Leslie Stephen (London: Smith, Elder, 1885), 60:260. Hereafter cited as *DNB*. John Wesley mistakenly identified his great-grandfather with Dr. John White, one of the

chairmen of the Westminster Assembly, *Letters*, 5:76; cf. Baker, "Wesley's Puritan Ancestry," 184.

42. *DNB*, 2:7. John A. Newton provides an extensive and helpful treatment of the work and contribution of Samuel Annesley in his *Susanna Wesley and the Puritan Tradition in Methodism.*

43. Calamy, *The Nonconformist's Memorial*, 2:104-5.

44. *DNB*, 2:7-8; Baker, "Wesley's Puritan Ancestry," 183.

45. Baker, "Wesley's Puritan Ancestry," 184.

46. Martin Schmidt, *John Wesley, A Theological Biography* (Nashville: Abingdon Press, 1962), 1:40. Schmidt also asserts that Wesley "owed a great deal to the Puritan emphasis upon the importance of repentance, conversion, and rebirth."

47. Maldwyn Edwards, *Family Circle* (London: Epworth Press, 1949), 30.

48. *Works*, 26:289.

49. Quoted by Newton, *Methodism and the Puritans*, 4.

50. Newton, *Methodism and the Puritans*, 5.

51. Newton, *Susanna Wesley*, 54-55.

52. Newton, *Susanna Wesley*, 6-7. Newton makes an interesting case for the essential Puritan cast of Susanna's character and thought in his comments in "Letters from Susanna Wesley to her Son John," *Wesley Chapel Magazine* (January, 1965): 8-12. See also his *Susanna Wesley*, Chap. 2, for further comments on her character.

53. Baker, "Wesley's Puritan Ancestry," 181.

54. *Letters*, 5:36.

2

Puritan Authors in Wesley's Publications

John Wesley's emergence in the early 1740s as a principal Evangelical Revival leader coincided with his recognition that the "power of the press" could be beneficially used as an evangelization tool. The importance of the printing press in spreading the Christian message had long been recognized, and, by Wesley's time, the number of religious works was myriad. Much of that material, however, was economically unavailable to the poor and not readily accessible for many other common people. Wesley's firm conviction that "reading Christians will be knowing Christians"[1] persuaded him to provide Christian literature to the less educated members of the societies through publication of tracts and small books. To accomplish this purpose, Wesley, in addition to publishing his own tracts, journals, and sermons, abridged numerous works authored by others.[2] These publications provided quality religious instruction for his followers and gave him an opportunity to supervise, at least to some extent, what they might be reading.

Among his abridgments Wesley included many drawn from sixteenth- and seventeenth-century Puritan authors and a few works from his Dissenter contemporaries. Examination of this material helps establish Wesley's relationship to the Puritan tradition by clarifying the extent of his familiarity with the Puritans, his evaluation of them, and the spheres of their thought and instruction he found most congenial.

The productive years of Wesley's literary life span the exceptionally long period from 1733 until his death in 1791. During the years 1749-55 Wesley edited *A Christian Library*, his largest single literary venture, consisting of fifty duodecimo volumes. This work provides valuable information relative to Wesley's purposes and methods in abridging the works of other authors and, more important for this study, is a principal source for examining and evaluating his use of Puritan materials.

A Christian Library

In August 1748 Wesley in a letter to a friend outlined his objectives in publishing *A Christian Library*:

> I have often thought of mentioning to you and a few others a design I have had for some years of printing a little library, perhaps of four-score or one hundred volumes, for the use of those that fear God. My purpose was to select whatever I had seen most valuable in the English language, and either abridge, or take the whole tracts, only a little corrected or explained, as occasion should require. Of these I could print ten or twelve, more or less, every year, on a fine paper, and large letter which should be cast for the purpose. . . . As soon as I am able to purchase a printing press and types I think of entering on this design. I have several books now ready; and a printer who desires nothing more than food and raiment. In three or four weeks I hope to be in London, and if God permit to begin without delay.[3]

By February 1749 Wesley had begun the work of abridgment while at Kingswood school.[4]

As Wesley intimates, the idea for such a library did not originate in 1748. On June 18, 1746, Dr. Phillip Doddridge, principal of a Dissenting academy in Northampton, offered Wesley his thoughts "on that little Collection of Books, which you seem desirous to make for some young preachers."[5] Wesley's inquiry to which Doddridge was responding demonstrates his active solicitation of aid in designing such a project.

Wesley's avowed purpose in *A Christian Library* was to publish the "choicest Pieces of Practical Divinity." Seventeenth- and eighteenth-century authors normally thought of Christian literature as falling into three main categories: doctrinal and speculative works establishing the truths of the gospel, controversial treatises arguing particular theological issues, and practical writings designed to help believers apply the truths of the Christian gospel to their daily lives. Works drawn from the last of these patterns of divinity constituted Wesley's library, works whose patterns reflected "Christianity reduced to *practice*."[6] Wesley's introduction to an early church commentary on the Scriptures stated his concern quite well: "That his acquaintance with those Sacred Writings was not merely *literal or speculative*, but that *it was a true and practical knowledge*."[7] Although practical divinity might, and usually did, incorporate biblical commentary and exegesis, that was not its primary concern; its objective in Wesley's understanding was to make the gospel "intelligible to plain men." Wesley did not disparage theological endeavors explaining the intricacies of doctrine; he simply sought to present, from among the variety of available writings, those most edifying. The ordinary believer with whom Wesley worked was often uneducated in anything more than the rudiments of reading and would have difficulty following the intricacies of many theological writings. Even the selections of practical divinity Wesley included required clarification, so he regularly eliminated and revised technical language and speculative theological argumentation. Clarification also required excising or explaining the theological controversy that often found its way into the writings of the scholars, their inconsistency of instruction, and their "mystical attempts to find hidden meanings in plain truths." Wesley was anxious to "separate the pure, genuine Divinity, out of this huge mingled mass."[8]

Wesley's approach to the task of abridgment is clearly outlined:

> I have also particularly endeavoured to preserve a consistency throughout, that no part might contradict any other; but all conspire together, "to make the man of God perfect, thoroughly furnished unto every good word and work."
>
> But in order to do this, I have been obliged, not only to omit the far greater part of several eminent authors, but also to add what was needful, either to clear their sense, or to correct their mistakes. And in a design of this nature, I apprehend myself to be at full liberty so to do. I therefore take no author for better, for worse; (as indeed I dare not call any man Rabbi,) but endeavour to follow each so far as he follows Christ. And not (knowingly) one step farther.[9]

Such liberties with the materials of other authors, though questionable by present-day standards, were much more common before the establishment of modern copyright laws. Nevertheless, Wesley's willingness to change any treatise as he saw fit certainly left him open to many questions and criticisms.

On the one hand, Church of England critics attempted to show that Wesley was a Dissenter,[10] and, on the other hand, his Evangelical Calvinistic opponents were anxious to find inconsistencies in his theological position.[11] Consequently, Wesley was forced to make public defense of the *Library*. He readily admitted mistakes caused by preparing the works as he could "snatch time in traveling, not transcribing them."[12] Perhaps more significant, he recognized that some mistakes were caused by trusting the ability of the printer to decipher his abridgment markings, as Wesley seldom examined the final copy before its publication. He also candidly acknowledged that "it is probable too, I myself might overlook some sentences which were not suitable to my own principles."[13]

After making these concessions, Wesley was ready to defend

himself against any attempt to make him responsible for all of the doctrines and views expressed in the *Library*. "I did believe and I do believe, every tract therein to be true, and agreeable to the oracles of God. But I do not roundly affirm this of every sentence contained in the fifty volumes."[14] He was willing to be counted as editor, not author, of these treatises.

Even if mistakes were inevitable, Wesley's willingness to "mind not who speaks but what is spoken" is the genius of the *Library* and, for that matter, of all his abridgments.[15] Although Wesley could reject the predestinarianism of Thomas Goodwin or the mysticism of William Law, he saw no valid reason for rejecting the truths that each might teach concerning the living of the Christian life and other congenial doctrines. This discriminating eclecticism allowed Wesley to seek helpful instruction wherever he might find it.[16]

Puritan Authors Included in *A Christian Library*

The first few volumes of *A Christian Library* were materials from the early church fathers and extensive martyrological accounts of the lives of exemplary Christians. Wesley characteristically provided few prefaces or introductions to his abridgments and consequently seldom gave the reader his valuable and incisive evaluation of their contents. Fortunately, one of the exceptions to this general practice is his preface to the rather large number of Puritan materials included in the *Library*. This revealing preface offers his most extensive comment on the Puritans and their experiences:

> After an account of the lives, sufferings, and deaths of those holy men, who sealed the ancient religion with their blood, I believe nothing would either be more agreeable or more profitable to the serious reader, than some extracts from the writings of those who sprung up, as it were, out of their ashes. These breathe the same spirit, and were, in a lower degree, partakers of the same sufferings. Many of them took joyfully the spoiling of their goods, and all had their names cast out as evil; being branded with the nickname of Puritans, and thereby made a byeword and a proverb of reproach.
>
> I have endeavoured to rescue from obscurity a few of the most eminent of these: I say a few; for there is a multitude of them, which it would be tedious even to name. Nor have I attempted to abridge all the works of these few; for some of them are immensely voluminous. The Works of Dr. Goodwin alone would have sufficed to fill fifty volumes. I have therefore selected what I conceived would be of most general use, and most proper to form a complete body of Practical Divinity.[17]

Wesley's esteem for Puritan writings and his respect for their sufferings is obvious in the statement,[18] as is his reason for selecting their writings for incorporation in the *Library*—they are preeminently works of practical divinity.

Many of Wesley's Church of England colleagues were especially distressed that *A Christian Library* should contain works of the Puritans. The November 1760 issue of *The London Magazine* carried a letter to John Wesley questioning his orthodoxy as a clergyman of the Church of England, inquiring whether *A Christian Library* was not simply an "odd collection of mutilated writings of dissenters of all sorts."[19] Wesley responded to this question in the next issue of the magazine: "No. In the first ten volumes there is not a line from any dissenter of any sort. And the greatest part of the other forty is extracted from Archbishop Leighton, Bishops Taylor, Patrick, Kenn, Reynolds, Sanderson; and other ornaments of the Church of England."[20]

This unequivocal answer is typical of Wesley, but it is doubtful that it was very satisfactory to his questioner. The problem arises in how one defines the word "Dissenter." This term had first been used to designate the "Dissenting brethren" of the Westminster Assembly (the Independents and Congregationalists) who disagreed with the concepts of church governance and some theological issues held by that predominantly Presbyterian body.[21] After the Act of Uniformity of 1662 and certainly in Wesley's own time, the term had become a popular label for all those persons who did not conform to the prayer book and remained outside the Church of England. This included most Presbyterians, Independents, Baptists, Quakers, and others of Puritan inclination. Wesley, however, appears to have distinguished in his own mind between two groups: (1) "Dissenters" who voluntarily removed themselves from the church, such as the Baptists and some Independents; and (2) those Church of England pastors who held Puritan sympathies before the Act of Uniformity as well as those who were "forced" out of the church by that act, all of whom he called Nonconformists or Puritans.[22] If in his response to Stephen Church, Wesley intended such a distinction, he could justly claim that the first ten volumes contained no Dissenters; nevertheless, these volumes do include a number of early Puritan authors.[23] Church must have also been aware that these early volumes contain Wesley's rather sympathetic introduction to the Puritan materials previously noted.[24]

Investigation of the remaining forty volumes demonstrates a reality that might have surprised Wesley himself. Authors of the Puritan tradition constitute the "greatest part" of the total, although a bare majority. Applying our broad definition of the term "Puritan" (including Dissenters) to the list of English authors in the *Library* reveals that thirty-one[25] are Puritans, whereas twenty-nine are Church of England authors.[26] In terms of bulk of material, or the actual space occupied by the writings of various authors, Puritan materials make up an even larger proportion of the *Library*.[27]

Among those listed in this study as Church of England men are some who display Puritan sympathies, even though they conformed to the Church of England in 1662. Archbishop Robert Leighton (d. 1684), the Scottish divine, would have qualified under Richard Baxter's classification as an "old Presbyterian" who accepted reordination while privately and knowingly understanding it in terms different from those of the officiating bishop.[28] Bishop Edward Reynolds (d. 1676) was a participant in both the Westminster Assembly and the Savoy Conference. He conformed, evidently thinking others would join him, and took a bishopric only after consulting with Baxter, Calamy, and other Puritan leaders.[29] Trained at Emmanuel College when its faculty was largely Puritan and in general sympathy with the political aspirations of the Commonwealth, most of the Cambridge Platonists were judged by the Westminster Assembly as "fitt to be fellows."[30] They differed at several major points with orthodox Puritan theology, but they shared the Puritan concern for vital personal religion displayed in everyday life. Of this group Wesley used Ralph Cudworth (d. 1688), Nathanael Culverwel (d. 1651), John Smith (d. 1652), John Worthington (d. 1671), and Henry More (d. 1687).

Wesley's selection from among the Puritan authors for inclusion in *A Christian Library* is principally confined to authors who were active after 1640. Only five of those who were leaders in the movement during its earlier days are included. Bishop Joseph Hall (d. 1656) was considered by Wesley to be one of these, although he noted that there might be some question about this.[31] The others are Robert Bolton (d. 1631), John Preston (d. 1628), William Whateley (d. 1639), and Richard Sibbes (d. 1635). John Foxe may also be counted among this number, even though his massive work, *Acts and Monuments*, carried its influence far beyond the confines of party and theological loyalties.[32] With only two exceptions, Wesley chose not to use works by Nonconformist authors of his own period, although a number had been suggested by Doddridge. Only John Howe (d. 1705) and Thomas Crane (d. 1714) lived in Wesley's century.

The extensive range of theological and ecclesiastical opinion among Puritans, which contributed significantly to their political and social difficulties during the Commonwealth, is found among the authors whose works Wesley selected for the *Library*. Wesley's own biases relative to some of their positions are perhaps evident in his selection. Of the twenty-seven Puritans from the latter half of the seventeenth century chosen by Wesley, only five are Independents or Congregationalists. This number includes three of their leaders, Thomas Goodwin (d. 1680), John Owen (d. 1683), and John Flavel (d. 1691), with Lewis Stuckley (d. 1687) and the layman Francis Rous (d. 1659) being lesser known members of the group. In addition to these five, the more radical wing of Puritanism gains representation by a lone Baptist, John Bunyan (d. 1688), whose literary contributions certainly transcended party lines.

The remainder of the Puritan authors were drawn from the ranks of the Presbyterians. These include many of the principal leaders of the church during the Commonwealth: Richard Baxter (d. 1691), Samuel Clarke (d. 1683),[33] Isaac Ambrose (d. 1663), Joseph Alleine (d. 1668), Richard Alleine (d. 1681), Samuel Annesley (d. 1696), and John Howe (d. 1705). Other Presbyterians included are Sir Matthew Hale (d. 1676), John Kitchin (d. 1662?), Matthew Pool (d. 1679), Thomas Crane (d. 1714), Samuel Charnock (d. 1680), William Dell (d. 1664), Thomas Manton (d. 1677), Herbert Palmer (d. 1647), and Samuel Shaw (d. 1696). Samuel Rutherford (d. 1661), Hugh Binning (d. 1653), and John Brown (d. 1679) represent Scottish Presbyterians.[34]

Numerical comparisons of the denominational or party affiliations of the Puritans should be used, at best, with caution. Wesley undoubtedly would have been surprised at such a calculation (no evidence suggests he ever made one), and he would claim that here, as elsewhere, he looked to what was said and not to who said it. Nevertheless, Puritans with Presbyterian sympathies were by far the largest group included, which seems to indicate Wesley's preference for the more moderate wing of Puritanism.

Exemplary Lives in *A Christian Library*

A large section of the *Library* is made up of "accounts" of exemplary Christian living. The popularity of diaries and biographical history was a common feature of the period, finding some of its most eloquent expression in Christian martyrology and hagiography.[35] Samuel Clarke, patterning his work on John Foxe's *Acts and Monuments*, was the major biographer of the Puritans. Although Wesley added some material from other Puritan sources, he principally depended on Clarke for the lives reproduced in the *Library*. Criticizing Clarke's selections for not giving adequate place, in his opinion, to some of the "most eminent men" of the Church of England, Wesley added a number of persons to Clarke's choices.[36] Even with these additions, however, Puritan lives number more than twice those drawn from the Church of England.[37] Just as Puritan authors were the major source for Wesley's choice of "practical divinity" included in the

Library, Puritan lives illustrating the application of those teachings in daily living predominate in Wesley's selections.

Wesley's appreciation of this type of material resulted in his extensive use of "accounts" of his followers' lives, and many gathered from other sources, in Methodist publications. Such lives became a hallmark of the Methodist societies, where, as among the Puritans, they were a major source of inspiration and proof of the Holy Spirit's work among Christians.[38]

Writings of Puritan Divines in Wesley's General Publications

Although *A Christian Library* was Wesley's most extensive abridgment project, he published many other abridgments during his career. As might be expected from the distribution found in the *Library*, works of Puritan divines also constitute a substantial portion of these publications.

Of the approximately fifty abridgments and abstracts printed as separate volumes, more than a third were from the Puritan tradition.[39] Although there was no set pattern in the types of literature published, selected writings on practical divinity, not unexpectedly, predominated—for example, Joseph Alleine's *Christian Letters* and *An Alarm to the Unconverted Sinner*, John Janeway's *Token for Children*, Richard Baxter's *A Call to the Unconverted* and *The Saint's Everlasting Rest*, and William Whateley's *Directions for Married Persons*.[40] Jonathan Edwards's three accounts of the revival in New England were understood by Wesley to be works providing practical instruction in Christian life and ministry. His abridgments of Milton's *Paradise Lost* and Bunyan's *Pilgrim's Progress* may be classified as practical divinity, as they were also understood by Wesley to provide useful instruction in Christian living.[41] To these should be added Isaac Watts's *Treatise on the Passions*, abridged by Wesley for *The Arminian Magazine* (1782).[42]

Wesley often published exemplary lives as separate tracts for easy distribution. Puritan lives printed in this manner include Jonathan Edwards's account of *The Life of the Late Rev. Mr. David Brainerd, Missionary to the Indians*, an extract from *The Life and Death of Mr. John Janeway*, and *The Life and Death of the Reverend Learned and Pious Mr. Thomas Halyburton*.[43]

Theological interests other than practical divinity were represented by such works as an abridgment of Jonathan Edwards's treatises *On the Religious Affections*[44] and *The Distinguishing Marks of a Work of God*.[45] Of more importance in terms of Wesley's own theological formulations are Richard Baxter's *Aphorisms of Justification* and John

Goodwin's *Treatise on Justification* and his *Exposition of the Ninth Chapter of the Epistle to the Romans*.[46] From Wesley's contemporaries was drawn Dr. Watts's *Serious Consideration Concerning the Doctrines of Election and Reprobation.*

The preface to Wesley's *Explanatory Notes upon the New Testament* discloses his primary dependence on the *Gnomon Novi Testamenti* by Johann Albrecht Bengel, the Württenberg Pietist. In addition, Wesley acknowledged his indebtedness to three English works, among which are treatises by two Dissenter authors: Phillip Doddridge's *Family Expositor* and the "work of Dr. Guyse" (presumably this is *An Exposition of the New Testament*).[47] Wesley's companion volume, *Explanatory Notes on the Old Testament*, was likewise dependent on Puritan biblical scholarship, since it uses as a major source Matthew Henry's *Exposition of the Old and New Testaments*.

The Arminian Magazine provided Wesley with an excellent vehicle through which to publish many brief tracts and exemplary lives, as well as such curious articles as *An Extract from Mr. Baxter's Certainty of the World of Spirits fully evinced by Unquestionable Histories of Apparitions and Witchcraft*.[48]

This cursory look at Wesley's general publications reveals essentially the same patterns in the use of Puritan materials as found in *A Christian Library*. A broad range of authors is represented, drawn largely from the latter half of the seventeenth century—although, to be sure, more of his contemporaries are represented. The most significant addition evident in these works is Wesley's acknowledged indebtedness to Puritan scholarship in the formulation of his biblical commentaries.

Wesley's Familiarity with Puritan Materials

Examination of Wesley's use of Puritan literature reveals many interesting and instructive features of Wesley's relationship to the Puritan tradition. However, the major contribution of any such examination is its demonstration of Wesley's thorough acquaintance with the wide range of Puritan literature. He was not only acquainted with the leaders of the Puritan tradition but knew the writings of some of its lesser known representatives.

This familiarity with the Puritans is surprising for a person of Wesley's education and vocation, and it must have raised some questions among his co-workers in the Church of England. The Presbyterian Phillip Doddridge's comment, in his letter to Wesley, is instructive at this point:

> I will not presume, Sir, to mention to you the Divines of the

> Established Church though to my Pupils I have given a larger enumeration of the principal of them, . . . But, as I may reasonably conclude, the Puritans, and the Divines of the Separation, less known to the Generality of those with whom you, Sir, may be concerned, you will pardon me, that I mention a few of them, and of the chief Pieces.[49]

Doddridge's subtle apology for including Puritans assumed that a person of Wesley's background would normally have little familiarity with, or interest in, the Puritans. Church of England men were usually loath to study or acquaint themselves with anyone under the stigma of separation. Although Wesley may have gained an appreciation for some writers of the Puritan tradition in his home, the prejudices of his formal education would not have encouraged pursuit of these materials. The breadth of his reading in these writers is, therefore, even more remarkable since familiarity with the tradition was largely gained after his formal education.

Like Doddridge, who did not allow party label to deter him from familiarity with the "valuable writings of the Established Church," Wesley, in contrast to most of his contemporaries, overlooked the points of separation to view the universal truths contained in the Puritan writings. In doing so he gave expression to the catholicity of his religious viewpoint.

Where or when Wesley gained an acquaintance with these works is largely a matter of conjecture. V. H. H. Green's listing of Wesley's readings in the period 1725-34 notes only a few of the more renowned materials: Milton's *Paradise Lost*, Bishop Hall's *Contemplation of the New Testament*, Isaac Watts's *On Predestination*, and the works of Richard Baxter, Edmund Calamy, and Samuel Clarke.[50] Perhaps Wesley's Georgia experiences with the Moravians whetted his interest in English writers who stressed justification by faith and the immediacy of contact with the Holy Spirit. In any case, Wesley's Georgia diaries indicate that in the winter and spring of 1737 he read such Puritan works as Bishop Hall's *Meditation on Heaven*, Clarke's *Lives*, the *Works* of John Owen, Milton's *Paradise Regained*, *The Life of Thomas Halyburton*, and the *Catechism of the Assembly* (presumably that of the Westminster Assembly).[51] In the autumn after Aldersgate (1738), he read Edwards's "truly surprising narrative of the conversions lately wrought in and about the town of Northampton, in New England."[52] May 1739 found him reading Daniel Neal's *History of the Puritans*,[53] and in October of that year he mentions reading *Bunyan's Life*, as well as his *Pilgrim's Progress* and, once again, Milton's *Paradise Lost*.[54] Examination of the titles referred to in his journals and letters until the publication of *A Christian Library* fails to reveal any broad reading among Puritans.[55] Those mentioned represent some of the more important and commonly read of the Puritan materials but give no indication of Wesley's knowledge of the far wider range of Puritan authors represented in *A Christian Library*. Doddridge's advice no doubt gave Wesley some direction in reading these authors, but comparison of Wesley's selection with Doddridge's list shows that these suggestions constitute only a small part of the writings finally included.[56]

The most plausible explanation for this familiarity is that, once Wesley was willing to drop the prejudices of education and background, he was open to materials explicating the "Christian life," no matter what their source. This concern must have led him to those writings with a heavy emphasis on practical divinity, which, of course, included the Puritan writers. His insatiable reading habits could well account for the wide range of authors. On the other hand, as we shall see, Wesley was willing to credit the Puritans with preeminence in this area, and, recognizing this, he may well have made a thorough and exhaustive examination of their writings. However their inclusion may be explained, Wesley clearly was not only familiar with the tradition, but also willing to permit their insights concerning the Christian faith and life to play a vital role in the instruction of his own people.

Notes

1. *Letters*, 6:201. Richard Baxter in the previous century had suggested that printing the gospel message had many advantages: people could read a powerful preacher whether or not they were privileged to hear one, books were available when preachers were not, and books could be read over and over. Richard Baxter, *A Christian Directory*: or, *A Summ of Practical Theologie, and Cases of Conscience* (London: By Robert White for Nevil Simmons, 1673), pt. 1, chap. 2, 60.

2. Frank Baker reports that John and Charles Wesley "issued some 450 literary works, which passed through about 2,000 editions." Frank Baker, *John Wesley: London Publisher, 1733-1791* (London: Friends of Wesley's Chapel, 1984), 1. See also Frank Baker, *A Union Catalogue of the Publications of John and Charles Wesley* (Stone Mountain, Ga.: George Zimmerman, 1991); T. W. Herbert, *John Wesley as Editor and Author* (Princeton: Princeton University Press, 1940), 2; James Joy, "Wesley: Man of a Thousand Books and a Book," *Religion in Life*, 8 (1939): 73.

3. *Works*, 26:323. In a letter to E. Blackwood, a London banker friend, on this same day Wesley suggested the project might include some 60 to 80 volumes that would include works already published, and commented that he was thinking of publishing some one hundred copies (*Works*, 26:322). This small publishing number suggests he intended it primarily for his preachers. In any case, there were no "whole tracts" included

without abridgments, and very few explanatory notes were added.

4. *Works*, 20:264.

5. Philip Doddridge "Letter to Mr. Wesley: A Scheme of Study for a Clergyman," *The Arminian Magazine*, 1 (1778): 419. Wesley may have gained his original idea for such a publication from an early work by his father. As a leading member of the Athenian Society, Samuel Wesley was a major contributor to one of their publications, entitled *A Young Student's Library*, a work of extracts and abridgments "of the most valuable books" on general knowledge (Tyerman, *Life and Times of the Rev. Samuel Wesley, A.M.*, 150). See also E. Martin, "The Christian Library," *WHSP* 2 (1899-1900): 191.

6. John Wesley, *A Christian Library*, 2nd ed. (London: Printed by T. Cordeux, for T. Blanshard, 1819-26), 2:3. Cited hereafter as *CL*. Wesley's inquiry to Doddridge requested such practical divinity: "I shall remember that your inquiry chiefly relates to books of practical divinity." Doddridge, "Letter to Mr. Wesley," 419.

7. *CL*, 1:69 (italics added). Professor Outler points out that this work was credited in the eighteenth century to "Marcarius the Egyptian" but was written by a fifth-century Syrian monk greatly dependent on Gregory of Nyssa (Albert Outler, ed., *John Wesley* [New York: Oxford University Press, 1964], 9).

8. *CL*, 1:viii. Wesley's concern to express the teachings of the gospel in the language of the people was most directly stated in the introduction to his sermons: "I design plain truth for plain people: Therefore, . . . I abstain from all nice and philosophical speculations; from all perplexed and intricate reasonings. . . . I labour to avoid all words which are not easy to be understood, all which are not used in common life; and in particular those kinds of technical terms that so frequently occur in bodies of Divinity; those modes of speaking which men of reading are intimately acquainted with, but which to common people are an unknown tongue" (*Works*, 1:104).

9. *CL*, 1:ix; cf. 4:106.

10. Stephen Church, "Letter to the Rev. Mr. Wesley," *The London Magazine* 29 (1760): 587.

11. Wesley recognized, after some debate, that a tract entitled *The Scripture Doctrine of Imputed Righteousness Asserted and Maintained by The Rev. Mr. John Wesley, Author of the Preservative against Unsettled Notions in Religion. Extracted from His Own Publications* had, in fact, been taken largely from *A Christian Library* and could on occasion be quoted in opposition to his own theological statements (*Letters* 4:207; *Works* [Jackson], 10:381ff.).

12. *Works* (Jackson), 10:382.

13. *Works* (Jackson), 10:382.

14. *Works* (Jackson), 10:381-82. Responding to these criticisms, Wesley attempted to correct the mistakes he recognized in the *Library*. He modified his own copy, and it is this hand-corrected copy that forms the basis of the second edition, issued under the editorship of Thomas Jackson in 1819-26. The present study uses this second edition of the *Library* in its references to the work. For comment on the second edition see Richard Green, *The Works of John and Charles Wesley: A Bibliography* (London: Methodist Publishing House, 1906), 95, cited hereafter as

Bibliography; Didymus [pseud.], "Mr. Wesley's *Christian Library*," *The Wesleyan-Methodist Magazine* 6 (1827): 313.

15. *Letters*, 4:121.

16. With all Wesley's fine plans and diligent work on *A Christian Library*, one might expect it to share the phenomenal success that most of his abridgments enjoyed; unfortunately, this was not the case. A melancholy entry in the *Journal*, dated November 6, 1752, noted that Wesley had lost money on the venture. The entry closed with the plaintive statement: "Perhaps the next generation may know the value of it" (*Works*, 20:443). In spite of this, he never ceased to insist that his preachers study it for their own instruction and share it with the societies (*Works*, 20:486; *Letters*, 4:272; 7:64, 83).

17. *CL*, 4:105.

18. Wesley's specific mention of Thomas Goodwin, a renowned leader of the Nonconformists, who was prominent in the latter half of the seventeenth century, suggests that Wesley intended to include in his comments the heroes of Nonconformity, along with the pre-1662 Puritans whose work is prefaced by this particular introduction.

19. Stephen Church, "Letter to the Rev. Mr. Wesley," 587.

20. "Letter to Mr. T. H., alias Philodemus, alias Somebody, alias Stephen Church, alias, R. W.," *London Magazine* 29 (1760): 651.

21. William Haller, *The Rise of Puritanism* (New York: Harper and Row, 1957), 16.

22. *Works* (Jackson), 8:114; 1:262; 2:49; *Works*, 20:485. R. Butterworth suggests that Wesley used the term "Dissenter" to refer to Independents as distinguished from Presbyterians ("Wesley and the Dissenters," *WHSP* 8 [1911-12]: 27).

23. Joseph Hall, Robert Bolton, John Preston, Richard Sibbes, Samuel Clarke, and John Foxe.

24. Volume 7 of the first edition of *A Christian Library* contains Wesley's comments on the Puritans.

25. To this number could be added the major work of joint Puritan authorship, *An Extract from the Assembly's Shorter Catechism*. See chap. 1 for additional comment on the definition of the term "Puritan."

26. A complete list of the authors included appears in app. 1. Classification of these authors into the various categories is dependent upon information obtained in the *Dictionary of National Biography*, Edmund Calamy's three lists of ministers ejected in 1662, A. G. Matthew's *Calamy Revised*, Benjamin Brooks's *Lives of the Puritans*, Daniel Neal's *History of the Puritans*, Samuel Clarke's various *Lives* and martyrologies, and other standard bibliographical reference works. For purposes of this calculation those persons from the early period when Puritanism constituted a "party" within the Church of England have been counted as Puritans; and those who conformed in 1662, even though some may have had Puritan sympathies, have been counted among the Church of England authors. I am indebted to Lawrence McIntosh, Theological Librarian at Drew University when the first edition of this study was published, for pointing out that I had mistakenly identified Benjamin Calamy, the author of one set of sermons, as Edmund Calamy, Benjamin's father (see app. 1, n. 10). This

changes the Puritan and Church of England totals given in the first edition.

27. According to a cursory count of the pages of the second edition of the *Library*, Puritan materials constitute some 7,150 pages, whereas the Church of England materials make up only 3,950.

28. *DNB*, 33:5. Baxter distinguished three kinds of conformists: the conformists proper, some of the old ministers formerly called Presbyterians, and the Latitudinarians. The Presbyterians in this group conformed and subscribed to the Act of Uniformity with the understanding that the bishop bade them "do it in their own sense." The Latitudinarians were mostly Cambridge men and included the Cambridge Platonists. According to Baxter, these were "ingenious Men and Scholars, and of Universal Principles and free, abhorring at first the *Imposition* of these little things, but thinking them not great enough to stick at when *Imposed*" (*Reliquiae Baxterianae, or Mr. Richard Baxter's Narrative of His Life and Times* [London: by Matthew Sylvester, 1696], pt. 2, 386).

29. *DNB*, 48:40. Henry Scougal (d. 1678), another Scottish divine with opinions close to those of Leighton, was reverenced among the Puritans as one of their own (*DNB*, 33:5). George Whitefield attributes his conversion to Scougal's *The Life of God in the Soul of Men*, which had been given to him by Charles Wesley (G. Whitefield, *Journal* [London: Banner of Truth Trust, 1960], 46-47).

30. *DNB*, 13:271; 53:74. Baxter judged them, along with the "old Presbyterians," to be the "honour of the Conformists" whose "profitable Preaching is used, by God's Providence, to keep up the Public Interest of Religion, and refresh the discerning sort of Auditors" (*Reliquiae Baxterianae*, pt. 2:386). For an examination of Wesley's use of the group, see John C. English, "The Cambridge Platonists in Wesley's 'Christian Library,'" *WHSP*, 35 (October, 1968): 161-68.

31. CL, 1:106; cf. *DNB*, 24:77. See Douglas Bush's *English Literature in the Earlier Seventeenth Century: 1600-1660* (Oxford: Clarendon Press, 1945), 323, for comments of one who did not consider Hall to be a Puritan.

32. John Foxe, *Acts and Monuments of the Christian Martyrs, and Matters Ecclesiasticall Passed in the Church of Christ, from the Primitive beginnings, to These Our Daies* (London: Printed for the Company of Stationers, 1641). Foxe was listed as a Puritan by Benjamin Brook, *The Lives of the Puritans* (London: Printed for James Black, 1813), 1:326; Daniel Neal, *History of the Puritans* (Dublin: Printed for Brice Edmond, 1755), 1:146-47; *DNB*, 20:142-48.

33. Samuel Clarke (1599-1683), the Puritan divine, is not to be confused with the famous metaphysician of the same name, Samuel Clarke (1675-1729). The latter was the chaplain to the Bishop of Norwick, whose theories on the Trinity caused him to be accused of Arianism (*DNB*, 10:441-42).

34. For comparative lists of Puritans in *A Christian Library* see Coomer, "Influence of Puritanism and Dissent on Methodism," 347, and Newton, *Methodism and the Puritans*, 8.

35. John Foxe's *Acts and Monuments*, Thomas Fuller's *The History of the Worthies of England*, and Samuel Clarke's *A General Martyrology* and *The Life of Sundry Eminent Persons in this Later Age* are some of the more re-

nowned works of this type. See Haller, *Rise of Puritanism*, 101, for Richard Baxter's comment on the importance of the spiritual character of such works.

36. "I have therefore been obliged to vary from my first design, both by omitting many lives which Mr. Clarke has inserted, . . . and by inserting those of some whom he has omitted, but who were men famous in their generations, and highly esteemed by all who love the image of God, in whomsoever it may be found" (*CL*, 15:3). Additions to Clarke's accounts include the lives of Richard Hooker (d. 1600), Sir Henry Wooton (d. 1639), John Donne (d. 1631), George Herbert (d. 1633), Bishop William Bedell (d. 1642), Archbishop Ussher (d. 1613), and Henry Hammond (d. 1660).

37. A complete list of exemplary lives may be reviewed in app. 2.

38. An examination of the first few issues of *The Arminian Magazine*, begun by Wesley in 1778, reveals a number of hagiographies drawn from the ranks of Methodist societies. Wesley's *Journal* is filled with what he usually terms a "remarkable account," that is, an account of the work of the gospel in the life of a sinner (*Journal*, 4:268-69, 381-87). See also Richard Green's items 89, 188, 215, in *Bibliography*; Herbert, *John Wesley as Editor and Author*, 12-13.

39. Richard Green's comprehensive *Bibliography*, with the corrections and additions to it found in the *Wesley Historical Society Proceedings*, is the basis of this survey (*WHSP*, 3 [1901-02]: 123-30; 21 [1937-38]: 132-33). Collections of hymns and psalms are considered in this calculation, although Clifford Towlson points out that Wesley's early (1737) *Collection of Psalms and Hymns* is largely dependent upon similar publications of Isaac Watts (*Moravian and Methodist* [London: Epworth Press, 1957], 196-98).

40. Several of these are also found in *A Christian Library*, although some are new abridgments.

41. Wesley, quite wisely, seldom attempted the abridgment of such renowned literary pieces as these works of Milton and Bunyan, and the general opinion of his few endeavors is negative. (See *Bibliography*, 28; Herbert, *John Wesley as Editor and Author*, 85-88.)

42. *Works*, 22:121. Wesley's understanding of the motivations underlying his publications compared to that of others became obvious as he commented on Watts's treatise: "I abridged Dr. Watts's pretty 'Treatise on the Passions.' His hundred and seventy-seven pages will make a useful tract of four-and-twenty. Why do persons who treat the same subjects with me, write so much larger books? Of many reasons, is not this the chief,--We do not write with the same view? Their *principal end* is to get money; my *only one* is to do good."

43. Wesley read Halyburton's life while in Georgia and made it one of his earliest publications (1739)(*Works*, 18:461-2). Along with *Pilgrim's Progress* and instruction to "transcribe and repeat select portions of Milton," it appeared in Wesley's plan for study at Kingswood School. See Ives, *Kingswood School*.

44. Edwards's work was characterized by Wesley's preface as a "dangerous heap wherein much wholesome food is mixed with much deadly poison." The poison, Calvinism, was naturally eliminated in the abridgment (*Bibliography*, 170). Wesley, in his treatise "Thoughts upon

Necessities," closely examined Edwards's famous *Freedom of the Will* and argued against its teachings (*Works* [Jackson], 10:460, 463, 475).

45. Charles Rogers's "John Wesley and Jonathan Edwards," *Duke Divinity School Review* 31(1966): 20-38, provides a suggestive examination of Wesley's relation to Edwards. See also Albert Outler's suggestions concerning Edwards's contribution to Wesley's doctrine of the Spirit (*John Wesley*, 15-16); Gregory Clapper, "'True Religion' and the Affections: A Study of John Wesley's Abridgement of Jonathan Edwards' *Treatise on Religious Affections*," *Wesleyan Theological Journal* 19 (1984): 77-89.

46. The latter work was published in successive issues of vol. 3 (1780) of *The Arminian Magazine*.

47. John Wesley, *Explanatory Notes upon the New Testament* (London: Epworth Press, 1958), 7-8. John Guyse (1680-1761) was an Independent minister well-known as a defender of orthodoxy against the Arian theories popular in his day (*DNB*, 23:394). For comment on Wesley's dependence on these sources, see *Bibliography*, 91-92; *Works*, 20:484.

48. *The Arminian Magazine* 6 (1785).

49. "Letter to Mr. Wesley: A Scheme of Study for a Clergyman," *The Arminian Magazine* 1 (1778): 421.

50. V. H. H. Green, *The Young Mr. Wesley* (New York: St. Martin's, 1961), 305-19.

51. *Works*, 18:461, 463, 473, 487, 503, 510.

52. *Works*, 19:16.

53. *Works*, 19:390.

54. *Works*, 19:410, 414.

55. "A Bibliographical Catalog of Books Mentioned in John Wesley's Journals," *WHSP* 4 (1903-04): 17-19, 47-51, 74-81, 107-11.

56. See app. 1 for this kind of a comparison. Isabel Rivers suggests several reasons for Wesley's attraction to Puritan authors and provides a most insightful comparison of the educational and publishing patterns of Wesley and Doddridge (I. Rivers, "Dissenting and Methodist Books of Practical Divinity," in *Books and Their Readers in 18th Century England* [New York: St. Martin's, 1982], 149-50).

3

Wesley's Abridgment of Puritan Literature

Commendable and beneficial abridgment is a work of art; John Wesley was a master of the medium. His methodology perhaps anticipated that of the modern-day digests, although his service as the entire editorial staff for such projects might challenge modern editors. The range and variety of his abridging Puritan authors is apparent from the previous chapter, but this material makes up only a part of his extensive abridgments. Almost any printed material in the field of religion was "fair game." Osborn's reported comment is certainly germane: "It is a wonder Mr. Wesley did not abridge the Gospel according to St. John."[1]

Wesley's primary objectives in editing, as stated in the preface to *A Christian Library*, explain his aspiration to clarify for the common reader a "practical divinity" that could be used in daily life. He was not interested in pursuing what he considered excessive attention to the arguments, illustrations, and general wordiness found in many treatises that he chose to abridge.[2] His modifications were often, therefore, technical in nature, for example, deletion of illustrations, elimination of foreign and specialized words, and modernization of language. Others, however, were clearly dependent on Wesley's theological biases and his desire to "preserve a consistency throughout" the writings. Detailed comparison of several original unexpurgated treatises and Wesley's editions of those works illustrates the complexity and variety of his abridging patterns.

For such an investigation four works have been chosen to provide comparative examples. John Preston's *New Covenant*, with its interest in Christian perfection, comes from the early seventeenth century, when the Puritan cause constituted one "party" within the Church of England.[3] An example of a substantial theological analysis is found in John Owen's *On Communion with God the Father, Son, and Holy Ghost.*[4] Richard Alleine's *Vindiciae Pietatis: or A Vindication of Godliness* provides an example of Puritan instructional patterns.[5] The Westminster *Shorter Catechism* allows examination of a major Puritan teaching tool modified by Wesley for use among Methodists.[6]

Most Puritan works used by Wesley were available in early editions during his own time; however, there is no reliable way to ascertain the editions he actually abridged. From his comments concerning their preparation for the printer, we can assume that he possessed copies that he could mark freely; thus the editions he used were likely current and in plentiful supply.[7]

Methods of Abridgment

Wesley's objectives in abridgment included retaining the truth of the publication, clarity of presentation, brevity within the bounds of conveying essential meaning, and readability for the typical Methodist society member. To accomplish his goals, he often chose to provide reading material for his followers in duodecimo pocket-books (5 by 7.5-inch pages bound in books that might hold up to 350 pages). These smaller books could be easily carried in one's pocket. Many theological books had traditionally been printed in oversize folios (12 to 15 inches in height) suitable for the university, but a book that size was effectively unavailable to the common person: "If Angels were to write books, we should have very few Folios."[8] To achieve his purpose Wesley chose to reduce substantially many theological works so that they might fit into the duodecimo limitations.

Effective and useful editing required Wesley to apply the many tools of abridgment expertly. The omission of material to secure brevity needs little explanation or comment; however, the methods employed by Wesley to accomplish such a reduction of materials are instructive. Brevity is normally obtained through three basic methods: omission of large sections of material, deletion of whole sentences, and exclusion of particular words and clauses. Wesley's editing pen masterfully applied each method, although he seems to have preferred the latter two. In Alleine's *Vindiciae Pietatis* there is thorough and meticulous modification sentence by sentence.[9] The material retained from Preston's *New Covenant* receives the same treatment, yet the total work is reduced by better than 90 percent—from an original 486-page treatise to a mere 45-page abridgment. When allowances are made for smaller type and a somewhat larger printed page used in Wesley's edition, the reduction is still extraordinary.

Deletion and Conflation

Wesley commonly deleted strictly illustrative, explanatory, or embellishing statements. The following example from Alleine's *Vindiciae Pietatis* is typical of Wesley's elimination of repetitious and superfluous words and clauses. (For purposes of this study Wesley's abridgments of original materials are illustrated through the following system of markings: The original words of the text that Wesley omitted are set in italics; Wesley's additions are in brackets; text used by both the original author and Wesley is set in boldface. Where Wesley does not modify the quoted passage, such markings are omitted.)

> **Fleshly Wisdom,** *a carnal* [or] **Policy; which consists in an understanding where the interest of the flesh lies, and in the ordering** *and managing* **of ourselves and our affairs so, that we may advance and secure this interest. By the interest in the flesh, I mean, all those things which please and gratify** [nature] *the flesh, and wherewith the fleshly minds of men are most delighted, and place their content and happiness in,* **as outward peace and quiet,** *outward ease and security, outward* **plenty and prosperity,** *outward* **credit and reputation.**[10]

Because most Puritan literature consisted of published sermons often full of such illustrative and explanatory commentary, this type of expurgation was common. Hortatory passages, so prevalent in sermon material, suffered the same fate.[11]

With the ordinary reader in mind, Wesley frequently eliminated foreign language words and phrases, retaining the English translation usually included in the original treatise.[12] Wesley often kept Greek and Latin terms, a mainstay in seventeenth- and eighteenth-century theological writings, but dropped extended discussions of the meaning and etymology of such words.[13] Where foreign language words were essential to the meaning of a passage, Wesley carefully retained them.

Still pursuing the interests of the common reader, Wesley made prime targets of his editorial pen those philosophical arguments supported by technical and scholastic exposition. Again, where such arguments formed an integral part of the treatises and could be omitted only to the detriment of the whole work, they were preserved. John Owen, for example, clothed almost every point in philosophical phrasing; therefore, Wesley tempered much of the treatise's academic pattern while retaining the salient points in more common speech. Where possible, he expurgated without hesitancy strictly philosophical arguments and explanations that played only a supporting role.[14] This practice is clearly evident when arguments from proportionality and a detailed discussion concerning the nature of God as simple, perfect without mixture, composition, or number were omitted from Preston's work.[15] Wesley, in most cases, as in this one, was satisfied simply to retain the statements concerning the nature of God, without including the philosophical argument. Technicalities of an involved theological statement were often reduced or omitted if they contained nothing that Wesley judged to be particularly instructive for his reader: **"The business of sending the Holy Ghost by Christ,** *which argues his personal procession also from him, the son,* **was a deep mystery which at once they could not bear; and therefore he thus instructs them in it by degrees."**[16]

Theological and philosophical controversy frequently has been dependent upon particular issues facing Christians or the church during a specific historical moment. Consequently, it often becomes dated quickly and, therefore, irrelevant to a later historical setting. True to his principle of deleting what he thought of as unnecessary controversy, especially that which was dated, Wesley omitted Alleine's derogatory reference to a "zealous Advocate for the lawfulness of sports on the Lord's Day."[17] In a similar vein Wesley omitted Owen's statements decrying the Church of England's decision to eject ministers who insisted upon free forms of worship.[18] Wesley could accept the sentiment of Owen's objection but perhaps hesitated to raise the issue in his own time, for he too was regularly accused of similarly modifying established worship patterns. Nevertheless, where controversial comments, written in the heat of earlier conflict, still had relevance to problems of Wesley's time, they were often preserved. Alleine's insistence on the significance and meaning of outward, public worship was retained, probably to instruct Wesley's readers, many of whom were also raising questions about such practices.

Preston's work furnishes a good example of Wesley's tendency to conflate what in the original may be separate chapters into one continuous narrative. *The New Covenant* was composed of fourteen separate sermons, but in Wesley's edition, divested of introductory and summary materials, it became one continuous treatise with no chapter or sermon divisions.

Such concern for brevity sometimes caused Wesley to create passages that were either confusing or that obviously changed the sense of the original. The deletion of a question and the retention of its explanation was, at best, confusing. Wesley's failure to eliminate or change pronouns resulted in their occasionally referring to the wrong antecedents.[19] Meaning was often therefore changed, albeit unintentionally. Such examples might be more readily excused if Wesley had intended to "correct" or amend the text, as he often allowed himself the liberty to do: but where they were evidently the consequence only of expurgation that does not carefully reorient the context, they might well have been avoided.

Transitions and Clarifications

Wesley clarified confusing and repetitious points by omission and, where necessary, the addition of transitional comments. Preston's tract was often confusing, since, when he moved from one point to another in the general outline, no indication was given of a new departure. Conversely, so many points were numbered serially that it became difficult for a reader to retain a clear understanding of what the numbers referred to. Wesley addressed this uncertainty by clarifying the transitions and eliminating many of the unnecessary references to series.[20] It may well be that this confusing aspect of Preston's work led Wesley to make the work one continuous treatise.

Clarification occasionally also made it necessary to insert explanatory comments. For example, Preston's comments on humanity's responsibility in the covenant with God gave no indication of the topic under discussion. No such ambiguity was present in Wesley's edition, wherein the passage was prefaced with this statement: "But here consider what is the condition of this covenant of grace on man's part."[21]

Modernization and Substitution

Antiquated words were modernized; Alleine's "phanatic" becomes Wesley's "enthusiast," a word that by Wesley's own day had taken on Alleine's meaning.[22] Crude expressions of an earlier age were changed to their more acceptable equivalents.[23]

The substitution of one word for another occasionally changed the emphasis of a statement, giving it added significance: "Your" became "our," broadening the scope of the passage; "soul" became "person" to give emphasis to the total being rather than to indicate only the spiritual "part" of a person; "saint" became "Christian," changing the nuance slightly but significantly.[24] Grammatical changes or corrections were commonplace, usually included to rectify antiquated practices.

On the whole, the additions were few and generally of this type, although simple explanatory sentences or phrases were occasionally interpolated.[25] A few summary sections may be noted wherein the full text was replaced by Wesley's comments, but this was also the exception rather than the rule.[26]

Paraphrasing and Rearrangement

Paraphrasing and rearrangement are always among the most effective means of obtaining clarity and brevity. In Wesley's hands they also offered additional opportunities to make changes that he thought might "improve" or correct the thought of the treatise. The following is a representative example:

> *The third thing to be expressed, is the manner of writing it; the apostle here compares himself and all other ministers to the pen, but it is Christ that writes the epistle, the epistle is His, fore these works he doth in it, it is He that takes the pen, it is He that handles it, and useth it, it is He that puts inke into the pen, it is He that applies it, so that though the minister be the immediate writer of these lawes in the heart, yet the inke is the Holy Ghost, and it comes originally from Christ, and besides they* **[Now you must observe that it is Christ that thus writes the law of God in the heart of man, which he doth ordinarily, by means of the minister (who is, as it were, the pen), through the power of the Holy Ghost (which is, as it were, the ink;) for the means] are not left to themselves, but the *Lord* must concurre with them immediately; *we* [the ministers] are but *coworkers with him*, he holds *our* [their] hands, as it were, when *we* [they] write the Epistle in any man's heart, it is he that guides the *penne*, [pen] as it is he that puts Inke into it,** *it comes originally from him*, **and therefore the Epistle is his.**[27]

Wesley's addition of the word "ordinarily" to the sentence, explaining Christ's working through the minister, left no question that there are other means by which the Holy Spirit might effect a change in the hearts of men, a point Preston would have readily admitted but which is not clear in his statement.[28]

Wesley's paraphrasing of the statement and the use of the words "as it were" also assured that the reader would not miss the metaphorical character of the statement.

Each of the foregoing methods of abridgment, when joined to the next, produces an instructive image of Wesley's employment of customary editing tools. Nevertheless, only in abstraction is one able to separate these technical patterns of abridgment from the preponderant influence of theological considerations in Wesley's modifications of another's work.

Theological Considerations in Abridgment

Although the usual methods of editing and abridging certainly account for much of Wesley's modifications of a treatise, perhaps of more import are the theological principles that guided many changes. The theological interest and personal allegiances of any religious editor obviously affect how that editor selects materials to be retained or excised. For purposes of this study, comparison of the original texts and Wesley's abridgments allow us, through attention to the *content* of deletions, changes, and embellishments, to identify specific areas of theological affinity and difference between Wesley and the Puritans.

In the bulk of this study I investigate Wesley's affinities with Puritan teachings and practice; however, before proceeding to consider those in detail, I examine in the remainder of this chapter Wesley's conspicuous differences with the Puritans on particular doctrines. Consistent omission of certain Puritan doctrines or concepts and the systematic modification of specific ideas serve to identify most of these differences.[29]

If it is granted that the Westminster *Shorter Catechism*, within the limits imposed upon it by its purpose, incorporates the major theological precepts of the Puritan tradition, this work may be taken as one guide to the theological divergencies between Wesley and that tradition. Examination of Wesley's abridgment of the catechism reveals several obvious differences. Wesley simply deleted from the catechism questions that considered election and predestination,[30] effectual calling,[31] and the decrees of God.[32] Such questions and their answers incorporated, or at least implied, a traditional Calvinistic interpretation of predestination and salvation. The questions suggested that God chose *some* persons for eternal salvation but not others—that is to say, God's grace is not universally offered. In Wesley's understanding God's saving grace is offered to all persons, not just some, so Wesley dropped those questions and answers.[33] Other references to election or predestination were similarly modified; for example, "God's elect" became "mankind,"[34] and "they that are effectually called" became "they that truly believe."[35]

Wesley's treatment of the election issue in the catechism was similarly applied to other works as he consistently deleted and corrected such passages.[36] A representative example is his alterations of Preston's comment: **"Even men, *they* do us not (without his** *commission* **[permission]) the least good, nor the least hurt."**[37] Passages that depended upon predestinarian concepts were omitted, such as Preston's argument that God directs every act of humanity.

A corollary to predestinarianism was the doctrine of perseverance; that is, if a person is one of the elect chosen by God's irresistible grace, that person may never completely lose his or her "reward"—eternal life—because for an "elect" person to turn completely away from God would not be possible. Wesley recognized that such a doctrine ultimately jeopardized responsible moral action, as salvation, under this scheme, is never threatened by one's own acts. The antinomianism Wesley so vehemently fought among his followers was a logical outgrowth of such teaching.[38] Accordingly, passages dealing with perseverance were generally dropped.[39]

Another important omission from *The Shorter Catechism* was its question concerning perfection: "Q. Is any man able perfectly to keep the commandments of God? A. No mere man since the fall is able in this life perfectly to keep the commandments of God, but doth daily break them in thought, word and deed."[40] The Westminster divines, acknowledging the nature of sinfulness even in the elect, effectively rejected the possibility of perfection. Wesley no doubt believed that the catechism statement unduly limited God's grace that, in his understanding, could make a person perfect in love within one's earthly life. Wesley agreed with the framers of the catechism that sinfulness often remained in believers; but, at the same time, he insisted that God's grace could, even so, "perfect" one's love. "If love is the sole principle of action" and if the believer has "the mind that was in Christ," all things are done in love.[41] The perfected believer made "mistakes" because of infirmities, ignorance, misjudgment, and so on, which are in fact morally imperfect; yet, because these are not contrary to perfect love, they are not "sins."[42] For Wesley this meant that perfection was a possibility, through God's grace, for every believer, although he never claimed to have received "perfection" himself. The catechism's denial of the possibility of perfection meant Wesley, true to his own beliefs, had to change it.

His doctrine of perfection also led to other alterations: **"Q. What benefits do Believers receive from Christ at [their] death? A. The souls of Believers** *are* **at their death** *made perfect in Holiness, and do immediately* **pass into glory; and their bodies,** *being still united to Christ, do* **rest in their graves till the Resurrection."**[43] Perfection is allowed, in this statement, at the moment of death but no earlier. Wesley, believing that perfection was an ever-present possibility, deleted those phrases that were contrary to his own opinion.[44]

Similarly, the *Catechism* question and answer that defined sanctification demanded a slight but significant omission. **"Sanctification is the word of God's free grace, whereby we are renewed in the whole man after the image of God, and are enabled** *more and more* **to dye unto sin, and to live unto righteousness."**[45] To retain the phrase "more and more" threatened the possibility of "entire sanctification" or perfection in this life.[46] "More and more" assumes that a person is never completely dead unto sin, an assumption Wesley was not willing to make. It should be noted, however, that Wesley understood that the sanctification operative in most believers, those not blessed with perfection, to be a gradual and continual process.

Another significant Wesleyan omission from the catechism was a question on the nature of adoption, and references to the doctrine in other questions.[47] This is a perplexing deletion because Wesley evidently held the traditional interpretation that believers are received into relationship with God through adoption as daughters and sons. Romans 8:14-16, the classic Scripture text for the doctrine, was the basis for his sermon "The Spirit of Bondage and Adoption."[48] Adoption was also incorporated into his order of salvation. James MacDonald suggests that the question was omitted for brevity and "in order to throw into bolder relief two great cardinal crises of the believer's experience, commonly called justification and sanctification."[49] MacDonald may be correct, as justification and sanctification were normally the poles supporting the other elements in Wesley's order of salvation. In the catechism the order is "justification, adoption, sanctification," apparently giving equal place to a believer's adoption as is given to justification and sanctification. Wesley may have sought, by deleting adoption, to place justification and sanctification in "bolder relief" with no intention of objecting to adoption. Another plausible explanation for its deletion is the close connection in the catechism between adoption and the decrees and election.[50]

The remaining changes made in the catechism generally represent concerns of clarity or brevity. One worthy of note is Wesley's modification of the catechism's definition of the Lord's Supper. In the phrase "according to Christ's appointment" Wesley changed "Christ's" to "God's," making the sacrament rest on the authority of the Godhead instead of on the Son.[51] Wesley evidently wanted to avoid any chance of misrepresentation or misinterpretation about the nature of the sacrament.

A few omissions that hinge on theological presuppositions other than those evident in *The Shorter Catechism* may be noted in the other three treatises examined. Wesley was always conscious of the distinction to be drawn between the life lived by the believer and that by the unbeliever, but he constantly guarded against a believer's interpreting this distinction as a cause for pride. Alleine was not always careful at this point; Wesley consistently deleted passages that might be misinterpreted.[52] The same was true for sections suggesting that a believer might personally profit, either spiritually or materially, from being faithful.[53]

In any comparison of an abridgment with the original, it is an artificial and false procedure to force every omitted passage (or for that matter every passage retained) into a reconstructed logical framework. No doubt, if questioned, the abridger might produce a logical reason for each deletion made, but inevitably some changes are matters of personal preference, interest, and prejudice that are not easily explained from the standpoint of the reader or investigator. As a consequence, some passages must remain puzzling. At times points that seem particularly cogent to the argument or to Wesley's general viewpoint were omitted, while repetitious material was occasionally retained. A partial explanation lies in the natural differing interests of any examiner of an abridgment and those of the person actually doing the abridging. What appears important to one may not seem so to the other. A few of Wesley's changes, therefore, raise tantalizing questions.

Wesley omitted the last eighty pages of John Preston's *The New Covenant,* although this section seems to support Wesley's views on how a believer knows that he or she is "within the fold" of the Christian community—in Preston's words, "if we have the Covenant."[54] Included were the witnesses of faith, the Holy Spirit, our own spirit, the fruits of the spirit, and our readiness to live a Christian life. All these Wesley used in his own treatises and sermons, and it would appear that he might well have retained at least the salient points in his abridgment.[55]

One of Owen's most instructive illustrations denoting the necessity of the Holy Spirit's witness was curiously omitted by Wesley. Using a court case as an illustration, Owen showed that an issue might finally turn on the appearance of a single but essential witness. So it is in the life of a believer; the case is finally decided when one receives the Spirit in his or her own life. The illustration is not only cogent to the context in which it is used but clarifies in commonly understood terms a significant point. It would appear that for Wesley's readers the illustration might have been particularly helpful. Perhaps Owen's "court" image used in reference to the Holy Ghost as Advocate seemed too legalistic for Wesley's understanding of the Spirit of Love.[56]

Alleine's "provisions" for those who could not successfully hold themselves to the rigors of the covenant pattern of life also appears as a curious omission.[57] Alleine outlined a definite pattern of disciplined study, questioning, prayer, and so forth, which is entered into by a covenant with God. In addition, he provided a shorter formula for those without the strength to follow the full course and a special "short-term" vow for those who could not hold themselves to the more demanding obligations. Wesley omitted all these provisions even though he must have recognized that few would be able to abide completely by the provisions of a covenant relationship, since, in his revision of Alleine's covenant service, he suggested it be renewed at least annually. Omissions such as these raise our curiosity but elude the more obvious explanations for omission or change.

These selected examples of Wesley's abridgments make it clear that his theological differences with major tenets of the Puritan tradition center on four principal issues: (1) divine election of believers, (2) the believer's active role in salvation, (3) perseverance of the saints, and (4) the time and extent of human perfectibility. These issues regularly guide his expurgation and modification of Puritan materials.

Patterns of abridgment dependent on technical methods and those denoting theological differences establish interesting and instructive features of Wesley's relationship to the Puritan tradition. However, because the theological abridgments we have considered concentrate on areas of divergence, their contribution, though important, provides only a partial view of Wesley's appropriation of the Puritan ethos and, therefore, do not provide a balanced representation of the relationship. I turn now to examine the significant areas of agreement between the two traditions and their teaching, practice, and thought.

Notes

1. Quoted by Green, *Bibliography*, 171. For further analysis of Wesley's editorial patterns and practices, see Rivers, *Books and Their Readers*, 152ff.; Henry Rack, *Reasonable Enthusiast: John Wesley and the Rise of Methodism* (Nashville: Abingdon Press, 1993), 346ff.

2. *CL*, 1:ix.

3. John Preston, *The New Covenant or The Saint's Portion* (London: Printed by I. D. for Nicholas Bourne, 1630), cited hereafter as *New Covenant*.

4. John Owen, *On Communion with God the Father, Son, and Holy Ghost*, vol. 10 in *The Works of John Owen*, ed. Thomas Russell (London: Printed for Richard Baynes, 1826), cited hereafter as *On Communion*. Owen was the most distinguished pneumatologist among the seventeenth-century Puritans.

5. Richard Alleine, *Vindiciae Pietatis: Or A Vindication of Godliness* (London: 1664), cited hereafter as *Vindiciae Pietatis*. This work also becomes a defense of Puritan tradition after the Restoration, when much of that tradition's popular appeal within the culture had been lost.

6. *The Shorter Catechism of the Westminster Divines: Being a Facsimile of the First Edition "with the Proofs thereof out of the Scriptures;" which Was Ordered to Be Printed by the House of Commons, 14th April, 1648*, ed. J. H. Cotton and J. C. Pears, Jr. (Nashville: Printed for Presbyterian Theological Seminary, Chicago, 1943), cited hereafter as *Shorter Catechism*.

7. *Works* (Jackson), 10:381.

8. *Arminian Magazine*, 4 (1781):iv.

9. Alleine, *Vindiciae Pietatis*, 11 [*CL*, 18:11], 59 [*CL*, 18:42]; *New Covenant*, 87-100 [*CL*, 6:15]. In order to provide adequate information, I include two page references wherever a direct comparison is made between Wesley's abridgment and the original material—the first refers to the page of the original treatise, and the second, in brackets, indicates the page of Wesley's abridged version.

10. Alleine, *Vindiciae Pietatis*, 52 [*CL*, 18:38].

11. Alleine, *Vindiciae Pietatis*, 98-100 [*CL*, 18:69], 109 [*CL*, 18:77].

12. **"And hath a great zeal about** ***the minima leges*****, the lower or more circumstantial matters"** (Alleine, *Vindiciae Pietatis*, 3 [*CL*, 18:7], cf. 29 [*CL*, 18:24]; Owen, *On Communion*, in *Works of John Owen*, 10:275 [*CL*, 11:83], 300 [*CL*, 11:97-98]).

13. Owen, *On Communion*, in *Works of John Owen*, 10:275-76 [*CL*, 11:83-84], cf. 307 [*CL*, 11:100]; Alleine, *Vindiciae Pietatis*, 14 [*CL*, 18:14].

14. Owen, *On Communion*, in *Works of John Owen*, 10:278-79 [*CL*, 11:86], 330 [*CL*, 11:115].

15. Preston, *New Covenant*, 37-42 [*CL*, 6:8], 73 [*CL*, 6:14], 365 [*CL*, 6:41].

16. Owen, *On Communion*, in *Works of John Owen*, 10:277 [*CL*, 11:85].

17. Alleine, *Vindiciae Pietatis*, 120 [*CL*, 18:83]. James I promulgated the *Book of Sports*, allowing certain sports on Sunday—a rude offense to Puritan sentiments that reverenced the Sabbath as a holy day to be observed without frivolity. The statement could also have been understood by Tory Wesley to be anti-Royalist and thereby repugnant, but it is doubtful that Alleine intended it to be so. The offense for Alleine was not political but religious.

18. Owen, *On Communion*, in *Works of John Owen*, 10:313-14 [*CL*, 11:104].

19. Owen, *On Communion*, in *Works of John Owen*, 10:285 [*CL*, 11:89], cf. 315-16 [*CL*, 11:105]; Preston, *New Covenant*, 295 [*CL*, 6:29].

20. Preston, *New Covenant*, 390 [*CL*, 6:42].

21. Preston, *New Covenant*, 360 [*CL*, 6:40].

22. Alleine, *Vindiciae Pietatis*, 95 [*CL*, 18:67], 108 [*CL*, 18:76].

23. **"Lusts are** ***big bellied*****, [prolific], a world of monstrous births are continually springing forth from them"** (Alleine, *Vindiciae Pietatis*, 105 [*CL*, 18:73], cf. 204 [*CL*, 18:144]).

24. Alleine, *Vindiciae Pietatis*, 214 [*CL*, 18:149], 88 [*CL*, 18:62]; Owen, *On Communion*, in *Works of John Owen*, 10:295 [*CL*, 11:94]. It may well be that in this latter case more than change in nuance is implied. For Wesley the word "saint" may have had a sectarian stigma, as in some Puritan usages it implied "the gathered church" rather than the national church.

25. Alleine, *Vindiciae Pietatis*, 300 [*CL*, 18:176].

26. Preston, *New Covenant*, 317 [*CL*, 6:31].

27. Preston, *New Covenant*, 324 [*CL*, 6:33-34], cf. 107 [*CL*, 6:15-16].

28. Wesley always left open the possibility of God's working through lay "instruments" of conversion—lay preachers and teachers.

29. The difficulty of distinguishing between what is omitted because of

basic theological disagreement and what is omitted merely for the sake of brevity calls for caution against overemphasis when one is using this methodology but does not eliminate the significant insights to be gained by it.

30. "Q. Did God leave all mankinde to perish in the estate of sin and misery? A. God, having out of his meere good pleasure from all eternity elected *some* to everlasting life, did enter into a Covenant of grace to deliver them out of the estate of sin and misery, and to bring them into an estate of Salvation by a Redeemer" (*Shorter Catechism*, 8, italics added).

31. "Q. What is Effectual Calling? A. Effectual Calling is the work of God's Spirit, whereby, convincing us of our sin and misery, inlightening our mindes in the knowledge of Christ, and renewing our wills, he doth perswade and inable us to imbrace Jesus Christ freely offered to us in the Gospel" (*Shorter Catechism*, 10).

32. "Q. What are the Decrees of God? A. The Decrees of God are, his eternal purpose according to the counsel of his will, whereby for his own glory, he hath fore-ordained whatsoever comes to pass. Q. How doth God execute his Decrees? A. God executeth his Decrees in the Works of Creation and Providence" (*Shorter Catechism*, 6).

33. The incessant struggle between Wesley and his Calvinistic Methodist contemporaries, who made up a major wing of the eighteenth-century Evangelical Revival, was over this very point of election. As Wesley suggested, his adversaries embraced an interpretation of the Westminster Confession wherein "some men and angels are predestined unto everlasting life, and others [are consequently] fore-ordained to everlasting death" (*Works* [Jackson], 10:206). The latter half of this statement is most offensive to Wesley. The classic statement of his own position is found in his sermon entitled "Free Grace": "The grace or love of God, whence cometh our salvation, is *free in all* and *free for all*" (*Works*, 3:544). Wesley understood all humankind to have an opportunity through "prevenient grace" to accept or reject God's offer of "saving grace." For a larger discussion of this doctrine see the section on "Wesley and Human Appropriation of Grace" in Chapter 4.

34. *Shorter Catechism*, 8 [*CL*, 14:393].

35. *Shorter Catechism*, 10 [*CL*, 14:398].

36. **"Carnal men often come before the Lord with mock praises, give thanks for their** *election*, **justification, sanctification"** (Alleine, *Vindiciae Pietatis*, 155 [*CL*, 18:108], cf. 134-36 [*CL*, 18:94]). **"Now the Holy Spirit is promised under a two-fold consideration. lst. as spirit of sanctification** *to the elect*, **to convert** *them* **[us] and make** *them* **[us] believers"** (Owen, *On Communion*, in *Works of John Owen*, 10:278 [*CL*, 11:85], cf. 294 [*CL*, 11:93-94]).

37. Preston, *New Covenant*, 3 [*CL*, 6:6].

38. For Wesley's criticism of the doctrine, see his tract, *Serious Thought upon the Perseverance of the Saints*, in *Works* (Jackson), 10:284-98, cf. 10:241-54.

39. The following passage illustrates the pattern: "But for the Elect, that can never fall quite away, this diligence is required, and is proper to them; they still look to themselves, lest they lose that which they have

wrought, lest they should not receive a full reward; for, though they cannot lose their reward altogether, yet they may lose a part of their reward" (Preston, *New Covenant*, 264-65 [*CL*, 6:29]). Preston is here attempting to retain responsibility by establishing degrees within the reward—because the comment assumes perseverance and raises the possibility of degrees of salvation, Wesley simply eliminated the statement (cf. Owen, *On Communion*, in *Works of John Owen*, 10:298 [*CL*, 11:97]).

40. *Shorter Catechism*, 17.

41. *A Plain Account of Christian Perfection*, in *Works* (Jackson), 11:383-85.

42. *Works* (Jackson), 11:395-96. For a more extended discussion of the doctrine of perfection and its presence among some Puritans see Chapter 5.

43. *Shorter Catechism*, 11 [*CL*, 14:400].

44. "As to the time, I believe this instant [of perfection] generally is the instant of death, the moment before the soul leaves the body. But I believe it may be ten, twenty or forty years before" (*Works* [Jackson], 11:466.; cf. *Works*, 2:19-20). Although Wesley in this passage accepted the traditional time of perfection to be the general experience of believers, his doctrine of perfection required that it *may be* present during life.

45. *Shorter Catechism*, 10 [*CL*, 14:399].

46. *Works* (Jackson), 8:294.

47. "Q. What is Adoption? A. Adoption is an act of God's free grace, wherebye we are received into the number, and have a right to all the privileges of the Sons of God" (*Shorter Catechism*, 10).

48. *Works*, 1:248-66. "You have not received the spirit of bondage again unto fear; but you have received the Spirit of Adoption, whereby we cry, Abba, Father" (Rom. 8:15; cf. *Works* 1:272, 309, 520).

49. James A. MacDonald, *Wesley's Revision of the Shorter Catechism* (Edinburgh: George A. Morton, 1906), 57. MacDonald provides a useful comparison of Wesley's abridgment of *The Shorter Catechism* with the original and occasionally gives some interesting notes on this abridgment. His purpose is to show "the connection of Methodist Doctrine with that of the Reformed Church, the Ancient faith, and the word of God," which leads him into a good deal of hortatory presentation.

50. Wesley also omits one of Owen's sections dealing with the "Spirit of Adoption," but there is no consistent pattern of eliminating this doctrine (Owen, *On Communion*, in *Works of John Owen*, 10:305 [*CL*, 11:99]).

51. *Shorter Catechism*, 20 [*CL*, 14:411]. Also in the interest of clarity, "heart" was changed to "thought" in the question on the seventh commandment, where it spoke of "the preservation of our own and our neighbor's chastity, in heart, speech, and behavior" (*Shorter Catechism*, 16 [*CL*, 14:405]). A similar change is made in one of Preston's statements: "*Jesus Christ, as he is a prophet of god* **[God] hath sent** *him* **[his Son Jesus Christ] to teach thee all things belonging to Salvation**" (Preston, *New Covenant*, 376 [*CL*, 6:37]).

52. Alleine, *Vindiciae Pietatis*, 219 [*CL*, 18:152], 239 [CL, 18:165].

53. Wesley omits both the following passages: "He bids a man *deny himself, and take up his cross*. Is it for him? No, my Beloved, it is for ourselves, and therefore when a man denies himself in his profit, in his

credit, when he denies himself in the satisfying of his lusts; all this is for his owne profit; as you have it clearly set down in Isay 48:17. *I am the Lord that teacheth thee to profit; therefore harken to my commandments*" (Preston, *New Covenant*, 106 [*CL*, 6:15]). "He hath promised outward riches, wee are heyres of all the world; so that it is likewise a part of his *Covenant*, when a Man wants any outward comfort, any outward helpe, any blessings, or deliverance, he may goe to Christ" (Preston, *New Covenant*, 381 [*CL*, 6:38]; Alleine, *Vindiciae Pietatis*, 395 [*CL*, 18:195]).

54. Preston, *New Covenant*, 403-86.

55. See Wesley's sermons "The Spirit of Bondage and the Spirit of Adoption," "The Witness of the Spirit, I," "The Witness of the Spirit, II," "The Witness of our Own Spirit," *Works*, 1:248-313. The marks of the "truly saved" are also omitted from Alleine, *Vindiciae Pietatis*, 274-86 [*CL*, 18:166].

56. Owen, *On Communion*, in *Works of John Owen*, 10:296 [*CL*, 11:96].

57. Alleine, *Vindiciae Pietatis*, 270-71 [*CL*, 18:166], 306 [*CL*, 18:180].

4

Theological Foundations: Experience, Justification, Assurance, Covenant

Wesley's usual objectivity when he evaluated the writings of others was not lost when he commented on the Puritan writings selected for *A Christian Library*. Not surprisingly we find him noting Puritan "blemishes": poor style, verbosity, repetitiousness, circumlocution, and propensity to controversy. These were to be expurgated from the abridgments. Yet Wesley found many "excellencies" in the treatises: strength of judgment, clear and just sentiment, comprehensiveness, exaltation of Christ, whom they made the fountain and sum of all things, and dependence on the Scriptures, which they honored "next to God himself" and used as the basis of all authoritative decisions. Perhaps equally as significant for Wesley: "They appear, one and all, to be quite possessed with the importance and greatness of their subject."[1]

Struggling with the antinomian teachers of his own day, Wesley found among Puritans those who shared his insistence on the necessity of "evangelical repentance" and holy living after justification: "They are continually tearing up the very roots of Antinomianism, by shewing at large, from the oracles of God, the absolute necessity, as of that legal repentance which is previous to faith, so of that evangelical repentance which follows it, and which is essential to that holiness, without which we cannot see the Lord."[2]

A Puritan propensity to emphasize "growth in grace" received his strongest commendation:

> But the peculiar excellency of these writers seems to be, the building us up in our most holy faith. It is frequently observed, that after the first joy of faith, wherein the young believer rides as upon the wings of the wind, he either suddenly, or gradually, sinks down, and meets as it were a vast vacuity. He knows not what to do with his faith, or how to

> exercise himself unto godliness. There appears a great gulph, an huge chasm between the first and the perfect love. Now this Mr. Bolton, Dr. Preston, Dr. Sibs, and their contemporaries, above all others, instruct us how to pass through: how to use the faith which God has given, and to go from strength to strength. They lead us by the hand in the paths of righteousness, and shew us how, in the various circumstances of life, we may most surely and swiftly grow in grace, and in the knowledge of our Lord Jesus Christ.[3]

Here was an accent on faith *and* practice constantly developing into a mature Christian life, which Wesley found compatible with his own interests.

One specific theological inadequacy was noted: "They generally give a low and imperfect view of sanctification or holiness."[4] This comment may seem incongruous with Wesley's praise of their instruction in the Christian life, but it apparently referred to Puritan failure, in his opinion, to carry the doctrine of sanctification to its culmination or pinnacle—Christian perfection.

For both the Puritans and Wesley, Christian faith inevitably leads to Christian living: Belief isn't complete until expressed in loving action. This dynamic interconnection between theology and practice became the basis of their consuming interest in practical divinity. Among Puritans, as with Wesley, doctrinal expression was hammered out in the course of daily living and not infrequently led to theological controversy with their contemporaries. Such controversy often arose from different emphases in the theological presuppositions on which their instructions for daily life rested. Because practice is normally motivated by conviction, theological principles and their doctrinal expressions assumed primary significance for the Puritans and for Wesley.

For the purposes of this study the theological undergirding that enlivened Puritan and Wesleyan teachings about living the faith daily is examined before proceeding to a detailed inquiry into the practices they taught. Central to all theological discussion for both movements, however, was a general assumption concerning the nature of Christian faith that demands our attention before we consider specific doctrinal teachings.

Experience

A foundational element of Christian living for both Wesley and the Puritans was religion's experiential nature. In their view religion could not simply be intellectual assent to doctrine or the formality of attending church services; it must include a uniquely personal encounter with and relationship to God.[5] A believer must perceive the presence of God in his or her own being. Wesley, speaking of a friend, commented, "Our conversation turned . . . upon *experimental religion*. . . .The theory of religion he certainly has. May God give him the living experience of it!"[6] Religion in this context is a dynamic, energizing force, arising from experiential contact with God. As such, it expresses itself continually in the believer's life. Daily actions, concerns, and patterns are transformed through the relationship established with God.

To appreciate the experiential emphasis among the Puritans, one need only read Baxter's description of a "true" minister:

> One can say more from the feeling and experience of his soul, than another can in a long time gather from his Books. And that which he saith will come warm to the hearers in a more lively experimental manner, than usual carnal Preachers speak.[7]

Bishop Joseph Hall, commenting on his own faith, expressed the same conviction:

> There is nothing more easy, than to say divinity by rote; . . . but to hear God speak it to the soul, and to feel the power of religion in ourselves, and to express it out of the truth of experience within, is both rare and hard. . . . It will never be well with me . . . till sound experience have really catechized my heart, and made me know God and my Saviour otherwise than by words.[8]

George C. Cell connected Wesley's own emphasis upon experience with that of Nonconformity through Wesley's mother, Susanna Wesley:

> Evidently Wesley's mother . . . was not wholly in the dark about the essential revelational and experiential nature of the Christian Faith. Both of Wesley's parents had become strongly Anglican in their attachments. But the conviction that experience is the stronghold of the Christian apologetic points unmistakably to their Nonconformist antecedents where in the nature of the case, external authority being reduced to a minimum, the higher significance of inner experience of necessity was pushed into the foreground of Christian doctrine. It was in the Nonconformist branches of English Christianity that the appeal to experience had its strongest and richest, though not exclusive, development.[9]

This statement overlooks and thereby minimizes the significant emphasis upon experience Wesley gained through the Moravians, but it correctly points to English antecedents of Wesley's own emphasis. Horton Davies recognizes these English precedents in his comment that Methodism's "evangelical passion and *experimental religion* were a revival of Puritan religion."[10]

Wesley and the Puritans shared the conviction that the gospel must be lived, which assumed an interconnection between the experiential nature of religion and its theological foundations. According to Wesley, the value of theological doctrine was neither in its formulation, its adequate dealing with all intellectual questions, nor its speculative nature, but in its relevance to life. Theological discussion and investigation of a particular doctrine, such as the nature and function of the Holy Spirit, were essential as they explained the what and why of Christian belief; at the same time discussion, comment, and formulation were of little purpose if they did not empower practical experience. Theology could not be separated from life.

Puritan understanding of the function of theology is essentially the same. In Owen's words, his treatise on the Holy Spirit is an attempt to "accommodate the doctrines treated of unto practice." Consequently, it assumed a "continual intermixture of practical applications which runs along in them all."[11]

Emphasis upon the experimental nature of religion, particularly stress upon a personal inner relationship with God, carries with it the danger of undercutting the authority of external form, practice, or tradition. Recognizing this danger, Wesley accompanied his stress upon experiencing religion with an insistence that experience itself be tested through a variety of checks and balances. The truths about God taught in Scripture, the well-tried doctrines formulated through tradition, the form of the Christian life as exemplified by other believers, and ultimately human reason itself, all stood along with personal experience as authoritative criteria for the Christian faith.

The Puritans generally were as anxious as Wesley to guard against the dangers of "experimental religion" without losing the thing itself—the real experience of God's love in the heart of the believer. More radical branches, particularly the Quakers, cast off the "external" authorities, insisting on the primacy of the Spirit. Most, however, affirmed that experience must be tested by other authorities. John Owen's exposition of the doctrine of the Holy Spirit, although written in another context, expressed his recognition of various "authorities": "In the substance of what it delivered, I have the plain testimonies of the Scripture, the suffrage of the ancient church, and the experience of them who do sincerely believe, to rest upon."[12]

For Wesley and the Puritans before him, external religious authorities were appropriated as a believer's own through experience that kept them from being only irrelevant externals.[13] In Colin William's phrase, "Experience . . . is the appropriation of authority."[14]

In guarding against overemphasis on any one source for religious authority and knowledge, the Puritans and Wesley were following long-established English theological practice correlating the religious authorities of Scripture, tradition, and reason. Geoffrey Nuttall suggests that the Puritan emphasis on experience added a new "authority" or dimension to this triad:

> Richard Baxter . . . declares the doctrine to be "a most practical article of our belief"; and the Puritan approach throughout the century is with practice clearly in view . . . . What is new . . . is the place given in Puritan exposition to experience, and its acceptance as a primary authority. . . . The interest is primarily not dogmatic, at least not in any theoretic sense, it is experimental. There is theology, but, in a way which has hardly been known since St. Augustine, it is a *theologia pectoris*.[15]

Wesley's parallel emphasis on experience as a primary religious authority appropriates for his own time this important Puritan emphasis. In some sense the Puritan combination of Christian experience with the Anglican use of Scripture, reason, and tradition as authorities for Christian theology and life anticipated what has recently come to be known as "the Wesleyan quadrilateral."[16]

The experiential nature of religion calls attention to how a human life must be a "living out" of the dynamic relationship between God and a believer, but its ultimate object is salvation—both present and future. Wesley and the Puritans generally followed English precedent when they considered the content of the doctrine of salvation, the *ordo salutis*.[17] As I continue to examine theological affinities and differences between Wesley and the Puritans, I will use this traditional outline as Wesley formulates it.

In a sermon entitled "The Scriptural Way of Salvation" (1765) Wesley's pattern for the order was carefully laid out: (1) the work of prevenient grace in natural man (2) repentance before justification (3) justification or forgiveness with its effects: peace, joy, and hope—assurance (4) new birth that brings a sense of God's love through the gift of the Holy Spirit and begins a real change in humanity—sanctification (5) repentance after justification (6) the gradual work of sanctification and (7) entire sanctification—perfect love.[18] Some of these "states" are not as neatly separated in Christian experience as they appear here, but the general order is evident. Certain of the stages in this order of salvation, particularly three, four, five, and six, are of special interest in relating Wesley's theology to that of the Puritan tradition.

Justification by Faith

Before turning to specific areas of theological affinity evident in

Wesleyan and Puritan presentations of *ordo salutis*, we should note that their respective doctrines of original sin (the condition of humanity that calls for salvation) were substantially the same. Wesley's treatise on this subject was, at least in part, a defense of Isaac Watts's formulation of the doctrine.[19] Quotations from John Howe's *Living Temple* were also used extensively in the treatise.[20] With the Puritans Wesley affirmed a traditional Protestant understanding of humanity's original sinfulness, the human condition that called for salvation. He used their literature as a support of his own interpretation of this universal sin, even though his corollary doctrine of prevenient grace would have been rejected by most of them.

Wesley's consistent exposition of faith as the one necessary condition of salvation also placed him squarely within the heritage of the Reformers. He criticized many of his Church of England contemporaries for having preached "our own holiness, or good works, as the cause of our justification" (1739). In doing so he insisted they had moved away from the traditional Church of England doctrine as found in its Articles of Religion and its homilies.[21] Scholars have often examined Wesley's exposition of the relationship between justification and sanctification. At one extreme some have insisted that in stressing sanctification Wesley embraced this aspect of Christian doctrine as the dominant feature of his theology.[22] Others agree with William Cannon's statement, "Wesley's doctrine of justification was the measure and determinant of all else."[23] However, neither of these extremes adequately accounts for the complexity of the issues involved.

We may more usefully discuss Wesley's understanding of justification (and sanctification) by following Richard Heitzenrater's helpful suggestion: "We would do well to distinguish between Wesley's spiritual pilgrimage and his theological development."[24] Wesley's spiritual pilgrimage, including Aldersgate, continually provided him with new experiences, which he then incorporated into his theology; as a result, his theology was constantly being modified, continually maturing throughout his ministry. At some points in that spiritual journey, often depending upon the circumstances and issues of the moment, justification was emphasized, at others sanctification, but most often both were held together as equally significant. Scholars such as Albert Outler and Colin Williams expressed the consensus of much recent scholarship when they affirmed that Wesley's mature doctrine of salvation retained its Reformation base wherein justification *and* sanctification are both necessary and are both appropriated by faith through grace alone.[25]

Many studies of Wesley, though emphasizing his insistence upon the primary role of grace and its appropriation through faith, fail to notice the English writers whom Wesley himself recommends as exemplary interpreters of the doctrine. Prominent among these are two Puritan authors whose treatises on justification Wesley abridged and repeatedly recommended, Richard Baxter's *Aphorisms of Justification* and John Goodwin's *Treatise on Justification*.[26]

The issues involved in an adequate understanding of justification were extensively discussed in Methodism's second annual conference (1745), and we find Wesley recommending, as "study material" for the deliberations, Baxter's work that he had abridged earlier in the year:

> Q. 4. Shall we read over together Mr. Baxter's "Aphorisms concerning Justification?"
>
> A. By all means. Which were accordingly read. And it was desired, that each person present would in the afternoon consult the scriptures cited therein, and bring what objections might occur the next morning.[27]

Wesley's abridgment of this treatise subsequently became a favorite theological resource among Methodists, enjoying four editions during the course of the eighteenth century.

John Goodwin's treatise was abridged and published twenty years later (1765) in the midst of Wesley's controversy with his Calvinistic evangelical colleagues.[28] In his preface to the work Wesley commented:

> Perhaps I should not have submitted, at least not so soon, to the importunity of my friends, who have long been soliciting me to abridge and publish the ensuing treatise, had not some warm people published a tract, entitled, "The Scripture Doctrine of Imputed Righteousness Defended." I then judged it absolutely incumbent upon me to publish the real Scripture doctrine. And this I believed I could not either draw up or defend better than I found it done to my hands by one who, at the time he wrote this book, was a firm and zealous Calvinist. This enabled him to confirm what he advanced by such authorities, as well from Calvin himself, as from his most eminent followers, as I could not have done, nor any who had not been long and critically versed in their writings.[29]

The closing sentence of this paragraph makes it clear that Wesley sought to identify his own interpretation with explanations of the doctrine that he perceived to be that found among the Reformers. Wesley chose this treatise because, in his understanding, Goodwin presented an interpretation of justification from within the Calvinist tradition that was similar to his own. If he was to argue with the Calvinists over the issue, he gladly sought the support of one from within their community.

Along with a number of their Puritan contemporaries (Joseph

Hall, John Owen, Daniel Williams, among others), Baxter and Goodwin were active opponents of what, in their understanding, was a revived form of antinominianism. This teaching suggested that believers were freed from moral law and its consequent human moral responsibility by virtue of Christ's righteousness being "imputed" into believers. Such a position, in the opinion of Baxter and Goodwin, threatened human moral responsibility. Because of their insistence that Christ's righteousness present in the believer did not relieve one of responsibility for his or her own righteousness, and that God's grace was offered to all persons, Baxter and Goodwin were accused of being Arminian and/or Pelagian. Heated debate on the role of "imputed righteousness" was not simply a Puritan issue, but it certainly raged among their ranks from the 1640s through the last decade of the century.[30] Baxter and Goodwin, though differing on numerous other theological and political issues, perhaps represent a minority among the Puritans in their championing of universal grace and some form of human cooperation with God's grace. Nevertheless, that these two Puritan leaders could take such a position confirms the diversity present in Puritan theological circles. It is not surprising that when Wesley entered into a similar theological battle with eighteenth-century antinomianism, he turned to those Puritan thinkers who defended a position similar to his own.

The *Aphorisms*, Baxter's first venture into publication, was not reissued during his lifetime after it received extensive negative comments from his contemporaries. Baxter admitted that some of its propositions "need correction, being not cautiously enough expressed."[31] The negative response to the work forced him to reconsider his expressions and to write extensively explaining his thoughts.[32] Nevertheless, in his subsequent writings on justification, Baxter restated, in perhaps a more cautious and circumspect manner, the primary content of the *Aphorisms*. He continued to insist that the grace offered in justification when appropriated by a believer requires good works for which one is then responsible at the final judgment before God.

The publication of John Goodwin's *Treatise on Justification* also raised a maelstrom of criticism, which Goodwin evidently expected, for he recognized that he was taking a position not shared by many of his colleagues. Most objections focused on Goodwin's refusal to allow Christ's righteousness to substitute for the believer's own righteousness and holiness.[33]

Wesley's publication of John Goodwin's treatise met with somewhat the same reaction that the *Treatise on Justification* had received from Goodwin's contemporaries more than a century earlier. John Erskine, using the treatise as authority, charged

Wesley with teaching justification by works. Wesley vehemently denied the charge and commented:

> I desire no one will condemn that treatise before he has carefully read it over; and that seriously and carefully; for it can hardly be understood by a slight and cursory reading. And let whoever has read it declare, whether he has not proved every article he asserts, not only by plain express Scripture, but by the authority of the most eminent Reformers.[34]

Wesley's use of these treatises to support his own position has been questioned,[35] as has the earlier edition of this book's use of Baxter and Goodwin to show Wesley's affinity with Puritan theology.[36] Baxter and Goodwin certainly illustrate distinctive interpretations from many of their Puritan contemporaries, interpretations that challenged or modified widely accepted explications of Calvin among their fellow Puritans. Although they may not be representatives of mainstream Calvinism on this particular issue, they clearly were Puritan leaders and understood themselves to be interpreters of the gospel from within, not outside, the Puritan fold.[37]

Is it not possible to see in Richard Baxter and John Goodwin the development, within the Puritan tradition itself, of an interpretation of justification that freed it from the rigid straitjacket of seventeenth-century Calvinism—a Calvinism that threatened a believer's moral responsibility to live a holy life and often led to an antinomian rejection of all good works? Can these men be understood as the precursors of a more adequate understanding of justification, while preserving the truth of the Reformers' emphasis on faith and grace? If so, they saved the doctrine of faith from the inadequacies of the "double decree" while guarding against the semi-Pelagian doctrines present in many of their Church of England contemporaries (and those of Wesley)—doctrines which were in danger of reinstating "works righteousness." In these men may be seen the breadth of the Puritan tradition, which allowed, contrary to popular understanding, widely differing positions and the possibility of new theological developments when rigidity of thought and practice threatened the central truths of the Reformed tradition.

Assurance: Witness of the Spirit

Experiential religious life has as its center a believer's awareness of God's acceptance—knowledge that what the gospel says and promises is actually true for *me*. Such personal awareness may be in part a rational deduction from the gospel promises but also, and of far greater significance, springs from contact with God in which the believer *experiences* the reality of this acceptance.[38] This conscious recognition of God's love and acceptance is foundational for the doctrine of assurance, a key doctrine in Puritan and Wesleyan theology. The general features of Wesley's interpretation of the doctrine are offered here so that his formulations may be compared to Puritan presentations.

Wesley's Interpretation of Assurance

An appropriate point to begin the discussion is Wesley's record of his Aldersgate experience, wherein, he incorporated the concept "I felt I did trust in Christ, Christ alone for salvation; and an *assurance* [italics added] was given me that He had taken away *my* sins, even *mine,* and saved *me* from the law of sin and death."[39] Wesley here identified the nature of the event as his own assurance of God's love. Whereas nineteenth- and early-twentieth-century Methodist perceptions of this seminal spiritual experience often interpreted the experience as Wesley's conversion to "real" Christianity, recent scholarship has more often described the event as Wesley's own experience of assurance.[40]

Richard Heitzenrater's careful chronicling of Wesley's spiritual pilgrimage and his related but distinct theological development suggests that Wesley came to Aldersgate after years of struggling with the question of how he could know (or be certain) that he was a Christian: What assurance or evidence did he have that he was "a child of God?"[41] At Aldersgate, Wesley experienced the assurance he had been seeking. Continuing under the influence of the English Moravians through 1738 and most of 1739, he preached that, as believers affirmed justification by faith, they would experience an assurance. Such assurance was expected to remove all movement of sin, doubt, and fear and, in its place, bring the full "fruits" of "joy, love, peace and good works." However, by late 1739 Wesley began to question a number of the Moravian teachings, including this interpretation of assurance. In the spring of 1740 he broke with them, establishing independent Methodist societies. His difficulties with the Moravians included a developing sense that though assurance may bring a believer real knowledge and confidence of God's love, because it is connected to both justification and sanctification, it cannot be essential for salvation; it must be distinguished from faith, the one requirement of salvation. The Moravians allowed no such distinction.[42]

This modification in Wesley's understanding of assurance, however, did not keep him from making it a mainstay of his preaching through the next several years. Many, besides the Moravians, questioned his interpretation, causing him in 1746 to publish a sermon on "The Witness of the Spirit" wherein assurance is shown to be part of the work of the Holy Spirit. In the sermon, with appropriate hesitancy but convincing clarity, he defines the witness in terms of an assurance:

> But what is that testimony of God's Spirit. . . . It is hard to find words in the language of men to explain "the deep things of God." Indeed, there are none that will adequately express what the children of God experience. But perhaps one might say (desiring any who are taught of God to correct, to soften, or strengthen the expression), the testimony of the Spirit is an inward impression on the soul, whereby the Spirit of God directly witnesses to my spirit, that I am a child of God; that Jesus Christ hath loved me, and given Himself for me; and that all my sins are blotted out, and I, even I, am reconciled to God.[43]

Wesley's hesitancy here to establish a definitive explanation was appropriate, for any such definition must be formulated so as to shelter a variety of individual experiences, each one differing from that of another believer. Additionally, any definition is an attempt to put into intellectual terms an event that is not simply rational but also emotional and spiritual, so the avenues of expression must contain these elements as well.[44] However difficult it might be to formulate a proper definition, Wesley remained convinced that preaching the doctrine was of particular consequence to the ordinary believer. A second sermon published under the same title some twenty years later (1767) stated his case:

> It is the more necessary to explain and defend this truth, because there is a danger on the right hand and on the left. If we deny it, there is a danger lest our religion degenerate into mere formality; lest, having "a form of godliness," we neglect, if not "deny the power of it." If we allow it but do not understand what we allow, we are liable to run into all the wildness of enthusiasm. It is therefore needful, in the highest degree, to guard those who fear God from both these dangers, by a scriptural and rational illustration and confirmation of this momentous truth.[45]

Wesley's insistence upon the possibility of such an assurance and its obvious comfort for ordinary Christians did not convince many contemporary Church of England critics. Most only saw in it the dangers of "enthusiasm."[46] Nonetheless, for Wesley its significant truth could not be discarded simply because it might be misunderstood as enthusiastic. Consequently, he continued to emphasize it as a central element of his theology. Early in his ministry he was willing to call assurance the "main Doctrine of the

Methodist." Later he affirmed, "It is one grand part of the testimony which God has given them [the Methodists] to bear to all mankind. It is by His peculiar blessing upon them . . . that this great evangelical truth has been recovered, which had been for many years wellnigh lost and forgotten."[47]

Together the two sermons on the witness of the spirit give Wesley's mature understanding of assurance. A letter dated 1768 further summarized his teachings:

> I believe a few, but very few, Christians have an assurance from God of everlasting salvation; and that is the thing which the Apostle terms the plerophory or full assurance of hope.
>
> I believe more have such an assurance of being now in the favour of God as excludes all doubt and fear. And this, if I do not mistake, the Apostle means by the plerophory or full assurance of faith.
>
> I believe a consciousness of being in the favour of God (which I do not term plerophory, or full assurance, since it is frequently weakened, nay perhaps interrupted, by returns of doubt or fear) is the common privilege of Christians fearing God and working righteousness.
>
> Yet I do not affirm there are no exceptions to this general rule. Possibly some may be in the favour of God, and yet go mourning all the day long. . . . Therefore I have not for many years thought a consciousness of acceptance to be essential to justifying faith.[48]

Several important features of Wesley's position became evident in this letter. First, the "assurance of faith" is a present reality; there is an immediacy about it that makes it a present event—one does not have to wait until a later time to know assurance. As such, in Wesley's words to his brother Samuel, "It is an assurance of present salvation only . . . Therefore, not perpetual, neither irreversible."[49] Second, it is a "common privilege" of the Christian believer but not necessary for salvation.[50] Third, the distinction between "assurance of faith" and "assurance of hope" (assurance of salvation) indicates Wesley's belief that there may be "degrees" of assurance—not all persons experience the same pattern of assurance. It may also be stronger or weaker in individual believers or within the same believer at different times. Whereas most can expect the assurance of faith, assurance of hope or final salvation is a rare event.[51] Fourth, although assurance normally eradicates doubt and fear in the believer, certainly both may return resulting in assurance being weakened on occasion.

As has been seen, for Wesley the doctrine was grounded in the "witness of the spirit." He insisted that the real difference between himself and those who opposed his position was over the reality of a direct witness from God. Most commentators in his day admitted some witness—usually understood as an indirect witness of the "fruits of the spirit" (good works)—but few affirmed there was a direct witness.[52] Wesley contended that there is, and that this is the essential meaning of the doctrine. As David Shipley indicates, Wesley always understood the important element in humanity's relationship to God to be that "God comes to man in this experience."[53] God's initiative in the relationship is preeminently important and formed for Wesley the "direct witness."

What, then, is the role of what Wesley termed the "indirect witness," traditionally referred to as the "fruits of the spirit?" Wesley's insistence on the direct witness was in part motivated by his perception that "fruits" in terms of simple good works could lead again to justification by works. A letter raised the issue:

> One of our preachers that was (I mean Hampson) has lately made a discovery that there is no such thing in any believer as a *direct, immediate* testimony of the Spirit that he is a child of God, that the Spirit testifies this *only* by the fruits, and consequently that the witness and the fruits are *all one*. Let me have your deliberate thoughts on this head. It seems to me to be a point of no small importance. I am afraid lest we should get back again unawares into justification by works.[54]

If such indirect fruits served as the "sign" or "evidence" of assurance, they could be misunderstood as works. So for Wesley those fruits could not be the only witnesses because they were dependent upon and intertwined with the direct witness.

The indirect witness of fruits was, nevertheless, essential. It allowed the believer (and others) testimony in daily life itself that one had experienced the assurance of the Spirit's witness. For Wesley these fruits were divided into two patterns: the inward, immediate fruits of "love, joy, peace, long-suffering, gentleness, goodness," and the outward fruits that, grounded in the inward witness, resulted in the "doing good to all men"—good works.[55] Good works as outward fruits were consequently indispensable and conjoined to the direct witness and the inward witness.[56]

Each of these points was scripturally based, in Wesley's understanding, and when pressed as to how assurance might be known to be true since it is essentially personal and, therefore, unknowable by others, he referred to the scriptural marks that precede, accompany, and follow the gift.[57] These include the following: (1) conviction of sin and repentance, Mark 3:2, Acts 3:19; (2) new birth or "a vast and mighty change; a change 'from darkness to light,'" Acts 2:5-6; (3) a humble joy—"a meekness, patience, gentleness, long-suffering. There is a soft, yielding spirit; a mildness and sweetness, a tenderness of soul, which words cannot express"; (4) keeping the Lord's commandments, I John 5:3; John 14:21.[58]

Wesley's proclivity for seeking signs and evidence for all

knowledge suggests that attention to the pattern of an inward witness may lead one to reasonable knowledge of one's relation to God. "Strictly speaking, it is a conclusion drawn partly from the Word of God and partly, from our own experience. The Word of God says, everyone who has the fruit of the Spirit is a child of God; experience, or inward consciousness, tells me, that I have the fruit of the Spirit; and hence I rationally conclude, 'Therefore I am a child of God.'"[59] In this syllogistic statement, Wesley combined the inward witness "of our own spirits," dependent upon a prior witness from God, with the customary eighteenth-century empirical search for objective evidence. For him inward as well as outward evidences formed the basis of reasonable proof.[60]

Wesley's constant effort was to retain the truth found in the gift of the Spirit without falling into the extremes of either formalism or enthusiasm. He sought to guard the doctrine by a closing admonition in the 1769 sermon—both the witness and its fruits are to be tested by each other:

> Let none ever presume to rest in any supposed testimony of the Spirit which is separate from the fruit of it. If the Spirit of God does really testify that we are the children of God, the immediate consequence will be the fruit of the Spirit. . . .
>
> Let none rest in any supposed fruit of the Spirit without the witness. There may be foretastes of joy, of peace, of love—and those not delusive, but really from God—long before we have the witness in ourselves, . . . but it is by no means advisable to rest here; it is at the peril of our souls if we do. If we are wise we shall be continually crying to God, until His Spirit cries in our heart, "Abba Father!" This is the privilege of all the children of God, and without this we can never be assured that we are His children. Without this we cannot retain a steady peace, nor avoid perplexing doubts and fears.[61]

These two, the witness and its fruits, were then to be joined together, and, as such, they offered a vital contact and relationship between God and the believer while serving as tests of each other. While these were conjoined, the fruit was dependent upon the witness, so that the whole relationship affirmed once again God's initiative and humanity's dependence.

Wesleyan and Puritan Explanations of Assurance

If Colin Williams is correct in suggesting that Wesley taught a doctrine of assurance before 1738, the following passage suggests he came to see his early comprehension of the doctrine to be inadequate:[62]

> When Peter Bohler, as soon as I came to London, affirmed of true

faith in Christ, (which is but one), that it had these two fruits inseparably attending it, "dominion over sin, and constant peace from a sense of forgiveness," I was quite amazed, and looked upon it as a new gospel. If it was so, it was clear I had no faith. But I was not willing to be convinced of this. Therefore I disputed with all my might, and laboured to prove that true faith might be where these were not; especially, where that sense of forgiveness was not; for, all the scriptures relating to this I had been long since taught to construe away, and *to call all Presbyterians who spoke otherwise*.[63]

As Wesley's own view of faith and assurance changed, he obviously reconsidered the teachings of English Puritans, as this passage notes. Among Puritans faith accompanied by a divine assurance had always communicated a real consciousness of God's witness.[64] In a response to critics of his own position Wesley's letter to the editor of *Lloyd's Evening Post* (December 20, 1760) observes:

You say: "No Protestant divine ever taught your doctrine of Assurance." I hope you know no better; but it is strange you should not. Did you never see Bishop Hall's Works? Was not he a Protestant divine? Was not Mr. Perkins, Bolton, Dr. Sibbs, Dr. Preston, Archbishop Leighton? Inquire a little farther; and do not run thus hand over head, asserting you know not what. By assurance (if we must use the expression) I mean "a confidence which a man hath in God that by the merits of Christ his sins are forgiven and he reconciled to the favour of God."[65]

If this statement is taken at face value, Wesley quite obviously believed that the doctrine of assurance he propounded was the same doctrine as had been taught by early Puritan divines as well as traditional Church of England representatives. In fact, in another letter he insisted that the doctrine was found among the early Reformers: "Luther, Melanchthon, and many other (if not all) of the Reformers frequently and strongly assert that every believer is conscious of his own acceptance with God, and that by a supernatural evidence."[66]

For Wesley the doctrine was not the "property" of any Christian party or group. In his more elaborate defenses of the doctrine against the charge of enthusiasm, he was concerned with showing that assurance was a legitimate part of the heritage of the Established Church. In *A Farther Appeal to Men of Reason and Religion* (1745), and in letters to Thomas Church (1746) and Bishop Warburton (1762), extensive sections demonstrated a doctrine of assurance of adoption. These passages also suggested that one could find affirmation of an authentic witness of the Spirit among the teachings of the Church of England's most honored representatives, particularly Bishop Pearson. He found the same doctrine in the church offices and sermons—especially the homilies.[67] Even so, as his reference to the concept as a Presbyterian doctrine indicates, he was quite conscious the doctrine was strongly represented among the Puritans and that he found their presentation of it attractive.

With the exception of William Perkins (d. 1602), all the "Protestant divines" listed by Wesley in the passage just quoted were included in abridgments found in *A Christian Library*. The authors mentioned were generally major leaders during the early period of the movement. Investigation of their works, those included in the *Library* and in other publications, allows us to compare Wesley's doctrine to that found among early English Puritans.

Assurance of Salvation

The most common Puritan formulation of assurance defines it as an "assurance of eternal salvation"[68]—or, to use Wesley's terminology, an assurance of hope. The Puritans assuming, as they normally did, a Calvinistic doctrine of predestination, this was a logical conclusion, as any assurance must include an assurance of eternal salvation or election.[69] Wesley did not reject an assurance of salvation but thought it to be the privilege of a few, and, working with a more Arminian concept of grace, he often emphasized an assurance of "present salvation."[70] Herein lies the major distinction between Wesley's doctrine and that of the Puritans. However, even though they did not distinguish, as Wesley does, between two forms of assurance (assurance of faith and assurance of hope), Puritan expressions of the doctrine still incorporated what Wesley defines as "assurance of faith."

A primary Puritan motive for accenting the doctrine was its immediate offering, through the Spirit's witness, affirmation of a believer's salvation:

> **You will say, What is the seale or witness of the Spirit? MY BELOVED, it is a thing that we cannot expresse, it is a certaine divine expression of light, a certaine inexpressible assurance that wee are the sonnes of God, a certaine secret manifestation, that God *hath received us*, and put away our sinnes.**[71]

> The Spirit, if it cometh, it subdueth all doubts. . . . In this witness hee taketh in no other testimony to confirm it, but witnesseth by himself. And hence ariseth joy unspeakable, and glorious, and peace which passeth all understanding, for it is an extract of heaven when we see our being in the state of grace, not in the effect only, but as in the breast and bosome of God.[72]

In these passages both Preston and Sibbes leave little doubt as to the importance of assurance as a present reality. The certainty of salvation draws its meaning and purpose from the knowledge of present salvation—it is living in such a comforting, certain, and stable relationship *now* that is of primary importance. Doubts and fears are normally driven out by it, and present life has a vitality that would be impossible otherwise.

For Puritans the strength of present assurance was connected to the assurance of eternal salvation. Sibbes remarked, "Our assurance is not only for the present, but for the time to come."[73] Perkins, chiefly concerned to distinguish true Christianity from that of the "papists," normally interpreted assurance as that of eternal salvation, yet also emphasized the present element since the whole question revolved around whether a person might be "certaine of his own salvation" in this life.[74]

The Puritan emphasis on a present assurance of salvation must, therefore, be distinguished from that of Wesley's, since a present consciousness of eternal salvation is certainly different from an awareness of present salvation only. Wesley's questioning of predestination allows no more than present knowledge for most believers, and the Calvinistic concept necessarily links both present and future knowledge even where the present aspect is highlighted and more often noted than that of a promised future salvation. Recognition of the difference between the positions should not obscure Wesley's acknowledging the Puritan presentation of the doctrine and his willingness to use Puritan expressions of it cleared, as always by Wesley the editor, of its predestinarian implications.

Personal Experience

The peculiarly personal aspect of this assurance—expressed by Wesley as "mine, even mine"—is also an emphasis of the Puritan interpretation. "**Now the Spirit doth not only teach the truths of the gospel, but the applications of those truths, that they are ours: this truth of the gospel is mine. . . . It is a Spirit of application, to bring home those gracious promises to everyone in particular; to tell us the things that are given *us* of God; not only the** particulars **[things] that are given to the Church, but to *us* in particular.**"[75]

The Place of Doubt

Experience taught Puritan divines that, however real and immediate the assuring witness of the Spirit might be at the moment, there were times when even the most faithful believer doubted his state of grace. Consequently, all the authors examined allow for periods of doubt and questioning when the assurance once seen so vividly may be "clouded over." They hesitated to affirm that this assurance was "lost" during these times, which would threaten their assertion of perseverance. Their answer to the phenomenon of doubt was usually that given by John Owen—the witness or assurance was present but simply not realized or appropriated by the believer.[76] *The Westminster Confession*, as we will see, conceded that assurance could be "shaken, diminished and intermitted." "Intermitted" used here certainly suggested that this assurance could be lost, at least for some period of time, but the confession also stated that other supports of faith (love, sincerity of heart) would bear one up until the time assurance was "revived."[77] Although such a statement raises the possibility that assurance may be "lost" or interrupted, the general tone of the statement suggests that it may be diminished rather than lost.

To admit the possibility of doubt was to affirm the existence of degrees of assurance. Some may have the witness to a stronger degree than others—those young in the faith were understood to have more doubt mixed with their assurance than those more mature. Sibbes distinguished three "ranks" of Christians wherein assurance progressively became more complete: those who believed, but out of fear, and who therefore had no real sense of acceptance; those who had some sense of assurance but were not completely free of fear; and those who were "fully assured."[78] These correspond roughly to one of Wesley's favorite descriptions of Christians as children, youth, and fathers.[79]

The Necessity of Assurance

The Puritan divines examined here display a variety of opinions about the necessity of assurance. For Preston the witness of the Spirit was "necessarily required" since man "shall not believe" until he knows that "God is thy Father."[80] Perkins also maintained that "an infallible certainty of pardon of sin, and life everlasting, is the propertie of every renewed conscience."[81] This was a logical position for those following strict predestinarian categories, for if one was truly elected and had appropriated this election through faith, assurance of this election would seem a corollary and necessary element.

Nevertheless, as Wesley saw in his mature years, to insist upon assurance or the witness of the Spirit as a prerequisite of salvation was to go beyond justification by faith alone. Richard Sibbes was quite aware of the dangers of confusing faith with assurance. "A man may be in the state of grace, by giving consent to Christ and relying on him for mercy, and yet want assurance of pardon and reconciliation." "Wee must know that faith is one thing, assurance another."[82] He spoke of assurance as a gift, similar to Owen's contention that the comforting work of the Spirit is at the discretion of God and not necessarily present in all.[83] Bolton commented, "Assuredly that assurance which is ever secure, is but a dreame."[84] Such a statement may also be interpreted to mean that assurance can be lost and, therefore, cannot be necessary to salvation.

Direct and Indirect Witness

Though they did not use Wesley's terminology to distinguish between two types of witnesses, Puritans insisted on the reality of both "direct" and "indirect" witnesses.[85] Preston's comment on the "witness of the spirit" illustrates the usual presentation:

> Now follows the testimony of God's Spirit, which we shall see described. . . . When a man hath believed, and tooke *Jesus Christ*; secondly, when he hath washed and purified himselfe; that is, hee hath gone about his work, and so his own spirit gathers a testimony hence, that he is in a good estate; after hee hath thus believed, then saith hee, comes the *Holy Ghost*, and seales the same thing unto you.[86]

Both witnesses are affirmed and, in this passage, the testimony of the Spirit comes as one which "secondeth and confirmeth" evidences of faith that one may recognize as already present in one's life. In this framework the good life and the accompanying testimony of the believer's spirit precede the receiving of God's direct witness. Wesley must have seen in this formulation a danger: If indirect witnesses are stressed, one may overlook or negate the direct witness. He omitted the passage in his abridgment, substituting the words "But above all of these is the testimony of God's spirit." In his own writings, Wesley continually maintained that the direct witness must precede the indirect.[87] Whatever the proper order of the witness in a believer's personal experience, for Wesley and the Puritans the crucial element was the recognition of the divine witness. John Owen made this quite plain:

> The Spirit worketh . . . it immediately by himself, without the imposition of any reasonings, or deductions and conclusions. . . . He immediately works the minds of men to a rejoicing and spiritual frame, filling them with exultation and gladness; not that this arises from our reflex consideration of the love of God, but rather gives occasion thereunto.[88]

Insistence on a direct witness distinguishes both the Puritans and Wesley from those who would confine assurance to the indirect witnesses alone.

Bolton reminded the believer that the two witnesses were to be tested by each other:

> Wherefore, if any man pretend to have this witness [the witness of the Spirit], and yet want the testimony of his conscience to the same purpose; the testimony of universal obedience; . . . I can give none but this cold comfort: he is miserably deceived by the devil's counterfeit glory of an angel . . . which in time of trial will vanish into nothing. . . .
>
> But though this last manner of assurance be more immediately from the Spirit; yet the others are not effectual upon the heart, without the excitation, illumination, and assistance of the same blessed Spirit.[89]

Wesley's own admonition to rest in neither witness without the confirmation of the other is strikingly similar.[90] For both men one without the other is delusion.

Scripture and Prayer

Wesley followed in the pathway of the Puritan tradition when he claimed the authority of the Scriptures for the whole doctrine. As has been indicated, the central text cited was Romans 8:15-16, and no exposition of the doctrine was complete without building upon this. The fruits of the Spirit were, as in Wesley, the scriptural marks; and every mark or testimony was grounded in scriptural support.[91] One was to distinguish between true witness and delusion through the avenues of the scriptural marks—the fruits of love, peace, joy, good works—and the witness of conscience in affirming these.

One of the results of the Spirit's witness, prayer, was emphasized by the Puritans but omitted by Wesley. Because the testimony of the Spirit allowed one to cry "Abba, Father"—to recognize and know oneself as a child—prayer became more intimate and meaningful. "It may be thou hast prayed to God before, but not as to a Father."[92] "The testimony of the Spirit is ever attended with the spirit of prayer."[93] Geoffrey Nuttall declares that the very foundation of prayer for the Puritans was the "conviction of God's Fatherhood"—the witness of the Spirit.[94] Here was established a reverent familiarity of children with their father. Wesley's exposition missed this altogether, except as he retained the references in his abridgments of Puritan materials. This, in some sense, is a loss, for the concept expresses so well the personal relationship that makes the whole doctrine of assurance appealing.

The treatises and authors examined here serve as a representative cross-section of the early period of Puritan thought. The doctrine found its way into the *Westminster Confession*, where its exposition provides a convenient summary.

> Such as truly believe in the Lord Jesus, and love Him in sincerity, endeavouring to walk in all good conscience before Him, may, in this life, be certainly assured that they are in the state of grace, and may rejoice in the hope of the glory of God, which hope shall never make them ashamed.
>
> This certainly is not a bare conjectural and probable persuasion grounded upon a fallible hope; but an infallible assurance of faith founded upon the divine truth of the promises of salvation, the inward evidence of those graces unto which these promises are made, the testimony of the spirit of adoption witnessing with our spirits that we are the children of God, which Spirit is the earnest of our inheritance, whereby we are sealed to the day of redemption.
>
> This infallible assurance doth not so belong to the essence of faith, but that a true believer may wait longer, and conflict with many difficulties, before he be partaker of it; yet, being enabled by the Spirit to know the things which are freely given him of God, he may, without extraordinary revelation, in the right use of ordinary means, attain thereunto. . . .
>
> True believers may have the assurance of their salvation divers ways shaken, diminished, and intermitted; . . . yet are they never utterly destitute of that seed of God, and life of faith, that love of Christ and the brethren, that sincerity of heart, and conscience of duty, out of which, by the operation of the Spirit, this assurance may, in due time, be revived; and by the which, in the meantime, they are supported from utter despair.[95]

In the *Confession* assurance was understood to be an essential part of faith, but the statement was ambiguous enough to indicate that some members of the Assembly must have shared Sibbes's formulation of faith's relation to assurance. The comment "Assurance doth not so belong to the essence of faith, but that a true believer may wait longer before he be a partaker of it" allowed the possibility that assurance was not of the "essence of faith" at all. If a "true believer" may be without assurance for any period, it is safe to assume that, should he or she die in this period, he or she would still be saved. Assurance is, therefore, not "of the essence of faith." On the other hand, to say "assurance doth not so belong to the essence of faith, but that a true believer may wait longer" indicates that it does belong in some fashion. Obviously, this statement could encompass a person of either opinion.

Significance of Assurance

The doctrine remained a major emphasis in Puritan circles throughout the seventeenth century. Owen treated assurance in his discussion of the Comforter and commented again on it in his *Concerning the Holy Spirit*.[96] Baxter and a host of others supported assurance through their commentaries on the witness of the Spirit,[97] but perhaps Bolton best expressed, in vivid imagery, the Puritan feeling for and appreciation of the witness.

> *A sound and undeceiving persuasion that thou are everlastingly lockt in the arms of god's mercy and love, grounded upon the lord, seconded and set on by the spirit,* **[The real testimony of the Spirit] is a most rare and rich Jewell, which doth infinitely** *outshine and overweigh in sweetness and* **[outweigh in] worth any rocke of Diamond,** *cristell mountaine, or this great creation, were it all converted into one unvaluable pearle.*[98]

Was Wesley correct in implying that his doctrine of assurance was the same as that taught among Puritans? Unquestionably a large measure of similarity is present between Wesley's presentation and that of the Puritan divines examined here. In a sense Wesley's exposition of the doctrine places him midway between the Puritans, who, insisting on the Spirit's witness, often implied, as a corollary, assurance of eternal salvation, and his contemporary Church of England colleagues who rejected the reality of a witness because it might imply "enthusiasm" and affirm assurance of eternal salvation. Wesley retained the important reality of the witness without necessarily implying eternal salvation. At the same time, with the Puritans, he guarded against enthusiasm and presumption through joining the necessity of "the witness of our own spirits," dependent upon fruits of the Spirit, with the witness of the Holy Spirit. Identification does not entail exact correspondence, and Wesley's doctrine does diverge at some points from that of the Puritans; nevertheless, identification of much of Wesley's presentation with those of exemplary Puritans may be sustained. Wesley clearly saw that what he pointed to—personal consciousness of salvation, which gives vitality and meaning to present life—was also affirmed by those of the Puritan tradition. This doctrine, a significant cornerstone in their affinity, points toward additional areas of relationship between Wesley and the Puritans.

Covenant Theology

Many Puritans found another basis for assurance in their revitalization of ancient Jewish/Christian patterns of covenant theology. Covenant and assurance were in some sense inseparable: God, by binding himself to a believer through the covenant promise, guarantees his steadfast love for the believer. Assured by the viability of the covenant relationship and dependent upon God's sovereign grace, a believer may thereby become confident of personal salvation.

Using Old Testament covenants as their pattern, Christians traditionally claimed Christ as a New Covenant (or testament) of God's steadfast love and presence. L. J. Trinterud has shown that emphasis on covenant theology came into prominence again during the sixteenth century, in the theologies of certain Rhineland Reformers (Zwingli, Oecolampadius, Bucer, Martyr, and others).[99] Reemphasized in conjunction with the emerging contract theory of government, "covenant theology," or as it came to be popularly known "federal theology," became a prominent feature of Reformed churches. Such continental precedents found expression as early as the 1530s in the English writings of William Tyndale, John Frith, and others.[100] In these works the covenant expressed the divine side of the relationship by seeing God's steadfast love as both a promise and a binding of God's mercy to the believer. On the believer's side this love was appropriated through personal commitment and responsible living. It was then conditional; it depended on a believer's continuing faithfulness to the gospel teachings.[101]

This covenant theology became, in the subsequent century, a key feature of Puritan teachings. For the Puritans central features of Christian salvation were encompassed in God's covenant, particularly its witnesses to God's steadfast love, mercy, and judgment. John Preston called it the point of "greatest moment that a minister has to preach to his flock."[102]

English Reformers who experienced the Marian exile (1553-58) in the Rhine valley and Geneva returned to England with new interpretations of God's sovereignty that they merged into the covenant tradition already present. One important theological modification occurred in the teachings they appropriated from John Calvin: "For Calvin . . . the covenant of God is God's promise to man, which obligates God to fulfill. Moreover, in the incarnation, death, and resurrection of Christ, God did actually fulfill that promise to which his covenant bound him. Therefore, the sacraments are witnesses . . . to the effect that God has long since fulfilled his covenant, his promise."[103] Because the covenant promise was God's promise, it did not depend on human cooperation. Consequently, Perry Miller suggests that the Puritan understanding of the covenant was an "extension" of what their orthodox Calvinism implied. It preserves the sovereignty of God by retaining his unmerited initiative in salvation and, at the same time, provides a rationale for man's obligation in terms of faith and moral duty.[104] Faith and duty are in this interpretation grounded in God's covenant promise, not human cooperation. It is this Calvinistic pattern of the covenant that becomes the dominant, though not exclusive, Puritan expression.[105]

A Puritan Pattern

Among Puritans John Preston's *The New Covenant, or the Saint's Portion* early became an exemplary Puritan formulation of the doctrine. Wesley, in selecting works for the *Christian Library,* chose to edit and publish this work. For the present study Preston's treatment of the doctrine and Wesley's abridgment of *The New Covenant* serve as our major comparative resource.

A principal feature of covenant theology was its reiteration of the Reformation emphasis on salvation through divine grace rather than good works. By the 1580s a "double covenant" theory had emerged, a "covenant of grace" and a "covenant of works."[106] Preston, following this precedent, states the idea thusly:

> **The Covenant of Workes runs in these terms, Doe this,** ***and thou*** **shalt** ***live*****, and I will bee thy** ***God.*** **This is the covenant that was made with Adam [in paradise.]** *and the covenant that is expressed by Moses in the morall law, doe this, and live.* **The** *second is the* **Covenant of Grace,** *and that* **runnes in these terms, Thou Shalt believe,** *thou shalt* **[and] take my Son** *for thy lord, and thy saviour,* **and** *thou shalt likewise receive* **[accept of] the gift of righteousness,** *which was wrought by him, for an absolution for thy sinnes, for a reconciliation with me,* **and** *therefore thou shalt grow up in love and obedience toward mee, then* **I will be thy** ***God*** and thou shalt bee my people.[107]

Preston continues, suggesting that the covenant of works was made in paradise before the fall and required perfect obedience on the part of Adam—"Doe this, and live." Adam and Eve, representing all humanity, broke this original covenant and, as a consequence, all persons have thereafter been hindered by prideful sin from fulfilling its requirements of perfect obedience to God's law. Nevertheless, God, in his gracious mercy and on his own initiative, established a new covenant with humanity in the Christ event. In order to obtain its blessings, humans were required only to believe in Christ. Through his death and resurrection Christ reconciled humanity to God, and Christ's righteousness was counted for a person's own righteousness; therefore, one who had faith would live righteously. Faith was the only condition of the new covenant, yet as a part of that faith good works and righteousness were expected to be the experience of a believer. Faith and works were both dependent on, and at the same time a consequence of, God's grace.[108]

Preston, following Paul, recognized an early pattern of the covenant of grace in Old Testament writings and suggested that Abraham and even Adam had their significant relationships to God through a covenant of grace and not works. Taking the concept a step further, Preston recognized Adam and Abraham as the only Hebrew recipients of God's "preaching" of an Old Testament covenant of grace.[109] Such early covenants, though being real covenants of grace because they depended upon faith, were but types, or shadows, of the final covenant revealed in Christ.[110]

Wesley and Preston's Interpretation

Wesley's agreement with much of Preston's exposition of covenant theology is evident in his sermon "The Righteousness of Faith" (1742).[111] Puritan understandings of grace affirmed that even the ability to believe—to perform this conditional act of faith—was the gift of the Spirit; only through this enabling gift could a believer appropriate the covenant and its blessings.[112] In this Wesley concurred; he also understood faith to be "the gift of God": "No man is able to work it in himself."[113] Humans having placed their confidence in their own capabilities and pride, best described as original sin, have lost their ability to be faithful and, therefore, must be enabled anew by God to respond to grace.[114]

Preston's exposition of the covenant of grace suggested it was Christ's righteousness that God accepts as the fulfillment of the human obligation to be obedient—never that of the believer. Christ's righteousness is not only obedience to the commandments but obedience even unto death, thereby making propitiation for human sin as well. Christ agreed to fulfill the obedience required, and the believer is able to have this righteousness counted as one's own, through faith in Christ.

> **Christ is the Mediator of the *Covenant*, it is he that declares the *Covenant* and, *secondly*, it is he that *by the intervention of a certaine compact, of certaine articles of agreement,* hath reconciled the disagreeing parties, he hath gone between them, as it were, and hath undertaken for both sides; he hath undertaken on *God's* part, these and these things shall be done, *all his promises are yea, and amen, in him* and *again*, he hath undertaken on our part to give satisfaction by his death, and likewise to make us obedient to his Father.**[115]

The Christocentric orientation of both the old and new covenants was an ancient understanding but accentuated by Preston and other Puritans because it removed any sense of "works righteousness." Wesley similarly affirms the Christocentric orientation of the doctrine.[116]

However, Wesley found that Preston's presentation required some editorial modification. Preston's limitations of Old Testament covenant revelations to Abraham and Adam were dropped by

Wesley. In this he followed other Puritan expositions, such as that initiated by William Ames (d. 1633) and expanded by Isaac Ambrose (d. 1663).[117] These Puritans, and Wesley, maintained that God progressively gave a fuller and clearer revelation of his covenant of grace from Adam through Abraham, Moses, David, and the prophets.[118]

Human Appropriation of Covenant Promises

Both Preston and Wesley, following the Protestant principle, affirmed the single condition of the covenant of grace to be faith in Christ's life, death, and resurrection, faith in the grace given through the new covenant. Through an act of faith the covenant is sealed and its benefits appropriated by each believer.[119]

As we have seen, however, Puritan stress on God's sovereignty led to the predestinarian belief that God elected some to salvation and not others. By its very nature this interpretation of election raised questions about the covenant relationship. How might a believer have the ability to respond in faith? How was one to meet the conditions of the covenant through affirming personal faith in God's gracious offer of salvation if indeed one was predestined to such faith? The usual Puritan answer was that faith came through the *promise* of the covenant. Nevertheless, the specific means of appropriation were constantly discussed among them.

John von Rohr notes that "Preston can say that the Covenant of Grace in its conditional provisions is offered to all, but in its absolute provisions only to the elect."[120] John Saltmarsh (d. 1647) and Tobias Crisp (d. 1643) argued that the covenant of grace was between God and Christ and therefore was not dependent upon human acceptance but was simply "applied" to the elect. Such an understanding left open the possibility of an antinomian interpretation in which believers are understood to be "freed" from moral law and its accompanying responsibilities. To counter such threats to personal responsibility, Richard Baxter, Daniel Williams, John Flavel, and others insisted humans must participate by some means in the conditions of the covenant. To accomplish this, one of the explanations offered by Williams and others was a "covenant of redemption" made between God and Christ in heaven. In this covenant Christ agrees to save humans (thereby providing particular election). This covenant is distinct from the covenant of grace established between God and the elect in the Christ event. The covenant of redemption was understood to be without condition for humans, but the covenant of grace retained the condition of faith.[121] The rudiments of this covenant of redemption are seen in Preston's statement previously quoted, referring to a "certaine compact, of certaine articles of agreement," although he was using the concept largely as a metaphysical framework for the whole doctrine of covenant.

Wesley eliminated the statement from Preston's work and spoke repeatedly against a covenant of redemption. He found no scriptural base for it; but, more important, in his own day such a covenant had become identified with a "covenant of eternal election," whereby God and Christ agreed to save the elect without human participation. Wesley had no use for this predestinarian pattern and, consequently, insisted in his own arguments with eighteenth-century Calvinists that only a covenant of grace and a covenant of works existed or were necessary.[122]

Wesley and Human Appropriation of Grace

Rejecting the usual Calvinistic explanations of how a believer was enabled by God's spirit to respond to the grace offered, Wesley revitalized a traditional Anglican perception of grace—the doctrine of prevenient grace. In this teaching *all* persons, estranged from God by their original sin and totally unable of their own volition to reestablish their relationship to him, are *enabled* by God's gift of "preventing grace" to accept or reject saving or convicting grace.[123] Such "enabling" grace *restores* to each person a measure of "free will" or, more correctly, a measure of responsibility for one's own salvation, as the universality of prevenient grace gives everyone the possibility of accepting or rejecting God's saving grace when offered.[124] In appropriating saving grace there is some "concurrence on man's part."[125] Synergism is qualifiedly admitted here but still within a Reformation context; even the restored human ability to respond is dependent on God's initiative and grace.[126]

In this formulation Wesley affirmed a Protestant doctrine of original sin, with its insistence upon total dependence on the mercy of God, and sought to avoid the pitfalls of a Pelagian "inherent" free will while, at the same time, restoring a measure of responsibility to humanity. Responsibility thus renewed by prevenient grace carried with it as a corollary the ability to distinguish right and wrong, good and evil. Part of the gift of prevenient grace was, then, human conscience.[127] Through prevenient grace a believer not only was empowered to respond faithfully to God's grace offered in Christ but also to become a responsible moral agent.

Wesley's doctrine, however, is not without its own problems. To distinguish between two aspects of God's grace and to offer an explanation of how humanity appropriates the second instance of grace (saving grace) still do not explain appropriation of the first instance of grace (prevenient grace). In his description of grace

Wesley had consequently provided only a partial explanation of its appropriation. Perhaps this is as much as is possible if, as in the Reformed tradition, humanity's total dependence on God was to be affirmed unequivocally and Pelagianism avoided. Prevenient grace in his description did not allow for human participation, because God "elected" all to receive it. In this explanation, has the question of a particular election only been pushed back one step through saving grace to prevenient grace? Perhaps, but such an election does not fall into the difficulties of a particular election since it eliminates distinguishing between persons—all are elected.

Other queries can, however, be raised about the doctrine. If conscience appears to be "strong" in some persons but "weak" in others, are there "degrees" within prevenient grace? Similarly, some persons appear to be more receptive to saving grace than others. Does prevenient grace equally prepare all persons for saving grace? Such questions suggest that the issue of unwarranted favoritism in God's election of some over others, so often leveled against predestinarianism, might have some relevance when examining Wesley's doctrine of prevenient grace.

Even if forced to admit the mystery of such discrepancies evident between persons in the state of prevenient grace, Wesley, unable to conceive that any person is totally void of conscience and contact with God, would probably answer these questions by pointing out that all persons, no matter how low their degree of conscience or receptivity to God, are nevertheless "elected" by God to respond in moral action and to saving grace. Although some may be more richly endowed through prevenient grace, none are without it—"in all and for all." All receive prevenient grace and through it the opportunity for saving grace even if in varying degrees; by the same token, all are made responsible no matter what their degree or state of receptivity. Wesley's construction may indeed leave one with unexplained discrepancies that appear to indicate degrees of election; yet at least it avoids the predestinarian limitation of God's grace whereby it is offered to some and withheld from others. In addition, it provides an explanation of how each person is responsible either to accept or to resist grace and to take responsibility as a free moral agent in daily life.[128]

As I have noted, Wesley's doctrine of prevenient grace was a renewal of a traditional Anglican pattern. It may surprise some to learn that it also had its precedent among Puritans. Richard Baxter could not accept an interpretation of God's grace that restricted it to a select few elected persons, so he insisted on the universality of what he termed "common grace."[129] According to David Shipley, "Baxter's description of common grace is a striking precursor of what is found in Wesley's conception of efficacious prevenient grace."[130] Baxter, like Wesley, insisted on the universality of "common grace" that enables humans to respond personally to God's offer of saving grace, thereby making one responsible for cooperation with God's grace. Baxter, using an uncredited quotation from St. Augustine, can affirm, "He that made us without us, will not save us without us."[131]

Human Accountability

In Wesley's view the concept of particular election removed both human cooperation with God's grace and personal accountability, but in the usual Puritan formulation accountability was restored to the believer through the covenant of grace. Such restoration was indeed one of its major functions. Not only was one empowered by grace to believe, but, under that same covenant, a believer was promised the motivation and ability to live a holy life; therefore, grace brought not only faith but a believer's performance of the moral obligations and duties originally required in the old covenant of works.[132] To enter into covenant meant to take on all the obligations, as Preston wrote, "though there were nothing but Faith, yet that believing, brings with it, and works sanctification, and holiness of life. . . . Let any Man believe as Abraham did, and of necessity it will produce good works."[133] When one has believed and been reconciled to God, then the Spirit "writes the Law in his inward parts, that is it that breedes in him a holy disposition, that enables him in some measure to keepe the Law; it prints in him all those graces that give him strength to observe the commandments that God hath given him."[134] The standard of the commandments given in the old law became again the standard of the new covenant, not on the basis of a covenant of works or humanity's ability to obey but as a natural consequence of faith.[135] The standard was still applicable to the believer's life; one was morally responsible for daily good works as a part of (or issue of) his or her faith.

Wesley, though not needing this explanation to restore man to moral responsibility, saw in this covenantal insistence upon the necessity of works issuing from faith an antidote to antinomianism. He also insisted one was bound to obey the commandments "under the covenant of grace, though not in order to his justification."[136]

The Puritan restoration of a believer's moral responsibility through the avenue of the covenant is open to the criticism that such a covenant is still restricted to the elect. Although it provided a defense against antinomianism among these elect, it failed to extend this understanding of the interrelation between faith and works to those outside the community of elected believers. Wesley's doctrine of universal prevenient grace allowed him to circumvent this problem; therefore, he was able to accept and use the insights and distinctions of covenant theology both to affirm humanity's dependence upon God's grace *and* to insist upon the necessity for moral responsibility and the holy life.

It is not surprising that Wesley found among Preston's formulations of covenant theology and those of others, properly edited, another resource to support his own teachings. Puritan covenant theology provides, then, yet another area of affinity between the two traditions.

Wesley's Use of a Puritan Covenant Practice

Along with Puritan covenant theology went its practical applications in church, national, and personal "covenants." For the community of Puritan believers, and their vision of national goverance, covenants established concrete evidence of commitment to particular standards. Consequently, in the Congregational wing of Puritanism, covenants committing each believer to God and incorporating each into a particular local group of believers became the standard means of establishing congregational governance. These covenants also came to take the place of creeds and confessions. The psychological value of committing oneself verbally and in written form to God contributed to personal covenants becoming a popular Puritan hallmark. Such statements served as a constant reminder of the covenant obligation solemnly entered into in public covenants.

Wesley's perception of both the limits and the value of such covenants is clearly expressed in his comment on II Chronicles 15:12 in *Explanatory Notes upon the Old Testament*: "The matter of this covenant was nothing but what they were before obliged to. And tho' no promise could lay any higher obligation upon them, than they were already under, yet it would help increase their sense of the obligation, and to arm them against temptations. And by joining all together in this, they strengthened the hands of each other."[137]

To aid the Methodist societies in keeping their obligations to God, Wesley also provided a formalized covenant service. Printed and available to all, the service depended on a covenant formulated by Joseph Alleine and first publicized by his father-in-law Richard Alleine, Puritan leaders of the previous century.[138] Interestingly, the earliest use of a public covenant service by Wesley in his societies coincided with the period during which he was laboring on the abridgments for *A Christian Library*, where he included the Alleine covenant formulations and directions for its use.[139]

Frederick Hunter correctly points out that Wesley had chosen out of the Puritan tradition a covenant form that was originally a personal covenant between a believer and God and not a church covenant. Perhaps Richard Alleine's form was intended to be used corporately within a church, but it was an individual covenant adapted by Wesley for use in the societies.[140] Its statements are individually oriented but were used by Methodists in a corporate society service. By the late 1760s, among Methodists, covenant services had become a traditional service of beginnings for each new year. Leslie Church presents evidence to show that, in addition to the corporate covenant service, some early Methodists also prepared and signed personal covenants declaring their relationship to God.[141]

There is little question that Wesley's advocacy of the covenant service among his followers came primarily out of the practical values he saw in its use, but Hunter also suggests the possibility that the covenant emphasis might be a carry-over from Wesley's Puritan ancestors. Wesley, in 1755, urged one of the societies to practice "another means of increasing serious religion, which had been frequently practiced by our forefathers, . . . namely, the joining in a covenant to serve God with all our heart and with all our soul."[142] Hunter takes the reference to "our forefathers" to be a recognition on Wesley's part of his own Puritan ancestors who used the covenant.

To support such a supposition, Hunter makes three suggestions: (1) that John Westley, paternal grandfather of John Wesley, may have proposed to Joseph Alleine the use of the personal covenant in corporate worship, (2) that Samuel Annesley "probably" derived the idea of a covenant service from Richard Alleine and used it in his church at Little St. Helens after his ejection in 1662, and (3) that John Wesley was possibly familiar with the use of the covenant by John White, another grandfather, in forming New England colonists into a church.[143] In all these, Hunter is dependent upon probabilities, and, therefore, the suggestion must be weighed accordingly. He is on safer ground in noting a real awareness and dependence upon the covenant relationship in the Wesley household when he points out that Susanna Wesley urged her sons, Samuel and John, to remember the covenant they personally made with God. Apparently Susanna urged upon her children an appreciation for the covenant theology and the personal covenant, which she may well have drawn from her Puritan forefathers.[144]

Wesley's adoption of the covenant service may, then, have been the result not only of its practical and religious value but also of his early appreciation, fostered by his family, of covenant patterns. In any case, in the use of both the covenant forms of dedication and the theological formulation upon which they were grounded, Wesley displayed a genuine appreciation for Puritan covenant formulations, suggesting again an affinity for Puritan precepts and practices.

Notes

1. *CL*, 4:105-6.

2. *CL*, 4:107. Wesley's distinction between the repentance before entering into faith and "evangelical repentance" is explained in his sermon entitled "The Repentance of Believers": "There is also a repentance and a faith (taking the words in another sense, a sense not quite the same, nor yet entirely different) which are requisite after we have 'believed the gospel'; yea, and in every subsequent stage of our Christian course, or we cannot 'run the race which is set before us.' And this repentance and faith are full as necessary, in order to our continuance and growth in grace, as the former faith and repentance were, in order to our entering into the kingdom of God" (*Works*, 1:336).

3. *CL*, 4:107-8.

4. *CL*, 4:106.

5. "On the one hand, are those who have not so much as the form of godliness; on the other, those who have the form only: there stands the open, there the, painted sepulchre. . . . The one having almost as little concern about religion, as if there were 'no resurrection, neither angel nor spirit'; and the other making it a mere lifeless form, a dull round of external performances, without either true faith, or the love of God, or joy in the Holy Ghost!" (*Works*, 1:57, cf. *Works*, 26:201).

6. *Letters*, 7:47 (italics added); cf. *Works*, 1:142ff. Theodore Runyon, Rex Matthews, and Frederick Dreyer helpfully examine Wesley's concept of experience (Theodore Runyon, "The Importance of Experience for Faith," in *Aldersgate Reconsidered*, ed. Randy Maddox [Nashville: Kingswood Books, 1990], 93-108; Rex Matthews, "'With the Eyes of Faith': Spiritual Experience and the Knowledge of God in the Theology of John Wesley," in *Wesleyan Theology Today*, ed. T. Runyon [Nashville: Kingswood Books, 1985], 406-15; Frederick Dreyer, "Faith and Experience in the Thought of John Wesley," *American Historical Review* 88 [February 1983]).

7. Baxter, *Christian Directory*, 918. Jerald Brauer notes this emphasis in his comment on the distinctive nature of Puritanism: "Now, what was so distinctive about this religious experience that it differentiated Puritanism from Anglicanism? Above all it was what the Puritan called 'experiential' or 'experimental'" (Brauer, "Reflections on the Nature of English Puritanism," 101). Geoffrey Nuttall understands this experiential emphasis to be a characteristic of the Congregationalists, differentiating them from the Presbyterians, yet the emphasis is present throughout all parties of the classical Puritan tradition (G. Nuttall, *Visible Saints: The Congregational Way, 1640-1660* [Oxford: Basil Blackwell, 1957], 112).

8. Joseph Hall, *Meditations and Vows*, in *The Works of Joseph Hall*, ed. Josiah Pratt (London: C. Whittingham, 1808), 6:43. Richard Alleine brands as a "Phanatick" the person who imagines he is a true Christian

merely because he carries out the forms of religion in every detail (Alleine, *Vindiciae Pietatis*, 152).

9. Cell, *Rediscovery of John Wesley*, 90.

10. Davies, *English Free Churches*, 141 (italics added). David Shipley compares the Methodist emphasis upon experience with British "sect" movements, such as the Anabaptists, early Independents, and Quakers, but he could have found evidence of this in the more conservative Puritans as well (Shipley, "Methodist Arminianism in the Theology of John Fletcher" [Ph.D. thesis, Yale University, 1942], 135-36).

11. John Owen, *Concerning the Holy Spirit*, in *The Works of John Owen*, 2:xii.

12. Owen, *Concerning the Holy Spirit*, in *The Works of John Owen*, 2:xiii. It should be noted that such external authorities as the *Westminster Confession* were also of particular consequence for most Puritans. This is a point George Cell apparently discounts in the statement referenced in note 9 of this chapter.

13. Wesley is clear in his concept of the relation between experience and doctrine: "Experience is not sufficient to prove a doctrine unsupported by Scripture," for this is only enthusiasm, but "experience is sufficient to confirm a doctrine which is grounded on Scripture" (*Works*, 1:259). Colin Williams, *John Wesley's Theology Today* (Nashville: Abingdon, 1960), 33-34, is correct in criticizing John Rattenbury for tending to make all doctrines and all authority for the Wesleys dependent upon experience even to the point of commenting, "There was, of course, much in their teaching that did not come out of their experience, but that is the commonplace and, to some extent, misleading part of it" (J. E. Rattenbury, *Wesley's Legacy to the World* [London: Epworth Press, 1928], 84).

14. Williams, *John Wesley's Theology Today*, 33.

15. Nuttall, *Holy Spirit in Puritan Faith and Experience*, 6-7.

16. Much has been written in recent years about "The Wesleyan Quadrilateral," whereby Wesley sought to test any aspect of Christian faith through dynamically balancing "scripture, reason, tradition and experience." See Albert C. Outler, "The Wesleyan Quadrilateral in John Wesley," *Wesleyan Theological Journal* 20 (1985): 7-18; Ted Campbell, "The 'Wesleyan Quadrilateral': the Story of a Modern Methodist Myth," *Methodist History* 29 (June 1991):87-95; William J. Abraham, *Waking from Doctrinal Amnesia* (Nashville: Abingdon Press, 1995), 44ff.; W. Stephen Gunter et al., *Wesley and the Quadrilateral: Renewing the Conversation* (Nashville: Abingdon Press, 1997). Some modern Anglican theologians have attempted to reclaim experience as a necessary element of theological formulations. See E. Radner and G. Sumner, *Reclaiming Faith: Essays on Orthodoxy in the Episcopal Church and the Baltimore Conference* (Grand Rapids, Mich.: W.R. Eerdman's, 1993), 38-40.

17. Chaps. 10-13 of *The Westminster Confession of Faith* give the order as Effectual Calling, Justification, Adoption, and Sanctification. This order was normative for most Puritans. See *The Confession of Faith of the Assembly of Divines at Westminster*, ed. S. W. Carruthers (London: Presbyterian Church of England, 1946); cited hereafter as *Westminster Confession*.

18. *Works*, 2:156-60. For another formulation of the order which gives fuller treatment to the bondage of man to sin and the necessity of the revelation of God through the gospel before repentance and justification, see Wesley's comments on Rom. 6:18 in Wesley's *Explanatory Notes on the New Testament*, 541-42; cf. *Works*, 1:161-65.

19. *Works* (Jackson), 9:327, 345-97.

20. *Works* (Jackson), 9:386-88. Many of the treatises included in the *Library* comment extensively on the doctrine; for example, Joseph Alleine's *An Alarm to Unconverted Sinners* (London: Printed by Nevil Simmons, 1672); Thomas Goodwin's *A Child of Light Walking in Darkness* (London: Printed by F. G. for R. Dawlman, 1659); and John Flavel's *Navigation Spiritualized or, A New Compass for Sea-men* (London: Printed for J.C. for Thomas Fabian, 1682).

21. *Works*, 19:96-97. Wesley's exposition of the doctrines of justification and sanctification is most clearly expounded in his sermons, particularly "Justification by Faith," "The Righteousness of Faith," and "The Scriptural Way of Salvation" in *Works*, 1:182-216; 2:153-69.

22. Maximin Piette, *John Wesley in the Evolution of Protestantism*, trans. J. B. Howard (New York: Sheed and Ward, 1937); Umphrey Lee, *John Wesley and Modern Religion* (Nashville: Cokesbury Press, 1936); Gregory S. Clapper, *John Wesley on Religious Affections* (Metuchen, N.J.: Scarecrow Press, 1989).

23. William R. Cannon, *The Theology of John Wesley* (Nashville: Abingdon Press, 1946), 14.

24. Heitzenrater, *Mirror and Memory*, 107.

25. Outler, *John Wesley*, 9-30; Williams, *John Wesley's Theology Today*, 186-88. For additional comments supporting this understanding of Wesley's theology, see Richard M. Cameron, "John Wesley's Aldersgate Street Experience," *The Drew Gateway*, 25 (1955): 210-19; Robert E. Chiles, "Methodist Apostasy: From Free Grace to Free Will," *Religion in Life*, 27 (1957): 438-49; David C. Shipley, "Wesley and Some Calvinistic Controversies," *The Drew Gateway*, 25 (1955): 195-210; Heitzenrater, *Mirror and Memory*, 135-36; Kenneth Collins, *The Scriptural Way of Salvation* (Nashville: Abingdon Press, 1997), 94-100.

26. Although here only Wesley's relationship to these Puritan writers as exemplified in his use of their treatises is discussed, a major reason for his attraction to these treatises appears in the discussion of "final justification" addressed in chap. 5.

27. *Minutes* (1745) in *Works* (Jackson), 8:282. Richard Green quotes Wesley as recommending this treatise as a "powerful antidote against the spreading poison of antinominianism" (*Bibliography*, 37).

28. Wesley's chief defender in the controversy with the Calvinists in the decade of the 1760s, John Fletcher, draws extensively on the works of Baxter, Goodwin, Flavel, Matthew Henry, and even John Owen to serve as witnesses to the Methodist interpretation of justification, particularly their insistence on works following justification (John Fletcher, *Checks to Antinomianism*, [New York: J. Soule & T. Mason, 1820], 1:66, 92, 276-85; *Works of John Fletcher* [New York: Carlton & Lanahan, n.d.], 1:576, 578.)

29. "Preface to a Treatise on Justification," *Works* (Jackson), 10:316.

See also Wesley's letter to Thomas Rankin concerning the publication of the treatise (*Letters*, 4:274). Rankin was evidently interested enough in the publication to attempt to find subscribers to finance its immediate publication (*Letters*, 4:279.)

30. C. F. Allison explores the intricacies of this long and tangled discussion within the Church of England in his *The Rise of Moralism* (New York: Seabury Press, 1966). Richard Heitzenrater recounts the historical development of these particular arguments and their predecessors, pointing out where the epithet "new Methodists" had been used against those insisting on human cooperation with God's grace ("What's in a Name," *Mirror and Memory*, 20-25).

31. Baxter, *Reliquiae Baxterianae*, 107.

32. Manuscript copies of Baxter's responses to numerous critics as well as the writings of the critics themselves are available in Dr. William's Library, London. These reveal the breadth and depth of the controversy caused by the work which Baxter says "cost me more than any other that I have written" (*Reliquiae Baxterianae*, 107). The cost was not only in the time it took to respond but also in the extent of "men's offense" at his position and its implications.

33. Goodwin's comments "To the Reader," which preface *A Treatise on Justification*, indicate that he clearly expected opposition to his position—"I can reasonably expect no better, than to see and heare it vexed from all quarters" (London: 1643). A portion of the title of one such work by Henry Roborough displays some of the reaction: ". . . an Examination of the said Mr. John Goodwin's *Treatise on Justification* Wherein the Inputation of Faith in a Proper Sense Is Denyed and Confuted; and the Inputation of Christ's Righteousness Is Affirmed and Proved" (London: 1650).

34. Wesley, *Remarks on a Defense of Aspasio Vindicated*, in *Works* (Jackson), 10:349.

35. Allison maintains that Baxter carried significant responsibility for an English drift toward moralism, and Wesley uncritically used Baxter, extending the trend further (*Rise of Moralism*, 194). For a more extended discussion of these issues see pages 105ff.

36. Paul Sanders, "The Puritans and John Wesley" (*Work Worship*, Whitsuntide, 1967): 16.

37. Baxter has historically been accepted as a leading exponent of the mature Puritan tradition (see Nuttall, *Holy Spirit in Puritan Faith and Experience*, 10; *DNB*, 3:429-37). Goodwin must also be placed in the tradition, for his general sympathies lay here, even though some of his theological and political ideas certainly brought him into conflict with others of the same tradition. (See *DNB*, 22:145-47; Matthews, *Calamy Revised: being a Revision of Edmund Calamy's Account of the Ministers and others Ejected and Silenced, 1660-1662*, [Oxford: Clarendon, 1934], 227; Wakefield, *Puritan Devotion*, 4.)

38. The inherent relation between experience and assurance in Wesley's thought is indicated in this statement when he refers to an "experimental assurance" (Wesley's *Explanatory Notes on the New Testament*, 622 [I Cor. 12:3]).

39. *Works*, 18:250.

40. Arthur Yates, *The Doctrine of Assurance* (London: Epworth Press, 1952), 3-11. Randy L. Maddox has helpfully traced the history of the Aldersgate discussion among Methodists, affirming that it is most congenially seen as Wesley's experience of assurance (*Aldersgate Reconsidered* [Nashville: Kingswood Books, 1990], 133-46). Colin Williams (*John Wesley's Theology Today*, 102-5) suggests that one of Wesley's early sermons, "The Circumcision of the Heart" (1733), expresses an early doctrine of assurance that is close to that developed later.

41. Heitzenrater, "Great Expectations: Aldersgate and the Evidences of Genuine Christianity," in *Mirror and Memory*, 106-49. This article, investigating the nature of Aldersgate, traces the complex development of Wesley's mature theology as it develops out of his spiritual journey.

42. Heitzenrater, *Mirror and Memory*, 139-41, 145.

43. *Works*, 1:274. Wesley comments on this definition in his second sermon on this topic (1767): "After twenty years' further consideration, I see no cause to retract any part of this. Neither do I conceive how any of these expressions may be altered, so as to make them more intelligible" (*Works*, 1:287). He is true to his willingness to be corrected or instructed, for he comments to Joseph Benson in 1781, "I do not insist on the term 'Impression!' I say again, I will thank anyone that will find a better; be it 'discovery,' 'manifestation,' 'deep sense,' or whatever it may" (*Letters*, 7:61).

44. "The manner how the *divine* testimony is manifested to the heart, I do not take upon me to explain. Such knowledge is too wonderful and excellent for me: I cannot attain unto it. . . . But the fact we know; namely, that the Spirit of God does give a believer such a testimony of his adoption, that while it is present to the soul, he can no more doubt the reality of his sonship, than he can doubt of the shining of the sun, while he stands in the full blaze of his beams" (*Works*, 1:276).

45. *Works*, 1:285.

46. See Yates, *Doctrine of Assurance*, 61-71, for a full exposition of the changes evident in the doctrine as taught by Wesley.

47. *Works*, 26:182; 1:285-86.

48. *Letters*, 5:358; cf. *Works*, 25:563, 622; 11:398.

49. *Works*, 25:645.

50. *Works*, 19:136; 26:254-55; *Works* (Jackson) 8:276, 291; *Letters*. 5:358.

51. *Works*, 25:563, 599-600; 26:157, *Letters*, 3:161. Cf. Heitzenrater, *Mirror and Memory*, 129.

52. *Works*, 1:288, 296-97.

53. Shipley, "Methodist Arminianism," 151.

54. *Letters*, 5:8.

55. *Works*, 1:283; 26:251; *Letters*, 5:364.

56. *Works*, 1:286, 221-25.

57. *Works*, 1:277, 273.

58. *Works*, 1:277-81, 221-25.

59. *Works*, 1:288.

60. For an insightful discussion of Wesley's appropriation and modification of eighteenth-century Lockean principles of knowledge, see Rex Matthews, "Religion and Reason Joined: A Study in the Theology of John Wesley" (Th.D. diss., Harvard University, 1986); Dreyer, "Faith and

Experience."

61. *Works*, 1:297-98.

62. Williams, *John Wesley's Theology Today*, 102-5.

63. *Principles of a Methodist*, in *Works*, 8:366 (italics added). Wesley, of course, later modified his opinion that this "sense of forgiveness" was necessary, or inseparable from justifying faith, but he never ceased to insist upon the possibility of such an experience and its occurrence as a "common privilege" of believers.

64. Gordon Wakefield declares the doctrine of assurance to be a "distinctively Puritan and evangelical contribution" and goes on to show that William Perkins calls it "A Case of Conscience the Greatest that ever was." Commenting that they often state it in syllogistic form, he points out that Wesley does the same (*Puritan Devotion*, 124-26). Compare Wesley's statement in *Works*, 1:276, and his abridgment of Bolton's *General Directions for a Comfortable Walking with God*, *CL*, 4:406.

65. *Letters*, 4:126. Wesley came to suspect the term "assurance" not only because it was not scriptural but because there was a tendency to understand it derogatorily, and it was identified most often with "assurance of perseverance" or final salvation (*Letters*, 3:228). See Howard Watkins-Jones, *The Holy Spirit from Arminius to Wesley* (London: Epworth Press, 1929), 318.

66. *Letters*, 3:159.

67. *Works*, 22:163-171; *Letters*, 2:233-35; 4:376-81.

68. William Perkins, *A Treatise of Conscience*, in *The Works of William Perkins* (London: John Legatt, 1616), 1:541; Robert Bolton, *General Directions for a Comfortable Walking with God* (London: 1641), 326 [*CL*, 4:408]; cited hereafter as *Walking with God*.

69. This is the concept of assurance that Wesley's brother Samuel so strenuously objected to—it obviously holds dangers of presumptuous pride and antinominianism (*Works*, 25:645).

70. *Letters*, 5:358.

71. Preston, *New Covenant*, 400 [*CL*, 6:44] (italics added). "A secret persuasion wrought in the heart whereby God assures you that he is yours, and you are his. . . . He hath said to your soul, 'I am your salvation'" (John Preston, *The Breast Plate of Faith and Love* [London: Printed by W. I. for Nicholas Bourne, 1630], pt. 2, 85 [*CL*, 5:86-87]).

72. Richard Sibbes, *A Fountain Sealed* (London: L. Chapman, 1637), 167. Thomas Goodwin clearly understood the immediate nature of the witness: **"First, the *immediate light of his countenance*, which is a clear evident beam and revelation of God's favour, immediately testifying that we are his; which is called the *sealing* [testimony] of the Spirit,** *received after believing*" (Goodwin, *Child of Light Walking in Darkness*, 14 [*CL*, 6:235-36]).

73. Sibbes, *Fountain Sealed*, 216.

74. Perkins, *Treatise of Conscience*, in *The Works of William Perkins*, 1:540.

75. Sibbes, *A Fountain Opened*, in *The Works of Richard Sibbes*, ed. A. B. Grossart (Edinburgh: James Nichol, 1863), 5:27 [*CL*, 6:65-66]; Sibbes, *The Nativity of Christ*, in *The Works of Richard Sibbes*, 6:353 [*CL*, 6:125]; Bolton, *On Walking with God*, 317 [*CL*, 4:404].

76. Owen, *On Communion*, in *The Works of John Owen*, 10:285-86; Preston, *Breast Plate of Faith and Love*, pt. 1, 126-27 [*CL*, 5:364-65]; Bolton, *Walking with God*, 335 [*CL*, 4:413]; Sibbes, *Fountain Sealed*, 233. Bolton, on the basis of the degrees of assurance, declares that assurance most often comes in times of prayer, special need, persecution, and so on. Wesley consistently eliminated such passages (Bolton, *Walking with God*, 336ff. [*CL*, 4:414 ff.]).

77. *Westminster Confession*, 15.

78. Sibbes, *Fountain Sealed*, 209-10.

79. *Works*, 2:105.

80. Preston, *Breast Plate of Faith and Love*, pt. 2, 53 [*CL*, 5:380]. This is true for Preston because he makes assurance in the believer a *reflex* action of faith that is strengthened or helped by the witness of the Holy Spirit (pt. 1, 63 [*CL*, 5:349]).

81. Perkins, *Treatise of Conscience*, in *Works of William Perkins*, 1:547.

82. Sibbes, *Salvation Applied*, in *Works of Richard Sibbes*, 5:393. "For it is one thing to believe and cast myself upon Christ for pardon of sins, and another thing upon that act to feel assurance and pardon. . . . We ought to labour for both, for affiance and consent in the will, to cast ourselves upon Christ, for salvation; and then upon believing we ought to find and feel this assurance" (*Salvation Applied*, in *Works of Richard Sibbes*, 5:393. Cf. Sibbes, *Fountain Sealed*, 211).

83. Owen, *On Communion*, in *Works of John Owen*, 10:297-98. "It is one thing to have holiness really thriving in any soul, another for that soul to know it, and to be satisfied in it; and these things may be separated." (Owen, *Concerning the Holy Spirit* in *Works of John Owen*, 2:470).

84. Bolton, *Walking with God*, 335 [*CL*, 4:413]. Cf. Baxter, *Richard Baxter's Confession of His Faith* (London: Printed by R. W. for Thomas Underhil, 1655), 208.

85. Wesley's inward and outward witnesses were occasionally interpreted by the Puritans as only two tests, examples, or marks among others as to how one is to recognize the validity of the covenant relationship and the true faith (Preston, *New Covenant*, 390-400 [*CL*, 6:42-44]; Owen, *On Communion*, in *Works of John Owen*, 10:294ff).

86. Preston, *New Covenant*, 400 [*CL*, 6:44]. Cf. Bolton, *Walking with God*, 317-27 [*CL*, 4:404-8].

87. *Works*, 1:274-75.

88. Owen, *On Communion*, in *Works of John Owen* 10:310 [*CL*, 11:102]. "This testimony of the Spirit containeth in it the force of all, word, promise, oath, seal, etc. This is greater than the promise, as a seal is more than our hand. . . . Our owne graces indeed, if we were watchful enough, would satisfye us. . . . Howsoever, the Spirit, if it cometh, it subdueth all doubts; in this witness hee taketh in no other testimony to confirm it, but witnesseth by himself" (Sibbes, *Fountain Sealed*, 167; cf. Bolton, *Walking with God*, 328 [*CL*, 4:409]).

89. Bolton, *Walking with God*, 328-29 [*CL*, 4:408-9]; Preston, *New Covenant*, 90. Richard Baxter's comment also joined the two witnesses: "And, if I am not mistaken, the testimony of the Spirit, and the testimony of conscience, are two concurrent testimonies, or causes, to produce one

and the same effect, and to afford the premises to the same conclusion, and then to raise our joy thereupon, so that they may well be said to witness together" (*Saints' Everlasting Rest*, in *The Practical Works of Richard Baxter* [London: James Duncan, 1830], 22:439-94).

90. *Works*, 1:298.

91. "A sound persuasion by the Spirit is ever answerable exactly to the word; . . . and therefore, if thy present state, wherein thou conceived thyself to be safe, be condemned by God's Word, thy confidence is vain" (Bolton, *Walking with God*, 329 [*CL*, 4:410]; cf. Preston, *New Covenant*, 390 [*CL*, 6:42]).

92. Preston, *Breast Plate of Faith and Love*, pt. 2, 105 [*CL*, 5:390].

93. Bolton, *Walking with God*, 336 [*CL*, 4:414].

94. Nuttall, *Holy Spirit in Puritan Faith and Experience*, 63ff.

95. *Westminster Confession*, 15.

96. Owen, *Concerning the Holy Spirit* in *Works of John Owen*, 2:470ff.

97. See Nuttall, *Holy Spirit in Puritan Faith and Experience*, 48-61, for a detailed discussion of the witness of the Spirit in the Puritan tradition and Watkin-Jones, *Holy Spirit from Arminius to Wesley*, 306-9, for a similar discussion noting both the Puritan and Anglican formulations.

98. Bolton, *Walking with God*, 333 [*CL*, 4:412]; Wesley's abridgment shows how occasionally his editorial pen, though retaining the meaning, loses the strength and vitality of the passage.

99. L. J. Trinterud, "The Origins of Puritanism," *Church History*, 20 (1951): 37. Trinterud's excellent treatment focuses on the genius of Puritanism in covenant theology.

100. William Tyndale, *Doctrinal Treatises and Introductions to Different Portions of the Holy Scriptures*, ed. Henry Walter for The Parker Society (Cambridge: University Press, 1848), 403.

101. For a detailed discussion of Puritan concepts of covenant and assurance, see John von Rohr's "Covenant and Assurance in Early English Puritanism," *Church History* 34 (June 1965): 195-202.

102. Preston, *New Covenant*, 351.

103. Trinterud, "Origins of Puritanism," 45.

104. Perry Miller, *The New England Mind: The Seventeenth Century* (New York: Macmillan, 1939), 367ff.

105. See Perry Miller, *New England Mind*, 374, for an evaluation of its significance among Puritans.

106. Trinterud, "Origins of Puritanism," 48-49.

107. Preston, *New Covenant*, 317-18 [*CL*, 6:31]. Preston also gives a helpful summary of the doctrine in *Breast Plate of Faith and Love*, pt. 1, 18-21 [*CL*, 5:329-31].

108. Preston, *New Covenant*, 359 [*CL*, 6:40].

109. Preston, *New Covenant*, 351-53.

110. Preston, *New Covenant*, 326 [*CL*, 6:34]; *Works*, 1:207.

111. *Works*, 1:200-16. For helpful treatments of Wesley's use of the covenants see John Deschner, *Wesley's Christology* (Dallas: Southern Methodist University Press, 1960), 112-13, and Lindström, *Wesley and Sanctification* (London: Epworth Press, 1950), 89-90.

112. W. Adams Brown, "Covenant Theology," in *Encyclopedia of Religion*

and Ethics, ed. James Hastings (Edinburgh: T. & T. Clark, 1912), 4:218.

113. *Works*, 2:47-48.

114. *Works*, 2:54-65.

115. Preston, *New Covenant*, 330 [*CL*, 6:36].

116. "Indeed, strictly speaking, the covenant of *grace* doth not require us to *do* anything at all, as absolutely and indispensably necessary in order to our justification; but only to *believe* in Him who, for the sake of His Son, and the propitiation which he hath made, 'justifieth the ungodly that worketh not,' and imputes his faith to him for righteousness" (*Works*, 1:207). See Williams, *John Wesley's Theology Today*, 84-87, for a discussion of Christ as mediator in Wesley and the use of covenant of works and of grace therein. See Deschner, *Wesley's Christology*, 156, 162, on the Christocentric nature of the covenants in Wesley.

117. William Ames, *The Marrow of Sacred Divinity* (London: Edward Griffin, 1642), 170-75; Isaac Ambrose, *Looking Unto Jesus*, *CL*, 8:116ff.; see Brown, "Covenant Theology," 4:218.

118. *Works*, 1:207-8.

119. See Miller, *New England Mind*, 378; *Works*, 1:207.

120. Von Rohr, "Covenant and Assurance," 201.

121. Shipley, "Wesley and Some Calvinistic Controversies," 205-9; Brown, "Covenant Theology," 218.

122. *Works* (Jackson), 10:238-42, 422-23. Wesley continually insisted that the covenant of grace required human participation in its conditions (*Works* [Jackson], 10:238, 309; *Letters*, 3:379).

123. *Works*, 3:207. See also "Free Grace," in *Works*, 3:544-45; *Doctrine of Original Sin*, in *Works* (Jackson), 9:196ff.

124. *Works* (Jackson), 8:285. Charles A. Rogers perceptively treats the doctrine in his "The Concept of Prevenient Grace in the Theology of John Fletcher" (Ph.D. thesis, Duke University, 1967). See also Randy L. Maddox, *Responsible Grace* (Nashville: Kingswood Books, 1994), 141ff.

125. *Works* (Jackson), 10:229-30.

126. Colin Williams (*John Wesley's Theology Today*, 72) points out that Wesley's synergism can only be correctly understood when it is noted that this does not allow, as in a Pelagian concept, an upward movement of man's natural will nor a required moral level or standard to be achieved. Man cooperates in his salvation only in the sense of accepting or rejecting saving grace, and even this ability—or responsibility—is given by God's free gift of prevenient grace. Lycurgus Starkey (*The Work of the Holy Spirit* [New York: Abingdon Press, 1962], 116ff.), wanting to point to this dependence on grace, suggests it may be called "evangelical synergism." Richard Heitzenrater (*Mirror and Memory*, 99, 244) and Albert Outler (*John Wesley*, 14) also accept Wesley's formulations as synergistic. David Shipley ("Methodist Arminianism," 417) and Robert Chiles (*Theological Transition in American Methodism* [Nashville: Abingdon Press, 1965], 108-10), on the other hand, are not willing to call this cooperative element by the title "synergism" since even this is dependent on grace. Perhaps Starkey's term of evangelical synergism best notes an element of "qualified synergism," but in the sense that it does imply cooperation by humanity, divinely bestowed, the term may be used legitimately.

127. *Works*, 3:481-82; 3:207.

128. Although Wesley rejected the limitation of election inherent in predestination, he affirmed election in the sense of "a divine appointment of some particular men, to do some particular work in the world" (*Works* [Jackson], 10:210). That he believed himself and his movement so appointed is without question. His famous comment about himself as a "brand plucked out of the burning" (from a fire in the Epworth rectory) to fulfill a special mission is only one example among many (*Works*, 20:482; *Letters*, 5:15). He was convinced that Methodism had been raised up to "reform the nation, particularly the Church, and to spread scriptural holiness over the land" (*Works* [Jackson], 8:299). Although Wesley denied, in response to one of his critics, that he felt such a "designation to extraordinary work," his constant affirmations contradict this denial (*Works*, 9:524; 2:285-86).

129. "Preface to the Readers," *Richard Baxter's Confession of His Faith*, vi.

130. Shipley, "Wesley and Some Calvinistic Controversies," 208.

131. Richard Baxter, *Aphorisms on Justification* (London: Printed for Francis Tyton, 1644), 95. Wesley in one of his sermons used the same quotation, crediting it to Augustine, and pointing out that Augustine was often thought of as favoring it to be the "contrary doctrine" (*Works*, 3:208 n. 64; cf. 2:490 n. 33). The author is indebted to Paul Sanders ("Puritans and John Wesley," 17) for noting Wesley's use of the phrase.

132. Von Rohr, "Covenant and Assurance," 196-97.

133. Preston, *New Covenant*, 362 [*CL*, 6:40]; see W. Adams Brown, "Covenant Theology," 217.

134. Preston, *New Covenant*, 345.

135. "In order that men should not presume upon the 'Absolute Promises' of the Covenant to give over trying, the federal God . . . perfected the adroit device of incorporating the Covenant of Works into the Covenant of Grace, not as the condition of salvation but as the rule of righteousness. . . . 'For the Morall Law, the Law of the ten Commandments, we are dead also to the covenant of that Law, though not to the command of it'" (Miller, *New England Mind*, 384).

136. *Letters*, 3:378; cf. *Works* (Jackson), 8:89; *Works*, 1:208.

137. John Wesley, *Explanatory Notes upon the Old Testament* (Bristol: Printed by William Pine, 1765), 2:1372.

138. Joseph Alleine prepared a form of prayer for making a covenant with God in *An Alarm to Unconverted Sinners* (printed posthumously, London: 1672). His father-in-law, Richard Alleine, incorporated Joseph's covenant prayer and its accompanying directions in his own more detailed pattern for personal covenanting in *A Vindication of Godliness* (London: 1664). Cf. David Lowes Watson, *The Early Methodist Class Meeting* (Nashville: Discipleship Resources, 1987), 36.

139. The first mention of "renewing in every point our covenant that the Lord should be our God" occurs in December 1747 (*Works*, 20:203), when Wesley was preparing materials for the *Library*. Covenanting was not mentioned again until 1755, after Wesley had published both of the Alleine formulas, and it had assumed by that time the form of a liturgical covenant service. After publication the covenant was frequently

mentioned and urged upon the societies, usually being credited to Richard Alleine. Wesley records in his *Journal*, almost each time the covenant is mentioned, how it brought special blessing to the congregation and to him personally (*Works*, 21:490; *Journal*, 7:133).

140. Frederick Hunter, "The Origin of Wesley's Covenant Service," *LQHR* 164 (1939): 81.

141. Leslie Church, *More about the Early Methodist People* (London: Epworth Press, 1949), 274-77.

142. *Works*, 21:23 (including n. 82).

143. Hunter, "Origin of Wesley's Covenant Service," 85-86.

144. Frank Baker ("Beginnings of the Methodist Covenant Service," 215) supports this assumption that much of the emphasis on the covenant came to Wesley through his mother.

5

Theological Foundations: Sanctification and Perfection, Sin in Believers, Final Justification

For Puritans and Wesley the witness of the Spirit and the bonding of faith through covenant theology activated a new life for the believer. It is in their teachings about this new life that we find additional theological congruence between the two traditions.

Sanctification and Perfection

Like the Puritans before him Wesley was extraordinarily interested in the evolutionary process that must take place for a simple believer to become an exemplary, full Christian—the Holy Spirit's transforming work of sanctification. For each, the personal relationship with God established through faith connoted little if it did not mean a constant transforming companionship of the Spirit and its guidance in the vicissitudes of daily life.[1] Continuous renewal and remolding constituted a distinct sanctifying of every believer.

Sanctification

The significant truth contained in a doctrine of sanctification was never lost in those branches of Protestantism most insistent on the priority and domination of justification by faith. To be sure, Luther essentially incorporated sanctification within justification without distinguishing between them, but the Reform tradition retained the distinction without losing the vitality of either.[2] The English Reformation, in all its branches, understood sanctification as a core component of the faith so the sanctified, holy life was constantly emphasized and taught. Both Puritans and Wesley, in accenting this doctrine, typified the mainstream of their joint heritage. The parallels between the two traditions are most obvious in their elaborate instructions for Christian living, yet these arose out of their emphasis on sanctification and their understanding of the doctrine itself.

For Puritans and Wesley sanctification was grounded on faith and not on human merit—to give it any other base would be to reinstate salvation through an order of merit. John Owen declared, "Faith is the instrumental cause of our sanctification; so that, where it is not, no holiness can be wrought in us. It is from faith in God through Jesus Christ, acting itself in obedience unto the gospel, that we purify or cleanse our soul, which is our sanctification."[3] Robert Bolton's *The Saints' Selfe-Enriching Examination* affirmed, "Saving faith is the root and fountain of sanctification."[4] The similarity of Wesley's position and his clarity on this feature of the doctrine is seen in his sermon "The Scriptural Way of Salvation":

> Faith is the condition, and the only condition, of sanctification, exactly as it is of justification. It is the *condition*: none is sanctified but he that believes; without faith no man is sanctified. And it is the *only condition*: this alone is sufficient for sanctification. Every one that believes is sanctified, whatever else he has or has not. In other words, no man is sanctified till he believes: every man, when he believes, is sanctified.[5]

The true import of Wesley's affirmation that sanctification is dependent solely upon faith comes when we apply Colin Williams's insight concerning Wesley's doctrine of Christian perfection to his concept of common or general sanctification. Williams, along with David Shipley, questions the widely held view of George Cell that Wesley had in fact established "a necessary synthesis of the Protestant ethic of grace with the Catholic ethic of holiness."[6] If it were true, Williams maintains, that Wesley accepted a Catholic doctrine of holiness, he must accept its essential elements: the ability of man, with the help of grace, to rise in a "ladder of merit" and to reach the goal or level of perfection. In the case of general sanctification a believer would be enabled and required to reach a certain moral level before he or she could be saved (in order to assure the possibility of this, the concept of purgatory had become an integral part of the system).[7] To accept these components of the doctrine required one to accept the corollary doctrine of grace; grace becomes essentially a helpmate to the natural ability of humanity. Wesley rejected these concepts, insisting that no merit is required or possible for believers, that salvation is a free gift of God without consideration of a standard or level of holiness. In doing this he not only affirmed a Protestant doctrine of grace but also a Protestant doctrine of sanctification wherein sanctification is, like justification, dependent on God's unwarranted grace appropriated by humans through faith.[8]

Wesley's formulation of the doctrine made it clear that sanctification is generally a gradual and lifelong process, even though "entire sanctification" or perfection is a possibility and a goal for all believers. In Wesley's understanding the normal pattern of sanctification, and as we shall see also of perfection, is constant spiritual and moral improvement of the Christian life: "How much soever any man hath attained, or in how high a degree soever he is perfect, he hath still need to 'grow in grace,' and daily to advance in the knowledge and love of God his Saviour."[9] Wesley's recognition of the importance of the gradual process and of his own task in cultivating it rang out clearly in his comment to his brother Charles (1766): "Go on, in your *own way*, what God has peculiarly called you to. Press the *instantaneous* blessing: then I shall have more time for my peculiar calling, enforcing the *gradual* work."[10]

The gradual or extended work of sanctification was expressed among Puritans in John Owen's chapter title: "Sanctification, a Progressive Work."[11] Through persuasive and constant work within the lives of believers the Holy Spirit is gradually "renewing in them the image of God," so that progressively, by degrees, one becomes more holy.[12]

Although Owen and Wesley follow traditional interpretations in their expressions of the progressive nature found in sanctification, Wesley's full doctrine, which included the possibility of an instantaneous present "entire sanctification," would have been rejected by most Puritans.[13] For them holiness could not be consummated within this life; therefore, entire sanctification came only at or after death.[14] Sanctification as a work of the Holy Spirit traditionally is rooted in Scripture (Rom. 15:16, I Cor. 6:11, II Tim. 2:13), and, as one might expect, Puritan and Wesleyan presentations emphasized the spirit's role in transformation of the believer. Wesley's fullest amplification of the spirit's action was developed in several early sermons, "The Circumcision of the Heart" (1733), "On Grieving the Holy Spirit" (1733), and "On the Holy Spirit" (1736).

> We are convinced, that we are not sufficient of ourselves to help ourselves; that, without the Spirit of God, we can do nothing but add sin to sin; that it is He alone who 'worketh in us' by His almighty power, either 'to will or do' that which is good—it being as impossible for us even to think a good thought, without the supernatural assistance of his Spirit, as to create ourselves, or to renew our whole souls in righteousness and true holiness.[15]

This conviction retained its force and expression throughout his ministry.[16] Tying the work of the Spirit to that of Christ, Wesley could exclaim, "As all *merit* is in the Son of God . . . so all *power* is in the Spirit of God; . . . all true faith and the whole work of salvation, every good thought, word, and work, is altogether by the operation of the Spirit of God."[17] The same accent on the spirit constituted a cornerstone of Puritan presentation. A comment by Owen typifies their insistence that "he [the Spirit] is the immediate author of every good or gracious acting in us."[18]

In understanding sanctification as a work of the Spirit, Wesley and the Puritans embraced traditional orthodox formulations. Wesley may have been able to give a wider scope to a believer's own cooperation in sanctification; nevertheless, the Puritans did not allow stress on the Spirit's action to negate a believer's responsibility. Owen asserted that, though the Spirit is the effective cause, it is "our own work also in a way of duty."[19] The antinomian affirmation that total dependence upon the Spirit removes the necessity of works was rejected by both traditions.

Perfection

Although the sanctification process culminated for the Puritans in a believer's moral and spiritual perfection at the moment of death, some of their number expounded a doctrine of perfection of "intent," "sincerity of heart," which may be fruitfully compared to Wesley's own doctrine. Gordon Wakefield, in *Puritan Devotion*, notes William Dell's teaching a doctrine of perfection, and that others such as Richard Greenham gave full credit to the scriptural inferences of perfection without affirming "absolute unspottedness in this life."

Wakefield's presentation suggests that among Puritan authors John Preston's *The New Covenant* was the work displaying the most complete treatment of perfection.[20] Once again, as in the foregoing discussion of the covenant, Wesley's abridgment of this work provides a readily available text for comparison. Preston's major characterization of the concept was "perfection of the heart"; that is, a heart dedicated singularly and solely to God:

> *So now* **he is a perfect man with God, that** first **hath a whole heart; that is, such a heart whereof every part, and facultie is sanctified; there is no part of it, but it is seasoned with grace, there is no wheele in all the soule, but it is turned the right way,** *According to that, I Thess. 5, he is sanctified throughout, in body, soule, and spirit, I say, when a man shall finde everything within him readie to prayse the lord, and to looke toward the lord, all that is within him.* **There is not anything within him, of which he can say, the bent of it is another way.**[21]

Wesley's definition closely paralleled this: perfection was "purity of intention, dedicating all the life to God. It is the giving God all our heart; it is one desire and design ruling all our tempers. It is the devoting, not a part, but all our soul, body, and substance to God."[22]

Wesley published his "sentiments of Christian Perfection" in *The Character of a Methodist,* and that exposition provides us with a strikingly similar explication to that found in Preston's work. In this tract Wesley listed characteristics for perfection that correspond exactly to those Preston used for the "sincere heart." For both, a perfected believer will have "purity of heart," a heart that casts out all sin; a "single eye," a heart that looks upon one thing; integrity of heart, every part and interest dedicated to God; and, finally, will follow all the commandments and ordinances of God without failing in any of them.[23]

The similarity in interpretation continued in their presentations of perfection as a higher level or stage to be sought and expected in the Christian life. Preston insisted that a believer's "constant and ordinary work" was "every day to make his heart perfect," a teaching that parallels Wesley's admonition to his followers to "go on to perfection."[24] Such statements should not be read as meaning that either author understood perfection as a state attained by human effort; rather, as we have seen, they both insisted that perfection was a gift of God's grace.[25]

A major distinction between Wesley and Preston lies in what each was willing to say about sin. Preston, recognizing that human infirmities continue in the believer, asserted that whatever perfection is available to the believer is only the perfection of intention, of dedication, of sincerity—it is perfect dedication toward the goal of life, God. Commenting on Phil. 3:12-14, he explained:

> **The meaning is this; this is my course, saith the apostle: I have not yet attained to perfection; but this I do, I aim at the utmost, even at "the prize of the high calling of God in Jesus Christ:" I aim even at the top of perfection, and *I follow hard to it*: and, saith he, not only I, but "as many as are perfect, let them be thus minded;" where, by the *perfect*, he means, you see not one that hath already a perfect heart, but one that is sound hearted.**[26]

Preston's perfection of the "sound heart" should perhaps be seen as an "imperfect perfection" pressing toward the goal of real perfection obtained when the taint of sin is taken from the believer at death; consequently, he never spoke of perfection as being completed in the present. Perfection of the sound heart was, in his understanding, an ideal sought in this life and expected of all believers when they are attuned to God.

Wesley, on the other hand, sought to circumvent the problem of sin in the perfected believer by distinguishing between two types of sin:

> To explain myself a little farther on this head: (1) Not only sin, properly so called, (that is, a voluntary transgression of a known law,) but sin, improperly so called, (that is, an involuntary transgression of a divine law, known or unknown,) needs the atoning blood. (2) I believe there is no such perfection in this life as excludes these involuntary transgressions which I apprehend to be naturally consequent on the ignorance and mistakes inseparable from mortality. (3) Therefore *sinless perfection* is a phrase I never use, lest I should seem to contradict myself. (4) I believe, a person filled with the love of God is still liable to these involuntary transgressions. (5) Such transgressions you may call sins, if you please: I do not, for the reasons above-mentioned.[27]

This definition gave him, like Preston, a "perfection that is imperfect."[28] By refusing to call sins those acts that are involuntary and those present because of man's "corruptible nature," he could and did maintain that "perfection" is presently available within this life. In this interpretation he intended to eliminate the confusion caused by presentations such as Preston's which, although talking about one "whose heart is perfect with God,"[29] actually push perfection into the future.

However, one may question whether Wesley had really moved beyond what Preston was attempting to formulate in his presentation of the doctrine. Without affirming complete moral perfection, Preston recognized a perfection of personal commitment that produces love and service and goes beyond occasional moral failures. That he called these failures sins, and Wesley did not consider himself obligated to do so, is not of major consequence. Both were concerned with an overarching perfection of the whole person, a perfection that becomes the motivating force of one's personality and that discounts occasional failures. Neither could accept a "perfection of degrees," which failed to demand continual increase.[30] Thus, although Wesley's perfection was a present possibility, it still had to improve or increase in love, just as Preston demanded a constant increase in love. Preston's concept of perfection, on the other hand, certainly allowed some sense of "present perfection" by his concentration on purity of intention or dedication present at any moment in a believer. Both authors sought a very similar, if not identical, end product—a pure, perfect, or sound heart in the believer. Richard Heitzenrater, speaking of Wesley's understanding, describes it in terms of value: "Perfection must be understood in the context of a value oriented ethic. The desired end is not perfect obedience to a standard of conduct; it is perfect conformity to a model of divine-oriented virtue. Being restored in the image of God is basic to the whole process."[31] The same sense of value can equally be applied to Preston's formulation.

The following passage exemplifies how close Wesley's concept corresponded to Preston's interpretation of the "essence" of a perfected heart. As can be seen, Wesley cut the passage extensively but retained the core of the message. The passage vividly illustrates how Preston conceived what Wesley termed humanity's "corruptible infirmities" and their place in the life of the perfected person.

> **Now what is it to be pure?** *That is pure which is full of itself, and hath no other heterogeneall thing mingled with it; so,* **that heart is pure,** *which hath no sinne in it,* **which is holy,** *which hath a renewed qualitie of grace, which hath an inward regenerate man, that* **[which] will mingle with no sin,** *that is full of itselfe, and admits not the mixture of any sinne. My beloved, I must be warily understood here, I say, it admits not the mixture of any sin.* **It is true, sin may cleave, and adhere to a man, as drosse doth to the silver,** *but it mingles not with the regenerate part, nor that constitution of a man's heart, it is not weaved into the texture of his heart; it is no ingredient into the very frame, and fabricke of it,* **but though sinne be here, yet the heart still casts it out of itselfe, it resists it, and rejects it, and purifieth and cleanseth itselfe from it,** *this properly is a pure heart.*[32]

John Peters suggests that the idea of love's expelling sin from the heart, so aptly stated here by Preston, was Wesley's most appropriate formulation; it voiced the essence of his doctrine. In Wesley's words, "It is love excluding sin; love filling the heart, taking up the whole capacity of the soul." "For as long as love takes up the whole heart, what room is there for sin therein?"[33]

Wesley's doctrine of perfection had many sources,[34] and it would be unrealistic to claim dependence upon Preston or any other Puritan expression. Nevertheless, there are distinct similarities and affinities between the doctrine of perfection taught by Preston, and other Puritans, and that taught by Wesley. The least that can be said is that models of the doctrine were present among the Puritans, and Wesley was not only familiar with some of these formulations but thought them significant enough to include one example of this Puritan presentation of perfection among his abridgments.

Sin and Repentance in Believers

Just as justification was consequent to a believer's recognition of his or her own sin, the spiritual and moral growth expected in sanctification included, for Puritans, constant self-examination, an examination that led a believer to become aware that sin continues to persist in her or his life. Such sin, like that prior to justification, required continual repentance in a believer.

Accent on this truth attracted Wesley to Puritan explications during his own struggle with English Moravians in the early 1740s. Moravian teaching asserted that once a believer was converted, "entire sanctification" occurred, sin was no longer a threat, good works were not necessary, and the sacramental means of grace were irrelevant because they were immaterial to salvation. In Wesley's opinion such teachings led to antinomianism. Consequently, he separated from the Moravians when it became clear he would not be able to counteract their insistence on such an interpretation.[35] The conflict was similar to that which had occurred the century before among Puritans when some, such as Tobias and Crisp, taught comparable antinomian doctrines. Though rejected and condemned by the majority of the Puritan divines, that struggle was intense. Puritans who in their writings fought antinomianism were commended by Wesley in the following passage, which, though quoted earlier, is also instructive for the present discussion:

> They are continually tearing up the very roots of Antinomianism, by shewing at large, from the oracles of God, the absolute necessity, as of that legal repentance which is previous to faith, so of that evangelical repentance which follows it, and which is essential to that holiness, without which we cannot see the Lord.[36]

The expressions "legal repentance" and "evangelical repentance" (or "gospel repentance") used here were technical theological terms of the Puritan era. Robert Bolton defined legal repentance as that which is "a necessary preparative to the infusion of faith."[37] The term "legal" was applied because such repentance arose when the preaching of the law drove one to personal consciousness of abject sin—a consciousness which, in turn, led to repentance and saving faith.

Evangelical repentance, according to John Owen, consisted of **"godly sorrow for sin,** *with its relinquishment,* **[and leaving of it] proceeding from faith, love, and abhorrency of sin,** *on account of father, son, and spirit, both law, and love.*"[38] It was necessary for continuance of a constant fellowship between the believer and God. Such insistence on the need for evangelical or gospel repentance presupposed the reality of sin in the lives of believers.

Several titles in *A Christian Library* suggest the general outlines of Puritan treatment of sin and repentance in believers: John Owen's *Of the Mortification of Sin in Believers: The Necessity, Nature and Means of It* and *The Nature, Power, Deceit, and Prevalency of the Remainders of Indwelling Sin in Believers*; Richard Alleine's *A Rebuke to Backsliders: And a Spur for Loiterers*; and Lewis Stuckley's

A Gospel-Glass: Representing the Miscarriages of English Professors, or, A Call from Heaven, to Sinners and Saints, by Repentance and Reformation, to Prepare to Meet God. The latter work suggested that "the great design of this publication is, to reduce *professors* to a more awful, humble, serious repentance towards God."[39]

Wesley's similar position elaborated on the concept:

> There does still *remain*, even in them that are justified, a *mind* which is in some measure *carnal*; . . . an *heart bent to back sliding*, still ever ready to "depart from the living God"; a propensity to pride, self-will, anger, revenge, love of the world, yea, and all evil: a root of bitterness, which, if the restraint were taken off for a moment, would instantly spring up; yea, such a depth of corruption, as, without clear light from God, we cannot possibly conceive. And a conviction of all this sin *remaining* in their hearts is the repentance which belongs to them that are justified.[40]

"Inward" sin is principally noted here, for Wesley assumed that the true believer would naturally cast off outward sin, though he recognized that a believer certainly remained capable of lapsing into both inward and outward sin. The carnal mind, the genesis of the sinful nature of humanity, is not eradicated upon justification but continues to produce sins that require constant recognition and repentance in order that one may "grow in grace."

Both Owen and Wesley based their concept of the "enmity" between humans and God on Gal. 5:7, "the flesh lusteth against the spirit." This sin, for Owen, was not, as in Wesley, primarily inward but encompassed the whole spectrum: "**Nor are these lusts of the flesh only whereby men act their sensuality in riot, drunkenness, uncleanness, and the like; but they comprehend all the actings** ***of the love*** **of sin whatever, in all the faculties and affections of the soul.**"[41] Owen's description of a believer's sin was quite elaborate, showing how it "wars" against the grace present in the believer, setting itself in opposition to the general purpose of the soul; how it deceived the soul by drawing its attention away to worldly things; and how any success it had in this work caused it to expand while grace diminished proportionately. The believer was then torn by a conflict between flesh and spirit, necessitating conscious acknowledgment of sin.[42]

Sin in believers necessitated true repentance (evangelical repentance) for this sin; in Wesley's words: "a conviction of all this sin *remaining* in *their hearts* is the repentance which belongs to them that are justified," or "one kind of self-knowledge, the knowing ourselves sinners, yea, guilty, helpless sinners, even though we know we are children of God."[43] Wesley's focus on recognition of sin in believers did not lead him to include in his discussion of repentance what Owen calls "a Godly sorrow for sin." He evidently assumed that recognition and conviction would bring contrition, which in turn allowed God, through grace, to establish holiness. For Owen and other Puritans repentance explicitly included contrition, or in Robert Bolton's words, "to bewaile our sins from the bottome of our hearts," which naturally entailed recognition.[44] Wesley's presentation perhaps served his immediate purpose, to convince one of sin's presence, but the Puritan emphasis on contrition rather than simple conviction was a more complete definition.

Bolton and Owen also suggested that a justified believer would be more sensitive to her or his remaining sin than would the person who, recently convinced of sin, was ready through repentance to enter into initial faith. Bolton affirmed that once a person becomes a believer, his or her eyes search further for sins. **"But comfort of remission must serve as a precious *Eye-salve*, both to cleare their sight, that they may see more, and with more detestation; and to enlarge their Sluices, as it were, to poure out repentant teares more plentifully."**[45] Wesley's exposition of repentance as conviction of sins, which range from unprofitable conversation to sins of omission, similarly stressed the believer's increased awareness of sin.

Several of the treatises abridged by Wesley gave elaborate directions for the eradication of a believer's sin. Owen outlined directions for mortification as the recognition of sin; conviction of one's guilt relative to this sin; repentance for the sin through consideration of the sin, particularly accompanied by meditation; and finally, through faith, dependence upon Christ's willingness to relieve one from this sin.[46]

Rather surprisingly, Wesley's treatment of the topic in his sermons omitted any such directions for overcoming sin, but he evidently found them usefully presented through these abridgments.

Another similarity between Wesley and the Puritans is their insistence that the regenerate are dependent in this repentance upon the work of grace through the Spirit, just as they are in their first repentance. As Wesley indicated, believers, for all of their newness and escape from their old lives,

> are no more able now *of themselves* to think one good thought, to form one good desire, to speak one good word, or to do one good work, than before they were justified. . . . They "can", it is certain, "do all these things"; but it is not by *their own strength*. . . . "it is the *mere* gift of God": Nor is it given all at once, as if they had a stock laid up for many years, but from moment to moment.[47]

Owen, pursuing his interest in the Spirit, also clearly marked evangelical repentance, with its resultant mortification of sin, as the work of the Holy Spirit. The Spirit convinces, reveals Christ as the relief for this sin, and is the "**author and finisher of our sanctification; gives new supplies in influences of grace for holiness** *and sanctification*."[48]

Clearly, in teachings on sin and repentance in believers, another affinity exists between Wesley and many Puritans. The affinity is demonstrated not only by the similarities between their respective instructions, but also by Wesley's specific commendation and use of Puritan materials in his own struggles against antinomianism.

Final Justification

Wesley's *ordo salutis* culminated in what he called "final justification." Wesley's doctrine of justification clearly retained its Reformation character through its insistence upon faith; however, his formulation of the doctrine differed from the Moravian and some Calvinistic patterns of his own day by giving positive value and importance to a believer's obedience and works in the final salvation event. His attraction to Richard Baxter's and John Goodwin's statements on justification was precisely at this point, for they had interpreted obedience and works as necessary to final justification.

Wesley's struggle to understand fully the relation of faith to morally responsible good works extended over a number of years. It was modified, codified, and continually restated from the time of early contact with the Moravians through the intense debates with Evangelical Calvinists in the 1770s. His developing understanding of justification is a good illustration of Heitzenrater's insight that Wesley's spiritual pilgrimage underlies every stage of the numerous twists and turns in his theological development.[49] The evolution of his theology becomes obvious as his spiritual pilgrimage challenged previous understandings, and as he defended his thoughts when they were questioned by the experiences and teachings of others.

Summarizing some of these stages in Wesley's developing doctrine of justification, Lindström demonstrates that immediately after 1738 Wesley tended to disparage any concept of a second or "final justification" that suggested obedience or good works as a condition of faith.[50] Rather quickly, however, he returned to his perennial interest in holiness, so we find an early comment referring to a form of justification that would be considered in "our acquittal at the last day."[51] In the antinomian controversies of the 1740s and 1770s Wesley not only reaffirmed such a final justification, interpreted in his own way, but used it as a chief weapon against his opponents. The nature of justification was discussed at length at the first Methodist Annual Conference (1744), and the minutes of that conference described the justification that was spoken of by St. Paul and St. James as being two different justifications—one indicating justification by faith alone, and the other justification at the point of judgment, which will include "those works which spring from it [faith]."[52] In *A Farther Appeal to Men of Reason and Religion* Wesley elaborated the point:

> With regard to the *condition* of salvation, it may be remembered that I allow not only faith, but likewise holiness or universal obedience, to be the *ordinary condition* [italics added] of *final* salvation; and that when I say faith alone is the condition of *present* salvation, what I would assert is this: (1) That without faith no man can be saved from his sins; can be either inwardly or outwardly holy and (2) that at what time soever faith is given, holiness commences in the soul. From that instant "the love of God" (which is the source of holiness) "is shed abroad in the heart."[53]

As this passage notes, Wesley shared the Puritan insistence that, by its very nature, faith must produce works. "Works do not give life to faith, but *faith begets works*, and then is perfected by them."[54] In all cases faith is present "together with" works.

The *Minutes of the Methodist Conferences* include records of the 1770 conference, held in the midst of Wesley's continuing struggle with evangelical Calvinists. In those records Wesley affirmed that a believer is saved not by "merit of works, but by works as a condition," yet he also wondered if it was not splitting a hair to question whether a believer was not saved "for the sake of our works."[55] Violent opposition arose in response to these minutes, leading the conference of the following year to issue a clarifying "declaration" signed by all but one of the 53 Methodist preachers present:

> Whereas the Doctrinal points in the Minutes of a Conference, held in London, August the 7th 1770, have been understood to favour Justification by Works: Now the Revd. John Wesley and others assembled in Conference, do declare, That we had no such meaning; and that we abhor the Doctrine of Justification by Works, as a most perilous and abominable Doctrine. And as the said Minutes are not sufficiently guarded in the way they are expressed, we hereby solemnly declare in the sight of God, that we have no trust or confidence but in the alone merits of our Lord and Saviour Jesus Christ, for Justification or Salvation, either in Life, Death, or the day of Judgment. And although no one is a real Christian believer (and consequently cannot be saved) who doth not good works, where there is time and opportunity, yet our Works have no part in meriting or purchasing our justification from first to last, either in whole or in part.[56]

The declaration interpreted justification in such a manner as to assure its Reformation base but just as clearly retained an emphasis on the necessity of works. The phrase "where there is time and opportunity" indicates, however, the secondary, though necessary, role of works. In a similar manner, commenting on the final judgment in Matt. 12:37, Wesley affirmed, "Your words as well as actions shall be produced in evidence for or against you, to *prove whether you was a true believer or not*."[57] John Deschner succinctly summarizes the position: "These works do not lay hold of eternal life; it is rather that the lack of them may cause God to withhold his grace."[58]

Lindström suggests that Wesley's distinction between "merit" and "condition" was made more precise by John Fletcher, Wesley's major ally in the 1770s struggle with the evangelical Calvinists, when he defined final justification as one in which the believer is "justified by the evidence of works."[59] Here, as in Wesley's comment, it is not on the merit but on the *witness* of the works that final justification rests.

The distinction between two justifications, which Wesley noted early in his Methodist ministry, crystallized over time into a doctrine that affirmed, first, a present justification totally dependent on faith in the righteousness and merit of Christ, and, second, a final justification incorporating obedience, holiness, and the good works that spring from that faith. Both are ultimately based on faith and are necessary if opportunity for works is present. Deschner maintains that through the avenue of final justification Wesley brought to bear the concept of judgment. Whereas in present justification forgiveness and reconciliation dominate, in final justification judgment is taken into full account.[60] In both justifications the central element is still Christ and his atoning work, for all works, no matter how they "evidence" a believer's faith, are ultimately dependent on the grace of God offered to humanity in Christ. Held in tension, the two justifications recognize God's judgment *and* his mercy in Christ as well as humanity's wretchedness *and* obedience, albeit appropriated through grace.

Is it possible to relate a twofold justification to the theories of justification present in Puritanism? David Shipley is convinced that "every element in Wesley's answer . . . to theoretical antinomianism, even to the precise detail of the concept of a double justification, had been set forth in the seventeenth century," that is, among English Presbyterians.[61] Shipley locates the concept of double justification in the works of Richard Baxter and John Flavel (d. 1691).

Among his Puritan contemporaries, Baxter's *Aphorisms of Justification*, discussed in chapter 4, offered an unusual, though not totally unique, justification teaching. One of its distinguishing features was its separation of two elements or stages in justification. Baxter, in vivid seventeenth-century phrascology, commented, "Justification is either 1. in Title or Sence of the Law, 2. or in

Sentence of Judgment. The first may be called Constitutive; the second Declarative; the first Virtual, the second Actual."[62] By "Title of Law" he understood "justification as done in this life. . . . a gracious Act of God, by the promise or grant of the New Covenant, acquitting the offender from the Accusation and Condemnation of the Old Covenant, upon consideration of the Satisfaction made by Christ and accepted by the sinner."[63] Justification by "sentence of Judgment" is, however, a "future thing, not yet done. . . . a gracious Act of God by Christ, according to the Gospel, by sentence at his publique Bar, acquitting the sinner from the Accusation and Condemnation of the Law, . . . upon consideration of the satisfaction made by Christ, accepted by the sinner, and pleaded for him."[64] This justification at judgment, although a justification by faith, is nevertheless dependent upon the performance of the human conditions of the new covenant; therefore, "the Justification which we have in Christ's own Justification is but as to the particular offenders, and none can lay claim to it, till he have performed the conditions; nor shall any be personally justified till then." Consequently, "men that are but thus conditionally pardoned and justified, may be unpardoned and unjustified again for their non-performance of the conditions."[65] Justification is, then, "not a momentaneous Act; begun and ended immediately upon our Believing: but a continued Act; which though it be in its kind complete from the first, yet it is still doing, till the finall Justification at the Judgment day."[66]

The conditions of the covenant are faith, but a faith incorporating the "necessary, immediate, inseparable products of Faith"—sincere obedience and works of love.[67] Therefore, "Faith only doth not justify in opposition to the works of the Gospel; but those works do also justify as the secondary remote parts of the condition of the covenant."[68] Baxter's metaphorical use of a marriage contract illuminated clearly what he (and Wesley) were striving to convey. "Actual Obedience (as part of the Condition) doth . . . goe before our justification as continued and confirmed. For though our Marriage Contract with Christ doth give us the first possession, yet it is the Marriage faithfulness and duties, which must continue that possession."[69]

Wesley's abridgment of the *Aphorisms* shortened Baxter's "Justification in Title of Law" to "justification," and justification "by sentence of Judgment" became "final justification." Baxter used the phrase "finall justification" and Wesley was certainly not misrepresenting him by substituting it for the phrase "by sentence of Judgment"[70] Clearly, Wesley could closely identify his own concept of final justification with Baxter's justification at judgment.

The attraction of Baxter's treatise for Wesley is obvious, as they agreed that (1) justification is not a "once for all" event but has two loci—initial justification affirmed in faith which gives assurance of God's grace *and* final justification; (2) final or complete justification, the culmination of the justification process, comes at the judgment event; (3) in this final justification a believer's obedience and good works count as a "secondary" condition, and consequently, human moral responsibilities are integrally related to justification itself; (4) yet both justification events are grounded in faith—it is the essential element; and (5) both justifications depend upon "the consideration of the satisfaction made by Christ." It is also significant that Wesley's own use of the term "final justification" followed his publication of Baxter's *Aphorisms* (1745), although, as we have seen, the basic concept was present before that time.

One would be going beyond the evidence to claim, as Shipley does, that "Wesley's phrase 'final justification' is taken from Baxter," for that suggests Wesley was directly dependent for his pattern of the doctrine on Baxter—a claim that certainly is difficult to sustain.[71] It is more plausible that Wesley's doctrine in its final form, shaped by the antinomian controversy, drew as usual from multiple sources; but he certainly found in Baxter's formulation congenial and familiar concepts, which, while perhaps contributing indirectly to his own formulation, were most useful among his preachers and societies as a model for understanding justification.

David Watson, in *The Early Methodist Class Meeting*, suggests Baxter's double justification did not "adequately emphasize" what Watson understands to be Wesley's "distinctive justification," justification clearly separated from sanctification. "Instead of linking these necessary good works with the doctrine of justification *per se* . . . he [Wesley] assigned them to the inseparable but quite distinct doctrine of sanctification."[72] Evidently, for Watson, Baxter's failure to emphasize such a distinction carried the danger of "tipping the balance" in such a manner that it would allow works an inordinate role in final justification. One must wonder, however, whether Watson adequately accounts for Wesley's clear emphasis on a justification consequent to sanctification. Whereas works may be "assigned" to sanctification, they are also part of this "secondary" justification—part and parcel of complete justification.

C. K. Allison's *The Rise of Moralism* argues that Baxter, along with John Goodwin, was among several seventeenth-century English theologians whose views of faith and justification after the civil war allowed the return of a "moralism masquerading as faith."[73] According to Allison these English theologians reestablished a Pelagian understanding of human responsibility and morality, shifting it away from faith. Perhaps if one sees the words "Constitutive" and "Declarative" or "virtual" and "actual," used in Baxter's definition, as suggesting that actual justification depends upon works, one can see him as a teacher of moralism and "works righteousness" in salvation. His writings are extensive, and his concern to preserve human responsibility in the midst of an intense antinomian struggle allows him to be quoted in such a manner, but to do so would miss or negate his insistence that works, while necessary, are a secondary cause for justification. Justification, for Baxter, was always dependent on faith and Christ's righteousness:

> We have no Righteousness of our own, . . . nor any which is instead of the Righteousness of Christ, . . . And the day of Judgment will not be to try Christ and his Righteousness, but (to honour it) and try us and ours. . . . Salvation or damnation will be adjudged us as we are found to have been personally righteous or upright, in respect to the terms of the Law of Grace.[74]

Clearly Baxter was here concerned to hold together faith, grace, and works without allowing any of the three to vitiate or substitute for the other; he insisted on the reality of each even as this meant holding them in tension with each other.

I have already noted that Shipley finds the meaning of a continuing and final justification also in the thought of John Flavel,[75] but is it possible to find it in other Puritans? John Fletcher thought so and devoted a generous section of his work *Checks to Antinomianism* to expounding the concept as found among the Puritan divines.[76] One would not expect to find in this group the esteemed John Owen, but, indeed, the following passage reveals why Fletcher could use Owen in defense of his own position:

> Suppose a person freely Justified by the Grace of God through Faith in the Blood of Christ, without respect unto any Works, Obedience, or Righteousness of his own: we do freely grant: (1) that God doth *indispensably require personal obedience of him*, which may be called his Evangelical Righteousness; (2) that God doth *approve* of, and accept in Christ this Righteousness so performed; (3) that hereby that Faith whereby we are justified is *evidenced*, proved, manifested, in the sight of God and men; . . . (5) that upon it, we shall be *declared Righteous* at the last day, and without it none shall be. And if any shall think meet from hence to conclude unto an *Evangelical Justification*, or call God's acceptance of our Righteousness by that name, I shall by no means contend with them. And wherever this inquiry is made, not how a sinner *guilty of death* and obnoxious unto the Curse, shall be pardoned, acquitted and justified, which is by the Righteousness of Christ alone imputed unto him; but how a man that professeth *Evangelical faith*, or Faith in Christ, shall be tried, judged, and whereon as such he shall be justified, we grant that it is and must be by his own personal obedience.[77]

Fletcher correctly recognized here a concept very close to his own, particularly as it stressed works as the *evidence* of the faith and as it allowed at least a qualified (evangelical) justification of the believer based on obedience. Owen, looking at the professing believer, could affirm this, yet his fear of justification by works would not allow him to affirm that works have a place in justification; therefore, in the last chapter of this treatise he specifically denied a second justification.[78] On one hand, one must reject Owen as a Puritan precursor of Fletcher's and Wesley's doctrine, but, on the other, it can be argued that in the passage quoted Owen expressed much of the underlying content of what Wesley and Fletcher were trying to formulate. Each of them had the same objective: salvation grounded on grace accepted by faith *and* a believer's responsible moral works growing out of that faith. The objective was the same, though the bulk of Owen's presentation stood against a twofold justification and is best understood as interpreting the same justification from differing perspectives.[79] Fletcher, in using the quote, was obviously selective, but it is a most intriguing and suggestive passage.

One must also note a curious similarity between one objective of Wesley's final justification and a primary intent of the Puritan insistence on the "perseverance of the saints." In Wesley's concept of the hope and promise of final justification, incorporating as it did moral responsibility dependent on God's sustaining grace, one finds a bulwark against a believer's "falling away" from the faith. Viewed as a sustaining agency, the doctrine had the same objective as the doctrine of perseverance. The *Westminster Confession* (chap. 17) affirmed God's sustaining love as the operative element in a perseverance that does not allow the elect to fall away from faith. The authors of this statement were, however, aware that this dependence on grace could become dangerously antinomian, so they called specific attention to the elect's moral responsibility and the possibility of damaging sinfulness even within the framework of perseverance. Wesley, no doubt, would object to any suggestion that his concept of final justification could be correlated with or compared to the doctrine of perseverance. He strenuously rejected all implications that believers *could not* "fall from grace," a major and inherent tenet of perseverance; therefore, he rejected the whole concept. Nevertheless, whether he would have recognized it or not, one objective of *both* final justification and perseverance is to sustain the faithful by providing an assurance of grace *and* a shield against falling away from one's "first faith."

What may be said in evaluation of Wesley's concept of final justification? One must agree with John Deschner that Wesley's "doctrine of justification . . . must not be read as a considered, balanced piece of doctrinal instruction" but is probably best understood as "a journal of his theological pilgrimage."[80] Using this insight as a framework one may raise several questions about Wesley's explication of the doctrine.

Deschner, speaking from a Christological perspective, raises the question of whether, insofar as Wesley fails to give full value to Christ's "imputed active obedience," he has not actually, in the doctrine of justification, strayed further from Calvin than he thinks.[81] Deschner is convinced that Wesley, in doing this, fails to see the full significance of the active obedience of Christ in his priestly office, particularly as "we participate in Christ's active as well as passive righteousness through the Holy Spirit, in the Church."[82] In this Deschner may be correct, and if Wesley had recognized a more legitimate role for this active obedience, he might have avoided "breaking justification in two"; with Owen he would have avoided distinguishing between two justifications and only affirmed that one must be clear what person—sinner or professor of the faith—one is talking about when speaking of justification. In other words, Wesley could have claimed that he speaks of the same justification but viewed from differing perspectives. Wesley, of course, then would be Owen and not Wesley, and we must evaluate him as he was and not as he might have been.[83] Whether one takes Wesley's or Owen's approach, such distinctions illustrate, once again, the subtleties and complexities of the discussion through the centuries.

In the context of the 1770s antinomian controversy, wherein final justification was extensively treated, Wesley may well have appropriated some formulations of John Fletcher, Methodism's principal theological spokesman in the debate. Fletcher, and occasionally Wesley, underemphasized Christ's active obedience, for, as he saw it, to do otherwise would be to vitiate any real "active obedience" or moral responsibility on a believer's part. Here their Arminian synergism, which affirmed a believer's active cooperation with God's grace, played a significant role in their formulation, just as similar concepts had for Baxter and Goodwin.[84]

John Knight goes further, suggesting that in overemphasizing human "free will" Fletcher led Wesley toward a "works righteousness" theology. In Fletcher's, and then Wesley's, anxiousness to guarantee a believer's moral responsibility, Knight suggests "the priority of grace unintentionally was made to appear to be secondary to man's responsible choice."[85] Steven Gunter, carefully reexamining the 1770s controversy and subsequent writings of Fletcher and Wesley, concludes that in Fletcher's works, though faith is always related to works, "on balance faith receives less attention than the necessity of works." If Fletcher was not as careful on this point as he might have been, Gunter suggests Wesley was. He notes that when Wesley's late sermons are carefully examined, although they certainly emphasize works, they continue to ground those works in faith and the righteousness of Christ without losing a balancing synthesis of faith and works.[86] If Knight and Gunter are correct in seeing Fletcher moving toward a form of moralism, it is curious that Fletcher's presentation of the relation of faith to works attracted Wesley to Fletcher. That Fletcher understood the difficulty of properly balancing the two is clear in the following:

> So work with that earnestness, constancy and unweariness in well doing, as if thy works alone were able to justify and save thee; and so absolutely depend and rely upon the merits of Christ for justification and salvation, as if thou never hadst performed one act of obedience in all thy life. . . . It is a difficult thing to give each of these its true due in our practice.[87]

Whether or not the balance is properly maintained by Fletcher, Wesley's appropriation of final justification offers a useful explanation of how faith initiated by God's grace must be witnessed to and confirmed by works responsibly carried out by believers—a continuing synthesis of faith and works.

Any doctrine of final justification inevitably raises several questions: Doesn't final justification, on the one hand, threaten the positive and continuing value of one's initial justification, making it less than truly complete? Conversely, does a final justification, which ultimately depends upon faith, threaten the real necessity of works? Obviously, we can defend Wesley here by affirming with Deschner that this is not a balanced piece of doctrinal instruction and, therefore, has its problems and inconsistencies. We may also answer with Fletcher that to claim grace *and* pursue works is difficult to practice in daily life, perhaps more difficult than to understand theoretically how they should be balanced. However, if the two justifications as presented by Wesley (and Baxter) can be held in dynamic tension in the demands of daily living, one always demanding a vibrant response from the other, we gain a Reformation doctrine of faith wedded to a genuinely fruitful human moral responsibility, whereas one without the other lacks an important truth.

Notes

1. One of Wesley's favorite distinctions between justification and sanctification was to call justification the "relative" change in humanity, and sanctification the "real" change (*Works* [*Jackson*], 2:158). Richard Baxter

provides a strikingly similar distinction when, in discussing salvation, he comments, "He [God] *never maketh a relative change, where he doth not also make a real change*" (*Aphorisms on Justification*, 95, italics added).

2. For discussion of the relation of Wesley's doctrine to that of the Reformation leaders see Lindström, *Wesley and Sanctification*, 91-92.

3. *Concerning the Holy Spirit*, in Owen, *Works of John Owen*, 2:488.

4. Robert Bolton, *The Saints' Selfe-Enriching Examination* (London: Printed by Anne Griffin for Rapha Harford, 1634), 132 [CL, 5:219]; cited hereafter as *On Self-Examination*.

5. *Works*, 2:163.

6. Cell, *Rediscovery of John Wesley*, 361. Others who generally support such a concept include John L. Peters, *Christian Perfection and American Methodism* (Nashville: Abingdon Press, 1956), 21; W. E. Sangster, "Wesley and Sanctification," *LQHR* 171 (1946): 219; Paul Sanders, "What God Hath Joined Together," *Religion in Life*, 29 (1960): 493.

7. Williams, *John Wesley's Theology Today*, 174-75; see also Shipley, "Methodist Arminianism," 267.

8. See Williams, *John Wesley's Theology Today*, 175.

9. *Works*, 2:104-5. One of Wesley's favorite images was the designation of the various stages as that of child or newborn babe, a young man, and finally, a father or mature adult, in the faith.

10. *Letters*, 5:16.

11. *Concerning the Holy Spirit*, in Owen, *Works of John Owen*, 2:453; cf. *Works*, 2:482-3, where Wesley also indicated that sanctification was to grow in the "image of God"; cf. Wesley, *Explanatory Notes upon the New Testament*, 900 (II Pet. 3:18); *Letters*, 5:81.

12. Owen, *Concerning the Holy Spirit*, in *Works of John Owen*, 2:453.

13. *Works*, 2:68-69; *Works* (Jackson), 11:380, 442. Although Wesley at times clearly distinguished between sanctification and perfection or entire sanctification (*Works* [Jackson], 1:388), he occasionally coalesced these "stages." Sanctification as both an instantaneous and a gradual process was identified with perfection as early as the 1744 conference and as late as 1770. Instead of perfection being the ultimate capstone of a gradual process of sanctification, it could be both "an instantaneous and a gradual work" (*Letters*, 5:215). "Whoever would advance the gradual change in believers should strongly insist on the instantaneous" (*Works* [Jackson], 8:329; cf. 8:293-94). This conflating of the two was possible because Wesley's perfection was never static but "admits of a thousand degrees" and thereby could be a constituent part of sanctification (*Letters*, 5:215). John Peters (*Christian Perfection*, 63-64) provides a helpful summary of Wesley's various meanings and usages of such words as "perfection," "sanctification," and "entire sanctification." See also Maddox, *Responsible Grace*, 176ff.

14. *Concerning the Holy Spirit*, in Owen, *Works of John Owen*, 2:477.

15. *Works*, 1:403-4.

16. *Works*, 1:236-7; 2:53; 26:199; 9:124; *Letters*, 5:7; 2:71.

17. *A Farther Appeal to Men of Reason and Religion*, in *Works*, 22:108.

18. *Concerning the Holy Spirit*, in Owen, *Works of John Owen*, 2:459; cf. *Westminster Confession*, 12; Isaac Ambrose, *The Practice of Sanctification*, in *The Works of Isaac Ambrose* (London: Printed by H. Fisher, n.d.), 78 [*CL*, 8:6].

19. *Concerning the Holy Spirit*, in Owen, *Works of John Owen*, 2:475. Wesley's appreciation of Owen was expressed in a letter to John Newton, where, commenting on how others fail to stress "zeal and care for practical holiness" when teaching imputed righteousness, he says, "They do not enforce it, as Dr. Owen does, with whom (though I do not like some of his opinions) I should never have disputed had he been alive now" (*Letters*, 5:5).

20. Wakefield, *Puritan Devotion*, 137-39; Samuel Shaw's *Communion with God* (Glasgow: Printed for William Collins, 1829), 303 [*CL*, 14:320] includes statements that suggest a belief in perfection, though no extended comment amplifies the doctrine. Wesley claimed that even Bunyan actually allowed in his *Holy War* a real sense of perfection, although he did not acknowledge it as such (*Works*, 3:86).

21. Preston, *New Covenant*, 229 [*CL*, 6:27-28].

22. *Works* (Jackson), 11:444. "Here is the sum of the perfect law, the circumcision of the heart. Let the spirit return to God that gave it, with the whole train of its affection—Other sacrifices from us he would not, but the living sacrifice of the heart hath he chosen. . . . Be no design, no desire admitted there, but what has Him for its ultimate object" (*Works* [Jackson], 11:368; cf. 371-72).

23. Preston, *New Covenant*, 220 et passim [*CL*, 6:26-28]; *Works* (Jackson), 11:372-73. For Wesley's expanded treatment of these explanations see his third sermon, "Upon Our Lord's Sermon on the Mount" (*Works*, 1:510ff.), and his eighth sermon of that series for comments on "singleness of eye" (*Works*, 1:612ff).

24. Preston, *New Covenant*, 259 [*CL*, 6:29]; *Letters*, 5:6; 6:103, 137.

25. Preston, *New Covenant*, 395. It should be remembered in any discussion of Wesley's doctrine of perfection that the doctrine in its fullest form guarded, on the one hand, against a concept of perfection that might dismiss the necessity of good works because of one's "perfected" state. On the other hand, it credited all perfection to the work of Christ so that the "perfected" were always in need of the "merits of Christ" and must always be in a constant communion with him. Any severance of communion with Christ was a threat to perfection, as was any pride "of achievement." Steven Gunter has carefully examined the dangers of perfection as Wesley experienced them within his movement and in his defense of the doctrine (W. Stephen Gunter, *The Limits of 'Love Divine'* [Nashville: Abingdon Press, 1989], 202-26).

26. Preston, *New Covenant*, 258 [*CL*, 6:28].

27. *Works* (Jackson), 11:396. It would be difficult to reconcile this concept of "involuntary transgression" with Wesley's own earlier criticism of a perfection that meant only that a believer does not willfully or habitually sin (*Works*, 2:107). Surely voluntary and involuntary transgression is what is meant by willingly and unwillingly sinning. For comment on the dangers of this definition of sin and Wesley's inconsistencies at this point, see R. Newton Flew, *The Idea of Perfection in Christian Theology* (London: Oxford University Press, 1934), 327; Williams, *John Wesley's Theology Today*, 179-80.

28. Williams, *John Wesley's Theology Today*, 168.

29. Preston, *New Covenant*, 259 [*CL*, 6:29].

30. Preston, *New Covenant*, 215; *Works*, 2:104.

31. Heitzenrater, *Mirror and Memory*, 101.

32. Preston, *New Covenant*, 219 [*CL*, 6:26-27]; cf. Alleine, *Vindiciae Pietatis*, 87.

33. Peters, *Christian Perfection*, 58-59; *Works*, 2:160, 167.

34. For Wesley's own description of these sources, see the early pages of *A Plain Account of Christian Perfection*, in *Works* (Jackson), 11:366-70. R. Newton Flew's *Idea of Perfection* traces these sources through various Christian traditions into the presentations of the early church.

35. For a careful and detailed analysis of Wesley's association with the Moravians, see Heitzenrater, *Mirror and Memory*, 121-38; Gunter, *Limits of 'Love Divine,'* 83-103.

36. *CL*, 4:107.

37. Bolton, *On Self-Examination*, 59 [*CL*, 5:201]. Wesley does not use these technical terms in his own exposition, but what Bolton described as legal repentance Wesley clearly outlined: "There is a repentance and a faith which are more necessary at the beginning: a repentance which is a conviction of our utter sinfulness, and guiltiness and helplessness, and which precedes our receiving that kingdom of God, which our Lord observes, is 'within us:' and a faith whereby we receive that kingdom, even 'righteousness, and peace, and joy in the Holy Spirit'" (*Works*, 1:335-36).

38. Owen, *On Communion*, in *Works of John Owen*, 1:241 [*CL*, 11:63].

39. Lewis Stuckley, *A Gospel-Glass: Representing the Miscarriages of English Professors or A Call from Heaven, to Sinners and Saints, by Repentance and Reformation, to Prepare to Meet God* (London: R. Edwards, 1809), x [*CL*, 19:232]. Italics added. Cited hereafter as *Gospel-Glass*.

40. *Works*, 1:341; cf. 321ff.

41. Owen, *The Nature, Power, Deceit, and Prevalency of the Remainders of Indwelling Sin in Believers*, in Owen, *Works* of John Owen, 13:45 [*CL*, 10:137].

42. For extensive catalogs of sin in believers see Owen, *The Nature, Power, Deceit, and Prevalency*, in *Works of John Owen*, 13:45 [*CL*, 10:137], and Lewis Stuckley, *Gospel-Glass*, 4ff. [*CL*, 19:239ff.].

43. *Works*, 1:341, 335.

44. Bolton, *On Self-Examination*, 129 [*CL*, 5:218].

45. Bolton, *Instructions for a Right Comforting of Afflicted Consciences* (London: Printed by Felix Kyngston for Thomas Weaver, 1631), 289 [*CL*, 6:61].

46. *The Mortification of Indwelling Sin in Believers*, in Owen, *Works of John Owen*, 7:425ff. [*CL*, 10:116ff.]; cf. Stuckley, *Gospel-Glass*, 367-83 [*CL*, 19:433-43]; Richard Alleine, *A Rebuke to Backsliders: And a Spur to Loiterers*, in *CL*, 18:306ff.

47. *Works*, 1:345.

48. *The Mortification of Indwelling Sin in Believers*, in *Works of John Owen*, 7:429 [*CL*, 10:118]; cf. Alleine, *A Rebuke to Backsliders*, in *CL*, 18:321.

49. Heitzenrater, *Mirror and Memory*, 107.

50. Lindström, *Wesley and Sanctification*, 205ff.

51. *Works*, 11:105.

52. *Works* (Jackson), 8:277; *Letters*, 4:178-79.
53. *Works*, 11:130.
54. Wesley, *Explanatory Notes upon the New Testament*, 862-63 (James 2:22), italics added.
55. *Works* (Jackson), 8:337-38; cf. Wesley's own question of the issue in *Letters*, 5:264.
56. *Works*, 22:285 n. 42. Ward and Heitzenrater, editors of this volume of the *Works*, in this note detail the circumstances surrounding the publications of the declaration. See also Gunter, *Limits of 'Love Divine,'* 251-54.
57. Wesley, *Explanatory Notes upon the New Testament*, 65 (Matt. 12:37), italics added.
58. Deschner, *Wesley's Christology*, 179.
59. Lindström, *Wesley and Sanctification*, 212. "Although from first to last, the merits of my life and death *purchase* or *deserve* thy justification; yet in the day of judgment thou shall be justified by thy works; that is, thy justification, which is purchased by my merits, will entirely turn upon the evidence of thy works, according to the time and opportunity thou hast to do them" (John Fletcher, *Checks to Antinomianism*, 1:107).
60. Deschner, *Wesley's Christology*, 178-79.
61. Shipley, "Wesley and Some Calvinistic Controversies," 205. It should be further noted that forms of a double justification concept were also found in Anglican circles (see Deschner, *Wesley's Christology*, 188). Wesley refers to this distinction in Bishop George Bull's *Harmonia Apostolica: Or Two Dissertations; in the Forms of Which the Doctrine of St. James on Justification by Works Is Explained and Defended: In the Latter the Agreement of St. Paul and St. James Is Clearly Shown* (*Letters*, 5:264).
62. Baxter, *Aphorisms of Justification*, 183.
63. Baxter, *Aphorisms of Justification*, 185.
64. Baxter, *Aphorisms of Justification*, 184, 188-89.
65. Baxter, *Aphorisms of Justification*, 196.
66. Baxter, *Aphorisms of Justification*, 233, 194. Baxter outlined some ten "steps toward our final and full Justification," calling the sixth ("The change of our Relation upon our actual Faith") and the tenth ("Our final Justification at the Great Judgment") those that are "directly and properly the Justification by Faith" (Baxter, *Aphorisms of Justification*, 195).
67. Baxter, *Aphorisms of Justification*, 241; cf. 235-36. As noted in chap. 4, Baxter's publication of the *Aphorisms* drew stinging attacks on his position. He responded to these, hoping to clarify the misunderstandings of his position, in a number of letters and treatises, and most completely in *Richard Baxter's Confession of His Faith*. In this latter work the distinctions between the justifications were reiterated, and obedience exemplified in works as a condition of final justification was ably defended (see particularly 47-55).
68. Baxter, *Aphorisms of Justification*, 289-90. "To conclude: It is most clear in the Scripture, and beyond dispute, that our Actual, most proper, compleat Justification, at the great Judgment, will be according to our Works, and to what we have done in flesh, whether Good or Evil: which can be no otherwise than as it was the Condition of that Justification."
69. Baxter, *Aphorisms of Justification*, 333. Richard Alleine's insistence

upon faith *and* works as necessary for salvation is very close to this exposition, though Alleine does not propose a second justification (*Vindiciae Pietatis*, 90ff.).

70. Baxter, *Aphorisms of Justification*, 195, 233.

71. Shipley, "Wesley and Some Calvinistic Controversies," 208. Shipley's statement is curiously incongruous with his concluding remarks that he has made no attempt "to prove that Wesley was in any way dependent upon or influenced directly by the English Presbyterians" unless he, with other commentators, does not judge Baxter to be a typical Presbyterian! (Shipley, 210).

72. Watson, *Early Methodist Class Meeting*, 52-53.

73. Allison, *Rise of Moralism*, 193. Allison is also disturbed that Wesley made "uncritical use" of Baxter's writings (Allison, 194).

74. Richard Baxter, *An Appeal to the Light* (London: Printed for Nevil Simons, 1674).

75. Shipley, "Wesley and Some Calvinistic Controversies," 209-10.

76. Fletcher, *Checks to Antinomianism*, 1:276-93.

77. John Owen, *The Doctrine of Justification by Faith through the Imputation of the Righteousness of Christ, Explained, Confirmed, and Vindicated* (London: Printed for R. Boulter, 1677), 222-23. Cf. Preston, *The Breast Plate of Faith and Love*, pt. 2, 101 [*CL*, 5:382].

78. Owen, *Doctrine of Justification*, 572. Owen, like Wesley after him, in discussing the reconciliation of Paul's and James's statements on works, pointed out that these two apostles, respectively, treat faith in two different senses. Paul interprets faith as "the means of our justification," whereas James interprets it as a description of a "dead" faith. He also allowed that they treat justification in different senses—Paul in terms of an "absolute justification before God," James as the evidence or manifestation of this justification as is shown in true "professors" of the faith. Wesley made this two justifications; Owen prefered to call it one (Owen, *Doctrine of Justification*, 557-82; cf. Wesley, *Letters*, 4:178-79; *Explanatory Notes on the New Testament*, 863 [James 2:24]).

79. Isaac Ambrose in his work *Practice of Santification*, recognizing that justification is not simply one event, distinguished between initial, progressive, and perfective justification. Here Ambrose attempted to guard against the dangers inherent in a justification that has already taken place and cannot therefore be counted as operative in terms of our present sin. His progressive justification then applied Christ's merits to forgiveness of daily sins. In the final day one is finally perfectly justified. Such a present application corresponds to Wesley's insistence upon a "moment by moment" relationship to God but does not attempt to take into account human responsibility in terms of obedience. Ambrose was at least aware of the problems of a "once for all" justification and attempted to deal with them constructively (Ambrose, *Practice of Sanctification* in *The Works of Isaac Ambrose* [London: Printed by Henry Fisher, n.d.], 76-78 [*CL*, 8:3-5]).

80. Deschner, *Wesley's Christology*, 180.

81. "I think on Justification just as I have done any time these seven-and-twenty years, and just as Mr. Calvin does. In this respect I do not differ from him an hair's-breadth" (*Works*, 21:509).

82. Deschner, *Wesley's Christology*, 183.

83. One should not assume that Deschner fails to recognize this. He points out that, for all its problems, Wesley's doctrine of justification still emphasized Christ's priestly work and, indeed, "Wesley is not Calvin here: Wesley is much more interesting simply as Wesley, even in his doctrine of justification" (Deschner, *Wesley's Christology*, 183).

84. John Goodwin in *Imputatio Fidei, or a Treatise on Justification* (London: Printed by O. and G. D., 1642) had an extended examination of Christ's imputed righteousness in which he rejected the imputation of Christ's active obedience "performed to ye moral law." In this work he distinguished between a constitutive and a declarative or pronunciative justification (111-12), which reminds one of Baxter's formulation. Goodwin intimated that the declarative justification, as an actual justification, must include the sense of Matt. 12:37 and James 2—that is, works will be considered in the declarative justification. Nevertheless, there is little made of this distinction by Goodwin, and it played no major role in his argument.

85. John A. Knight, "John Fletcher's Influence on the Development of Wesleyan Theology in America," *Wesleyan Theological Journal*, 2 (1978): 19.

86. Gunter, *Limits of 'Love Divine,'* 261; cf. 261-66.

87. Fletcher, *Works of John Fletcher*, 2:397; cf. *Works*, 3:504-5.

6

The Nature and Significance of Christian Living

Among the legacies for the common people of England's seventeenth-century civil war were vast social, economic, and philosophical changes. These continued in the eighteenth century, wherein new occupational patterns and population shifts threatened conventional social patterns. Customary religious beliefs and worship practices were especially endangered, contributing to widespread religious and moral unease and disquiet. In such a climate emphasis on strong traditional Christian discipline often promised security and hope where little conventional certainty existed. English Christianity for the common people had normally given careful attention to instruction in Christian living, yet in times of such disquiet explicit guidance became even more significant. Puritans and Methodists working in these centuries were especially eager to offer Christ and a clear and disciplined Christian life in the midst of what had become widespread cultural malaise and hopelessness. They were convicted that as faith extended hope, it also expressed itself in better lives both here and in the hereafter. Teaching a true, pure, consistent, and dynamically active life of love modeled on Christ's life became a hallmark for each group. They presumed that their followers would be recognized by the Christ-oriented lives they lived among their neighbors.

A late eighteenth-century commentator, perhaps derisively, identifies this trait as a shared one: "They who go now under the name of Methodists, were in the days of our forefathers called *Precisians*, terms of their own devising, importing that the bearers of them had carefully squared out their religion by line and level."[1] This joint accent on Christian living provides much fruitful material to give us insights into what Wesley found most congenial among the Puritans and supportive of his own message.

The Printing Press and Christian Instruction

Puritan appropriation of the printing press as a principal means of communicating instruction and theological debate led to their authorship of a multitude of tracts, books, and broadsheets throughout the seventeenth century, but particularly after the restoration of Charles II. Chief among these were works on Christian living. Wesley, early in his public ministry, also recognized the proverbial "power of the press" that Puritans had discovered earlier. Making publication a major feature of his movement, Wesley's greatest income ultimately would come from use of the press, income which he often turned into more books and tracts.

For Puritans and Wesley it was crucial that the common person should have readily affordable printed instruction for Christian living. Richard Baxter, as we will see, suggested that those believers who could afford it would do well to purchase and distribute books of instruction among "the unsanctified that need them."[2] Always careful to publish literature at a minimal cost to the reader, Wesley late in his career was able to carry out Baxter's suggestion. In January 1782 Wesley and his able assistant, Thomas Coke, established a society for the distribution of reading materials among the poor, with little or no cost to the reader. Wesley's object is seen in his comment upon the establishment of the society: "I cannot but earnestly recommend this to all those who desire to see true, scriptural Christianity spread throughout these nations. Men wholly unawakened will not take the pains to read the Bible. They have no relish for it. But a small tract may engage their attention for half-an-hour; and may, by the blessing of God, prepare them for going forward."[3] The plan was to subsidize the publication of various tracts containing "true, scriptural Christianity" and to distribute these to the poor and to those "unconverted" or uninterested souls whom one might have opportunity to contact.[4]

Thirty tracts appeared in 1782 under the auspices of this society, on which were printed, according to Green, the words "This book is not to be sold, but given away."[5] Wesley seemed quite pleased with the success of this project. He comments later in that same year to Thomas Davenport:

> Our little Society for dispersing religious books among the poor has now spread them through all England. Two of the books which they disperse are *Alleyne's Alarm* and *Baxter's Call to the Unconverted*. Any person that subscribes half a guinea or a guinea yearly will have

> four times as many books sent down as he could otherwise purchase with that sum. It seems this is one of the most excellent charities that we can be concerned in.[6]

Of the thirty tracts distributed in this manner, twenty-one were Wesley's own sermons and tracts. These ranged from his sermon "The Almost Christian" to various "words" such as his "Word to a Drunkard." The other tracts included two contemporary sermons by Fletcher and Oliver; three tracts by Wesley's mentor, William Law, including his *A Serious Call to a Holy Life*; and four Puritan pieces. Alleine's and Baxter's works are joined by Wesley's abridgment of two works related to the Puritan John Janeway: *John Janeway's Life* and Janeway's *Token for Children*, which Wesley had published as early as 1749. In publishing these works, Wesley was once again printing his evangelistic message *and* providing instruction in Christian living as Puritans had before him.

Christian Living

In view of these publishing endeavors, the number and range of Puritan and Methodist materials on Christian living available for comparison and analysis are phenomenal. Any investigation of affinities among these works is immediately confronted with the problem of selection. A full survey would require a complete catalog and systematic analysis of teachings that touch practically every imaginable life situation. To limit the inquiry and to examine relatively concrete instances of correspondence between the two traditions, I have selected representative teachings from three sources: (1) those Puritan treatises that Wesley related to his own teachings through recommendation and use; (2) those in which both movements display a peculiar interest or emphasis; (3) those in which, through Wesley's action or practice, can be identified as incorporating Puritan precepts or practice.

Because Wesley so appreciated Puritan teachings concerning Christian life, it is well to review again his evaluation of that "peculiar excellency" among the Puritan divines: "[They] instruct us . . . how to use the faith which God has given, and to go from strength to strength. They lead us by the hand in the paths of righteousness, and shew us how, in the various circumstances of life, we may most surely and swiftly grow in grace, and in the knowledge of our Lord Jesus Christ."[7] The dominant concern for Wesley was that such instruction ultimately led one to closer conformity to Christ's example and teachings. They provided a climate or setting for "growth in grace."

Evangelical Invitations to Christian Faith

Although neither Wesley nor the Puritans were especially original in their instructions for Christians, the successes of both their movements witness that they were masters in the art of its application. Central to the teachings were two foci: *evangelism*, works intended to convert unbelievers and awake nominal Christians who failed to practice their faith; and *instruction*, works meticulously detailing how a Christian could and should live out the faith. Often these two concerns were not carefully separated, for in practicality that is most difficult, but one or the other often received special attention in any one tract. We begin by examining the evangelical works.

For evangelism Wesley found special significance in two Puritan works that, as we have seen, he republished for his tract series: Joseph Alleine's *An Alarm to Unconverted Sinners* and Richard Baxter's *A Call to the Unconverted.*[8] Alleine's work, first published in 1672, was widely acclaimed and cherished. Edmund Calamy notes that twenty thousand copies of the tract were sold in this first edition, and fifty thousand more three years later under the title *The Sure Guide to Heaven.*[9] Whether or not these figures are accurate, the work was, without question, exceptionally popular both in England and America well into the nineteenth century. Wesley not only included this treatise in *A Christian Library*, but he also used it as a source for the covenant service and instructions concerning covenanting that he prepared for Methodists. His *Journal* entry of April 3, 1757, records: "On Good-Friday, in the evening, at the meeting of the society, God was eminently present with us. I read over and enlarged upon Joseph Alleine's 'Directions for a Thorough Conversion to God', and desired all who were able would meet me on Monday that we might 'perform our vows to the Lord.'"[10] He also recommended the version included in the *Library*, along with Richard Alleine's *Vindiciae Pietatis*, to Samuel Furly for a good example of instruction in Christian piety.[11]

Baxter's treatise was the only one of the thirty tracts specifically abridged by Wesley for this series, although the abridgment of Alleine was a new one and not a reprint of the abridgment included in the *Library*. Baxter's *A Call to the Unconverted* was first printed in 1657, and, like Alleine's *Alarm*, enjoyed renown as a popular Puritan set of instructions. In fact, Baxter, late in life, acknowledges it as an "unexpected success, beyond all the rest that I have written, except *The Saints' Rest*."[12]

The similarity of these two treatises is obvious from their titles. They were both originally addressed to local congregations that these men served and were likely preached before being published.

The printed tracts, though designed for a wider audience, retained their sermonic intimacy. Baxter voiced his intent in publication:

> The use this Part is published for, is 1. For Masters and Parents to read often in their Families, if they have servants or children as yet unconverted. 2. For all such unconverted persons to read and consider themselves. 3. For the richer sort, that have any pitty on such miserable souls, to give to the unsanctified that need them: (if they have not fitter at hand to use and give.)[13]

Although Baxter's tract was directed toward those outside the community of the faithful, the text of the treatise cried out to lackadaisical Christians to recognize their true state. The latter persons concerned Alleine most, for in his words, "The numbers of unconverted Souls among you [nominal Christians] call for my most earnest Compassions and hasty Diligence to pluck them out of burning."[14]

To clarify to whom the treatises were addressed, both Baxter and Alleine included elaborate descriptions of the unconverted. Obviously, those who lived in open sin, that is, the drunkards, the thieves, the openly covetous, and so forth, were unconverted; yet many who assume that they are converted testify through their lives the frailty of their assumption. Such a person, though not living in outward evil, is inclined to self, making the "principal business of his life to prosper in the world."[15] Religion that is used to one's own ends is no religion at all.[16] The formality of religious practice should also not deceive one:

> **Friends and Brethren,** ***be not deceived, God is not mocked,*** **Gal. vi. 7. Whether it be your Baptism, or whatever else you pretend, I tell you, from the Living God, that, if any of you be prayerless Persons, or unclean, or malicious, or covetous, or riotous, or a Scoffer, or a Lover of evil Company,** *(Prov. xiii. 20)* **in a word, if you are not holy, strict, and self-denying Christians,** *(Heb. xii. 4 Matt. xvi. 24)* **you cannot be saved,** *except you be transformed by a farther work upon you, and renewed again by repentance.*[17]

In Alleine's theologically stated description of the unconverted, the Puritan insistence on holy living was clear: "Regeneration and remission are never separated: the unsanctified are unquestionably unjustified, and unpardoned."[18]

Having established the nature of the unconverted, our authors then explain conversion. Alleine succinctly defined it as "the thorow change both of the heart, and life."[19] "**He saith it must be a total change, and you must be holy, and new creatures,** *and born again;* **and you think that it is enough to patch up the old man, without becoming new.**"[20] The converted believer will have a new direction to life—mind, will, affections, fears, joy, love, sorrows, every aspect of life now receives new direction. A believer desires "nothing in all the world so much as that Christ may be magnified in him."[21]

Using the fear of eternal damnation and the promise of new life, as well as contrasting God's judgment with his mercy and compassion, Alleine and Baxter appealed to both emotion and reason. Baxter was sure that "God taketh Pleasure in Men's Conversion and Salvation, but not in their Death or Damnation: he had rather they would Return and Live, than go on and die."[22] Therefore, God promises, commands, admonishes, and reasons with humans in order to convince them of their need for salvation. Alleine, although concentrating more on the miseries and danger of the one who refuses to accept conversion ("Turn or burn")[23] also emphasized God's joy over one who accepts his grace.

Baxter contributed a helpful section answering common objections to the emphasis Puritans placed on active Christian faith: despite the fact that all are sinners why one should endeavor to live a holy life; "we will have a store of company" in hell; "professors are not any better than other men"; we are not gross sinners; "you would make men mad under the pretense of converting them"; and you make "too much ado" about religion.[24] Although Wesley omitted some of these from his abridgment, he included those of most consequence. It is not difficult to imagine his recommending Baxter's answers as credible responses to those who ridiculed his Methodist followers.

Guidance for Those Seeking Faith

Wesley no doubt found the evangelical portions of these treatises useful, but it was their detailed instructions that attracted him. Often these were "directions," or extensive lists of instruction, for those seeking the blessedness of a Christian life. Baxter's formulation, with which one may assume Alleine was familiar, was written a decade before Alleine's. The treatises closely resembled each other, with some variance in order of presentation. Beginning with a caution that one must recognize the nature and necessity of conversion, Baxter's directions laid out a plan that, through serious meditation, prayer, and study of the Word, would bring one to renounce all sin. Believers were thereby able to deliver themselves, through Christ, to God, and give themselves "unreservedly, absolutely, and universally" to God. This commitment shouldn't be delayed and must be accompanied by shunning evil company whose influence endangered such firm resolutions.[25] Alleine's presentation provided expanded comment on each direction, and he emphasized recognition of one's state while affirming that, for a converted believer, the laws of holiness were to be accepted willingly. For Wesley one of Alleine's most important contributions was, as we have seen, the outline of a covenant by which a believer might objectively bind himself or herself to God after conversion.[26] Wesley's abridgments of the respective treatises retained the entire set of directions with the usual abbreviation of hortatory elements he evidently considered to be unnecessary expansion of particular points.

Wesley's attraction to these treatises lay in (1) their clear and precise appeal to all, churched and unchurched, to recognize the absolute necessity of a changed and holy life, (2) their description of both the converted and the unconverted, and (3) their method of direction by which a person might offer herself or himself to God in order that the Holy Spirit could effect major change in the individual's life. They ideally prepared a person for the Christian message and then presented the new Christian life in such a manner that one might, with God's help, willingly appropriate it.

Wesley's own presentation of the gospel to the uncommitted, or the falsely committed, was distinguished from these treatises by his emphases. For instance, in his writings there was little description of hell's fiery torments, spelled out so vividly by Alleine,[27] and Wesley tended to emphasize salvation's promised blessedness, particularly as related to this life.[28] Furthermore, Wesley was perhaps more successful in striking a balance between an emphasis on inward holiness and its outward manifestations.[29]

Each of these authors, including Wesley and many others, was faced with the dilemma of how to insist upon inward holiness as the essential criterion of Christian conversion, whereas in reality one can judge only the outward actions of another, inferring from these the believer's inward condition. As a result, although stress may be placed on the necessity of a change in the heart, the common yardstick by which one distinguishes the unconverted person from the converted is in his or her outward actions. If most members of a congregation were evaluated as unconverted, as both Baxter and Alleine continually insisted, one must, out of necessity, make this judgment on the basis of outward manifestations. Therefore, Baxter and Alleine appear to stress outward manifestations, even though that may not have been their intention. Wesley was far from escaping the same charge but seems to have made a more conscious effort to guard against the dangers inherent in such a situation.[30] Finally—and perhaps this is simply a matter of changing preaching styles over the century that had intervened between his time and that of the Puritans—Wesley did not use Baxter's and Alleine's long and involved discourses pleading with the people to accept the faith.[31] Wesley admonished and advised each believer to examine one's self and to accept the gospel, but not with the same verboseness or pleading fervor found in these Puritan authors. Yet Wesley could indeed see precedents for his own preaching style among the Puritans.[32]

The Direction and Destiny of Christian Living

The most widely known Puritan statement of humanity's purpose is found in the Westminster *Shorter Catechism*: "Man's chief end is to glorify God and enjoy him forever." Such glorification may be completed or fulfilled in the future, but "enjoyment of God" suggests this is not simply a future heavenly event. Glorification takes place in one's life—in daily loving service to God and neighbor. Both the present course of a believer's life and one's ultimate destiny are bound up in the glorification of God.

Neither Puritan authors nor Wesley were interested in Christian living simply on moral grounds, as "morality for morality's sake" simply seeks a better or more congenial personal and social life. The Christian life is, rather, as we have seen repeatedly in this study, the product of a true faith in Jesus Christ, which by its very nature issues forth in an active life of obedience and love, love directed toward God and loving service of the neighbor—not simply because one ought to do good but because a believer *must* do good. Seen from this perspective, the purpose and aim of the Christian life is to carry the intimate personal relationship that exists between God and the believer into one's daily life so that one's faith *and* life glorify the divine.

Although such a presentation of God's glorification was the foundation of Puritan understanding, inherent in the concept lay another subtle perspective: If one lived a life glorifying God, salvation was promised and the promise contained within itself duties, the living of a holy life; so one's salvation in some sense was sustained, reinforced by the "living out" of these duties. The anticipation of God's fulfilling of the promise, which included duties, in turn became another important motivation for right living. The direction and destiny of Christian life presented in this manner subtly shifted attention toward the eternal salvation that a holy life will bring a believer. Puritan teachings on Christian living, as a consequence, often concentrated on directions and explanations of Christian living, which were oriented toward an anticipated personal salvation. Faith was still, in this formulation, the sole condition of salvation because the sanctified Christian life was ultimately dependent on God's grace for its inception and continuation; but the rewards of personal salvation were also significant as motivations for doing good.

Although the Puritan treatises Wesley incorporated in *A Christian Library* included both emphases and perspectives, the goal of personal salvation often predominated. With proper reservations against understanding such teaching as a new salvation by works, Bolton's presentation of the direction and destiny of a Christian life of obedience and love was clear:

> There is no greater encouragement, or stronger motive to *stirre* [excite] a man to an eager and earnest pursuite of the meanes, than to propose unto him an end wherein at length his heart may repose; as in a concurrence of all comforts and contentments. To which, there is no possibility of attainment, but by purenesse of heart, holinesse of life, constancie in course of sanctification, which onely leade unto the face, and presence of God; where, and with whom alone is the highest perfection of blisse, a river of infinite pleasures, the well of life, and endless rest of all created desires.[33]

Thomas Manton's formulation similarly emphasized an eternal salvation:

> The gospel is not a naked, unconditionate offer of pardon and eternal life in favour of sinners, but upon most convenient terms, for the glory of God, and the good of men, and enforced by the strongest obligations upon them *to receive humbly and thankfully these benefits*. The promises are attended with commands to repent, believe, and persevere in the uniform practice of obedience. . . . His [Christ's] end was to enable and induce us to return to God, as our rightful Lord and proper felicity, from whom we rebelliously and miserably fell by our disobedience, in seeking for happiness out of him. Accordingly the gospel is called "the law of faith" as it commands those duties upon the motives of eternal hopes and fears.[34]

Richard Baxter, as we have seen, emphasized works as a secondary condition of faith, thus, in *The Saints' Everlasting Rest*, his stress fell on the necessity of a righteous life for salvation.

> I call a Christian's happiness the end of his course, thereby meaning, as Paul, (2 Tim. iv. 8,) the whole scope of his life. For salvation may, and must be, our end, so not only the end of our faith, though that principally, but of all our actions; for as whatsoever we do, must be done to the glory of God, *whether eating, drinking, etc.*, so must they all be done to our salvation. *That we may believe for salvation, some will grant, who yet deny that we may do, or obey for it.*[35]

Baxter's emphasis here, and others like it, opened the Puritans to charges that they were reinstituting legalism. Baxter, responding to an accusation that "to make salvation the end of duty, is to be a legalist," simply responded by insisting that duty is a necessary element in a person's participation in the salvation process.[36] Nevertheless, Baxter, though admitting that the text of his discourse ("There reemainth, therefore, a rest for the people of God." Heb. 4:9) may refer to the rest (salvation) that one enjoys in this life as well as the "rest of eternal glory," insisted that one must consider the future rest toward which life is moving to be "the very first stone in the foundation of religion."[37] In these passages the anticipation of future salvation does not negate the present emphasis on glorification of God by daily holy living, but personal salvation looms large in the presentations. For Puritans, then, Christian life was most advantageously presented as leading to its crowning glory, eternal salvation, be it defined as true happiness, everlasting rest, or "seeing God."[38]

Wesley shared with the Puritans their emphasis on the direction and destiny of human life being the glorification of God:

> Devote and employ all ye have, and all ye are, entirely unreservedly and forever, to His glory.
>
> In all things whatsoever, whether of a religious or civil nature, in all the common, as well as sacred, actions of life, keep the glory of God in view, and steadily pursue in all this one end of your being, the planting or advancing the vital knowledge and love of God, first in your own soul, then in all mankind.[39]

Like the Puritans, however, he often expressed the purpose of Christian life in terms of its obligation and its necessity for salvation. A Christian life of love and good works was a secondary, "remote" condition of salvation; nevertheless, it was a necessity and as such becomes a means of sustaining salvation.[40]

> "Without holiness no man shall see the Lord," shall see the face of God in glory. . . . No, it cannot be done; none shall live with God, but he that now lives to God; none shall enjoy the glory of God in heaven, but he that bears the image of God on earth; none that is not saved from sin here can be saved from hell hereafter; none can see the kingdom of God above, unless the kingdom of God be in him below.[41]

Wesley did make a conscious effort to hold present and future salvation together. "It is not something at a distance: it is a present thing; a blessing which, through the free mercy of God, ye are now in possession of." Salvation may, then, be extended "to the entire work of God, from the first dawning of grace in the soul till it is consummated in glory."[42] This presentation of salvation including both present and future life allowed a full recognition of both aims of Christian life—glorification of God and personal salvation.

Wesley's inclusion of the Puritan formulations, properly edited, meant he obviously found them useful instruction for his own followers. Comparing the abridgments with passages from his own works shows that he was in essential agreement with their understanding of the direction and destiny of Christian life. The possibility of present and future reward for holy living does not exclude genuine glorification of God by such a life. They are simply different facets of one objective—Christian living—a central concern for Wesley and the Puritans.

Holiness: The Design of a Christian Life

Whatever the direction and destiny of the Christian life, its character, for the Puritans and for Wesley, was most often described as "holiness" or godliness, conformity to God's love expressed in Jesus Christ by a believer's every inward and outward act declaring anew that love. Wesley's attraction to holiness as the appropriate characterization of Christian living began as early as 1725 during his Oxford experiences.[43] By 1729 his studies of the ancient church and the teachings of Jeremy Taylor, William Law, Henry Sougal, and Thomas à Kempis served to mold this image into a lifelong conviction. In his later explanation of Methodism's rise, its centrality is clear:

> In 1729, two young men, reading the Bible, saw they could not be saved without holiness, followed after it, and incited others so to do. In 1739 they saw holiness comes by faith. They saw likewise, that men are justified before they are sanctified; *but still holiness was their point*. God then thrust them out, utterly against their will, to raise a holy people.[44]

Among Puritan works Wesley selected for the *Christian Library,* the same characterization is abundantly displayed.

For both traditions true religion was threatened if it faltered in producing loving service of God and neighbor. On one hand, intellectual acquiescence to gospel truths which failed to relate to one's daily actions jeopardized its reality. Richard Sibbes commented, **"For, religion is a *truth 'according to godliness,'* not according to *speculation* only, and *notion*. Wheresoever these fundamental truths are embraced, there is godliness with them; a man cannot embrace religion in truth, but he must be godly."**[45] At the opposite extreme genuine holiness was threatened by hypocrites who carried on the outward forms of true religion, living upright moral lives graced with performance of outward religious duties, but did so for their own selfish ends rather than from inward dedication to God.[46] To these were added the antinomian who interpreted faith as freeing one from the obligations of good works and moral law. Any of these misinterpretations of true Christian life threatened the vitality of present religion as well as its ultimate object:

> O study to get the image and impress of Christ upon you within. Begin with your hearts, else you build without foundation. Labour to get a saving change within, or all external performances will be to no purpose. And then study to show forth the power of godliness in your life. Let piety be your first and great business. . . .
>
> But piety without charity is but half of Christianity, or rather impious hypocracy. We may not divide the tables. See therefore that you do justly, and love mercy; and let Equity and Charity run like an even thread throughout all your dealings.[47]

Joseph Alleine here made clear that inward *and* outward aspects of the Christian life, distinguished but not separated, assume the priority of inward holiness. Outward acts of good must be grounded in inward love, charity, and compassion. Together, inward and outward holiness constituted the foci of the Puritan treatment of the Christian life. To promulgate specific instructions, as they constantly did, was to expand on one or the other of these aspects of life.[48] Wesley's instructions similarly insisted on the joint nature of the two aspects.[49]

How, then, should one characterize such inward and outward elements? As we have seen, Alleine's call for a believer "to get the image and impress of Christ upon you within" gave definition of the inward holiness (and was much the same as Wesley's formulation).[50] In Sibbes's phrase it was "the inward bent of the soul."[51] The love of God permeating all the interests, affections, and "tempers" of the person was regarded as inward holiness. For Wesley such inward holiness constituted the immediate fruits of new birth when God's love begins to expel "the love of the world, the love of pleasure, of ease, of honour, of money, together with pride, anger, self-will, and every other evil temper; in a word, changing the 'earthly, sensual, devilish' mind, into 'the mind which was in Christ Jesus.'"[52]

Outward holiness consisted of all that characterized a person in her or his relationship to God and to the world, but particularly to human companions. Included here are all religious, political, occupational, and social relationships that make up life. Outward holiness acts in all these situations out of love and in obedience to God's commands. Bishop Hall summed up both inward and outward holiness in his comment on good works, which, though not all inclusive, indicated the direction a holy life should take: "**The fruits of faith are good works: whether inward, within the roof of the heart, as love, awe, sorrow, pity, zeal, joy, and the rest; or outwards toward God, or our brethren: obedience and service, to the one; to the other, relief and beneficence. These he bears, in his time: sometimes, all; but, always, some.**"[53] The outward works noted here correspond roughly to Wesley's own distinction between "works of piety" and "works of mercy."[54]

The character of a Christian life, though most appropriately defined in terms of inward and outward holiness, is grounded in one's relationship with God. Wesley's attraction to Samuel Shaw's formulation was perhaps its elaborate treatment of the communion and fellowship with God that stand behind all true religion.

> Right [real] **fellowship with God is a communion of hearts and natures, of will and affections, of interests and end: to have one heart and will, the same interest and ends with God, is to be truly godly; a God-like man is the only godly man: a Christ-like nature brought into the soul** *doth only* [does alone] **denominate a man a** *living* [true] **Christian. It is not speaking together, but loving and living together, that brings God and the soul into one.**[55]

Wesley's own descriptions of Christian perfection—the believer in whom true holiness has become a reality—were based upon such a communion and conformity of man to God.

The following passage from Shaw serves as an eloquent and informative summary of the character of a true Christian life:

> **As to the outward acts of service which the true Christian** *doth* **performs, he is freely carried out toward them, without any constraint** *or force*. **If he keeps himself from the evils of the place, and age, and company wherein he lives** *and converses*, **it is not by restraint, which is upon him merely from without him, but by a principle of holy temperance planted in his soul: it is the seed of God abiding in him that preserves him from commission of sin,** I *John* III. 9. **He is not kept back from sin as a horse by a bridle, but by an inward** *and spiritual* **change made in his nature. On the other hand, if he employs himself in any external acts of moral or instituted duty, he does it freely, not as of necessity, or by constraint. If you speak of acts of charity, the godly man gives from a principle of love to God, and kindness to his brother;** *and so* **cheerfully, not grudgingly, or of necessity,** 2 Cor. IX. 7. . . . **If you speak of righteousness or temperance, he is not over-ruled by power, or compelled by laws, but** *indeed acted* [actuated] **by the**

power of that law which is *written and* engraved upon his mind. If you speak of acts of worship, whether moral or instituted, in all these he is also free, as to any constraint. Prayer is not his task, or a piece of penance, but it is the nature cry of a new born soul; . . . he prays, because he wants, and loves, and believes.[56]

Conscience: The Guide to Christian Living

An authentic Christian life that embodies holiness depends on distinct guidance and direction. This study's earlier discussion of covenant theology noted that for Wesley and the Puritans God's law, expressed in Scripture, became through Christ incorporated into the gospel and served as a primary standard for Christian living. The law present in Christianity, therefore, included the Ten Commandments as well as the commandments of Jesus buttressed by his own example of living love. Though no longer required as the condition of justification or sanctification, the Christian law of love comprised the standard defining good works, understood always as a natural consequence of faith.[57]

How is such a standard to be made applicable in the life of the individual believer? It could not be adequately applied by some external authority such as the minister, a friend, or the congregation, for, though they may judge the outward manifestations, they can never truly judge the inward motivation. Hence, for Wesley and the Puritans, the conscience of each individual Christian became the means by which one evaluated conformity to the standard; its significance for both traditions can hardly be overstressed.

Because conscience held such a pivotal role in Christian life, Puritan literature often examined conscience and its operations in the life of the individual. Natural outgrowths of such concern and interest were continual endeavors to define how a true Christian conscience should interpret the various situations of life. Such efforts produced a vast Puritan casuistical literature. Although this casuistry was extensively elaborated in the latter half of the seventeenth century, its significant foundations may be found in the works of William Perkins, *A Discourse of Conscience* (1595), *The Whole Treatise of the Cases of Conscience* (1606), and William Ames, *Conscience, with the Power and Cases Thereof* (1639). The standard format for Puritan ethical application became specific "cases of conscience," which provided parishioners with a practical guide to a "tender" conscience. Richard Baxter and his contemporaries represent the full flower of Puritan instructions for the average church member, explaining how conscience should determine true Christian action.[58]

Even though Wesley does not follow the general Puritan form, "cases of conscience," in his own writings, he carried out the intent of such work in many of his ethical writings, particularly various instructions and "words" ("Of Riches," "On Dress," "A Word to a Freeholder," and others). For purposes of this study, however, I turn to one of Wesley's most obvious borrowings from Puritan authors. For his own followers Wesley recast a sermon, "How May We be Universally and Exactly Conscientious?" authored by his maternal grandfather, Samuel Annesley.

Beginning in 1661, Annesley sponsored in his church at Cripplegate a series of early-morning lectures by prominent Puritan divines. Following a pattern established by Thomas Case, these lectures were originally designed to provide opportunity for extemporaneous corporate prayer and Christian instruction, specifically in "practical godliness." Such lectureships were sporadically continued by Annesley and others through the next thirty years. Edited by Annesley and published in four volumes, these lectures, *The Morning Exercises at Cripplegate*, became an important resource for Christian theology and guidance among Puritans.[59]

The lecture used by Wesley introduced the whole series and is intended by Annesley to define conscience, thereby establishing a foundation for the following lectures. In doing so, he hoped the "select cases of conscience" might be better understood and applied.[60] Wesley abridged this lecture and included it in *A Christian Library*.

In introducing his own sermon on the topic, "On Conscience," Wesley commented that conscience is one of the most familiar expressions of humans and yet grossly misunderstood. He pointed out that there have been numerous treatises written upon the subject (many only confusing the issue), yet "there is still wanting a discourse upon the subject, short, as well as clear. This by the assistance of God I will endeavour to supply, by showing, first, the nature of conscience; and, then, the several sorts of it; after which, I shall conclude with a few important directions."[61] Although there were a multitude of treatises on conscience, Wesley's attraction to his grandfather's treatment must have been at least in part Annesley's wish to keep the discussion practical.[62] Annesley tells us that he intended "to wave the determination of that school-dispute, whether it [conscience] be an act, or an habit, whether of the understanding, or will or both; whether it be a distinct faculty, or power, how far born with us, and far acquired. I willingly let pass all that doth not further the design I drive at, namely, an universal and exact conscientiousness."[63] No doubt such a sentiment struck a responsive note in Wesley, anxious as he was to jettison speculation wherever possible. He shared Annesley's wish to occupy oneself with definitions only insofar as they offered clarity and a basis of application.

Wesley began his sermon by quoting Dr. Annesley's definition of conscience:

> This word, which literally signifies, "knowing with another", excellently sets forth the scriptural notion of it. So Job 16:19 "My witness is in heaven;" And so the Apostle Rom. 9:1, "I say the truth, my conscience also bearing me witness in the Holy Ghost." In both places it is as if he had said, God witnesseth with my conscience. Conscience is placed in the middle—under God, and above man. It is a kind of silent reasoning of the mind, whereby those things which are judged to be right are approved of with pleasure; but those which are judged evil are disapproved of with uneasiness.[64]

In Annesley's lecture this quotation was an expansion of an earlier brief definition of conscience: "Conscience is man's judgment of himself, of his estate and actions as they are subjected unto the judgment of God."[65] Wesley's own formulation states quite simply what the conscience is for the Christian: "It is that faculty of the soul which, by the assistance of the grace of God, sees at one and the same time, (1), Our own tempers and lives—the real nature and quality of our thoughts, words, and actions; (2), The rule whereby we are to be directed, and, (3) The agreement or disagreement therewith."[66]

Conscience used to discover a Christian's conformity to God's law and judgment, however, leaves little place for "natural conscience," or the ability of all persons to discern right and wrong. Both Annesley and Wesley allowed such a natural conscience, but it was of secondary importance to them. Annesley defined this natural ability in the more traditional sense as "the relics of the image of God after the fall," and made no additional comment on it.[67] From Wesley's perspective there was a more useful and convenient explanation. Humanity's ability to distinguish good and evil is "a branch of that supernatural gift of God which we usually style preventing grace. . . . For though in one sense it may be termed 'natural,' because it is found in all men, yet properly speaking it is not *natural*; but a supernatural gift of God, above all his natural endowments."[68] Wesley, using this explanation, insisted not only that conscience is dependent upon God, because it is a gift, but also that it is activated by the Holy Spirit. "In all the offices of the conscience, the 'unction of the Holy One' is indispensably needful."[69]

Wesley's understanding of prevenient grace as the first step in the salvation process led him in this sermon to conflate two states or categories of conscience, that of the natural human, and that of the Christian:

> This is properly the account of a *good* conscience, which may be in other terms expressed thus: a divine consciousness of walking in all things according to the written word of God. It seems, indeed, that there can be no conscience which has not a regard to God. If you say, "Yes: there certainly may be a consciousness of having done right or wrong without any reference to him," I answer, This I cannot grant. I doubt whether the very words, "right and wrong" according to the Christian system, do not imply, in the very idea of them, agreement and disagreement to the will and word of God. If so, there is no such thing as conscience in a Christian if we leave God out of the question.[70]

Wesley here followed Augustine, who in a strikingly similar passage commented: "The virtues which it [the soul] seems to itself to possess, and by which it restrains the body and the vices that it may obtain and keep what it desires, are rather vices than virtues so long as there is no reference to God in the matter."[71]

If, then, conscience is restored to fallen humans by prevenient grace, Wesley may be correct in declaring that there is no conscience "which has not a regard to God." Yet this is certainly not the same *enlightened* conscience that guides one into "walking in all things according to the written word of God." A true Christian conscience defined, as both Wesley and Annesley insist, as one aware of "the rule [the law and commandments] by which we are to be directed" is far different from the ordinary unbeliever's conscience, which may still be able to discern good and evil.[72]

It must be remembered that Wesley's conflation of the two types of conscience was framed as he defined the word within the Christian community; therefore, his insistence that all knowledge of good and evil must refer to God was quite adequate, framed as it was within a theological context. It is doubtful, however, if his answer would have been accepted by the fledgling empiricism of his own day, which claimed that the terms "good" and "evil" have a legitimate application in situations that are not specifically religious and have no primary reference to ultimate ends.[73] In contrast, the theological understanding of good and evil, deriving its meaning essentially by reference to God, is concerned predominantly with the ultimate end and religious significance of any particular action.

Wesley's insistence that the conscience cannot function without the activation of the Holy Spirit—and his application of this statement even to natural conscience, as it is a "branch" of prevenient grace—had no equivalent in Annesley. Annesley assumed the Holy Spirit's activation of the Christian conscience, but he lay no stress on this reality. Neither was there any need for the Holy Spirit to be peculiarly operative in the conscience of the natural human, unless, of course, one wanted to point out that creation itself assumed some operation of God in the life of every person. In any case, Wesley was more insistent upon the role of the Spirit in activating and sustaining the conscience of all people.

Another aspect of these definitions is significant. Annesley's statement, apparently approved by Wesley, that conscience is somehow "in the middle, under God and above man," suggested that conscience is in some sense a separate entity external to humanity, judging it. This reflected a tendency among some to hypostatize conscience as the judge of humans.[74] Conscience is somehow "over-against" humanity in this presentation. Wesley's own comment that conscience is not natural but "above all his natural endowments" might also reflect such tendencies, yet such hypostatization should not be given too much weight. Perhaps allowance should be made for literary license in these expressions, as the burden of both Annesley's and Wesley's presentations leave little doubt that conscience is a part or faculty of our own nature, judging our actions. It does, however, indicate the extremely important place that conscience held in the thinking of Puritan authors and Wesley.

Moving beyond the definition of conscience, Annesley treated the "kinds" of conscience, and Wesley considered the "sorts of consciences," but there is no significant dependence in Wesley upon his grandfather's work in this section of his sermon. Annesley's treatment was quite extensive, giving definition, cause, and cure for six types of conscience (sleepy, seared, erring, doubting, scrupulous, and trembling) that are inadequate. The section closed with brief statements concerning a proper or true conscience, that is, the "good honest" conscience and the "good quiet" conscience. Wesley added to his general definition comments on a tender conscience, or one that is "exact in observing any deviation from the word of God." This understanding corresponded roughly with Annesley's comments on a good conscience. Wesley considered only two of Annesley's several negative types of conscience. The hardened or seared conscience may discern correct action but dismisses, without self-condemnation, the failure to act in accordance with its insights. The overly scrupulous conscience fears when there is no reason to do so and, consequently, either condemns without cause or fails to act, fearing that the judgment might be wrong.[75]

Wesley returned to direct dependence on Annesley's sermon as he closed his own treatise. Here he extensively quoted Annesley's "directions" for acquiring a good conscience, giving credit in a footnote to the fact that they were the work of his grandfather. Annesley gave ten directions and then, in closing, added four more that are "generally sufficient, when others cannot be had"; these latter he considered to be the "spirit," or summary, of the more elaborate set. Wesley condensed the fourteen to ten and then liberally abridged them for his own sermon, which he does not do in the *Christian Library* edition. Annesley conveniently summarized the ten directions, allowing one an insight into the nature of the instruction:

> For the *integrity* and *quiet* of your consciences, observe the rules proposed, as punctually as you would physicians' bills in a tedious sickness. (1.) Avoid sinning, as you would a train of gunpowder. (2.) Be as quick in your repentance, as in a pleurisy. (3.) Live under the apprehended presence of the jealous God. (4.) Examine your hearts, as princes sift out treason. (5.) Pray for suitable grace, as starving persons cry for food. (6.) Let every action be as an arrow shot at a mark. (7.) Think of God as a wise physician. (8.) Be as vile in your own esteem, as you are in the eyes of a captious enemy. (9.) Live upon Christ, as the child of the womb lives upon the mother. (10.) Love God (as near as possibly you can) as God loves you.[76]

Wesley omitted four of these and included those that Annesley had added as expressing the spirit or essence of the directions: consult duties, not events; what advice you would give to another, take yourselves; do nothing on which you cannot pray for a blessing; think and speak and do what you are persuaded Christ himself would do in your case, were he upon the earth. The directions were, of course, good instruction for any Christian believer and might have been applied to many areas besides the conscience, but they typify the kind of practical instruction that was so much the concern of the Puritans and so attractive to Wesley.[77]

In addition to the analysis of conscience found in the sermons of Annesley and Wesley, another Puritan use of conscience is noteworthy. Investigating and commenting upon all areas and situations of life, the Puritans were led to deal with those of their congregations who suffered an "afflicted conscience." Because of the importance of such a state, which might threaten the whole tenor of a Christian life, the subject is a recurring theme in their writings and merits the attention of whole treatises. Representative works in the area are Robert Bolton's *Instructions for Rightly Comforting Afflicted Consciences*; Bishop Hall's *Heaven Upon Earth, or, Of True Peace of Mind*; and Thomas Goodwin's work, *A Child of Light Walking in Darkness; Or, a Treatise Shewing the Causes by Which, the Cases Wherein, and the Ends for Which God Leaves His Children to Distress of Conscience.*

Those suffering from an afflicted conscience were treated by the Puritans as two differing groups. First, there were those whose afflicted consciences signified their readiness to receive the comforting message of the gospel. Such a state usually resulted when a person, having had the reality of personal sin presented to him or her, desired the peace of the gospel. In Bolton's terms the responsibility of a minister in this case was "first, to wound by the *Law*, and then heal by the *Gospel*."[78] It was primarily this type of afflicted conscience with which Bolton and Hall were concerned. Bolton's treatise might well serve as the manual for the Christian minister in dealing with one in a state of affliction, for it is not only full of advice about how to apply comfort but, just as important, how to avoid the errors of offering comfort to those who are not ready to embrace Christian understandings of conscience.

The second type of afflicted conscience was found in the believer who has experienced conversion and the life of faith but is now suffering doubt and temptation. Thomas Goodwin's treatise dealt specifically with this condition, describing it in his comments on light as it is used in Eph. 5:13:

> When therefore here he says he hath no *light*, the meaning is, he wants *all present* [the] sensible testimonies of God's favour to him; he sees nothing that may give *sensible* present witness of it to him; God's favour, and his own graces, and all the sensible tokens and evidence thereof, which are apprehended by spiritual sight, are become all as *absent things*, as if they were not, or never had been; that light which ordinarily discovers these as present he is clean deprived of.[79]

As the subtitle of Goodwin's work indicates, he assumed that there is always purpose in such afflictions; therefore, he emphasized God's justice and purpose in these situations, God's mercy for one who keeps faith during such trials, and the duty of offering comfort to such, and closed with the expected "directions for those who are deeply troubled." Bolton's treatise dealt with this type of affliction, though concentrating on the first type. He also instructed believers in the way to rectify the situation. Central in both sets of instructions was the admonition to seek by every means possible to know why one is so afflicted, that is, examine by the use of the conscience itself the state of one's life that might have led to this disturbed moment. Whether or not one is able to discover the problem this way, the solution to an afflicted conscience is true dependence upon the promises of the Scripture and a steady attendance upon these Scriptures. Added to this is the use of prayer (Goodwin emphasized seeking the prayers and help of others as well) and the ability to wait "in the constant use of all ordinances and means of comfort"[80] for the relief that will assuredly come to the one who seeks it. Wesley's inclusion in the *Library* of these treatises, designed specifically for those facing such a situation, witnesses to his appreciation of their work and his use of it in his own instruction.

Wesley's incorporation into his own sermon of Annesley's treatment of conscience, its definition, and its instructions for attaining and nurturing a good conscience provides another incident of clear dependence on Puritan antecedents. His particular commendation of the Puritan treatment of the disturbed conscience further illustrates his affinity with the Puritan tradition in his treatment of this topic.[81] The situation in which Wesley worked forced him to deal more extensively with other topics, so he did not emphasize conscience to the extent the Puritans had; nevertheless, its important function in Wesley's theology is obvious. He was at least partially dependent upon the Puritan tradition for his own understanding and presentation of it.

Notes

1. Quoted by T. E. Owen, *Methodism Unmasked: Or the Progress of Puritanism* (London: Printed for J. Hatchard, 1802), ix; see also Richard Heitzenrater's article tracing much of this identification ("What's in a Name?" *Mirror and Memory*, 13-32).

2. Richard Baxter, *A Call to the Unconverted to Turn and Live* (London: Printed by R.W. For Nevil Simmons, 1669), introduction. Cited hereafter as *Call*.

3. [H. R. O.], "Tract Societies," *The Wesleyan Methodist Magazine*, 70 (1847): 270.

4. "'A Plan of the Society, instituted in January, 1782, to Distribute Religious Tracts among the Poor.' 1. Every member must subscribe half-a-guinea, a guinea, or more, annually. 2. A proportionable quantity of tracts shall be delivered yearly to each subscriber, according to his subscription, and as nearly as possible at prime cost, and carriage paid. 3. Every subscriber shall have a right to chuse his own tracts, if he please: otherwise he will receive a proportionable variety of the whole" ([H. R. O.], "Tract Societies," 70 [1847]: 270).

5. *Bibliography*, 217.

6. *Letters*, 7:155.

7. *CL*, 4:107-8.

8. These works are used in this study as representative Puritan treatments of this topic, although several other treatises included in Wesley's *Library* quite adequately deal with this subject: Robert Bolton's *On Self-Examination*; Hugh Binning's *Fellowship with God*; Richard Alleine's *Vindiciae Pietatis*; Isaac Ambrose's *The Doctrine of Regeneration*; and Lewis Stuckley's *A Gospel-Glass*.

9. Calamy, *Nonconformist's Memorial*, 2:319.

10. *Works*, 21:91. This reference to "Directions for a Thorough Conversion to God" is evidently a reference to one of the chapters in Alleine's tract.

11. *Letters*, 3:207.

12. He continues, "In a little more than a year there were twenty

thousand printed by my own consent, and about ten thousand since, besides many thousands by stolen impressions, which poor men stole for lucre's sake. Through God's mercy, I have information of almost whole households converted by this small book, which I set so light by: and as if all this in England, Scotland, and Ireland, were not mercy enough to me God (since I was silenced) hath sent it over in his message to many beyond the seas; for when Mr. Elliot had printed all the Bible in the Indian language, he next translated this my *Call to the Unconverted*, as he wrote us here. And yet God would make some further use of it, for Mr. Stoop, the pastor of the French Church in London, being driven hence by the displeasure of superiors, was pleased to translate it into French; I hope it will not be unprofitable there; nor in Germany, where it is printed in Dutch" (Baxter, *Call to the Unconverted,* iv).

13. Baxter, *Call* , introduction. [Wesley's Abridgment, 2nd ed. (Dublin: Printed by R. Napper, 1795).] Hereafter W.A. in the bracketed references indicates Wesley's abridgment of the treatises.

14. Alleine, *Alarm to Unconverted Sinners,* 1; cited hereafter as *Alarm.* [Wesley's Abridgment, 2nd ed; (Dublin: Printed by R. Napper, 1794)].

15. Baxter, *Call*, 31-35 [W.A., 14-16].

16. "When they have so much as will save them (as they suppose,) they will look no farther, and so shew themselves short of true Grace, which will ever put men upon aspiring to further perfection" (Alleine, *Alarm*, 97 [W.A., 70]).

17. Alleine, *Alarm*, 12 [W.A., 29].

18. Alleine, *Alarm*, 122 [W.A., 82]; cf. Ambrose, *Practice of Sanctification*, in *Works of Isaac Ambrose*, 79 [*CL*, 8:7].

19. Alleine, *Alarm*, 19 [W.A., 32].

20. Baxter, *Call*, 135 [W.A. 46].

21. Alleine, *Alarm*, 30 [W.A., 37].

22. Baxter, *Call*, 69 [W.A., 28].

23. Alleine, *Alarm*, 81 [W.A., 63]; Baxter used the same phrase (Baxter, *Call*, 186 [W.A. 58]), yet without the same emphasis.

24. Baxter, *Call*, 144-54 [W.A., 49-51].

25. Baxter, *Call*, 224-37 [W.A., 67-72].

26. Alleine, *Alarm*, 136-77 [W.A., 89-107]. His advice given to the one who would join in the covenant indicates how he thought it should be used: "This Covenant I advise you to make, not only in Heart, but in Word; not only in Word, but in Writing; and that you would, with all possible Reverence, spread the Writing before the Lord, as if you would present it to him as your act and deed; and, when you have done this, set your hand to it, keep it as a Memorial of the Solemn Transactions that have passed between God and you, that you may have recourse to it in Doubts, and Temptations" (Alleine, *Alarm*, 170 [W.A., 104]).

27. See Alleine's section titled "The Furnace of Eternal Vengeance Is Heated Ready for Thee," (Alleine, *Alarm*, 128 [W.A., 83]).

28. *Works*, 1:432.

29. *Works*, 1:435-41; 541.

30. Wesley's sermon on the dangers of judging others shows his concern that one should be careful in this area (*Works*, 1:650-63).

31. For discussion of the changes in preaching styles and interests in the period, see Charles Smyth, *The Art of Preaching* (London: SPCK, 1953); E. C. Dargan, *The History of Preaching,* vol. 2 (London: Hodder and Stoughton, 1905); F. R. Webber, *A History of Preaching in Britain and America,* vol. 1 (Milwaukee: Northwest Publishing House, 1952); R. C. Petry, *No Uncertain Sound* (Philadelphia: Westminster Press, 1948).

32. *Works*, 1:20 n. 33.

33. Robert Bolton, *A Discourse about the State of True Happiness* (London: Printed by Felix Kyngston for Thomas Weaver, 1631), 1 [*CL*, 4:243]; cited hereafter as *True Happiness*.

34. Thomas Manton, *Twenty Sermons*, in *The Works of Thomas Manton* (London: James Nisbet, 1871), 2:175-76 [*CL*, 7:166].

35. Baxter, *Saints' Everlasting Rest*, in *Practical Works of Richard Baxter* 22:36 [*CL*, 12:11-12].

36. **"It is not a note of a legalist neither; it hath been the ground of a multitude of late mistakes in divinity, to think that 'Do this and live,' is only the language of the covenant of works. It is true, in some sense it is; but in other, not: The law of works only saith, 'Do this,' that is, perfectly fulfil the whole law, 'and live,' that is, for so doing: but the law of grace saith, 'Do this and live' too; that is, believe in Christ, seek him, obey him sincerely, as thy Lord and King; forsake all, suffer all things, and overcome; and by so doing, or in so doing,** *as the conditions which the gospel propounds for salvation*, **you shall live. . . . In a word, you must both use and trust duty in subordination to Christ, but neither use them nor trust them in co-ordination with him."** *Saints' Everlasting Rest,* in *Practical Works of Richard Baxter*, 22:32-33 [*CL*, 22:9-10]).

37. Baxter, *Saint's Everlasting Rest*, in *Practical Works of Richard Baxter*, 22:20.

38. Bolton, in the passage previously quoted (see note 33), incorporated the concept of the "vision of God," which was a common expression of the nature of salvation for both the Puritans and Wesley. For a detailed study of the development and importance of this classical medieval view of Augustine and Aquinas, see K. E. Kirk's *The Vision of God* (London: Longman, Green, 1931).

39. Wesley, *Explanatory Notes upon the New Testament*, 602-3 (I Cor. 6:20); 617 (I Cor. 10:31).

40. *Works*, 2:163; 166-69.

41. *Works* (Jackson), 10:364.

42. *Works*, 2:156; cf. *Explanatory Notes upon the New Testament*, 22 (Matt. 3:2).

43. In establishing holiness as the character of the Christian life, Wesley and the Puritans are joining an ancient tradition reaching back to the earliest Christian eras, as R. Newton Flew ably shows in his work *The Idea of Perfection in Christian Theology*. L. J. Trinterud ("Origins of Puritanism," 40) maintains that the emphasis on piety was an English religious trait, principally Augustinian in character and present in medieval English Church life. ("Origins of Puritanism," 40.)

44. *Works* (Jackson), 8:300 (italics added). Joseph Alleine states the same sentiment: "He [the Christian] pitches upon God his blessedness,

and upon Christ as the principal, and holiness as the subordinate means, to bring him to God" (Alleine, *Alarm*, 30 [W.A., 37]).

45. Richard Sibbes, *Fountain Opened*, in *Practical Works of Richard Sibbes*, 5:461 [*CL*, 6:56]; cf. Ambrose, *Looking Unto Jesus*, in *Works of Isaac Ambrose*, 144-46 [*CL*, 8:102-4].

46. Robert Bolton indicated that there is a "Formall Hypocrit" who lives by deception because in times of trial or suffering one quite honestly pledges to live a true Christian life but fails to carry this out when the spiritual affliction has passed (Bolton, *Instructions*, 290 [*CL*, 5:62]; Bolton, *True Happiness*, 67ff. [*CL*, 4:278 ff.]).

47. Joseph Alleine, "A Counsel for Personal and Family Godliness," in *Christian Letters* (London: Printed by J. Darby for N. Simons, 1672), 113-14 [*CL*, 14:173-74]. **"If thou have respect onely to the Commandments of the first table, and outward performance of religious services; but neglect duties of the second,** *And conscionable carriage to thy brethren*; **Thou art but a Pharisie, and formall Professour: If thou dealest justly with thy neighbor, and yet bee a stranger to the mystery of godliness,** *canst not pray, sanctifie the lords day, submit to a sincere and searching ministrie, etc. which the first table enjoynes*; **Thou art but a meere civill man"** (Bolton, *Walking with God*, 22 [*CL*, 4:334]).

48. Hugh Binning, *Fellowship with God*, in *The Works of Hugh Binning* (London: A. Fullarton and Co., 1851), 307 [*CL*, 17:54]; Manton, *Twenty Sermons*, in *Works of Thomas Manton* 2:238 [*CL*, 7:234]. Samuel Shaw, *Immanuel: or a Discovery of True Religion* (Glasgow: Printed by R. Urio, 1749), 68 [*CL*, 14:296-97].

49. *Works*, 1:531-33, 592.

50. *Works*, 4:354-55.

51. Richard Sibbes, *Fountain Opened*, in *Practical Works of Richard Sibbes*, 5:460 [*CL*, 6:55].

52. *Works*, 2:158. Cf. Bolton, *Walking with God*, 58-59 [*CL*, 4:342-43].

53. Joseph Hall, "Letter to My Lady Mary Denny," in *The Works* of Joseph Hall ed. Josiah Pratt (London: Printed by C. Whittingham, 1808) 7:234 [*CL*, 4:195].

54. "Works of piety, such as public prayer, family prayer, and praying in our closet; receiving the supper of the Lord; searching the Scriptures, by hearing, reading, meditating; and using such a measure of fasting or abstinence as our bodily health allows. . . . Works of mercy, whether they relate to the bodies or souls of men; such as feeding the hungry, clothing the naked, entertaining the stranger, visiting those that are in prison, or sick, or variously afflicted; such as the endeavouring to instruct the ignorant, to awaken the stupid sinner, to quicken the lukewarm, to confirm the wavering, to comfort the feeble-minded, to succour the tempted, or contribute in any manner to the saving of souls from death" (*Works*, 2:166).

55. Shaw, *Communion with God*, 211 [*CL*, 14:303].

56. Shaw, *Immanuel*, 75 [*CL*, 14:231-32].

57. "Nor yet do we so establish the moral law (which, it is to be feared, too many do), as if the fulfilling it, the keeping all the commandments, were the condition of our justification. If it were so, surely 'in his sight

should no man living be justified'. But all this being allowed, we still, in the Apostle's sense, 'establish the law,' the moral law" (*Works*, 2:34).

58. For a thorough exposition of Richard Baxter's casuistical endeavors, see James M. Phillips, "Between Conscience and Law: The Ethics of Richard Baxter" (Ph.D. dis., Princeton University, 1959).

59. In 1844 James Nichols edited a new edition of these volumes, adding two others originally edited by Thomas Case. Collating the various impressions or editions (because later editions published during the lifetime of the various authors were corrected and expanded), Nichols produced a "standard" text. He provides an informative introduction on the occasion and importance of the lecture series in the Nonconforming community. Nichols's edition is the resource used in this study. (Samuel Annesley, *The Morning Exercises at Cripplegate, St. Giles in the Fields, and in Southwark*, ed. James Nichols, 5th ed. ([London: Printed for Thomas Tegg, 1844]), 1:vi; cited hereafter as *Morning Exercises*.)

60. "How May We be Universally and Exactly Conscientious?" in *Morning Exercises*, 1:1. In the first edition of *A Christian Library,* Wesley credits this sermon to Matthew Pool, another Puritan ejected in 1662. The first edition of *Morning Exercises* does not include author designations but later editions published in Annesley's lifetime credit the work to Annesley. Wesley may not have had adequate information at the time of the first edition or simply mistakenly credits the work to Poole. For a more complete discussion of the issue see app. 1 n. 13.

61. *Works*, 3:480.

62. Not only were the Puritans interested in the role of conscience, but it was a common topic among theologians of the period. Wesley could easily have drawn from the Anglican works such as Bishop Sanderson's *Lectures on Conscience and Human Law* and Jeremy Taylor's *Rule of Conscience*, to mention only two. Wesley commented that the "best treatise on the subject which I remember to have seen is translated from the French of Mons. Placette," but he continued suggesting that this is much too long and therefore not likely to be very useful (*Works*, 3:480). Wesley's sermon "On Conscience" was a late production, according to his *Journal* written in 1788 (7:359). Before this he seems to have recommended his grandfather's sermon as found in *A Christian Library* for instruction in the area (*Letters*, 5:200).

63. Annesley, "How May We Be Universally and Exactly Conscientious?" in *Morning Exercises*, 1:3.

64. *Works*, 3:481. Wesley in this quotation is not completely accurate in transcribing Annesley's statement, nor does he note that part of the statement is quoted by Annesley from Brockmand, but there are no significant changes or omissions.

65. Annesley, "How May We Be Universally and Exactly Conscientious?" *Morning Exercises*, 1:3.

66. *Works*, 3:485.

67. Annesley, "How May We Be Universally and Exactly Conscientious?" in *Morning Exercises*, 1:5.

68. *Works*, 3:482. As Lindström indicates, there are occasional instances in which Wesley expressed "the opinion that a certain residue of

knowledge of the law was preserved after the Fall" (Lindström, *Wesley and Sanctification*, 47; see also *Works* 1:551-52; 2:7). In doing so, he followed his grandfather and many others. In his sermon "The Heavenly Treasure in Earthern Vessels," Wesley in a passage discussing the remains of the image of God after the Fall suggested that whether conscience is a "natural attribute" or "superadded by the grace of God," it is present in all (*Works*, 4:163). For Wesley it was possible to understand both explanations as necessary and complementary if one is seen as the gift of creation and the other as part of the gift of sanctification. In any case, Wesley's normal formulation was that conscience is a part or branch of prevenient grace (*Works*, 2:156-7).

69. *Works*, 3:485.

70. *Works*, 3:485-86.

71. Augustine, *The City of God*, in *Basic Writings of St. Augustine*, ed. Whitney J. Oates (New York: Random House, 1948), 2:504. Wesley, in reflecting Augustine here joined the Puritans and other theologians. Baxter stated it thusly: "There is no virtue, truely so called, which is not theological as well as moral" (*Saints' Everlasting Rest* in *Practical Works of Richard Baxter*, 23:36).

72. Annesley's presentation does not contain the same confusion of two types of conscience. Along with his definition of natural conscience as a relic of the image of God, he defined a believer's conscience as one activated by "the light of Divine revelation" in "the standing rule of Scripture, and God's extraordinary discoveries of himself, whether by dreams, visions, or prophecies, or other spiritual communications" ("How May We Be Universally and Exactly Conscientious?" in *Morning Exercises*, 1:5).

73. In fact, it is just such a sentiment expressed by "Professor Hutcheson, late of Glasgow" that Wesley is attempting to refute. Francis Hutcheson (1694-1746), moral philosopher at Glasgow, correspondent of David Hume, and effective lecturer "on the evidences of Christianity" was well-known in his time as a defender of Christianity among philosophers. Wesley dismisses him as an atheist since he would not allow that good action must always refer to its reward. His theology was decidedly liberal for that day, and he may be considered an originator of British utilitarianism, which, of course, in later hands slipped from its Christian moorings (*DNB*, 28:333).

74. For a discussion of such hypostatization in Baxter and other Puritan divines, see J. M. Phillips, "Between Conscience and Law," 182-83.

75. Annesley, "How May We Be Universally and Exactly Conscientious?" in *Morning Exercises*, 1:23-37; *Works*, 3:487-88.

76. Annesley, "How May We be Universally and Exactly Conscientious?" in *Morning Exercises*, 1:34.

77. The almost compulsive use of "directions" throughout Puritan literature appears to have been an important element in his choice of their works. Directions for covenanting, for conversion, and now for gaining a true conscience have already played a significant role in this study. Other sets of directions are included in the *Library*, such as Bolton's *Walking with*

God and Whateley's *Directions for Married Persons*.

78. Bolton, *Instructions*, 131 [*CL*, 5:17]. Wesley's appreciation for the treatise is witnessed by his recommendation of it to answer the questions of one of his followers (*Letters*, 7:64).

79. Goodwin, *Child of Light Walking in Darkness*, 14 [*CL*, 6:235]. Wesley's own description of this state is similar: "But he [God] now 'hides His face and they are troubled'; they cannot see Him through the dark cloud. But they see temptation and sin—which they fondly supposed were gone never to return—arising again, following after them again, and holding them in on every side. It is not strange if their soul is now disquieted within them, and trouble and heaviness take hold upon them" (*Works*, 1:484).

80. Goodwin, *Child of Light Walking in Darkness*, 312 [*CL*, 6:300].

81. *CL*, 4:107.

7

Christian Life: The Individual and the Family

In the seventeenth and early eighteenth centuries not only were Puritans or Dissenters interested in how a believer lived out his or her Christian faith, but the issue also dominated the writings of Anglican divines. From both traditions came innumerable directions, instructions, calls, duties, memorials, and sermons designed to ensure that ordinary believers, sustained and helped by the Holy Spirit, patterned their lives after that of Jesus and thereby lived in the "image of God." Such Anglican instruction, presupposing an Arminian base, included human moral responsibility and capacity in the appropriation of one's own salvation. Puritan instruction, with, as we have seen, no less emphasis on good works, subordinated these works to faith and grace. Unfortunately, such teachings, whatever their presuppositions concerning the role of human cooperation with or response to God's grace, could be and often were easily turned into rationalistic legalism. Though such teachings started from somewhat different presuppositions among both Puritan and Anglican writers, a substantial amount of strikingly similar, and in some cases almost identical, ethical instruction was characteristic of the period. To credit Wesley's teachings on a particular subject to either tradition by itself, one would be in danger of misrepresentation. For example, Wesley used the presentations of William Law and Jeremy Taylor when he taught about the responsible use of time, although it was a major emphasis of the Puritans as well.[1] Examples need not be multiplied in order for one to appreciate the problems of any study seeking to identify Wesley's affinities with Puritan teachings on Christian living. Either or both traditions, and other resources such as the early church fathers, obviously influenced many of Wesley's specific teachings.

Modern Wesleyan scholarship generally affirms a Wesleyan blending of the Anglican and Reformed presuppositions and emphases in Wesley's own teachings, although it may occasionally question some of the implications of such a combination.[2] As we have seen, in describing the beginnings of Methodism, Wesley recalled that while he and his brother Charles discovered (in 1738) justification by faith as the entrance to Christian life, nevertheless, holiness, which they had earlier been convinced was the way to salvation, was still their goal. The end result was the same—holiness of thought and life. In the metaphor of John Deschner, Wesley's avid search for holiness was cut off the old tree of Anglican tradition and grafted upon a new tree—Reformation faith.[3] Nourished by different roots, the fruit was still holiness. Though holiness might have a new root, none of its imperative nature was lost for Wesley, and what had always been a primary concern was simply reinforced.

The theological presuppositions that might underlie a particular teaching was never a primary concern for Wesley: He was much more interested in the truth of the instruction and its applicability to the lives of the common people. To avoid the pitfalls inherent in any attempt to distinguish where Wesley may have gleaned a particular teaching, this study is limited (1) to specific areas of Christian instruction incorporated in the Puritan literature that Wesley recommended and used, (2) to selected issues within each sphere of the Christian life where Wesley shared a Puritan interest and emphasis, and (3) to those areas where Wesley's practice reflected Puritan emphases.

With this caution in mind, and working within these limitations, I will discuss specific teachings as they relate to the various "spheres" of everyday life suggested in Richard Baxter's *A Christian Directory*—the spheres of the individual, the family, the church, and the world. Obviously, while each sphere of life may be distinguished from the others, they are not to be separated, for each reflects and involves the others.

Individual or Personal Christian Life

> ***I desire to have my Affections molded by Religion, and towards it*; my thoughts, and words, and deeds, to be all *exercises of Religion*, and my very *cessation* from *works commanded by Religion*, and *limited* and *circumstantiated* by Religion. My eating, drinking, sleeping, journeying, visiting, entertaining of friends, to be all *directed* by *Religion*: and that, above all, I may be *serious* and *Basie* in the *acts* of *Religion*, about the Word, Prayer, Praises, Singing, Sacraments, not only that the duties in each kind be**

> **performed, but *religiously* performed, with life, and vigor, with Faith, Humility, and Charity.[4]**

Herbert Palmer gives in this passage a representative Puritan portrayal of how faithful Christians should live. Christian principles and love will permeate all areas and aspects of a believer's life—none will be exempt from its direction. Consequently, Puritan writers often turned to "self-examination" to raise awareness of one's spiritual and moral condition.

Self-Examination

Self-examination appeared in some fashion among the topics of most Puritan authors Wesley included in *A Christian Library*, but he particularly appreciated and commended an extensive commentary on the subject, Lewis Stuckley's *A Gospel-Glass*. Soon after the publication of the *Library*, Wesley noted, "I began reading that excellent book, *The Gospel Glass*, to the morning congregation—a method which I find more profitable for 'instruction in righteousness' than any other manner of preaching."[5] We do not know how extensively Wesley practiced this type of instruction or how often this particular work was used. However, his continuing appreciation for the work is clear, for in January of 1791, only a few months before his death, he notes having one of the more active of his society members, Elizabeth Richie, read it again to him.[6]

As one may surmise from the title, Stuckley attempted to place before the believer a mirror, a special mirror silvered with the gospel in which one's likeness reflected either conformity or deviation from gospel standards of conduct. With this aid one's conscience was to examine itself to commend or rebuke, whichever was appropriate. Stuckley's elaboration often concentrated on negative patterns that might be discovered in the "mirror." Consequently, the treatise often stresses major deviations from the proper Christian path, yet throughout he recognized that careful and honest examination would carry one beyond identified sins to repentance and renewal. The central importance of such self-examination is articulated in his comment

> **There are few things more commanded *us*, than to try and examine our *habits* [hearts] and lives: *examine yourselves, etc. prove yourselves, etc.* We are apt to be strangers to ourselves, to cheat ourselves with vain *presumptuous* hopes, to rest in notions; therefore *Examine yourselves*, take an experimental knowledge of yourselves: we are apt to prove others, and censure them;**

> **therefore, *Prove your own selves* [yourselves]; begin at home, try your state, try your actions, bring the metal to the touchstone, see whether it be sound or counterfeit; try your faith, whether it be temporary or saving; prove your repentance, whether it be thorough or superficial; examine your love, whether it be sincere or hypocritical; and your obedience, whether it be universal or partial.**[7]

This passage makes it clear that self-examination was, for Stuckley, a constant, never-ending task.[8] Self-examination led one inward, trying one's heart to see if it is truly set on Christ and if it has produced faithful outward or public actions. Every personal activity during each day was to be examined to see if it complied with Scriptural instruction.[9]

Sir Matthew Hale, a prominent Puritan layman, began each day with resolve to set a "watch over my own infirmities and passions" and closed the day by casting "up the accounts of the day."[10] Wesley's grandfather Annesley provided a similar scheme for daily examination:

> **How few are there amongst us, that can say as David, 'I have thought on my ways, and turned my feet unto thy testimonies?' . . . If you do, that is not enough, unless you do it frequently, daily. Every evening ere you sleep, review your carriage in the day, what you have done, or spoke, or thought, that is so much as indecent. Whether your hearts have been intent on religion, and indifferent to the world. Briefly, have special care of two portions of your time, vis. morning and evening, the morning to foreshank what ought to be done, and the evening to examine whether you have done what you ought.**[11]

Robert Bolton's *A Treatise on Self-Examination* suggested another and special use when he detailed how it may prepare one to receive the Lord's Supper. Used thus, it became for the believer "**an holy works of the soul, whereby it casteth its eye,** ***and reflecteth upon itselfe, and so looks through itselfe, makes an exact survey and search into every corner, and takes a true*** *scantling and* **estimate of its spiritual state.**"[12] The object of this self-examination was to test the authenticity of one's faith and actions and seek renewal and restoration where one was deficient. Richard Sibbes counseled that examination extends beyond simple morality, for, relying on the Holy Spirit's guidance, it helps judge how well one lives by the gospel pattern of love. It is not an examination of acts alone, but of motivation and intent.[13]

Wesley's appreciation for self-examination was deep-seated, having begun in the Epworth household and become further elaborated during his Oxford teaching experiences. It became a mainstay of the Holy Club and pattern for later Methodists in its published form, *A Scheme of Self-Examination: Used by the First Methodists in Oxford*. Here, as in the Puritan writings, were presented questions that might bring before a person every action and thought, religious and secular, personal and social.[14] Martin Schmidt sees the Holy Club structure of self-examination as "an example of the way in which the Puritan practices of self-control and self-criticism have been intensified and formulated into an extra-ordinarily exacting oversight of the individual's affairs."[15]

Expanding on his interest in self-examination, Wesley made it an important part of Methodist patterns for Christian living. Throughout his ministry Wesley admonished preacher and layman alike to "watch" and "try" oneself.[16] Self-examination was essential for determining the cause of "spiritual darkness"—those times of afflicted conscience that Wesley graphically described in his sermon "The Wilderness State."[17]

Wesley's emphasis on self-examination may have many sources, but his mother Susanna exposed him, as a child, to it. John Newton credits Susanna Wesley with establishing a routine of self-examination in the Epworth parsonage. Having assimilated this practice from her own Puritan childhood, she brought similar disciplines into the lives of her children. Susanna's later instructions to her sons emphasized the pattern: "Keep the mind in a temper for recollection, and often in the day call it in from outward objects, lest it wander into forbidden paths. Make an examination of your conscience at least three times a day, and omit no opportunity of retirement from the world." [18]

Whether Newton and Schmidt are correct in grounding in Puritanism Wesley's extraordinary interest in self-examination, it is certain he found among the Puritans significant formulations of the discipline. As usual, he did not hesitate to use these resources for instruction among his society members.

Diaries and Self-Examination

Methods of self-examination may vary, but among Puritans a principal means supporting such personal scrutiny lay in the keeping of a daily diary. Diaries provided not only records of daily events but the opportunity to evaluate those events. Here it was that one recorded the results of "casting his accounts." William Haller maintains that the diary served as the Puritan confessional and thereby played a singularly important role in their spiritual lives.[19] Theirs was an age of renewed popular interest in biography and history, which explains much of their interest in diaries; but keeping a diary had far more than simple literary interest for

Puritans. It served as the daily record of their relationship to God.

Wesley's own careful diary records reflect his lifelong discipline of self-examination as they chronicled his daily activities. Richard Heitzenrater's extensive work on the early Oxford diaries provides valuable insight into the role self-examination played in Wesley's spiritual development.[20] These and later diaries serve as the lodestone for Wesley's printed *Journal* that provides a most interesting road map to the unfolding of Methodism through the century.

Adam Clarke, one of Wesley's preachers and biographers, and Nehemiah Curnock, editor of the 1909 edition of Wesley's *Journal* suggested that an example of diary keeping was set for Wesley by his Puritan grandfather, John Westley, who seems to have recorded "not only the most remarkable events of God's providence in his behalf, but more especially the operations of the Divine Spirit upon his heart."[21] John Newton notes that Susanna kept a "spiritual journal" following the precedent of her father Samuel.[22] Wesley's own account of his diary and journal keeping credited Bishop Taylor's *Rules of Holy Living and Holy Dying* with being his inspiration to "take a more exact account than I had done before."[23] Curnock claimed that this later phrase suggested that, most likely, following the precedent of his forefathers and mother, Wesley kept a journal before he read Bishop Taylor.[24] Though none of these comments can offer conclusive evidence of direct influence upon John or Charles stemming from their Puritan forefathers' and from their mother's practice, the suggestion is attractive. Evidence showing that the Puritan pattern of diary keeping was a significant part of the family heritage at least allows one to consider this practice as one factor encouraging Wesley's own use of a diary.

Self-Denial

Self-examination leads naturally to self-denial, or the denial of the selfish interests and motivations discovered through the process of examination. For Wesley self-denial was an "indispensable necessity" in Christian living. Consequently, in his sermon on the subject, he criticized, on the one hand, the predestinarians, antinomians, and Ranters of his own day, who either discounted it altogether as a reinstitution of "salvation by works" or failed to appreciate its significance. Similarly he also censured mystics, for they spoke in perplexed and intricate terms most "likely to cancel its meaning." General treatises on the subject did not satisfy him because they "deal in generals only" without coming to the particulars that affect common men, or they detail the "particulars" such as imprisonment, tortures, the giving up of lands, and so on, which were not likely to be the lot of common people in the eighteenth century.[25] His intent was to provide an exposition of the topic that would not err by embracing any of these extremes.

If the predestinarians of Wesley's own day were not willing to proclaim the necessity of self-denial, as he asserted, they had at that point strayed from their Puritan heritage. Such denial is a recurring theme throughout Puritan literature. Puritans treated the topic in many of the works Wesley included in the *Library*, but it received special attention in Isaac Ambrose's tract *The Practice of Sanctification*, wherein self-denial was defined as

> a total, thorough, utter abnegation of a man's own ends, counsels, affections, and a whole prostration of himself, and of all that is his under Christ Jesus. And thus we have the meaning of Christ, *If any man will come after me, let him deny himself*; i.e. let him lay aside his own wisdom as an empty lamp, his own will as an evil commander, his own imaginations as a false rule, his own affections as corrupt counsellors, and his own ends as base and unworthy marks to be aimed at . . . ;so in the regenerate man, all the supernatural gifts and graces, all the moral endowments and abilities, all the natural powers and faculties of the soul, with all the members of the body, and all the labours of the life . . . must do obeisance, and be made subject to Jesus Christ. And this is true self-denial.[26]

This characterization of self-denial as the turning of a believer from one's own will, goals, purposes, and inclinations to those of God corresponds to Wesley's definition of self-denial as "the denying or refusing to follow our own will, from a conviction that the will of God is the only rule of action to us."[27] Wesley's description was even closer to that of Richard Alleine, who pointed out that one cannot serve both Christ and self at the same time: "If you will not deny yourselves, you deny your Lord; and if you can deny yourselves in anything, you will deny Christ in nothing."[28] Wesley concentrated on one's will, but certainly intended to include not simply the will but all affections, goals, abilities, capabilities—the entire person was to be completely consecrated to God.

Ambrose enumerated various patterns of self-denial showing that a believer must be willing to deny (1) sinful self or corruptions and concupiscence (Wesley's "corrupt nature of humanity"); (2) external relations or those natural human relations even of family that may stand between a person and God; (3) special gifts or endowments, such as learning, wisdom, and power, if they interfere with singular service of God; (4) worldly profits and pleasures when these tend to selfish sin instead of service to God and others; (5) honor, praise, and a good name when they are "snares or baits unto sin"; (6) one's very life if this is required; and finally (7) any spiritual pride or any credit for the graces of God that may be present in one.[29] He carefully indicated that whatever is denied may be good and useful in itself but must be cast away when it interferes with one's following God. When graces or blessings are used or sought for what they may do for the self, they are sinful and must be denied.

Wesley, though not specifying each of these patterns of self-denial, commented on most of those enumerated by Ambrose. As he demonstrated in his criticism of the typical handling of the subject, he was more concerned with pride, self-will, seeking after place and wealth—attitudes that tend toward worldly position—than he was with those realities that he doubted the common person will be called upon to abandon, such as family or life itself. Many seventeenth-century Puritans, however, had been called upon to make the kind of self-denying sacrifices that Ambrose indicated; consequently, the self-denial that might lead to actual sacrifice of property and life was much closer and more real to them than they were to the average eighteenth-century Methodist. In any case, the "particulars" of self-denial are evident throughout the Puritan treatises, and Wesley could easily recommend Stuckley's delineation of what was to be denied as "all your sinful lusts, . . . all your worldly advantages, . . . all self, self-will, self-righteousness, self-sufficiency, self-confidence, and self-seekings."[30] Self-denial served as a major touchstone of true Christian life, and the Puritans, as well as Wesley, were convinced that without self-denial one could hardly expect to lead a Christian life.[31]

Growth in Grace

Wesley's commendation of the Puritans' ability to teach a believer how to "grow in grace" or to go from "strength to strength" arose from his perception of their recurrent emphasis on spiritual growth.[32] They were convinced that a believer does not stand still in a state of "achieved" faith but must move forward in a continuing process of sanctification. Discussed in many of the treatises, such growth was Thomas Goodwin's topic in *The Tryall of a Christian's Growth*.[33] Convinced that "there is therefore as great a necessity to grow as to be born again or else we cannot enter into heaven," Goodwin, in typical Puritan style, gave instruction and tests by which one could ascertain the nature of such personal growth. True growth in grace included expanding one's Christian life through building on such foundations as love, faith, and humility.[34] Growth on these foundations enlarged one's opportunities for fruitful service to others. In a believer renewal and increase also expand the graces that are already present in substance. Credit for such increases must be given to God; it is his work and not that of the believer's, even though he "doth proportion his influence to our endeavours." In this limited sense believers may be seen as "fellow-workers" with God.[35] Other Puritan divines joined Goodwin in his insistence that growth in grace is a necessary element in Christian living. Bolton saw it as a test of conversion and "an inseparable companion of spiritual life."[36] Sibbes picturesquely commented, "He [God] doth not only give them a stock of grace at the beginning, but also helps them to trade. . . . He not only plants graces, but also waters and cherishes them."[37]

Examples need not be extended to show that growth in grace was a constant theme in these Puritan works used by Wesley. As he indicated, he was strongly attracted to them because of their exemplary treatment of personal growth in Christian living.

Wesley's affinities with Puritan teachings on self-examination, self-denial, and growth in grace show only representative areas of mutual concern and interest in the religious life of an individual Christian. He offered at least one specific recommendation of Puritan patterns that would be useful for guidance in expanding one's personal religion. In the 1763 edition of the *Minutes of the Methodist Conferences* and the two editions that followed, Wesley, questioning his preachers about their own personal religious practice, asked them if they follow the "instituted" means of grace, such as prayer, reading the Scriptures, and "meditating: at set times? How? By Bishop Hall's, or Mr. Baxter's rule? How long?"[38] It is possible that he was suggesting here the use of Bishop Hall's *Meditations and Vows*, which he had made available to his followers in *A Christian Library*. The reference to Baxter's rule may indicate several treatises, as meditation was essentially the subject of *The Saints' Everlasting Rest*, also available in the *Library*, and was included in the instructions found in *Gildas Salvianus, The Reformed Pastor*. Wesley in other connections recommended each of these to his preachers. It is intriguing that he recommended Puritan sources for this instruction because his Anglican mentors emphasized similar instruction. Perhaps the practical nature of the Puritan instruction, principally designed to reach the common believer, made it, from Wesley's viewpoint, more acceptable and appealing to Methodist laypersons and preachers.

Wesley's own teachings on personal morality range over such diverse areas as, among many others, marriage, vocation, dress, time, conversation, recreation, and, of course, money. Tracts and sermons that treated these provide a fertile field for comparing his teachings with the Puritans' teaching in the same areas, but to pursue them would unduly extend the scope of this study. The similarities in areas we have considered are obvious and no doubt account for Wesley's contemporaries' comparing his work and teaching with those of the Puritans. Professor Davies cogently suggests that "in effect, Wesley's ethical sermons provided for the spiritual illiterates what another Arminian, Baxter, had given the Puritan élite in his *Christian Directory*."[39]

Family Religion

Recognizing the immense significance of the inherently close relationships of a home, Puritan divines made counsel concerning family religion and training a primary element of their teachings. Wesley shared this vision of a Christian home even though Methodist band meetings and class meetings supplemented family relationships and served as an additional intimate fellowship for individual Christians. Leslie Church suggests that this emphasis on family religion was a significant characteristic of Wesley's followers: "The first Methodists were distinguished for many things, but nothing more became them than their 'sense of family.'"[40]

Puritan works included in the *Library* provided numerous commentaries on proper conduct of family religion, as well as instruction in the proper relationship between family members, and the shared responsibility of each member for all other members. The treatises of Anglican and other authors included in Wesley's *Christian Library* include similar instructions, but their handling of these concerns does not highlight the subject with the same intensity. The number of Puritan commentaries on the topic in the *Library* significantly outnumber treatments by Anglicans or others.[41]

Family Responsibility

Convinced that the household should be a fundamental model for all other social relations, Puritan divines maintained that the master of the house carried privileges and responsibilities similar to those of a civil governor. Instruction in family religion and responsibility began, therefore, with an affirmation that the governors of the household, the father *and* his helpmate, must realize the gravity of their positions. John Kitchin stated the responsibility thus:

> That father that does not correct his child when he goes amiss, is justly corrected for his faults; and it is the pattern of God's judicial proceedings. As He visits the iniquities of the fathers upon the children who *imitate* them; so He visits the iniquities of the children upon the fathers, who *countenance* and indulge them. . . . Thus must family governors be accountable to God for every lamb in the fold, for every child in the family, for every servant in the house. . . . God will one day cry aloud in thine ears . . . "Husband, father, master, wife, give account of thy husbandship and give account of thy fathership, give account of thy mastership, give account of thy wifeship."[42]

Richard Alleine's comment puts the case in more direct terms: "Now, where there is a charge of Souls, there must be an account given of Souls. . . . If any in the house perish through thy neglect, thy life shall go for his life, thy Soul for his Soul."[43] The religious care of the child was, then, part of the express command of God—a duty that one could not overlook or escape.

Puritans, employing a metaphor that gave the family a sacred image, did not think they could overstress its significance. The family itself, because of the centrality of its religious training, served as a minichurch. "Why hath God given the name of Churches to Christian families, but because of those holy services which are to be done publikely in the family? Whereby they are all sanctified, and become even houses of God to dwell in."[44] "He that makes his House a *little church*, shall find, that God will make it a *Little Sanctuary*."[45]

Wesley shared much of this Puritan understanding of family responsibilities before God, and he was especially appreciative of another of their insights: Through family religion and education God will raise up a new generation to carry on his church and a well-ordered society.[46] William Whateley contended that only through the progeny of fruitful and legitimate marriage can there be a "flourishing estate of every church and commonwealth."[47] Richard Baxter agreed: "The very welfare of Church and State lieth mainly on this duty of well educating children; and without this, all other means are like to be far less successful."[48] Family worship and religion, the very cornerstone of a good education and proper training of the child, was then more than merely a personal affair, having much larger implications. Wesley took these insights a step further when he suggested, as some Puritans had done before him, that family religion and training were also pivotal to the continuation of the religious revival he was witnessing among his followers—without such training the revival would "in a short time die away."[49]

Wesley's sermon "On Family Religion" corresponds to much of

the general Puritan teachings on the topic.[50] The necessity of constantly keeping family religion before his pastors made it a recurrent theme in his instructions: "Do all you can herein, if not all you would. Inquire in each house, Have you family-prayer? Do you read the scripture in your family? Have you a fixed time for private prayer? Examine each as to his growth in grace, and discharge of relative duties."[51]

Family Worship

For a pattern of Christian family worship, Wesley turned to the Puritan Philip Henry. Henry's "Method of Family Prayer" was part of the "particular" instructions that the Methodist preachers were to give in the families under their care.[52] Printed as a part of *The Life of Mr. Philip Henry*, the work had been abridged for the *Library*.[53] Wesley does not appear to have published it separately; therefore, we may assume that he expected his people to use the *Library* edition, for he consistently recommended it as a pattern for Methodist families.

Philip Henry's method of family worship was a classical Puritan treatment of the subject and may serve as a representative treatise. Insisting that one follow the practice of private worship, or "Closet-worship," as the first step in religious cultivation, Henry additionally urged his parishioners to join together as husband and wife in prayer. "This Sanctifies the Relation, and fetcheth in a Blessing upon it, makes the Comforts of it the more sweet, and the Cares and Crosses of it the more easie, and is an excellent Means of preserving and encreasing Love in the Relation."[54] Such parental prayer would then serve as an exemplary pattern for all the household.

All family worship was to be practiced daily.[55] An early-morning worship experience began the day, before the cares of the day crowded in, and another preceded supper in the evening before the family became sleepy. Attended by all in the household, including servants, field-workers, sojourners, and the children, they were to begin with a short introductory prayer followed by a psalm and Scripture reading. A short exposition accompanied Scripture, and the children were questioned concerning it. Family prayer followed this and was "usually most full in giving Thanks for Family-Mercies, confessing Family-Sins, and begging Family-Blessings."[56] Here were offered prayers for the children, any special occasion or event, and the sojourner who might be in the household. At the close of this prayer the children were dismissed after asking for a blessing from their father and mother.

Catechizing the children and servants or examining them "in

some other useful Book" replaced reading of the Scripture one evening of the week, usually Thursday.[57] Saturday night in Philip Henry's plan brought a scriptural review of passages read during the week, accompanied by an examination of the children on their meaning and an explanation of what had not been fully understood. Matthew Henry gave credit to these sessions, conducted with "prudence and sweetness," for instilling in him and the other children a love for the Scriptures and providing them with extensive scriptural knowledge.

The Sabbath, however, was to be the crowning day of family worship. Although the regular form was followed, family prayers were expanded and Psalms sung after dinner and supper. The evening brought another catechetical session with the children and servants, to which was added a review of the sermons of the day to be sure that all remembered and understood.[58] Sabbath prayer was also expanded, with particular attention given to the exemplary role of the family in its larger community. The Henry family was to be especially aware of their role as examples in the community, as they were children of a minister.

To these family-worship patterns Henry added regular instructions for his children in the meaning of their baptism and the Lord's Supper. Supplementing other instructions, Henry prepared for the children a Baptismal Covenant, which they repeated and reaffirmed weekly. The children were also taught to pray, sometimes as a group without adult supervision, and, of course, to read the Scriptures as early as they were able.[59]

Summarizing the discussion of family worship, Matthew Henry comments on Philip's example:

> **He managed his daily Family-Worship to make it a Pleasure and not a Task to his Children and Servants; for he was seldom long, and never tedious in the Service; the variety of the Duties made it the more pleasant; so, that none who join't him had ever any reason to say, 'Behold what a Weariness is it!'. . . He did not burthen his Children's Memories by imposing upon them the getting of Chapters and Psalms without Book; but endeavored to make the whole Word of God Familiar to them,** *(especially the scripture stories)* **and to bring them to understand it and love it,** *and then they would easily remember it.*[60]

Such worship was carried on "in the most lively method" to guard it against becoming a dull formal matter.[61]

From the hints given in Susanna Wesley's own plan for her children's education, recorded in Wesley's *Journal*, it may be seen that this daily pattern of family worship was closely followed in the Wesley home.[62] Not surprisingly, therefore, Wesley recognized an affinity with Puritan teachings on this point and heartily recommended it by strongly suggesting that his followers pattern their own family worship after it.

Wives and Husbands

William Whateley's *Directions for Married Persons* illustrates another important example of Puritan family instruction. Whateley was interested in providing "good instruction to Young and Unmarried people" as well as to married couples who needed to "become acquainted" with the duties of marriage.[63]

Wesley's commendation of the work shows his admiration of the instructions:

> I have seen nothing on the subject in any either ancient or modern tongue, which is in any degree comparable to it;—it is so full, so deep, so closely, so strongly written, and yet with the most exquisite decency, even where the author touches on points of the most delicate nature that are to be found within the whole compass of divinity. I cannot therefore but earnestly recommend it to the most serious and attentive consideration of all those married persons, who desire to have a conscience void of offence, and to adorn the gospel of God our Saviour.[64]

This tract was first issued by Wesley, from the same plates used to produce the *A Christian Library* edition, as a separate publication in 1753 and then reprinted again in 1760 and 1768.[65] Such multiple editions suggest it enjoyed wide usage as marriage instruction material by the Methodists.

For Whateley marriage was to be kept inviolable, with divorce granted only on the offense of adultery. However, the physical relationship was blessed and in proper order when it was "sanctified, seasonable, temperate, and willing."[66] Anything less than this threatened the marriage itself.

"Love is the life and soul of marriage, without which, it differs as much from itself, as a carcass from a living body." This statement sounds quite modern and agrees with present-day marriage counseling; however, Whateley's understanding of love's source or foundation may appear archaic and perhaps threatening to many modern interpreters.

> **Love must be built** *chiefly and* **principally upon the** *will and* **commandment of God, the only sure** *and steadfast* **foundation of it. . . . A Christian man must love his wife not only** *or principally*, **because she is beautiful, wittie,** *housewifely,* **dutiful, [and] loving**. *And every way wel conditioned*; **but chiefly, because the Lord of Heaven and**

> **earth,** *to whom all hearts should stoope, and all affections yield*, **hath said, Husbands, love your wives. The wife also must love her husband, not only or chiefly because he is a** *proper* **[comely] man of good meanes, and** *or good* **parentage, kind to her,** *of good courage*, **and of good carriage** *in every respect*; **but because he is her husband, and [because] God the soveraigne of all soules hath told women, that they ought to be lovers of their husbands.**[67]

Obviously in this passage, love's source does not lie within the person but in the command and grace of God. Although love of the partner is "chiefly" because it is commanded, this is at the same time the most intimate and meaningful of human loves. In Bolton's words it is **"a sweet, loving, and tender-powring out of their hearts, with much** *affectionate dearenesse* **[affection], into each others bosomes; in all passages, carriages, and behaviours, one towards another."**[68] Based on the command of God *and* mutual human love, the married state is characterized by the "pleasingness, faithfulness, and helpfulness" of each partner for the other. It results in the closest of communities that, though cognizant of faults and sins, will not allow these to interfere with the relationship and will be one in which the partners are always looking for the best in each other.[69] It will keep inviolable the secrets and problems shared, while offering all of the help, encouragement, and direction possible. Through all aspects of the relationship they work together for common piety.

Reflecting the social forms and understanding of the day, Whateley, along with the other Puritan divines, could not discuss the family without detailing the structure of authority and responsibility within it. As noted previously in Henry's comments on family worship, they understood the husband was the "head" and sovereign of the wife, master of the household with unquestioned authority.[70] Abuse of his headship was, at the same time, thought to be a gross sin. "No woman can endure her husband's government with comfort, if gentlenesse does not temper it."[71]

> **Compassion,** *love*, **kindnesse, the declaration of ones sorrow for** *her* **[the] fault [of the person reproved], desire of his good, care of his amendment** *that is reproved*; **these** *be* **[are] the things that** *frame* **[dispose] the will to accept of an admonition, and** *doe* **much helpe the kindly working thereof. I am not against the wholesome earnestnesse of reproving, and that sharpnesse of rebuking, which in some cases the Lord himselfe commands; but this may well** *stand* **[be] without bitternes, without** *the* **violence of words** *and gesture*, **and without** *the* **fiercenesse** *against which we speake*.[72]

Authority could neither be neglected nor abused in the proper Christian household.

Whateley was, on the other hand, concerned about the dangers of a household wherein the wife might be dominant, for her "peculiar duties" included her acknowledgment of her "inferiority" and her recognition that "she must carry herself as an inferior."[73]

In the choice of a marriage partner the Puritans insisted that primary consideration be given to the religious character of the person: "**Let pietie be the first mover of thine affection,** *the prime and principal ponderation in this great affaire*; **and then** *conceive of personage, parentage, and* **[consider person,] portion,** *as they say*, **and** *such* **outward things** *and worldly additions, as a comfortable accessory, consideration* **onely in a second place.**"[74]

Wesley also feared the consequences of marrying "unbelievers." In addition, he warned against the dangers of attempting to seek "a good match," meaning a worldly good one.[75]

Parental Responsibility

Parents were to remember their responsibility before God for their children's spiritual and moral development. They were also cautioned to set a good example, since example is the true test of teaching.[76] Parents were not only responsible for their children's spiritual nurture, but for their total education and occupation as well; and, consequently, for their whole demeanor. Parental discipline in the family was fundamental, and neither partner could forsake responsibility. **"Both must discountenance those that** *miscarry* **[carry] themselves [ill], and both must** *give commendation and good allowance to* **[commend] them of good behaviour; that so they may both maintaine each others authority to the full."**[77]

The children were to respect and obey their parents. To maintain proper relationships, a child must have "a loving fear, and a fearing love" for the parent. Such love would naturally result in reverence of speech and carriage, obedience to the "commands, instructions, reproofs, and corrections of their parents," and a true recompense for the care and love they have received from the parent.[78] Wesley, reiterating this view, extended a child's obligation even to the obedience of a grown child: "Those only who obey their parents when they can live without them, and when they neither hope nor fear anything from them, shall have praise from God."[79]

Wesley's use and recommendation of William Whateley's work on marriage takes on added significance when we remember Wesley's own troubled love life and less than outstanding marriage which most would agree could hardly be recommended as an example. His turning to a Puritan description and pattern suggests that he found there an ideal, for Puritans held the blessedness of the married estate to be God given. Therefore, such blessedness was primary to a meaningful and useful Christian life, whether within the family or within the larger culture.

Education of a Child

For the Puritans and Wesley parental responsibility centered in education of the whole person: moral, spiritual, and (at least the rudiments of) academic. They understood that a parent's teaching role was the most challenging of all his or her responsibilities. Wesley notes Baxter's comment that "whoever attempt to profit children will find need of all the understanding God has given them."[80] This familiar anecdote from Wesley's own family expresses the difficulty quite well: "I remember to have heard my father asking my mother, 'How could you have the patience to tell that blockhead the same thing twenty timesover?' She answered, 'Why, if I had told him but nineteen times, I should have lost all my labour.' What patience indeed, what love, what knowledge is requisite for this!"[81] Still, the need for patience and the difficulty of the task in no way negated its urgency.

Wesley appropriated his mother's educational pattern for his instructional model when, as a leader of Methodism, he designed the spiritual and academic program for Kingswood school.[82] These instructions, illustrating the discipline and educational patterns of the Epworth household, have often been seen as outlining the loving but usually stringent regimen that marked a Puritan home.[83] Wesley's own formulations were often austerely stated and, therefore, lack the warmth found, for instance, in the admonitions of Whateley and Philip Henry even when they were giving exacting instructions.[84]

Wesley's instructions for children's spiritual development closely resemble those of Richard Baxter's that Wesley had abridged for the *Christian Library*. Both noted that training of children often meant going against a child's nature, which, in their understanding, is imbued with love of self, pride, and love of the world.[85] To accomplish this, one must, in Baxter's terms, "rectify their wills."[86] For Wesley, as for his mother, this was the primary task. If the self-will of a child could be broken and brought under the control of the parent, it was Wesley's logic that it could more readily be given to God; therefore, "a Wise parent, . . . should begin to break their will the first moment it appears." One should, then, "never, on any account, give a child any thing that it cries for."[87] To conquer their natural pride, one was not to praise them "to their face." Wesley seems to have reconsidered this last admonition once he had stated it, for in the next paragraph he tempered this advice by allowing commendation to be given but with the "utmost caution."[88] The sharpness of such sentiments may certainly cause a modern psychologist to shudder, but one needs to remember that, for the Puritans and Wesley, these measures were always to be carried out within the broader perspective of love and compassion. They were considered to be in the best interest of the child, and how they might be judged certainly depends on the context within which such insights were applied—be it loving compassion or simple authority. In their starkest forms they are obviously open to the charge of endangering the child's development and, if followed strictly, of making the household a regimented prison, a charge sometimes leveled against both movements.[89]

It is also significant that, in his maturity, Wesley never carried primary responsibility as a parent. He never personally experienced the challenges of daily parental care where these instructions would have, no doubt, been tempered and perhaps adjusted. Although, such instructions about breaking a child's will may appear abusive to some modern educators and parents, they are, at the same time, appealing to others who judge many of our present societal problems to rest in the loss of parental care and control in our children's lives. In the eighteenth century close parental control was the normal understanding of family authority and responsibility.

With Baxter, Wesley insisted that training must be started as soon as the child begins to reason, and that instruction of the child must be frequent and with the utmost perseverance.[90] Though Wesley did not follow Baxter in detailing the doctrinal and practical religious matters that must be taught the child,[91] he generally agreed with Baxter and certainly approved the manner in which the instructions were to be applied: "And for the manner, you must do all, 1. Betimes, before sin get rooting. 2. Frequently. 3. Seasonable. 4.Seriously and diligently. 5. Affectionately and tenderly. 6. And with authority: compelling, where commanding will not serve; and adding correction, where instruction is frustrate."[92]

In summary, investigation of teachings concerning the family reveals a close affinity between Wesley and the Puritans and, in the areas of family worship and marriage relationships, actual dependence upon Puritan materials for instruction of the Methodist people. To say that Wesley was dependent upon this tradition for his own understanding of these matters is perhaps to go beyond the evidence, although a case might be made for his having acquired his understanding through the Epworth household. Certainly, that home appears in the evidence available to us to have been a household closely resembling those portrayed by Puritan authors. In any case, in Puritan teaching and practice he recognized the expression of views congenial to his own, and he clearly used these as patterns for the people called Methodists.

Notes

1. Wesley's sermon entitled "On Redeeming the Time" quotes extensively from William Law's treatise *Redeeming the Time from Sleep*; see *Works* (Jackson), 7:71ff. The first rule of Jeremy Taylor's *Rules and Exercises for Holy Living* also deals with the subject. On the Puritan side, Sir Matthew Hale discusses the redemption of time in his *Contemplations, Moral and Divine* (London: Printed by William Godbid for William Shrowsbury, 1676), 15ff. [*CL*, 17:225ff.]. It is a concern for Herbert Palmer in his *Memorials of Godliness and Christianity in a Discourse of Making Religion Ones Business* (London: Printed for Samuel Crouch, 1681), 14-18 [*CL*, 12:10-11].

2. For a detailed discussion of such blending see the sections "Wesley and Human Appropriation of Grace" in chapter 4 and "Sanctification" in chapter 5 of this study.

3. This metaphor is drawn from John Deschner's perceptive analysis of the interrelation of the Anglican and Reformed theologies in Wesley (Deschner, *Wesley's Christology*, 177, 185).

4. Palmer, *Memorials of Godliness*, 2 [*CL*, 12:5]; cf. Bolton, *Walking with God*, 29 [*CL*, 4:335].

5. *Works*, 21:80. Wesley used Bolton's treatise, *Walking with God*, for the same purposes, and comments, "I wish all our preachers would herein follow my example, and frequently read in public and enforce select portions of the *Christian Library*" (*Works*, 20:486).

6. *Journal*, 8:122.

7. Stuckley, *Gospel-Glass*, 158-59 [*CL*, 19:330].

8. Stuckley, *Gospel-Glass*, 162-63 [*CL*, 19:332-33]; cf. Bolton, *Walking with God*, 150 [*CL*, 4:372].

9. Stuckley, *Gospel-Glass*, 161 [*CL*, 19:332].

10. Gilbert Burnett, *The Life and Death of Sir Matthew Hale* (London: Printed for W. Shrowsbury, 1682), 11-12 [*CL*, 17:109-10]. CF. Palmer, *Memorials of Godliness*, 32 [*CL*, 12:8].

11. Annesley, *Morning Exercises*, 20-21 [*CL*, 21:468].

12. Bolton, *On Self-Examination*, 17-19 [*CL*, 5:188].

13. Richard Sibbes, *Bowels Opened, or A Discovery of the Neere and Deere Love, Union, and Communion betwixt Christ and the Church*, in *Works of Richard Sibbes*, 2:47 [*CL*, 6:160]; cited hereafter as *Christ and the Church*.

14. *Works* (Jackson), 11:521-23.

15. Schmidt, *John Wesley*, 1:97.

16. *Works* (Jackson), 8:315, 323.

17. *Works*, 2:202ff.; *Letters*, 8:241. As might be expected, such use is

made of self-examination in Puritan treatises also. See Goodwin, *Child of Light Walking in Darkness*, 263-64 [*CL*, 6:288].

18. Newton, *Susanna Wesley*, 142.

19. Haller, *Rise of Puritanism*, 98.

20. Richard Heitzenrater, "John Wesley and the Oxford Methodists, 1725-35" (Ph.D. dis., Duke University, 1972). See also Heitzenrater and Reginald Ward's meticulous and insightful recounting of the development of dairies and journals, *Works*, 18:1-119.

21. Clarke, *Memoirs of the Wesley Family*, 23; *Journal*, 1:42-44; cf. Whitehead, *Life of the Reverend John Wesley*, 1:2.

22. Newton, *Susanna Wesley*, 140.

23. *Works*, 18:121.

24. *Journal*, 1:43.

25. *Works*, 2:239-41.

26. Ambrose, *Practice of Sanctification*, in *Works of Isaac Ambrose*, 87 [*CL*, 8:20]; cf. Joseph Alleine, *Divers Practical Cases of Conscience Satisfactorily Resolved* (London: Printed for Nevil Simmons, 1672), 24 [*CL*, 14:191].

27. *Works*, 2:242.

28. Alleine, *Vindiciae Pietatis*, 315 [*CL*, 18:186-87].

29. *Ambrose, Practice of Sanctification*, in *Works of Isaac Ambrose*, 87-107 [*CL*, 8:20-47]. Cf. Bolton, *Walking with God*, 52 [*CL*, 4:340]; Goodwin, *Tryall of a Christian's Growth* (London: Printed for R. Dawlman, 1643), 14ff.

30. Stuckley, *Gospel-Glass*, 31-32 [*CL*, 19:255].

31. "**No Walking with God, no sweete communion, and sound peace at his Mercy-Seate, except for his sake,** *and keeping a good conscience,* **thou be content to denie thy selfe**" (Bolton, *Walking with God*, 52 [*CL*, 4:339-40]; cf. 313 [*CL*, 4:12]; Ambrose, *The Practice of Sanctification* in *Works of Isaac Ambrose*, 87 [*CL*, 8:20]).

32. *CL*, 4:108.

33. Goodwin, *Tryall of a Christian's Growth* [*CL*, 7:49ff.].

34. Goodwin, *Tryall of a Christian's Growth*, 70 [*CL*, 7:56].

35. Goodwin, *Tryall of a Christian's Growth*, 167 [*CL*, 7:86].

36. Bolton, *On Self-Examination*, 287 [*CL*, 5:244]; cf. *Walking with God*, 312, 339-40 [*CL*, 4:400, 416]; Stuckley, *Gospel-Glass*, 378 [*CL*, 19:441].

37. Sibbes, *Christ and the Church*, in *Works of Richard Sibbes*, 2:13 [*CL*, 6:139]; cf. Preston, *New Covenant*, 258-60 [*CL*, 6:28-29].

38. *Minutes* (1763), in *Minutes of the Methodist Conferences, 1744-1798* (London: John Mason, 1862), 550; cited hereafter as *MMC*.

39. Davies, *Worship and Theology in England*, 156.

40. Leslie Church, *The Early Methodist People* (London: Epworth Press, 1948), 222.

41. Wesley included only two Anglican treatises that extensively treated the subject in *A Christian Library*: Jeremy Taylor's *The Rules and Exercises of Holy Living*, *CL*, 9:186-88, and Anthony Horneck's *The Happy Ascetic*, *CL*, 16:367-73.

42. John Kitchin, "How Must We Reprove, That We May Not Partake of Other Men's Sins," in *Morning Exercises*, 1:135 [*CL*, 21:434]; cited

hereafter as "How Must We Reprove." Cf. Stuckley, *Gospel-Glass*, 222 [*CL*, 19:370].

43. Alleine, *Vindiciae Pietatis*, 353 [*CL*, 18:209]; cf. Baxter, *Saints' Everlasting Rest*, in *Practical Works of Richard Baxter*, 23:146 [*CL*, 22:216].

44. William Whateley, *A Bride-Bush: or a Direction for Married Persons* (London: Printed by Bernard Alsop for Beniamin Fisher, 1623), 91 [*CL*, 12:295]; cited hereafter as *Directions for Married Persons*. "It will never be said to your glory, *the church in your house:* but may it not be said, there is a nest of snakes, a cage of devils in your house?" (Stuckley, *Gospel-Glass*, 241 [*CL*, 19:383]).

45. Matthew Henry, *An Account of the Life and Death of Mr. Philip Henry*, 3rd ed. (London: Printed for J. Lawrence, J. Nicholson, et al., 1712), 59 [*CL*, 28:291]; cited hereafter as *Philip Henry*; cf. Kitchin, "How Must We Reprove," in *Morning Exercises*, 1:135 [*CL*, 21:434].

46. Wesley, *On Family Religion*, in Works, 3:337-38.

47. Whateley, *Directions for Married Persons*, 17 [*CL*, 12:263].

48. Baxter, *Saints' Everlasting Rest*, in *Practical Works of Richard Baxter*, 23:150 [*CL*, 22:218].

49. *Works*, 3:335; *Works* (Jackson), 8:316.

50. *Works*, 3:334-46.

51. *Minutes* (1763), *MMC*, 456. The first sentence of this quotation is almost a paraphrase of Baxter's admonition on this same subject: "O Sirs, if you cannot do what you would do for them, do what you can" (*Saints' Everlasting Rest*, in *Practical Works of Richard Baxter*, 23:165 [*CL*, 22:228-29]. Cf. *Works* (Jackson), 8:302ff).

52. *Works* (Jackson), 8:315.

53. In the *Minutes* (1766) Wesley identifies this "Method" with that printed in *Philip Henry*: "Read publicly that part of Mr. Philip Henry's life, enforcing it as a pattern" (*MMC*, 53).

54. Henry, *Philip Henry*, 58 [*CL*, 28:291]. See also Whateley, *Directions for Married Persons*, 49 [*CL*, 12:275]; Bolton, *Walking with God*, 255 [*CL*, 4:389]; *Works*, 3:337-38.

55. Henry, *Philip Henry*, 59 [*CL*, 28:292ff.]; cf. Ambrose, *Practice of Sanctification*, in *Works of Isaac Ambrose*, 126 [*CL*, 8:74]; Kitchin, "How Must We Reprove," in Annesley, *Morning Exercises*, 1:136 [*CL*, 21:435].

56. Henry, *Philip Henry*, 63 [*CL*, 28:295].

57. Henry, *Phillip Henry*, 64 [*CL*, 28:296-97]. Catechizing was important but should not be considered sufficient for complete instruction, according to Lewis Stuckley, for he asked, "How seldom do you converse personnally with everyone in your families concerning the practical part of religion?" (Stuckley, *Gospel-Glass*, 221 [*CL*, 19:369]; cf. Alleine, *Vindiciae Pietatis*, 353 [*CL*, 18:209]).

58. Henry, *Philip Henry*, 65 [*CL*, 28:297]. Stuckley lamented the failure of most to follow such a pattern of Sabbath worship (Stuckley, *Gospel-Glass*, 153-58 [*CL*, 19:326-30]).

59. Henry, *Philip Henry*, 67-71 [*CL*, 28:299-303].

60. Henry, *Philip Henry*, 64 [*CL*, 28:296]; 67-68 [*CL*, 28:300].

61. *MMC*, 53. Bolton commented on family worship in the same vein: **"In the discharge of which maine dutie of Christianitie, utterly**

neglected by the most, and empoysoned to many, by their resting onely in the works wrought, take heed of *growing* **[Declining] into [a] forme, [or] customarinesse,** *performatorinesse*, **which will most certainely draw the very life-blood and** *breathing* **[breath] out of those holy businesses"** (*Walking with God*, 67 [*CL*, 4:345]).

62. *Works*, 19:286-91.

63. Whateley, *Directions for Married Persons*, 216 [*CL*, 12:335-36].

64. *CL*, 12:253.

65. Green, *Bibliography*, 82. The following appeared as the preface to the separate edition: "I am persuaded, it is not possible for me to write anything so full, so strong, and so clear on this subject, as has been written near an hundred and fifty years ago, by a person of equal sense and piety."

66. Whateley, *Directions for Married Persons*, 15 [*CL*, 12:262].

67. Whateley, *Directions for Married Persons*, 32 [*CL*, 12:269]; cf. Ambrose, *The Practice of Sanctification*, in *Works of Issac Ambrose,* 131 [*CL*, 8:82].

68. Bolton, *Walking with God*, 239 [*CL*, 4:381].

69. Whateley, *Directions for Married Persons*, 54-60 [*CL*, 12:278-93]; cf. Stuckley, *Gospel-Glass*, 224-29 [*CL*, 19:371-75].

70. Whateley, *Directions for Married Persons*, 97ff. [*CL*, 12:299ff.]; cf. Bolton, *Walking with* God, 244-50 [*CL*, 4:384-87].

71. Whateley, *Directions for Married Persons*, 156 [*CL*, 12:320].

72. Whateley, *Directions for Married Persons*, 168 [*CL*, 12:324]. In the words of Isaac Ambrose, "If he shall have occasion to reprove her, he must keep his words until a convenient time, not [do it] in the presence of others, and then in the spirit of meekness and love" (Ambrose, *Practice of Sanctification*, in *Works of Isaac Ambrose,* 132 [*CL*, 8:82]).

73. Whateley, *Directions for Married Persons*, 189-91 [*CL*, 12;328-30].

74. Bolton, *Walking with God*, 236 [*CL*, 4:379]. Herbert Palmer, writing before he was married, desired "that I may never marry with any whom I have reason to judge not to be truly religious, whilst yet I conclude, 'That religion alone is not sufficient to make any match'" (Palmer, *Memorials of Godliness*, 27 [*CL*, 12:14]; cf. Alleine, *Vindiciae Pietatis*, 354 [*CL*, 18:210]).

75. *MMC*, 483; *Works*, 3:344-45.

76. Whateley, *Directions for Married Persons*, 98 [*CL*, 12:300]; Alleine, *Vindiciae Pietatis*, 354 [*CL*, 18:210]; Stuckley, *Gospel-Glass*, 222 [*CL*, 19:370]; *Baxter, Saints' Everlasting Rest*, in *The Practical Works of Richard Baxter*, 22:166 [*CL*, 22:230].

77. Whateley, *Directions for Married Persons*, 95 [*CL*, 12:298]; Stuckley, *Gospel-Glass*, 230-35 [*CL*, 19:375-80]; Works, 3:339-41, 3:347-60.

78. Ambrose, *Practice of Sanctification*, in *Works of Isaac Ambrose,* 134 [*CL*, 8:84-85]; Stuckley, *Gospel-Glass*, 235 [*CL*, 19:380].

79. *Works*, 3:364.

80. *Letters*, 5:335; cf. *Saints' Everlasting Rest*, in *Practical Works of Richard Baxter*, 23:147 [*CL*, 22:217].

81. *Minutes* (1766), *MMC*, 69; *Works*, 3:342-41.

82. *Works*, 19:286ff.

83. See John Newton's *Susanna Wesley*, 108ff., for an expanded discussion of the household and its educational patterns.

84. Whateley, *Directions for Married Persons*, 156ff. [*CL*, 12:320ff.]; Henry, *Philip Henry*, 67-71 [*CL*, 18:299-303].

85. *Saints' Everlasting Rest*, in *Practical Works of Richard Baxter*, 23:147 [*CL*, 22:217]; *Works*, 3:351-52.

86. *Saints' Everlasting Rest*, in *Practical Works of Richard Baxter*, 23:166 [*CL*, 22:230]; *Works*, 3:353-54; *Journal*, 3:35.

87. *Works*, 3:354.

88. *Works*, 3:356.

89. For a general evaluation and criticism of Wesley's educational system as it was applied outside the home, particularly at Kingswood, see Alfred H. Body, *John Wesley and Education* (London: Epworth Press, 1936). See A. G. Ives, *Kingswood School in Wesley's Day and Since* for additional evaluation of Kingswood. F. C. Pritchard maintains that Wesley's plan for Kingswood was modeled, to some extent, upon the Dissenting academies, particularly as these were proposed by Milton's *Treatise on Education*, to which Wesley refers in his *Plain Account of Kingswood School* (Pritchard, *Methodist Secondary Education*, 64-65).

90. *Saints' Everlasting Rest*, in *Practical Works of Richard Baxter*, 23:152, 166 [*CL*, 22:219, 230]; *Works* (Jackson), 7:81-82.

91. *Saints' Everlasting Rest*, in *Practical Works of Richard Baxter*, 23:166-70 [*CL*, 22:230-34].

92. *Saints Everlasting Rest*, in *Practical Works of Richard Baxter*, 23:170 [*CL*, 22:234].

8

Christian Life and the Church

The church constituted an indispensable third component of Christian living in both Puritan and Wesleyan teaching and practice. Related to all areas of a Christian's life, the church was, for both groups, one of the instituted means God establishes on earth to convey love. As such, it provides a community of support and guidance necessary for a full life of faith, a principal channel by which one receives Christian instruction, and a context through which one normally comes to embrace faith itself.

In every age the church, as the earthly institution representing Christ, symbolizes and expresses the gospel itself; therefore, its outward form represents its spiritual and inward character. The church's spiritual nature is, consequently, inexorably related to its outward expressions of governance, patterns of teaching, forms of worship, and social countenance. For seventeenth-century Puritans the outward patterns they found in the Church of England represented centuries of "human additions." In their attempts to purge the church of these additions, they sought to reestablish the "pure," early church patterns revealed, as they understood it, in the Word of God. Similarly, though Wesley remained a loyal son of the Church of England, he did not hesitate, as the Puritans before him, to question and modify church forms if he thought they restricted the proclamation and spread of the gospel's good news. Both traditions understood such actions to be subservient to the gospel's spiritual demand that Christ's love be applicable to and available for all persons.

This chapter considers several issues that arise out of Puritan and Wesleyan willingness to alter or add to traditional church practice. First, what do Wesley's writings reveal about his attitude toward and evaluation of the Nonconformist's struggle to reform the church? Second, how may his understanding and practice of ordination be related to Nonconformity? Third, what relationship existed between Puritan practice and understanding and Wesley's own practice in his organization of the Methodist societies? Finally, do Wesley's teachings relative to certain aspects of the ministerial office indicate dependence upon Puritan teachings?

Wesley and Nonconformity

Albert Outler's insight that Wesley's voracious reading habits and his constantly changing pastoral experience were continually molding his theology reminds us that "experience," in its broadest sense, was the touchstone of Wesley's theology.[1] When new insights came, by whatever avenue, he willingly reformulated and revised both thought and practice. His attitudes toward church governance and its biblical bases clearly illustrate this pattern.

In January 1746 Wesley read a book that, along with other experiences, changed his attitude toward church governance and authority, an encounter that subsequently had momentous repercussions for his movement.

> On the road I read over Lord King's *Account of the Primitive Church.* In spite of the vehement prejudice of my education, I was ready to believe that this was a fair and impartial draught. But, if so, it would follow that bishops and presbyters are (essentially) of one order, and that originally every Christian congregation was a church independent on all others![2]

The *Minutes of the Methodist Conferences* (1747) incorporate insights gained from Lord King's study of the early church and the ministerial experiences of the decade that followed Wesley's 1738-39 reorientation of his ministry. The first question proposed in this section of the minutes obviously paraphrases criticism of Wesley and Methodism offered by some of his contemporaries:

> Q. You [Wesley] profess to obey both the governors and rulers of the Church, yet in many instances you do not obey them; how is this consistent? Upon what principles do you act, while you sometimes obey and sometimes not?
>
> A. It is entirely consistent. We act at all times on one plain uniform principlewe will obey the rulers and governors of the Church, whenever we can consistently with our duty to God, whenever we cannot, we will quietly obey God rather than man.
>
> Q. But why do you say, you are "thrust out of the churches?" Has not every Minister a right to dispose of his own church?

A. He ought to have, but in fact he has not. A Minister desires I should preach in his church. But the Bishop forbids him. That Bishop then injures him, and thrusts me out of that church.

Q. Does a church in the New Testament mean "a single congregation?"

A. We believe it does. We do not recollect any instance to the contrary.

Q. What instance or ground is there then in the New Testament for a *National* Church?

A. We know none at all. We apprehend it to be a merely political institution.

Q. Are the three orders of Bishop, Priests, and Deacons plainly described in the New Testament?

A. We think they are; and believe they generally obtained in the churches of the apostolic age.

Q. But are you assured that God designed the same plan should obtain in all churches, throughout all ages?

A. We are not assured of this; because we do not know it is asserted in Holy Writ.

Q. If this plan were essential to a Christian church what must become of all the foreign Reformed Churches?

A. It would follow, they are no parts of the church of Christ! A consequence full of shocking absurdity.

Q. In what age was the Divine right of Episcopacy first asserted in England?

A. About the middle of Queen Elizabeth's reign. Till then all the Bishops and Clergy of England continually allowed and joined in the ministrations of those who were not episcopally ordained.

Q. Must there be numberless accidental varieties in the government of various churches?

A. There must, in the nature of things. For, as God variously dispenses His gifts of nature, providence, and grace, both the offices themselves and the officers in each ought to be varied from time to time.

Q. Why is it, that there is no determinate plan of church government appointed in the Scripture?

A. Without doubt, because the wisdom of God had a regard to this necessary variety.[3]

Wesley's reading of another treatise a decade later further confirmed the position taken in these minutes.

> That it [episcopal order] is prescribed in Scripture I do not believe. This opinion (which I once heartily espoused) I have been heartily ashamed of ever since I read Dr. Stillingfleet's *Irenicon*. I think he has unanswerably proved that neither Christ nor His Apostles prescribed any particular form of Church government, and that the plea for the divine right of Episcopacy was never heard of in the primitive Church.[4]

These passages clearly show Wesley's willingness, rather early in his evangelical career, to recognize as authentic differing patterns of church order. This recognition was not, however, foreign to Anglican divines either in Wesley's own time or during the preceding two centuries, as Norman Sykes has ably shown.[5] Such staunch advocates of episcopacy as Jewel, Hooker, Bancroft, Andrewes, and Laud willingly recognized that, where the necessities of history deprived a church of the episcopacy, valid ministries and sacraments were present under other patterns of ordination even though these were most often considered "defective" forms. Sykes asserts that the early Anglican apologists argued for episcopacy on the grounds of its apostolic lineage, appealing to history and tradition as their authority; but, facing pressures generated by Puritan advocacy of divine inspiration for the Presbyterian order, the Anglican position moved toward a more rigid affirmation of episcopacy as divinely established.[6] Nevertheless, among all but the most extreme advocates, episcopacy "was held to be not of dominical but of apostolic appointment, and as *divino jure* only in that sense; as necessary where it could be had, but its absence where historical necessity compelled did not deprive a church of valid ministry and sacraments."[7] Wesley's intimation, in the minutes just quoted, that "foreign Reformed Churches" would necessarily be rejected as "no parts of the church of Christ" under Anglican formulations was evidently unfounded, though it may have been a common opinion shared by many of his contemporaries.[8]

Anglicans accepted as authentic the ministerial orders of some "foreign" churches if they could be related to the early church. Such recognition was not extended, however, to the English Dissenters because, in postrevolution Anglican understanding, Dissenters had been under no imperative of historical necessity to separate. By their voluntary rejection of episcopacy they were in error, thereby bringing on themselves the condemnation and restrictions they sustained in England. Wesley generally shared this Anglican interpretation, yet he parted from many of his contemporaries by carefully distinguishing Nonconformists (those ejected by the Act of Uniformity of 1662) from Dissenters (those voluntarily choosing to leave the church).[9] Consequently, he could recognize the validity of the church order established by the Nonconformists even as he affirmed the Church of England order to be the "best" among the various patterns.

Wesley's statement previously quoted that "both the offices themselves and the officers in each [church] ought to be varied from time to time" goes beyond general Anglican opinion. To admit various forms where "necessity demanded" was not to admit that such orders "ought" to be. An even more important departure was Wesley's explanation of the principle that guided his attitudes toward church governance: "We will obey the rulers and governors of the Church, whenever we can consistently with our duty to God, whenever we cannot, we will quietly obey God rather than man." This express willingness to disobey "the rulers and governors of the Church" where he thought obedience would be inconsistent with the will of God was doubtless viewed by his contemporaries as undercutting the real authority of the episcopacy and church order as regularly established. The principle is very close, if not identical, to that guiding moderate Puritans in their refusal to conform in 1662.

Wesley, in Methodist annual conference minutes of 1745, affirmed another position that can be interpreted as being at variance with traditional episcopal order:

> Q.6. Is mutual consent absolutely necessary between the pastor and his flock?
> A. No question. I cannot guide any soul unless he consent to be guided by me. Neither can any soul force me to guide him if I consent not.
> Q.7. Does the ceasing of this consent on either side dissolve this relationship?
> A. It must, in the very nature of things. If a man no longer consents to be guided by me, I am no longer his guide. I am free. If one will not guide me any longer, I am free to seek one who will.[10]

At the very least, such a sentiment of voluntary association of a pastor and parishioners raised questions relative to traditional patterns of episcopal authority, an authority that allowed episcopal appointment of pastors to a local parish without reference to "voluntary consent" by the parishioners.[11] Although the comment does seem to raise such questions, Wesley appears to be speaking about the mutual consent of pastor and parishioners within the principles of episcopacy. Nevertheless, this line of reasoning concerning mutual consent was very similar to the justification used by the Puritans of congregational persuasion for their separation from the Established Church.[12]

Wesley's comment on voluntary consent describes his understanding of the nature of his Methodist societies. The societies were voluntary associations in which each person participated only as long as he or she agreed to be led by Wesley.

Thus, some of Wesley's opinions on church order were at variance with dominant Anglican interpretations and were similar to those prevalent among moderate Puritans. However, we should not assume that any of these opinions meant Wesley condoned or encouraged separation from the Church of England. They were later to bear fruit in his willingness to ordain, but, a true son of the Church of England, he never relinquished his opinion that it was "the best constituted National Church in the world" and must be stood by at all costs.[13]

Wesley's sentiments relative to those who made up the varied groups among the Nonconformists were clearly stated in the following passage. Having commented that the Quakers and Baptists caused much disturbance and trouble by arguing about "opinions and externals," he chastened them for separating themselves from the Established Church, then continued:

> The same occasion of offense was, in a smaller degree, given by the Presbyterians and Independents; for they also spent great part of their time and strength in opposing the commonly-received opinions concerning some of the circumstantials of religion; and, for the sake of these, separated from the Church.
>
> But I do not include that venerable man, Mr. Philip Henry, nor any that were of his spirit, in that number. I know they abhorred contending about externals. Neither did they separate themselves from the Church. They continued therein till they were driven out, whether they would or no. I cannot but tenderly sympathize with these; and the more because this is, in part, our own case. Warm men spare no pains at this very day to *drive* us out of the Church.[14]

The crux of the matter always lay in separation. Wesley had little sympathy for those who willingly separated; yet he could readily identify himself with those who were forced out. The ejections of Philip Henry, Richard Baxter, and others in 1662 were undoubtedly more complex than presented here by Wesley and in some sense were dependent upon "opinions"; yet Wesley's statement reveals the touchstone by which he distinguished between the Puritan factions and indicates those he could and could not readily accept.

The same principle guided his evaluation of early Puritanism:

> That "the irregularities of Mr. Cartwright did more harm in the course of a century than all the labours of his life did good" is by no means plain to me. . . . I look upon him and the body of Puritans in that age (to whom the German Anabaptists bore small resemblance) to have been both the most learned and pious men that were then in the English nation. Nor did they separate from the Church, but were driven out, whether they would or no. The vengeance of God which fell on the posterity of their persecutors I think is no imputation on Mr. Cartwright or them, but a wonderful scene of divine Providence.[15]

His sympathy for the Nonconformists was further confirmed on several occasions as we can see in this *Journal* entry of April 3, 1754:

> In my hours of walking I read Dr. Calamy's *Abridgment of Mr. Baxter's Life*. What a scene is opened here! In spite of all the prejudice of education, I could not but see that the poor Nonconformists had been used without either justice or mercy, and that many of the Protestant Bishops of King Charles had neither more religion, nor humanity, than the Popish Bishops of Queen Mary.[16]

"In spite of all prejudice of education" Wesley came to appreciate the Nonconformists.[17] He was quite conscious of breaking with the traditional pattern set for a minister of the Church of England; nevertheless, he was willing to take up differing opinions and forms when convinced of their legitimacy.[18]

Responding to his Dissenting contemporaries, who wrote defending separation, Wesley commented, "You do not write as did those excellent men, Mr. Baxter, Mr. Howe, Dr. Calamy, who seem always to speak, not laughing, but weeping."[19] Here again was revealed sympathy for "reluctant" Nonconformists.

Wesley returned to Philip Henry for an illustration of how the Methodists should look upon their relation to the Church of England: "Should we go to church to hear ourselves abused, by railing, yea, and lying accusations? What said that blessed man Philip Henry when his friend said (after hearing such a sermon), 'I hope, sir, you will not go to church anymore'? 'Indeed, I will go in the afternoon; if the minister does not know his duty, I bless God I know mine.'"[20] The Methodists were to follow Henry in attending and participating in the church, even where unwelcome and persecuted.

What may be said in evaluating these passages? Wesley's acceptance of a broad view of church government distinguished him from many of his fellow Church of England ministers. At the same time, his reasoning as to certain aspects of church order brought him close to moderate Puritan opinions on the topic. He stood, therefore, somewhere between the more rigid Anglican and Puritan positions. Unwilling to make any form of church government exclusive of all others (as had been the case of many moderate men in both parties the century before), he recognized the validity of the type of church government found among many Puritans. This allowed him, while believing the episcopal form to be preferable, to use the Puritan understanding where necessary for his own purposes. The passages just quoted also reveal his genuine sympathy for more conservative Nonconformists and establish his willingness to identify himself with their situation. Perhaps motivated in part at least by his own recognition of the similarity between their persecutions and his own, identification is present and provides another bond between the two traditions. His extensive use of Philip Henry and Richard Baxter to suggest proper attitudes toward the church again gave his people instruction patterned after a Puritan example.

Ordination

What relation did Wesley's understanding of church order, revealed in his evaluations of Nonconformity and the ordination practices found there, have to Wesley's own ordination, late in his life, of Methodist preachers to the ministerial office? This much-discussed topic is of particular interest to the present study since Wesley's ordinations effectively appropriated Presbyterian understandings and forms of ordination.

Wesley's ordinations, though legal and valid in his own understanding, were defended by him as the result "not of choice, but necessity" and would not have been carried out at all had there been any other alternative, an argument often used by Puritans in the previous century.[21] There was no question in Wesley's mind that the practice that he appropriated was that of the early church where, in his understanding, "presbyters" and "bishops" constituted a single ecclesiastical order. Similarities, therefore, between his ordinations and those exercised in Presbyterian churches were, in his mind, only coincidental. Nevertheless, the fact remains that he had been led to this understanding through the insights and writings of a Presbyterian author (Lord King). In addition, he could hardly ignore the reality that his practice was popularly identified with contemporary Presbyterians since this pattern of ordination had been practiced in the Scottish church and among English Presbyterians since the time of Queen Elizabeth.

Wesley expressed his justification and reasoning concerning the original ordinations for America in his letter to the American Methodists, wherein he applied the insights already noted:

> Lord King's *Account of the Primitive Church* convinced me many years ago that bishops and presbyters are the same order, and consequently have the same right to ordain. For many years, I have been importuned from time to time to exercise this right by ordaining part of our travelling preachers. But I have refused, not only for peace sake, but because I was determined as little as possible to violate the established order of the National Church to which I belonged.
>
> But the case is widely different between England and North America. Here there are bishops who have a legal jurisdiction: in America there are none, neither any parish ministers. So that for some hundred miles together there is none to baptize or to administer the Lord's Supper. Here, therefore, my scruples are at an

> end; and I conceive myself at full liberty, as I violate no order and invade no man's right by appointing and sending labourers into the harvest.
>
> I have accordingly appointed Dr. Coke and Mr. Francis Asbury to be Joint Superintendents over our brethren in North America; as also Richard Whatcoat and Thomas Vasey to act as elders among them, by baptizing and administering the Lord's Supper.[22]

Here Wesley clearly stated his conviction that he was acting both within the primitive church pattern and through the impetus of necessity, the cardinal Anglican criteria for "irregular" ordinations.

Wesley's equation of bishop and presbyter corresponded to the Presbyterian insistence that "presbyter" and "episcopos" were "only different designations for the same church officials."[23] Presbyterian equation of presbyter and bishop, following the general Reformed church tradition, allowed them to eliminate the position of bishop and retain only one title for the ministerial office, that of presbyter. The offices to which Wesley ordained, however, followed the Anglican practice of a two-stage structure "deacon" and "presbyter." Wesley generally substituted the designation "elder" for presbyter, yet in several instances used presbyter as the title.[24] Wesley ordained by the presbyterial pattern that called for the laying on of hands by at least three ordained presbyters. Such ordinations were a clear move beyond the ordinary Church of England pattern that required that a bishop, even though he was joined by presbyters, lay his hands on a candidate for an ordination to be authentic.

The rejection of episcopacy for Presbyterians meant denial of any concept of apostolic succession that might suggest an unbroken line of consecration. James Ainslie points out, however, that the Westminster Assembly's regulation concerning ordination[25] may be interpreted as incorporating some sense of "transmission" or "conveyance" of authority and doctrine.[26] Using this perception, the presbyters, through ordaining, pass on to others what they themselves have received both in authority and in doctrine; consequently, the rite is limited to "preaching presbyters"—those who had also received ordination to this office. Conversely, one may interpret the regulation as simply providing a form of ordination wherein presbyters plead for God to authorize the one they ordain without assuming this means "transmission" of authority. In either case ordination is regulated and carried out by those who have also received it. Ainslie has also shown that, though this restriction was written into the Westminster forms and, therefore, became the common practice, there was widespread difference among the Reformed churches on restrictions as to who might ordain—lay elders sometimes being included. The intent behind the Westminster pattern was clearly to establish standard ordinations providing unity and authority for the ministerial office.[27]

Wesley, too, rejected a linear concept of apostolic succession that depended on an uninterrupted succession of bishops because he doubted it could ever be proved; he considered it a "fable."[28] This opinion did not, however, require Wesley to reject an element of authoritative transmission being present in ordination. Rattenbury points out that Wesley's views here were "more akin to those of the Presbyterian Divines." He writes:

> There is no evidence at all that he [Wesley] thought "orders" could be given by any other persons than bishops and presbyters. He was, in this matter, not a High Church Episcopalian, but a High Church Presbyterian. Whether he taught that there was a special grace bestowed or transmitted by the laying on of hands is undemonstrable, but he obviously thought that authority to administer sacraments could only be transmitted by this method.[29]

Rattenbury's designation of Wesley as a high church Presbyterian in matters of ordination is useful, as it identifies him with those Presbyterians who held a restrictive view of the ministry and ordination and at the same time were willing to modify the Anglican pattern. According to Ainslie, some high church Presbyterians embraced a distinct linear-succession doctrine, claiming church power to have descended to them from Christ through the Roman Church and being no less effective or valid because of this.[30] Perhaps Colin Williams is correct when he suggests Wesley intended, in his criticism of succession, to reject any notion of a "mechanical succession" but not some form of succession itself, a position embraced by "high church" Presbyterians as well.[31]

Frederic Platt quotes Richard Whatcoat, one of those ordained by Wesley for America: "Rev. John Wesley, Thomas Coke, and James Creighton, presbyters of the Church of England, formed a presbytery and ordained Richard Whatcoat and Thomas Vasey deacons; and the next day by the same hands they were ordained elders."[32] The similarities between these ordinations and those of the Presbyterians are obvious. Ordination is a corporate act requiring the participation of more than one presbyter. It was the action of a presbytery signifying the unified body.[33] The Presbyterians insisted on ordination as the action of the whole presbytery in order to avoid the problems they saw in the "free" ordinations of the Independents, but in any case, they took, in general, the same form used by Wesley. Of course the Presbyterians claimed, like Wesley, the precedent of the early church.

Wesley, however, took ordination a step beyond what the

Presbyterians were willing to do. English and Scottish Presbyterians, following the pattern of joint ordination by peers, limited their ministerial office to that of a presbyter. According to John Simon, Wesley understood the early church presbyters at Alexandria to have joined together not only to ordain their peers but also to ordain a new bishop, chosen from their own number, so that they might avoid outside interference from other bishops.[34] Following this Alexandrian pattern, Wesley extended his ordinations to that of a superintendent (bishop).

Whether or not Wesley intended to retain the office of bishop by his designation of Thomas Coke and Francis Asbury as "superintendents" raised a fundamental question for English Methodists and resulted in much contention between various Methodist factions after Wesley's death. The consensus among scholars today is that Wesley intended to establish a modified episcopal system as the normal Methodist order, because that order "generally obtained in the churches of the apostolic age."[35] Certainly, in his own ministerial supervision of his preachers, he assumed the role of a scriptural "episcopos," and the pattern of Methodism he established conformed to an episcopal structure. For purposes of this study it is sufficient to note that when he became convinced he would have to ordain if his followers in America were to have the sacraments, he turned to the presbyterial pattern for his authorization.

Charles Wesley, much to his chagrin, recognized the clear implications of this step and its similarity to the Presbyterian form:

> I can scarcely believe it, that, in his eighty-second year, my brother, my old, intimate friend and companion, should have assumed the episcopal character, ordained elders, consecrated a bishop, and sent him to ordain our lay preachers in America! . . .
>
> Had they patience a little longer, they would have seen a real bishop in America, consecrated by three Scotch bishops who have their consecration from the English bishops, and are acknowledged by them as the same with themselves. . . . But what are your poor Methodists now? *Only a new sect of presbyterians*.[36]

We see the depth of Charles's bitterness over this action as he expressed himself in his most congenial medium, poetry:

> So easily are Bishops made
> By man's, or woman's whim?
> Wesley his hands on Coke hath laid,
> But who laid hand on Him?[37]

Though Wesley seemingly intended to establish an episcopal order, even if through the means of an essentially Presbyterian concept and pattern of ordination, his followers in England failed to carry out his plan. The Conference of 1794 eliminated ordination by simply ruling that "the distinction between ordained and unordained preachers shall be dropped."[38] Thereafter admission to full conference connection was considered sufficient ordination. Ordination by the imposition of hands was not resumed until 1836. When it was reinstated, the conference assumed this function with the "President, ex-president, secretary, and three of the other senior ministers" laying on their hands.[39] This form, of course, eliminated the necessity of a bishop and made ordination the function of the "presbyters" or "elders" acting for the conference. In British Methodism ordination is still considered to be a function of the conference.[40] In this it is again similar to Presbyterianism, for, as we have seen, Presbyterians always insisted that, though the preaching presbyters are the instruments or conveyors of ordination, it is the Presbytery that ordains.[41] However, other elements of British Methodism are not Presbyterian; thus, in the words of Edgar Thompson, it has "a constitution which is neither Episcopalian nor Presbyterian, but a unique composition of both."[42]

It has not been my intention in this review of Wesley's ordinations to suggest any dependence upon the Presbyterians, but to note that, as the historical situation developed in which he believed he had to ordain, Wesley invoked a presbyterial order and understanding. Once again there are similarities between the situation and practices of Puritan Presbyterians and Wesley that denote affinities between the two traditions, whether or not Wesley publicly recognized them or they would have been accepted as such by him.

For all of Wesley's vehement denial that his actions separated Methodism from the Church of England, he always defined separation in its strictly legal terms, an explanation that was inadequate in the eyes of the Church of England authorities.[43] In 1784, the year that he first ordinated, he obtained legal status for the Methodist Conference by a "Deed of Declaration" providing for a structure of conference leadership to succeed him. Both acts witness to his own recognition, never publicly admitted, that an almost certain separation would come after his death.[44] However, his ordinations were what finally put him and his movement beyond the pale of the Church of England, for this was a violation of a fundamental Anglican rule of order.[45] To take such a step was in reality to separate himself and his societies from that church, whether or not he would admit it. In Frank Baker's words, "By his ordinations John Wesley proclaimed himself in deeds if not in words a schismatic, though with the best of intentions and the clearest of consciences."[46]

The Societies

The Methodist societal system has long been recognized as a key element in its success. It gave the strength of communal spiritual fellowship to the movement and provided a structural framework peculiarly adapted to the needs of the common people. Here it was that the individual believer gained encouragement and guidance so necessary for continued growth in the faith.

The developed system or "connexion" of Methodist societies, firmly and permanently entrenched on the English scene by the late eighteenth century, was the result of more than a half century of development under the diligent and firm hand of John Wesley. It expressed his early conviction that *together*—through Christian fellowship—members discover, confirm, and grow in their faith.

The establishment of Wesleyan societies was, like so much of Methodism, a matter of historical circumstance. In both Bristol and London, according to his account, Wesley found himself sought out as a leader by small groups of people, who, responding to his preaching as well as that of George Whitefield and others, sought to enrich their faith and Christian life.[47] The earliest societies grew out of these requests as Wesley responded to persons seeking spiritual guidance.

The basic organizational pattern for such groups, however, had long been a part of Wesley's heritage. Samuel Wesley organized and led a "religious society" at Epworth that John must have recognized as a pattern for his own groups.[48] John and Charles's Oxford "Holy Club" incorporated into its patterns many of the structures and goals of earlier and contemporary Anglican religious societies. Wesley, in another accounting of the beginnings of the Methodist societies, traced them to the Holy Club.[49] In America, John formed a comparable group among his parish members. A similar structure was found among the Moravian Christians Wesley first encountered during his trip to America. Upon his return from America, Moravian societies in London significantly influenced his understanding of faith and fellowship. Numerous societal designs and patterns were then readily at hand.

John Simon's first work in his monumental series on Wesley, entitled *John Wesley and the Religious Societies*, contains his persuasive attempt "to show the affinities between the Religious and the Methodist Societies."[50] Here it becomes clear that, in many respects, Wesley consciously or unconsciously revived in his societies the principal features of these predecessor Anglican groups. Originally formed to encourage their members to seek spiritual "holiness," they, by design, avoided doctrinal controversy while insisting on a high degree of disciplined spiritual study and practice. Led by Anglican clergymen, they were influential in reemphasizing traditional Anglican spirituality, though they were often limited in their appeal to a select group within local parishes. From these groups, however, arose such far-reaching mission and evangelical work as that promoted by "The Society for Promoting Christian Knowledge," and "The Society for the Propagation of the Gospel in Foreign Parts." Simon, though certain that Wesley moved beyond the interest and abilities of these earlier societies, understood him to have preserved their "best characteristics" and to have been at one with their purpose—to promote holiness.[51]

A principal difference between Wesley's societies and similar Anglican groups was the Wesleyan societies' openness to all who might seek the fellowship, particularly the common people of the time. Wherever one might be in the social and economic spectrum, and at whatever stage of faith development, one could be part of Wesley's groups. Wesley clearly intended to distinguish his groups from the exclusiveness found among the Anglican groups.

Early within his societial work Wesley adopted a system of "bands" within the local societies. In these bands five to ten persons met frequently to "confess their faults one to another, and pray one for another, that they may be healed."[52] Clifford Towlson has convincingly argued that this system was a direct import from the Moravian practice instituted by Count von Zinzendorf at Herrnhut and followed by Böhler in London.[53] David Watson suggests that what Wesley gained from the Moravian patterns was the genius of the band, its "spiritual nurture the guiding to maturity of a faith which was received as a gift, by grace."[54] Such nurture incorporated confession, mutual accountability among members for the spiritual lives of each participant, and mutual encouragement-all within the context of a clear affirmation that such spiritual fellowship could be valid only if dependent on God's grace. Wesley's later disenchantment with the Moravians led him to question some aspects of the bands; some individuals could easily misuse them to monitor others and, unfortunately, this often led to a sense of spiritual elitism. As Methodist societies grew, the use of bands declined, but their positive contribution of an emphasis on mutual support and accountability were incorporated into the Methodist classes that succeeded them.

Although the identification of Wesley's societies with Anglican or Moravian precedents may be more obvious, another English form of religious society displays striking similarities to Wesley's groups: the Puritan "gathered church." Horton Davies notes that Wesley's societies may be "an amalgam of two great Puritan concepts namely 'the gathered church' and 'the priesthood of all believers.'"[55] Methodist appropriation of the Protestant principle often designated the "priesthood of all believers" included use of lay preachers, lay leaders in the societies, bands, and classes, and mutual sharing of responsibility among laypersons for one another's spiritual life. Such use calls for little additional comment. However, the similarities between Wesleyan societies and "the gathered church" merit investigation.

In early Puritanism the most obvious distinction between the Presbyterians and the Independents (Congregationalists) arose in differing interpretations of "the church." Independents insisted that a church was formed when redeemed believers *voluntarily* joined themselves together for mutual fellowship and worship. Local control and autonomy lay with the group. This principle rejected any "inherited, nominal, birthright type of Christianity" as found in the Church of England.[56] The Presbyterian form of church organization with its synods and presbyteries, in the understanding of the Independents, also infringed on local control and the voluntary nature of each church. Much controversy and debate resulted from these distinctions and lay at the root of Puritan inability to establish a unified church during the Interregnum. Davies notes, however, that "the ejection of the Puritan divines in 1662 and the failure to comprehend them in 1689 led all the Nonconformists to approximate to the Congregationalist conception of a 'gathered church.'"[57] With the ejection Puritans of whatever stripe were forced to "gather" their followers into homes and other meeting places for the functions of fellowship and worship.

Mutual Concern and Fellowship

Salient to this study are the characteristic features of these groups that resemble specific traits found in Wesley's societies. The church as a fellowship of mutually concerned individuals is the first of these features.

As Geoffrey Nuttall insightfully comments, a small group consciously separating from a larger body, and often persecuted by such, normally has a heightened appreciation of and demand for fellowship.[58] Such was the case for both Congregationalism and Methodism. Central to genuine fellowship, however, is the mutual help, encouragement, and support members draw from one another. Speaking of the Congregationalists, Nuttall declares: "This mutual care and 'watchfulness over each other's conversation' are precisely what we find recorded again and again in the church books and histories, from the first day of their formation."[59] The church covenant of Norwich was typical: "We will, in all love, improve our communion as brethren, by watching over one another, and as need shall be, counsel, admonish, reprove, comfort, relieve, assist, and bear with one another."[60] Similarly, Wesley characterized his societies as "a company of men having the form and seeking the power of godliness, united in order to pray together, to receive the word of exhortation, and to watch over one another in love, that they might help each other to work out their salvation."[61] The spiritual fellowship patterns developed among Puritan and Methodist groups are clearly analogous when one compares these descriptions. That Wesley recognized such similarity is evidenced by his response to an accusation that Methodists were Dissenters: "Although we frequently use extemporary prayer, and unite together in a religious society; yet we are not Dissenters in the only sense our law acknowledges."[62] Consistent with his rejection of any implication that Methodists were legally Dissenters, he does not deny similarity of his societal patterns to those of the gathered churches.

Along with the Congregationalists' mutual consent of members to watch over and be responsible for one another went an expectation of similar mutual consent between pastor and congregation. Without a traditional episcopal appointive system, such mutual understanding was necessary in the Congregational system. As we have seen, Wesley insisted on voluntary consent between pastor and parishioners. In doing so, he expressed a fundamental Congregational precept and, as Frank Baker asserts, indicated his essential agreement with the Congregational understanding. The 1745 annual conference minutes allowed either the preacher or a people to leave the other if "convinced it is for the glory of God and the superior good of their souls."[63] This expression of a Congregational principle did not, however, lead Wesley to reject a comprehensive appointive system. His understanding of the mutual consent present for pastor and parishioners assumed that an agency other than the local congregation would appoint the pastor. Consequently, in the pragmatic application of the theory by Wesley and his successors, Methodism characteristically subordinated mutual consent by relying on an authoritarian appointive procedure.

Personal Testimony

A second prominent feature of the Puritan fellowships was the sharing of one's religious experience through personal testimonials. Wesley does not make the testimonial of one's experience a requirement of admission to the community as did the Congregationalists; nevertheless, personal testimonials were a prominent feature of the Methodist societies.

Public expression of religious views and experiences was

unusual among common Englishmen, giving the testimonial another important and unanticipated consequence. Nuttall maintains the Congregationalists' requirement for public testimony trained an articulate laity, who quickly used this newly found aptitude outside the church.[64] The same was true for Methodism, where the small-group weekly meeting demanded public religious self-expression. Such lay testimony became an important factor in the spread of the gospel and trained members to offer spiritual guidance and support to fledgling converts. According to G. M. Trevelyan, these Puritan and Methodist attributes added to those of personal discipline, learned to a significant degree in these small groups, contributed a great deal to the character and self-reliance of nineteenth-century Englishmen.[65]

Holiness

Puritan congregations and Wesleyan societies shared a third characteristic: their perception of holiness as an essential testimony or witness to Christian faith. As we have seen, Puritan theology understood God's covenanted grace to manifest itself in holy living. Among Congregationalists this expectation took on another attribute. Church membership required not only a personal testimony confirming conversion but required additional verification through the witness of a holy life. Indeed, one had to become a "visible saint" to gain admittance, as indicated by this article from the church covenant at Altham: "We thus apprehend, that they only are worthy that are Saints visible to the eye of rational charity, or such as, professing faith and repentance, live not in the neglect of any Christian duty or in commission of any known notorious sin; having such a measure of knowledge as to lead Christ into the soul, and the soul to Christ."[66] Such visible holiness, required for admission, naturally was expected for continuation in good standing. Holiness became, then, for Congregationalists not only a witness to faith but an essential feature of membership.

In contrast, Wesley never made his insistence on holiness an entrance requirement to the societies. In fact, Methodist societies were known for their openness, requiring of an inquirer only a desire "to flee from the wrath to come, to be saved from their sins." This contrast signals a major difference between the Congregationalist understanding of holiness and that of Wesley. Nevertheless, the "Rules" for Wesley's United Societies stated, "Wherever this [desire] is really fixed in the soul, it will be shown by its fruits. It is therefore expected of all who continue therein, that they should continue to evidence their desire of salvation."[67]

Wesley's expectation that "fruits" would be shown in a Christian's life had the same consequence, if not the same motivation, as the Congregational insistence on a testimony or witness in holy living. Wesley continued in the "Rules" to chronicle in detail the inward and outward testimonies that characterize such a life. One worthy of continuing in the fellowship of the Methodist societies would no doubt have qualified as a Congregational "visible saint."[68] Holiness is, then, a common tenet for both Congregationalists and Methodists. Wesley's own passion for holiness must be traced to sources other than Puritanism, but it is one clearly shared with it.[69]

Freedom of Opinion

A fourth trait common to Congregational and Methodist societies was insistence upon freedom of opinion, a bulwark of Congregational thought and polity. Liberty of conscience, or the ability to choose voluntarily one's associations without the compulsion of forced belief, was inherent in the Congregationalists' whole understanding. It was quite natural, then, that they strongly asserted the corollary to liberty of conscience, freedom of opinion or independence of judgment in matters of religion. Because personal religious experience rather than doctrinal belief was the criterion of membership, the principle by which they accepted and continued persons in membership was "Faith in Christ; and Holiness of Life, without regard to this or that circumstance, or opinion in outward, and circumstantiall things."[70] This independence of thought led to a great variety of opinion among the Congregationalists and to many conflicts, but they vigorously sustained it.

Wesley's well-known description of a Methodist suggests his comparable appreciation for differences of opinion:

> The *distinguishing marks* of a Methodist are not his *opinions* of any sort. His assenting to this or that scheme of religion, his embracing any particular set of notions, his espousing the judgment of one man or of another, are all quite wide of the point. . . . But as to all opinions which do not strike at the root of Christianity, we "think and let think."[71]

Wesley's definition of "the root of Christianity," and the Congregationalist "Faith in Christ, and Holiness of life" statements, do in fact put restrictions upon their seemingly liberal sentiments. In both personal and congregational settings both Methodists and Congregationalists were much more circumspect in their acceptance of various "opinions" than these quotations might indicate; yet both traditions sought to allow freedom of opinion in all matters but those that lay at the very core of the Christian faith. It was this freedom of opinion, particularly as it applied to church polity, that George Eayrs sees as a principal affinity between the Nonconformists (including the Congregationalists) and Wesley.[72]

Wesley's openness to all, which included his unwillingness to judge doctrinal understandings, and his attitude toward "opinion" have often been cited to claim that Methodism makes no distinction between opinion or doctrine, nor insists on particular belief. Such usage misappropriates Wesley's insight expressed in these statements, which assert that God's grace is offered without regard to any conditions, including "opinion." His struggle with Moravian and Calvinist alike revolved around his attempt to keep doctrine from limiting God's grace and, in the midst of these conflicts, he hammered out his distinctive interpretation (and doctrine). Wesley most clearly formulated his doctrinal beliefs through the *ordo salutis*, where, as we have seen, repentance followed by faith initiated Christian life, which, when fully fruited, culminated in "entire sanctification."[73] This Wesleyan and Methodist order of salvation required clear and definitive belief but left no room for God's grace to be bound by human formulations.

Covenanted Discipline

Similarity between Congregational Puritanism and Wesleyan understandings of covenant, and of the call for close personal discipline in a member's daily living, form the fifth shared trait. Wesley's modification of the Puritan personal covenant for use in a corporate service provides useful data concerning the correlations between Methodist and Congregational use of church and personal covenants.

The most obvious difference in function of a covenant for the two groups lies in the use of covenants by Congregationalists to define articles of incorporation for their churches. A Congregational church covenant was personally accepted and usually signed or recited by all members.[74] It required faith and demonstrable holiness: In this sense holiness became an entrance requirement along with faith and commitment to the covenant itself. Wesley, on the other hand, used Joseph Alleine's personal covenant in the corporate setting of worship to help members renew and reevaluate their commitment to Christ and neighbor. Nevertheless, making the covenant a public and corporate service, prepared for by personal spiritual discipline, was similar to Congregational use. Although for Methodists it had no corporate enrollment implications, its objective was much the same as those of the Congregationalists: clear personal examination and commitment within a corporate setting. Congregationalism took this commitment into the structures of church organization, but the basic intent was the same: personal commitment (or recommitment) publicly proclaimed.

For the Congregational churches covenant was also used as a disciplinary tool. The covenant entered by a member had a twofold function: first, it represented the commitment between God and the believer and second, it was a commitment between the member and fellow members within the congregation. Any transgression of the covenant—usually through failure to live a holy life and sometimes in matters of belief—constituted grounds for expulsion from the church. Article 19 of the Savoy Declaration stated the procedure for correction and expulsion among the Congregationalists:

> Whereas some offenses are or may be known only to some, it is appointed by Christ that those to whom they are so known do first admonish the offender in private (in public offenses where any sin, before all), and in case of non-amendment upon private admonition, the offense being related to the Church, and the offender not manifesting his repentance, he is to be duly admonished in the Name of Christ by the whole Church, by the Ministry of the Elders of the Church; and if this Censure prevail not for his repentance, then he is to be cast out by Excommunication, with the consent of the Church.[75]

Based on the scriptural admonitions about reproof of one's neighbor, the failure to modify behavior led ultimately to breaking relationship with Christian neighbors.[76] Public acknowledgment that a member had broken the covenant, accompanied by the failure to repent within the formularies of the congregation, resulted in excommunication, the ultimate church construct of discipline. Such use of covenant made it a primary disciplinary tool among Congregationalists and other Puritan groups.

Although Methodists did not use covenant for the purpose of excommunication, there certainly were disciplinary implications to their societal commitments. Wesley understood the societies to be voluntary groups wherein one entered simply to "seek salvation." Covenant, though not required for membership, incorporated commitment to a lifestyle that required intense personal discipline. Requirements for continuation in the societies, therefore, looked much like the expectations found among Puritan churches: maturing faith and holiness of life. To enter a Methodist society was to commit oneself to definite societal and personal responsibilities. One agreed to abide by Methodist discipline; attend the class, band, and society meetings; and, most important, lead a holy life. Therefore, expulsion for failure to abide by this pattern was a definite and often-used method of regulation. Wesley and his preachers, also applying the scriptural formulary quoted in the Savoy Declaration, often found themselves "clearing the society rolls."[77] Development by the Methodists of the class ticket to "separate the precious from the vile" gave the pastor another powerful disciplinary tool to ensure faithful membership.[78] Authoritarian use of the class ticket occasionally bordered on the autocratic, as it placed in the hands of Wesley or his preachers almost total responsibility for judgment of whether a member conformed to the societal rules. Duncan Coomer suggests such authoritarianism had a precedent in Independence, where the "church meeting" could "wield quite as despotic an oversight of the lives of its members."[79]

Community discipline, grounded in expectations of holy living, was an obvious mark distinguishing both Puritans and Methodists. It provided a primary justification, in the minds of Wesley's contemporaries, for the identification of the two groups. Nevertheless, an important difference existed between their uses of expulsion. Wesley, because he understood his societies simply to be groups within the larger church, never perceived expulsion from a Methodist society to result in any significant change in the church relationship of that person nor in any lessening of its ministrations to him or her. Excommunication for Congregationalists, however, essentially put one "outside" the communion of the faithful. Wesley's understanding of the societies as only groups within the church, and his openness to all genuine seekers, lead Geoffrey Nuttall to credit Wesley with providing the basis for a world church, whereas Congregational exclusiveness tended to draw the parish closer, thereby limiting its appeal to the world at large.[80]

Gathered Communities

A final area of similarity, and a most important one, is that of the "gathered" nature of Methodist societies and Congregational churches. Nuttall maintains, and Haller supports him, that the earliest Congregationalists sought to establish their groups within the parochial framework, being in these situations "gathered" communities within the larger group.[81] In time they were forced out or willingly left the Established Church because of the strictures and impediments placed on their ministries. When this happened all Nonconformist groups, no matter their previous affiliations, were of necessity forced to form themselves into "gathered" communities. Their separation led them to defend their concepts. One of William Dell's sermons, included by Wesley in the *Christian Library,* defended such "gathered" churches, as well as their requirement of holiness:

> **There be some that talk much against New Doctrine, which is the old reproach of the Gospel; but surely there was never newer Doctrine than this, *that the Spiritual Church of the New Testament, should be made up of all the People that live in a Kingdom; and that all that are born in such a Nation, should necessarily be stones for the building up of the New Jerusalem.* This is a new Doctrine indeed, which neither the Old nor the New Testament owns;** *but was conveyed into the world by the spirit of antichrist.* **For God doth not now make any People, or Kindred, or Nation his Church; but gathers his church out of every People, and Kindred, and Nation; and none can be stones of this Building, but those that are** *first* **Elect, and** *after made* **precious, through a new Birth, and the gift of the Spirit.**[82]

A major criticism of the Congregationalists by men such as Baxter and Philip Henry before the Act of Uniformity (1662) was that they disregarded parish lines "gathering" their members indiscriminately.[83] However, when Baxter and Henry were ejected from the Church, they had little choice but to appropriate the pattern and perhaps see Dell's description in a more congenial light.

Wesley's movement had its share of trouble over just such charges, and Methodists often found themselves compared with the "gathered" churches in the earlier century. Like the Congregationalists before them, Methodists' disregard of parish lines and other ecclesiastical restrictions was seen by those of the Established Church as a clear Puritan pattern. Parish churches and some dioceses were, not surprisingly, declared closed to Methodist preachers over this issue.

When we turn to Wesley's *Advice to the People Called Methodist*, we find that he occasionally referred to his own societies as "gathered" communities. "Another peculiar circumstance of your present situation is that you are *newly united* together; that you are just gathered, or (as it seems) gathering rather, out of all other societies or congregations": "You are gathered out of so many other congregations."[84] Wesley openly advocated "gathering" members from whatever their religious community if they were obviously unbelievers or inactive believers. Could he have used the term "gathered" during his own time without raising the image of the earlier "gathered churches," so much a part of the English religious scene? It hardly seems possible. Indeed, he recognized this likely identification when, in defense of his movement later in the same treatise, he commented: "Whereas every other *religious* set of people, as soon as they were joined to each other, *separated themselves* from their former societies or congregations; you on the contrary, do not; nay, you absolutely disavow all desire of separation."[85]

On another occasion, in discussing the truth of the common

accusation that he was "gathering churches out of churches," he recognized that such identification would often be made: "If you mean only gathering people out of buildings called churches, it is. But if you mean, dividing Christians from Christians, and so destroying Christian fellowship, it is not."[86] It is interesting, however, to note that in this expanded statement his description of other churches strongly suggested that they did not contain Christians, nor were they places of Christian fellowship. In this assertion he pointedly used the same reasoning the Puritans employed in "gathering" new Christian communities in the previous century, but his dedication to the Church of England would not allow him to take the step of separation. No matter how clearly he could enunciate the ineffectiveness of the Church of England and other groups and recognize the reasoning that underlay previous separations, separation was not the only logical step—at least for himself. He could only be a critical son still respecting and honoring the parental institution no matter how wayward it might be. Coomer is therefore correct when he says that Wesley never accepted the "gathered church" principle in the sense that he never accepted separation as a part of that principle, but he certainly used the pattern and some elements of its justification in forming his own societies.[87] Horton Davies can, consequently, assert that Methodism was eventually forced by circumstance to become "a connection of 'gathered' churches."[88]

In view of these real similarities between the "gathered church" and Wesley's societies, are we able to claim relationship between the two? Wesley clearly recognized and accepted some more obvious parallels but did not allow any attempt to identify Methodism with the Congregationalists or other Dissenters. To do so would have vitiated his personal commitment to the Church of England. That he also recognized the other similarities discussed here seem self-evident: fellowship, holiness, freedom of opinion, personal and corporate discipline, and the principles that called for a gathered community; yet the dangers of identification and his personal understanding of the Church of England led him to deny what seemed obvious to others. Even denial did not, however, keep him from commending the Puritan tradition and the contributions of its leading advocates of the "gathered church," such persons as John Owen, William Dell, and Lewis Stuckley. We may, therefore, legitimately claim some areas of true affinity, possibly neither as pronounced nor as direct as can be seen in his relation to the Anglican and Moravian religious societies, but still present.

Rupert Davies, reflecting recent British Methodist scholarship, understands attempts to identify Wesley's movement with patterns of Nonconformity to exhibit a predominantly nineteenth-century pattern of interpretation. Davies emphasizes Wesley's natural affiliation to be with the Anglican establishment and its religious societies.[89] Perhaps this is the current Methodist interpretation, but, as we have seen, contemporary Congregational scholars Horton Davies and Geoffrey Nuttall might disagree as they point to significant affinities with the gathered churches. Whatever judgment is made regarding modern interpretations of Wesley's relationship and affinity to preceding groups, the distinctive similarities between Methodist societies and the "gathered church" tradition suggest that the tradition deserves attention and consideration in any comprehensive study of Methodism.

The Ministry

True to his principle of using profitable material or example wherever he found it, Wesley's instructions for his preachers directly appropriated Puritan sources when he turned to the subject of pastoral duties. Late in 1749 Wesley read the recently published *Account of the Life of the Late Rev. Mr. David Brainerd*, edited by Jonathan Edwards.[90] This description of a Puritan missionary working among Native Americans enjoyed great popularity in England. Wesley, impressed with Brainerd's faith, abridged the work soon after its publication, and this work became a favored Methodist tract reprinted many times over the next few years.[91]

Throughout his ministry, when faced with local pastors' chafing under the exigencies of their condition or lagging in dedication to their tasks, Wesley turned to Brainerd.[92] Indeed, the recommendation was included in Methodism's earliest ministerial handbook, *The Minutes of the Conferences*, and retained its place there throughout the several editions and revisions made during Wesley's lifetime.

> Q. What can be done in order to revive the work of God where it is decayed? A. (1) Let every Preacher read carefully over the "Life of David Brainerd." Let us be followers of him, as he was of Christ, in absolute self-devotion, in total deadness to the world, and in fervent love to God and man. Let us but secure this point, and the world and the devil must fall at our feet.[93]

For Wesley, Brainerd's dedication under adverse and discouraging conditions and his ministry spent for others served as an example of a totally dedicated minister.

Of more consequence for the actual training of pastors, however, was Wesley's inclusion in the *Minutes* of a substantial set of instructions drawn directly from Richard Baxter's *Gildas Salvianus: The*

Reformed Pastor. This treatise, written by Baxter at the height of Puritan power and control in the English church, appealed to pastors to dedicate themselves to "private instruction and catechizing." Providing an agenda for pastoral ministry, it became the principal work of its kind among Puritans, serving as a significant manual for Nonconformist ministers. Wesley adopted its main features and methods to guide the Methodist preachers in the all-important responsibility of house-to-house visitation and instruction.

While he recommended the work as early as 1755, it was in the 1766 revision of the *Minutes* that he incorporated a succinct abridgment of large sections of the treatise with the following introduction:[94]

> We must instruct them from *House to House*: Till this is done, and that in good earnest, the *Methodists* will be little better than other People.
>
> Can we find a better Method of doing this than Mr.Baxter's? If not, let us adopt it without delay. His whole Tract, entitled *Gildas Salvianus*, is well worth a careful Perusal. A short Extract from it I have subjoined. Speaking of visiting from House to House, he says, p. 351.[95]

Wesley then inserted into the *Minutes* some six pages of abridged materials from Baxter's work. Though reduced somewhat in later editions of the *Minutes*, this abridgment was to stand throughout Wesley's lifetime as the standard Methodist direction for visitation and private spiritual instruction. The Puritan demand for the religious cultivation of the whole person wherein a most intimate and exacting relationship could be developed between pastor and parishioner was almost identical to that of Wesley's own teachings. It is not surprising, therefore, that Baxter's Puritan pattern became an example for Methodists and in the *Minutes* is the very instruction itself.

Baxter's directions included in Wesley's *Minutes* illustrate some of Wesley's most careful and, at the same time, extensive abridging. Following his usual pattern, Wesley freely paraphrased and condensed the major points. Because the work was to be used as specific instruction for Methodist pastors, Wesley made changes adapting the instruction to the societies rather than the parish system within which Baxter worked.[96] He also eliminated comments relative to the situation of the church in Baxter's own time. Wesley's personal preferences are evident in his recommendation that, while each morning was to be spent in study, each afternoon should include house-to-house visitation. Baxter's recommendation had been that visitation occupy two days of the week. Omitted was an extensive section in which Baxter gave some twenty reasons for the necessity of pastoral visitation, ranging from its arising out of scriptural precept to comments reflecting seventeenth-century English perceptions of ministry.[97] Evidently Wesley assumed that its necessity was self-evident, or perhaps his own requirement that his preachers carry out such personal instruction was considered sufficient justification.

On the whole, however, Wesley was substantially true to Baxter's major instructions, even to the point of including apt illustrations and casual comments. Although a detailed examination of these instructions is not necessary, a summary of the major points gives insight into why these men considered such work to be imperative and illustrates how the Methodists, through Puritan instruction, were to carry on their visitation.

Wesley's abridgment begins with Baxter's catalog of the human foibles that hinder such work. Pastors would be hampered in the work, for they would discover themselves to be lazy and dull; bashful; of a "base, man pleasing temper"; unwilling to jeopardize their own "fleshly" interests, that is, their tithes or financial support; unskillful in the work; and, most important, unfaithful or weak. All of these make it most difficult to convince and sustain others in the faith. Besides these difficulties, a pastor often finds among the people an unwillingness to be taught, dullness that makes it difficult to teach them anything, ignorance to the point of inability to understand the pastor, and when "desirable impressions have been made on their hearts," they may soon die away because they do not receive continuous cultivation.[98] Difficult as the task might be under these conditions, it is absolutely necessary; for, Baxter suggested, many of those who have attended services regularly and heard good sermons for many years did not really understand their own sinful condition or the nature of the gospel. **"I have found by experience that [one of these]** *an ignorant set that hath been an improfitable hearer so long,* **hath** *got* **[learned] more** *knowledge and remorse of conscience* **in half an hour's close discourse, than** *they did* **from ten years' public preaching."**[99]

In his usual verbose style Baxter included a series of objections that were often raised against this kind of pastoral work and proceeded to answer them in detail. Of the two Wesley included, the first examined the objection that such intensive private instruction would leave no time for necessary study. Baxter answered by pointing out that "saving of souls" was more important, or in Wesley's version, "gaining knowledge is a good thing, but saving souls is a better."[100] One might also find such work actually practical, as it contributes to better understanding, and, if given the correct amount of time, there will still be time enough for study. But if a choice must be made between the two, **"I would throw by all the**

libraries in the world, rather than be guilty of the perdition of one soul; *at least I know this is my duty.*"[101] Such was the opinion of Baxter and Wesley, both of whom, in other settings, strongly recommended and required rigid study patterns for the minister. The other objection used by Wesley was Baxter's comment on the supposition that the people would not submit to such a course of instruction. Here Wesley takes only one of Baxter's several answers: **"If some** *refuse our help* **[do not], others will** *accept* it **[gladly]; and the success with them may be so much, as may answer all our labour."**[102] Without question this task would tax all the skill of the minister and was in many ways far harder than study or preaching.

Correctly handling a visit or consultation with a family, one should, after speaking with them together, "take then the persons one by one, and deal with them as far as you can in private, out of the hearing of the rest."[103] In this private discussion one was to hear what each knew of the catechism (or for Wesley, what the children knew of the "Instructions for Children").[104] Such discussion was followed by asking (presumedly the more mature) "some of the weightiest points" of the gospel. Because private instruction was designed primarily as a learning experience, questions might be accompanied by suggesting appropriate answers, particularly where an individual did not seem to understand and/or to be able to answer. Having ascertained what all members of the family knew of correct religion, the pastor was prepared to instruct them "according to their capacities." If a person was unconverted, the pastor should seek to help that individual understand his or her condition. All persons in the household were to receive a "strong exhortation" to duty and to the use of every means available to secure a right relation with God. Before leaving the house, according to Baxter, one may comment, "I pray you take it not ill that I have put you to this trouble, or dealt thus freely with you! It is as little pleasure to me as to you. If I did not know these things to be true and necessary, I would have spared this labour to myself and you."[105] This must have appeared too much like an apology to Wesley, for he omitted it from his abridgment. One was to close by asking the head of the house to carry on this work of instruction by examining the household at least each Sunday evening.

All of this should be done in the best spirit. One must remember to "speak differently according to the difference of the persons that you have to deal with." Hence, it was to be done in plain language with "Scripture proof for all you say" and with due seriousness.[106] Here, in capsule form, we see the Puritan outline (usually elaborated in much more detail) of proper spiritual instruction.

In later years Wesley added the comment, "Do this in earnest, and you will soon find what a work you take in hand, in undertaking to be a Travelling Preacher!"[107] Puritan instruction had become the criterion by which Methodists would measure their traveling preachers.

Because Wesley's helpers were, for the most part, lay pastors without the opportunity to administer the sacraments, this pastoral work assumed even greater importance. Supplementing the fellowship and discipline of societal and class organization, it contributed to the genius of the movement. Wesley's dependence on Puritan precept and teaching in this important pastoral function is, therefore, of major relevance.

As we have repeatedly seen, Wesley's image of the Christian life and his instructions in its practice reflect strong affinities with the Puritan ethos. Although some may not have been consciously recognized by Wesley, they are nevertheless clearly evident. Others he readily accepted and appropriated. In the case of ministerial instruction, he was unquestionably dependent on the Puritan pattern. Wesley's tenacious refusal to separate from the Church of England—though it has been shown he may have seen separation not only as a threat but perhaps inevitable—could only retard but not stop Methodism from moving toward a closer identity with Nonconformity. Only a truly unique combination of intense dedication to the Church of England and affinity with and sympathy for some aspects of Puritanism could produce one who so vigorously held the two together and lived with the resultant tensions.

Notes

1. Albert Outler, "John Wesley: Folk-Theologian," *Theology Today*, 34 (July, 1977): 150.

2. *Works*, 20:112. Lord Peter King, a Dissenter, wrote *Enquiry into the Constitution, Discipline, Unity, and Worship of the Primitive Church* (1691) to justify the comprehension of Dissenters in the Church of England at the close of the seventeenth century. King recognized both bishop and presbyter and a distinction in their offices but saw them equal "in order." King's equation of the orders was to have profound influence on Wesley's understanding of church governance throughout his ministry. (See Edgar W. Thompson, *Wesley, Apostolic Man: Some Reflections on Wesley's Consecration of Dr. Thomas Coke* [London: Epworth Press, 1957], 23-9, and Frank Baker, *John Wesley and the Church of England*, 147-48.)

3. *MMC*, 35-36.

4. *Letters*, 3:182. It is not clear when Wesley read Stillingfleet's work *The Irenicum, a Weapon Salve for the Church's Wounds* (London, 1659) but certainly by the time of this letter, July 3, 1756. Stillingfleet, Bishop of

Worcester, had written the work to show all church parties emerging from the civil war that neither the New Testament nor the early church prescribed a particular form of church government. See Baker, *John Wesley and the Church of England*, 145-46, for further information on Stillingfleet's position.

5. Norman Sykes, *Old Priest and New Presbyter* (Cambridge: University Press, 1956). Sykes provides an extended and valuable investigation of Anglican interpretations of church order.

6. Sykes, *Old Priest and New Presbyter*, 60. Wesley is, therefore, correct in noting that only from the middle of Elizabeth's reign had the divine right argument become dominant.

7. Sykes, *Old Priest and New Presbyter*, 81.

8. Recognition of such churches allowed the Archbishop of Canterbury to approve the use of the Moravians in a Church of England missionary enterprise. When inquiry was made as to "whether anything in their [the Moravians] Doctrines was so far repugnant to those of the Church of England as to make it improper to employ some of the Brethren in instructing the Negroes in Christianity," his opinion was "that he had long been acquainted by Books with the Moravian Brethren, and that they were apostolical and Episcopal, not sustaining any Doctrines repugnant to the thirty-nine Articles of the Church of England; and that he was confirmed in these sentiments of them by the Conferences he had lately had with the Count of Zinzendorf." Peter Böhler was one of the missionaries appointed under this approval. (*Minutes of the Associates of the Late Dr. Bray* [Library of Congress Microfilm No. 665], 3:13.)

9. *Works*, 3:474-75. See Chapter 1 of this study for a more detailed discussion of Wesley's attitude toward Noncomformists.

10. *MMC*, 27.

11. Colin Williams (*John Wesley's Theology Today*, 220) maintains that Wesley used this argument to justify "his invasion of the parishes of other presbyters on the ground that they had refused to give true guidance to their parishioners, and that therefore the parishioners were no longer obliged to submit to their guidance."

12. See Nuttall, *Visible Saints*, 88ff.

13. *Letters*, 7:239.

14. *Works*, 11:319-20. "We believe it utterly unlawful to separate from the Church unless sinful terms of communion were imposed; just as did Mr. Philip Henry, and most of those holy men that were contemporary with them" (*Letters*, 6:326).

15. *Works*, 26:235.

16. *Works*, 20:485. The same sentiment was expressed, as well as his opinion of the "circumstantials" over which the Puritans argued, in this *Journal* entry: "I snatched a few hours to read *The History of the Puritans*. I stand in amazement: First, at the execrable spirit of persecution which drove those venerable men out of the Church, and with which Queen Elizabeth's clergy were as deeply tinctured as ever Queen Mary's were. Secondly, at the weakness of those holy confessors, many of whom spend so much of their time and strength in disputing about surplices and hoods, or kneeling at the Lord's Supper" (*Works*, 20:163).

17. For Wesley's opinion of the Act of Uniformity and the Act against Conventicles, as well as another expression of his deep sympathy for those who suffered under the strictures of these measures, see his tract *Thoughts upon Liberty* in *Works* (Jackson), 11:39.

18. Wesley hoped to modify the "prejudices of education" he had experienced as he designed his own educational enterprises. He included Daniel Neal's *History of the Puritans* among the textbooks of the Kingswood School, where the sons of his preachers were trained (Newton, *Methodism and the Puritans*, 8-9).

19. *Letters*, 3:251. "I finished the 'Gentleman's Reasons' (who is a Dissenting minister in Exeter). In how different a spirit does this man write from honest Richard Baxter! The one dipping, as it were, his pen in tears, the other in vinegar and gall. Surely one page of that loving, serious Christian weighs more than volumes of this bitter, sarcastic jester" (*Works*, 21:10).

20. *Letters*, 7:333. This evidently was a favorite illustration, for Wesley records it as his own reason to attend church after a poor sermon (*Works*, 22:23). In *An Account of the Life and Death of Mr. Philip Henry* it is recorded thus: "Once when one of the Curates preached a bitter Sermon against the Dissenters, on a Lord's Day Morning; some wondered that Mr. Henry would go again in the Afternoon, for the second part; *But* (saith he) *if he do not know his Duty, I know mine; and I bless God I can find Honey in a Carcase*" (Henry, *Philip Henry*, 121 [*CL*, 28:340]).

21. *MMC*, 192.

22. *Letters*, 7:238-39.

23. James L. Ainslie, *The Doctrines of Ministerial Order in the Reformed Churches of the 16th and 17th Centuries* (Edinburgh: T. & T. Clark, 1940), 92.

24. Baker, *John Wesley and the Church of England*, 268.

25. "Every minister of the Word is to be ordained by imposition of hands, and prayer, with fasting, by these preaching presbyters to whom it doth belong" (*The Form of Presbyterial Church Government and of Ordination of Ministers Agreed upon by the Assembly of Divines at Westminster* [Edinburgh: Printed by E. Robertson, 1766], 535, cited hereafter as *Westminster Form of Church Government*).

26. Ainslie, *Doctrines of Ministerial Order*, 217. Ainslie is rather reluctant to incorporate this interpretation of the Assembly's rubric, for he evidently would like to dismiss any concept of "transmission" when it relates primarily to the office of the minister and his authority to administer the sacraments, although he makes an interesting case for "doctrinal succession," placing the emphasis on the succession of ministers who have taught a "true" doctrine. Norman Sykes (*Old Priest and New Presbyter*, 38) credits Bishop Jewell with interpreting apostolic succession "as a succession of doctrine, not of office."

27. Ainslie, *Doctrines of Ministerial Order*, 186-90.

28. *Works*, 21:307.

29. J. Ernest Rattenbury, *Wesley's Legacy to the World* (London: Epworth Press, 1938), 193.

30. Ainslie, *Doctrines of Ministerial Order*, 217-18.

31. Williams, *John Wesley's Theology Today*, 226.

32. Frederic Platt, "Wesley's Ordinations—A Retrospect," *LQHR* 160 (1953): 65-66.

33. "Ordination is the act of a presbytery, the power of ordering the whole work of ordination is in the whole presbytery. . . . The preaching presbyters orderly associated . . . are those to whom the imposition of hands doth appertain" (*Westminster Form of Church Government*, 534; cf. Ainslie, *Doctrines of Ministerial Order*, 188-89).

34. John Simon, *John Wesley, The Last Phase* (London: Epworth Press, 1934), 229.

35. *MMC*, 36. Luke Tyerman expressed the opinion of much of early English Methodism when he stated that Wesley, in ordaining Coke, only intended this as a "mere formality to recommend his delegate to the favour of the Methodists in America: Coke, in his ambition, wished and intended it to be considered as an ordination to a bishopric" (*Life and Times of the Reverend John Wesley*, 3:434). This, however, leaves much to be explained, for (1) if Wesley had not intended some form of the episcopacy, why did he participate in the "laying on of hands" for Coke, who was already a presbyter in the Church of England and presumably would have the same powers as Wesley, for whom only an introduction would have been necessary to establish the office of superintendent? (2) Why was it necessary for Wesley in 1788 to consecrate Alexander Mather to the superintendency in England instead of merely appointing him to the office if it was not to be a consecrated office distinct from the other ministers? Even though a bishop or superintendent might carry only equivalent powers of ordination with presbyters and is, therefore, distinguished from a presbyter only in terms of function, the office is nevertheless distinct and one to which a candidate is installed through consecration or ordination. It seems to have been Wesley's intention that Mather be responsible for carrying on the ordinations when that became necessary after Wesley's death.

Interestingly, in both the cases of Coke and Mather, Wesley's personal diary records the word "ordained" when referring to these events (Baker, *John Wesley and the Church of England*, 269, 280). Edgar Thompson quotes Pawson, one of the preachers Wesley ordained for Scotland: "In order, therefore, to preserve all that was valuable in the Church of England among the Methodists, he ordained Mr. Mather and Dr. Coke bishops. These he undoubtedly designed should ordain others. Mr. Mather told us so at the Manchester Conference, but we did not then understand him" (Edgar Thompson, "Episcopacy: John Wesley's View," *LQHR* 181 [1956]: 117).

It should also be noted that Wesley's term for this office "superintendent" was that used in some of the European Reformation churches and in Scotland for a period and is, in fact, the Latin equivalent of the word "bishop." Many early Anglican divines evidently would have preferred this designation and understood the European churches to have retained the office of bishop under a different designation (Sykes, *Old Priest and New Presbyter*, 14-15, 246). Wesley perhaps intended to do the same thing. At least his participation in ordination and the changing of the designation of "bishop" to "superintendent" and that of "presbyter" to "elder" would indicate a modified episcopal form and order. According to Frank Baker, in the case of the two men Wesley ordained besides Mather for work in England, Henry Moore and Thomas Rankin, Wesley used the term "presbyter" because these ordinations were intended to be valid in England, where this term would be more congenial (Baker, "Wesley's Ordinations," *WHSP* 24 [1943-44]:76). In any case, a modified episcopacy seems to have been Wesley's intention. Frank Baker's *John Wesley and the Church of England*, 256-82, provides the most comprehensive recent investigation of the issue.

36. Tyerman, *Life and Times of the Reverend John Wesley*, 3:439-40 (italics added: C. Wesley's original drafts may be found in the Methodist Archives, John Ryland's Library of the University of Manchester). As the rest of the letter indicates, Charles sees no future for the Methodists, for they, through "vain janglings," will, "like other sects of Dissenters, come to nothing." The dissensions among the Methodists immediately following Wesley's death almost substantiated Charles's prediction.

37. Frank Baker, *Representative Verse of Charles Wesley* (Nashville: Abingdon Press, 1962), 368.

38. George Smith, *History of Wesleyan Methodism* (London: Longman, Green, Longman, & Roberts, 1863), 2:24, cf. 234-35.

39. Smith, *History of Wesleyan Methodism*, 3:327.

40. Thompson, "Episcopacy" *LQHR* 181 (1956): 117.

41. Exact correspondence would require that the Presbyterian General Assembly ordain, but in either case those ordaining are acting as instruments of the governing body.

42. Thompson, "Episcopacy" *LQHR* 181 (1956): 117.

43. Commenting on his ordinations, he defines his concept of separation: "If anyone is pleased to call this *separation from the Church*, he may. But the law of England does not call it so; nor can anyone properly be said so to do, unless out of conscience he refuses to join in the service, and partake of the Sacraments administered therein" (*MMC*, 192).

44. *Works* (Jackson), 8:329-31.

45. Thompson, "Episcopacy" *LQHR* 181 (1956): 116. George Eayrs points out that not only did this ordination "dissent from the Church as by law established" but Wesley's use of extemporaneous prayer, his introduction of "unauthorized" services, and his disregard for parish lines and the authorization of bishops to preach in appointed places, as well as his establishment of a conference as the ecclesiastical authority over Methodism, must also be considered. These actions established in reality a separate Methodism whether or not Wesley recognized it. In each of these practices he stands close to the Puritan tradition. (Eayrs, "Links between the Ejected Clergy," 116-18.)

46. Baker, "John Wesley's Churchmanship," *LQHR* 185 (1960): 272.

47. *Works*, 9:69.

48. Watson, *The Early Methodist Class Meeting*, 72.

49. Wesley, *A Short History of Methodism*, in *Works* (Jackson), 8:348.

50. John Simon, *John Wesley and the Religious Societies* (London: Epworth Press, 1921), 10. See also chap. 1, "The Religious Societies," and chap. 23, "A New Society" of this study.

51. Simon, *John Wesley and the Religious Societies*, 27.
52. *Works*, 18:292; 9:77.
53. Clifford Towlson, *Moravian and Methodist* (London: Epworth Press), 184ff.
54. Watson, *Early Methodist Class Meeting*, 74. Watson helpfully discusses the contribution of both Anglican and Moravian societies to Wesley's groups.
55. Horton Davies, "Epworth's Debt to Geneva—a Field of Research," *The Livingstonian* (1960): 6.
56. Davies, *Worship and Theology in England: 1690-1850*, 25.
57. Davies, *Worship and Theology in England: 1690-1850*, 25.
58. Nuttall, *Visible Saints*, 70.
59. Nuttall, *Visible Saints*, 74.
60. Quoted by Nuttall, *Visible Saints*, 81.
61. *Works*, 9:69. See Wesley's "Rules of the Band-Societies" for a description of the intimate inquiry into the spiritual status of one another (*Works*, 9:77ff.).
62. *Works* (Jackson), 8:321.
63. Baker, "John Wesley's Churchmanship," 270.
64. Nuttall, *Visible Saints*, 111.
65. "The real strength and felicity of the Victorian age lay . . . in the self-discipline and self-reliance of the individual Englishman, derived indeed from many sources, but to a large extent sprung from Puritan traditions to which the Wesleyan and Evangelical movements had given another lease of life" (G. M. Trevelyan, *English Social History* [London: Longmans, Green, 1958], 509). G. P. Gooch, *English Democratic Ideas in the Seventeenth Century*, 2nd ed. (New York: Harper & Row, 1957), provides a detailed study of the molding of English political thought and self-reliance by those of the Puritan tradition.
66. Quoted by Nuttall, *Visible Saints*, 132.
67. *Works*, 9:70.
68. Wesley's *Character of a Methodist* expands the description of inward and outward holiness (*Works*, 9:32-46).
69. See the section on "Holiness: The Design of a Christian Life" in chapter 5 of this study. Holiness was the focus of much of Wesley's early discipleship arising out of his study of Jeremy Taylor and William Law and was the primary motivation for the Anglican Religious Societies (Simon, *John Wesley and the Religious Societies*, 10-12). See also Gunter, *Limits of 'Love Divine,'* 202-8.
70. Covenant at Bedford, quoted by Nuttall, *Visible Saints*, 114.
71. *Works*, 9:33-34, 130. For Wesley's strongest statements on freedom of conscience see his tract *Thoughts upon Liberty*, where he notes the stripping of freedom from the Puritans by the Act of Uniformity (*Works* [Jackson], 11:39-40).
72. Eayrs, "Links between the Ejected Clergy," 114.
73. See Outler, *John Wesley*, and *Theology in the Wesleyan Spirit* (Nashville: Discipleship Resources, 1975); Williams, *John Wesley's Theology Today*; Maddox, *Responsible Grace*. Renewed interest in Wesleyan and Methodist doctrinal formulations is reflected in works such as

Thomas Oden's *Doctrinal Standards in the Wesleyan Tradition* (Grand Rapids, Mich.: Zondervan, 1988) and William Abraham's, *Waking from Doctrinal Amnesia* (Nashville: Abingdon Press, 1995). Abraham urges renewed recognition and commitment to doctrinal standards in the face of what he sees as an erosion of doctrinal understanding and commitment among modern Methodists. This same concern has also recently been displayed among some United Methodists whose "Confessing Movement" urges commitment to a "confession of faith" incorporating distinctive Wesleyan doctrines.

74. Nuttall, *Visible Saints*, 74-75.

75. "The Savoy Declaration, 1658," in *The Creeds of Christendom*, ed. Philip Schaff, 6th ed. (New York: Harper & Brothers, 1931), 3:727.

76. Matt. 18:15-17.

77. *Works*, 19:185, 240. See also "The Cure of Evil Speaking," *Works*, 2:252-62.

78. *Works*, 9:265.

79. Coomer, "Influence of Puritanism and Dissent," *LQHR* 175 (1950): 349.

80. Nuttall, *Visible Saints*, 159.

81. Nuttall, *Visible Saints*, 134. "All this [Puritan Reform], we must remember, was done or attempted primarily within the church, and with no admitted intention save to inspire and reform the people through the church. Independence and separation in all their organized forms developed only as the authorities at successive stages placed more and more serious impediments in the way of the reformer's efforts" (Haller, *Rise of Puritanism*, 53).

82. William Dell, *Several Sermons and Discourses* (London: Printed by J. Sowle, 1709), 94-95 [*CL*, 7:123].

83. Nuttall, *Visible Saints*, 108.

84. *Works*, 9:126, 128.

85. *Works*, 9:127.

86. *Works*, 9:258

87. Coomer, "Influence of Puritanism and Dissent," 349.

88. Davies, *Worship and Theology in England: 1690-1850*, 30.

89. *Works*, 9:23-24. Rupert Davies's introduction to *The Methodist Societies* (vol. 9 of the *Bicentennial Edition of the Works of John Wesley*) extensively examines the development of Wesley's societies, including their antecedents.

90. *Works*, 20:315.

91. Green, *Bibliography*, 143.

92. *Letters*, 6:57. "Methodist preachers cannot have always accommodations fit for gentlemen. But let us look upon D. Brainerd, and praise God for what we have" (*Letters*, 5:282).

93. *Works*, 8:328; Wesley helped raise money for the Native American work and commented on how it could only be effective if preachers could be found "of David Brainerd's spirit" (*Works*, 22:98). Though Wesley always recommended Brainerd, he could still be critical: "God hath once more 'given to the Gentiles repentance unto life!' Yet amidst so great matter of joy I could not but grieve at this, that even so good a man as Mr.

Brainerd should be 'wise above that is written,' in condemning what the Scripture nowhere condemns, in prescribing to God the way wherein He should work, and (in effect) applauding himself and magnifying his own work, above that which God wrought in Scotland, or among the English in New England; whereas in truth the work among the Indians, great as it was, was not to be compared to that at Cambuslang, Kilsyth, or Northampton" (*Works*, 20:315).

94. Telford quotes Wesley as recommending the work to the 1755 Conference (*Letters*, 6:271.)

95. The 1766 *Minutes* are used as the resource for this study, since they incorporate the original abridgment. In these *Minutes* the abridgment is not clearly credited to Baxter by quotation marks, though its source is clearly noted by Wesley. In the 1770 *Minutes* quotation marks have been inserted around the first six "difficulties," but the remaining five pages of abridgment are not so marked. Thomas Jackson, in editing his fuller version of *The Works of the Rev. John Wesley,* which remained the "standard" edition until the modern revision, perpetuates the error by marking with quotations only the "difficulties," so one is left with the impression that only that portion of the material was drawn from Baxter. Although perhaps a printing error, this failure to mark clearly the total six pages of abridgment easily causes one to mistake the author of the instructions. Such is in fact the case even with the renowned scholar Leslie Church. In his article "The Pastor in the Eighteenth Century" *LQHR* 181 (1956): 19-23, he quotes much of Wesley's instructions on visitation as if it were Wesley's own; but it is in reality Wesley's careful reworking of Baxter.

96. Baxter, *Gildas Salvianus: The Reformed Pastor*, in *Practical Works of Richard Baxter*, 14:316 [*MMC*, 66]; cf. 14:278 [*MMC*, 65].

97. Baxter, *Gildas Salvianus*, in *Practical Works of Richard Baxter,* 14:276-96 [*MMC*, 64].

98. Baxter, *Gildas Salvianus,* in *Practical Works of Richard Baxter,* 14:273-75 [*MMC*, 63-64].

99. Baxter, *Gildas Salvianus*, in *Practical Works of Richard Baxter,* 14:276 [*MMC*, 64].

100. Baxter, *Gildas Salvianus,* in *Practical Works of Richard Baxter,* 14:296-98 [*MMC*, 65]. Objections to this type of work omitted by Wesley include (1) the supposition that this pattern of visitation would destroy health in leaving no time for recreation (an objection Baxter and Wesley could make short work of); (2) an understanding that it was not required that ministers "make drudges of themselves," making their lives "a burden and a slavery"; (3) the very idea that such instruction was the prerogative and responsibility of a preacher; and (4) the concept that faith comes by hearing the word preached, and, therefore, preaching was a far more important aspect of the work (Baxter, *Gildas Salvianus,* in *Practical Works of Richard Baxter,* 14:296-312).

101. Baxter, *Gildas Salvianus*, in *Practical Works of Richard Baxter,* 14:298 [*MMC*, 65]. That such a statement expressed Wesley's opinion is seen in a letter to Joseph Benson: "Many persons are in danger of reading too little; you are in danger of reading too much. Wherever you are, take

up your cross, and visit all the society from house to house. Do this according to Mr. Baxter's plan, laid down in the *Minutes* of the Conference: The fruit which will ensue (perhaps in a short time) will abundantly reward your labour" (*Letters*, 6:65).

102. Baxter, *Gildas Salvianus*, in *Practical Works of Richard Baxter*, 14:309 [*MMC*, 65-66].

103. Baxter, *Gildas Salvianus*, in *Practical Works of Richard Baxter*, 14:319 [*MMC*, 66].

104. Baxter, *Gildas Salvianus*, in *Practical Works of Richard Baxter*, 14:320 [*MMC*, 67].

105. Baxter, *Gildas Salvianus*, in *Practical Works of Richard Baxter*, 14:333 [*MMC*, 68].

106. Baxter, Gildas Salvianus, in *Practical Works of Richard Baxter*, 14:334 [*MMC*, 68].

107. *Works* (Jackson), 8:307. "In the afternoon follow Mr. Baxter's plan. Then you will have no time to spare: You will have work enough for all your time. Then, likewise, no Preacher will stay with us who is as salt that has lost its savour. For to such this employment would be mere drudgery. And in order to it, you will have need of all the knowledge you have, or can procure" (*Works* [Jackson], 8:315).

9

Christian Life within the World

From New Testament times until the present, one of Christianity's most enigmatic tasks has been maintenance of a strong faithful community of believers who must live in the midst of a profane, self-centered world. St. Paul's double-edged instructions relating to whether a Christian should eat food offered to idols (I Cor. 8:1-13) are complemented by St. James's admonitions to protect the faithful from involvement with the world (James 4:4). As the New Testament writers struggled with how one was to live in the world and yet not be overcome by it, so did the hosts of early church fathers and mothers. Medieval monasticism, responding to the difficulties of faithful living in a secular world, offered escape from the temptations of such a world and yet demanded that the monks be responsible for sustaining the faith within that world. Clearly, the experience of the church from its beginning demonstrates that adequate instruction in Christian living necessarily includes tutelage in a Christian's proper attitude toward, and participation in, the everyday world in which one lives.

Wesley and the Puritans repeatedly addressed the topic and, as we will see, their instruction on these issues reflected the specific context and situation they were addressing at any particular moment. Attitudes toward the world depended on whether one's focus centered on cultivating a community of faithful believers within a dangerous and evil world, or on evangelizing the unbelievers and half believers of the world while living as their neighbors and ministering to their physical and spiritual needs.

Their teachings relative to the world consequently contained contrasting, and sometimes opposing, positions, leading both Puritans and Wesley to statements that often appeared to those outside the movements as contradictory and ambiguous. At their best these instructions embodied positions that occasionally sanctioned significant tension between the alternatives offered. Both movements recognized that humanity has been placed, in the providence of God, in a material world that is good if used for its proper purposes—that is, for God's glorification. So the Puritans and Wesley could urge Christians to participate fully in the world by setting examples of disciplined, responsible living. Such living was understood to incorporate service, both spiritually and materially, of all one's neighbors, including unbelievers and the downtrodden, poor, disenfranchised persons of the society. Nevertheless, living within the world and offering service to it exposed believers to its inherent dangers. Christians could never completely separate themselves from its risks and temptations. Consequently, believers were repeatedly warned of the world's dangers, its evil nature, and urged to separate themselves from its temptations. Teachings that incorporated both patterns of instruction could easily be taken by sceptics as contradictory. Turning now our attention to how Wesley and the Puritans handled specific teachings about Christian involvement in the world, we begin by looking at their treatment of the difficulties and opportunities Christians encounter in their daily living.

The Individual Christian in His or Her World

Dangerous Associations

Because for the seventeenth- and eighteenth-century Christian the ultimate meaning and purpose in life comes from relation to God, and not, as in the case of other humans, from the world, a primary Christian concern was the substitution of divine interests and values for those of worldly rewards. Contamination by the world was to be removed. Teachings concerning such dangers were common in the ethical instructions of the day among all branches of the church, but Puritans and Methodists emphasized the dangers of worldly contamination to such an extent that it became one of the characteristics distinguishing them from their contemporaries.

It is no surprise to find one of the most prominent of Puritan attitudes toward the secular world in this sentence from John Flavel: "What is a saint, but a stranger and a pilgrim upon earth, a man in a strange country traveling homeward."[1] John Bunyan's *Pilgrim's Progress* epitomized this attitude, expressing the

Christian's goal and consuming desire to be turned heavenward rather than toward the earth. The traps and snares along the way were principally those connected with worldly pleasures and desires. Wesley's sympathy with this concept is evident not only in his publication of *Pilgrim's Progress* but also by his comment to his niece that everything is a blessing "which disengages us from transient things and teaches us to live in eternity."[2] However, his conviction that the blessed life may be lived now in this world did not allow him to overemphasize the spiritualization of the Christian life—a trait sometimes found among the Puritans.

When we examine instructions about the dangers of inappropriate personal relations, we find Robert Bolton's advice to his congregation setting the standard:

> **That thou never cast thy selfe into wicked company,** *or presse amongst the prophane, especially* **upon choice,** *voluntarily and delightfully* **and abide no longer with them at anytime** *upon any occasion*, **then thou hast sound warrant,** *and a calling thereunto. It is uncomely, and incompatible with good conscience* **[to do], It is not for the honour or comfort of Gods children, to** keepe company, or **familiarly converse with gracelesse men. . . . There is a strange** *attractive and imperious* **power in ill company, to empoyson and pervert even the blest dispositions: . . . let a Christian but for a while abandon his** *holy conference, and comfortable* **communion with Gods children, and** *plunge himselfe into* **[stay in] the company of those who are** *but* **cold and carelesse,** *lasie and luke warme professors;* **and he shall in very short time finde his zeale to be very much cooled,** *his forwardnesse abated,* **the tenderness of his conscience** *too* **much qualified with worldly wisdome; much dullness of heart, deadnesse of spirit, drowzinesse, and heartlessnesse in his affections to holy things, and a universal decay of his graces insensibly to grow upon him.**
>
> **In this respect many Christians doe themselves much** *wrong, and afflict their soules with many unnecessary spiritual miseries* **[injury]. For they** *doe* **sometimes unadvisedly, by reason of kindred, [or] for old acquaintance,** *advantage, and carnal contentment, because of worldly wisdome, immunity from grosse sinnes, and other good parts of the parties,* **hold a too neare,** *intimate and delightful* **correspondence with such as are** *but* **[at best] only civill men.**[3]

Stuckley affirmed the same sentiment and warned that the wicked are not simply the "loose" but also the "formal"—meaning those who are formally Christians but really wicked.[4]

Wesley's sermons "On Friendship with the World" and "On Leaving the World" were similar commentaries upon the dangers inherent in a Christian's necessary contact with worldly persons. They expressed the same concerns as the passage from Bolton, particularly warning against the almost unconscious way in which association with persons of the world undercuts resolute concentration upon God. Aware of the particular situations wherein this danger is greatest, Wesley specifically admonished believers not to marry anyone who lacked religion, for in this closest of human ties, it would be almost impossible to live in a situation where "they are subjects, not only of two separate, but of two opposite kingdoms. They act upon quite different principles; they aim at quite different ends."[5] Equally dangerous, in his understanding, was association with one's kinspeople or old acquaintances who were not religious. These constituted special danger, for it is "contrary . . . to flesh and blood" to reject such, but, to avoid the danger these relations entail, it is nevertheless advisable. One may out of courtesy and natural affection visit such a relative but, "it should certainly be as seldom as possible."[6] Like Stuckley, Wesley compared such association with the futility and unthinkable act of associating with one who had the plague; it was even more dangerous, for it endangered the soul and not simply the body.[7]

Clearly, these instructions were fashioned to protect the faithful in weak moments and to shield them from the obvious temptations of a nonbelieving world. When one remembers that among Puritans and Methodists many had been drawn into the faith from lives of sin, often compounded through poor associations, these teachings spoke to a real need among their members. Although they may sound harsh and separatist by modern standards, they are familiar, as we often similarly instruct our children concerning their associations. Stringent as such teachings may seem, empathy and concern for nonbelievers and quasi-believers were constantly exhibited by both the Puritans and Wesley. Necessary contacts with worldly folk, dangerous as they might be, were to be made in courtesy, patience, and love.[8] Such teachings, intended to protect Puritans and Methodists from the dangers of the world and not particularly distinctive from traditional Christian instruction, were often seen, unfortunately, by those outside the groups as attempts to separate themselves from the world—to create a "holy" people removed from the world.

The two traditions, through other emphases, further distanced themselves from the values and patterns of the general society that surrounded them. Puritan "preciseness," discipline, instructions pertaining to sobriety and austerity in dress, criticism of the theater, and a general depreciation of the arts (particularly the theater) were all matched in Wesley's instructions.[9] Whether intended or not, such teachings built a group of believers with at least outward characteristics that distinguished and separated them from the general society. These noticeable characteristics doubtless contributed to "Puritan" and "Methodist" being terms of derision among many contemporaries. Certainly these similarities, in the popular mind, identified Wesley with the Puritans.

Cognizant that such distinctions from others would lead to persecutions, Wesley and the Puritans often interpreted such events as God's providence granted to them in order to strengthen their faith.[10] Another perilous consequence of this distinction was for those easily recognized as "different" to adopt attitudes of being "holier than thou." The Puritan ministers and Wesley continually warned against such an attitude, yet the pervasive temptation to display such an attitude remained a persistent difficulty for their followers.

Although Wesley's teachings and Methodist practice clearly paralleled much of the Puritan instruction, it is curious that Wesley included few Puritan teachings regarding such matters in *A Christian Library*, nor did he use them as examples to be followed. The two treatises in the *Library* that admonish their readers to sobriety in dress are those of circumspect Anglicans: the anonymous treatise *The Whole Duty of Man*, and Dr. Cave's *Primitive Christianity*.[11] Robert Bolton's treatise, *General Directions for a Comfortable Walking with God* commented extensively on associations with evildoers, yet Wesley's selections from it and other Puritans in the *Library* and elsewhere concentrate on such issues as the spiritual nature and vitality of the Christian life, and the purity of its holiness, rather than on instruction in such things as dress, plays, and the arts.

Reproof

Puritan and Wesleyan teaching and practice included another emphasis: the "duty of reproof"—an emphasis that modern Christians find "quaint" and perhaps difficult to appreciate. The teaching was, nevertheless, grounded in the gospel admonition to care for and seek to aid one's neighbor. It required the believer to be responsible not simply for oneself but equally for the state of one's neighbor's spiritual and ethical life.

As we have seen in the discussion of Wesley's societies, one of the most important functions of Christian fellowship was the opportunity to help and encourage one another, but an equally important role was the duty to call into question the thoughts or actions of a fellow member who appeared to be openly, but perhaps unconsciously, sinning. Methodist classes and bands thereby functioned confessionally and as a forum for loving and humble criticism. Such groups of frequent and intimate fellowship were ideal for carrying out this duty of reprehension, and, within this context, it was easily understood and appreciated. However, this duty, as understood by Wesley and the Puritans, had larger consequences. It was to be applied to the community as a whole and not simply to one's Christian neighbors. A Christian could not comfortably live in a sinful community, nor would the sense of responsibility for others allow a believer to countenance sin without at least attempting to warn and admonish the sinner concerning that sin. A Christian was duty bound under the command of God to rebuke, admonish, and chastise one's associates, with the objective of bringing them to the better life of Christian faith in Christ. Consequently, instructions relating to this duty were applicable to both the Christian brother and sister *and* the secular acquaintance, though the particular approach should vary according to the condition and status of the one being admonished.

Wesley identified his own treatment of reproof with that of Richard Baxter:

> How striking is Mr. Baxter's reflection on this head, in his *Saints' Everlasting Rest*. "Suppose thou wert to meet one in the lower world to whom thou hadst denied this office of love when ye were both together under the sun; what answer couldst thou make to his upbraiding? At such a time and place, while we were under the sun, God delivered me into thy hand, I then did not know the way of salvation, but was seeking death in the error of my life; and therein thou sufferedst me to remain, without once endeavouring to awaken me out of sleep: Hadst thou imparted to me thy knowledge, and warned me to flee from the wrath to come, neither I nor thou need ever to have come into this place of torment."[12]

Wesley's quote of Baxter's illustration provided an introduction to his own comments on the subject, but he also found other Puritan examples to be useful.

John Kitchin's sermon on the topic, "How Must We Reprove," gives us a convenient statement that we may use to compare Wesleyan and Puritan teachings on this duty. Reproof was naturally directed toward any sin or, for Wesley, toward any error that might lead to sin. It was to be applied to unbelievers where admonishment of outward sin was necessary, for example, obvious sins such as drunkenness, cursing, Sabbath breaking, among others.[13] However, Kitchin warned that one must be sure that the accused were truly sinful—one ought not be reproved on supposition or hearsay.[14] In Wesley's words the circumstance should not be "anything of a disputable nature, that will bear much to be said on both sides."[15]

This duty could be correctly undertaken only in love; therefore, concern for the individual's salvation should characterize it, instead of any scorn or pride on the part of the accuser.[16] It follows that such admonition will be done humbly, meekly, compassionately, and with a recognition of one's own faults. Nevertheless, it must be done, to use Baxter's terms, "seriously, zealously, and effectually."[17] One should not mince words in calling attention to the serious nature of the sin but must speak plainly. "A ludicrous reproof makes little impression, and is soon forgot. Besides, that many times it is taken ill, as if you ridiculed the person you reprove." Wesley allowed some exception to this general rule of seriousness, for "a little well-placed raillery will pierce deeper than solid argument" with some "who are strangers to religion."[18]

One was to reprove with prudence and discretion so that it varied according to the occasion, and according to the relation one had to the accused. For instance, one was not to reprove a superior, whether parent or magistrate, in the same manner as one might one's peers, nor was one type of reproof as effective for one person as another might be.[19] Reproof should also be seasonable, when the accused were most likely to accept it. On this matter of occasion, though Wesley accepted the principle, he differed from Baxter and Kitchin, for he asserted that even a drunk man might be justly and compassionately reproved to good effect and, in his typical pattern, proceeded to give instances thereof.[20]

The Christian was also to assure that "reproofs and exhortations are backed with the authority of God. Let the sinner be convinced that you speak not from yourselves, or of your own hand. Show them the very words of Scripture for what you say."[21] Kitchin added the psychologically sound admonition to take an occasion when you can "**commend a man for something, and then *rub* [reprove] him *up* for his faults.**"[22] For Wesley the same purpose was served if one prefaced "a reproof with a frank profession of good will."[23]

Baxter and Kitchin insisted that the one approaching a brother or sister for the purpose of reproving was also to be upright and righteous, setting an example by one's own life, or the admonition would be hypocrisy.[24] Though Wesley failed to note this instruction in his sermon, he doubtless sympathized with the caution. Wesley, guarding against the dangers inherent when any person sought to help others recognize their faults and sins, reminded his readers that the outcome of a reproof or exhortation was finally in the hands of God. Any success in the duty was to be credited to God's action in the life of the person one seeks to help.[25]

Each author was thoroughly convinced that adequate and

helpful reproof was the work of a wise and prudent believer who could handle the matter without undue offense to a neighbor, yet "none is exempted from this duty for unfitness: No: This ought ye to have done, and not to have left the other undone."[26] By this method and in the context of these cautions one was to take up the task. Wesley ended his sermon with this impassioned plea to his followers, which illustrates his own emphasis on the duty:

> I have now only a few words to add unto you, my brethren, who are vulgarly called "Methodists". I never heard or read of any considerable revival of religion which was not attended with a spirit of reproving. I believe it cannot be otherwise; for what is faith unless it worketh by love? Thus it was in every part of England when the present revival of religion began about fifty years ago: all the subjects of that revival—all the Methodists, so called, in every place, were reprovers of outward sin. . . . Come, brethren! In the name of God, let us begin again! Rich or poor, let us all arise as one man! And in anywise let every man "rebuke his neighbor, and not suffer sin upon him!" Then shall all Great Britain and Ireland know that we do not "go a warfare at our own cost:" Yea, "God shall bless us, and all the ends of the world shall fear him."[27]

Wesley's reappropriation of this teaching concerning Christian responsibility for reproving sinners undoubtedly, perhaps more than other similar teachings in the eyes of his contemporaries, revived an image of the earlier Puritans. As he expressed it, the charge against Christians, understanding here his own movement, was that they would not "keep their religion to themselves."[28] So it had been with the Puritans. Their similar teachings illustrate their common view of this significant Christian expression of one's accountability for the world in which one lives.

Responsibility for Others

Separation for the development of the faithful, and evangelization that included reproof, certainly drew negative responses against Puritanism and Methodism from many. However, both movements were also attractive to many. The reasons for their appeal were several. Their revitalization of an emphasis on personal faith and salvation gave hope to many whose traditional securities were rapidly evaporating. This hope was matched by the genuine concern of both groups for their neighbors, whether believers or not. Such loving involvement with others brought Puritans and Methodists to the attention of their neighbors who experienced society as indifferent, unloving, and sometimes cruel.

From their understanding of the gospel, they concluded that a Christian's active role in everyday life involved the believer inextricably in society and its issues, both positive and negative. As a consequence, Wesley and the Puritans objected to any understanding that effectively separated Christians from the world, even when they were, as we have seen, consciously warning against the temptations of that same world. In taking such a position Wesley parted with both the pietist and mystic traditions that influenced his early ministry. He stated his position thusly: "Christianity is essentially a social religion. . . . It cannot subsist at all, without society,—without living and conversing with other men."[29] How could a Christian do good to *all* persons if associated only with other Christians? How could one be a peacemaker among Christians, who presumedly would not need such service? The heart of the matter lies, then, in this: Though one should not have any "particular familiarity or any strictness of friendship with them," this does not mean that one is to "renounce all fellowship" with unbelievers or those who fail to practice their Christian duties.[30]

A number of the Puritan works used by Wesley note the Puritans' active concern that a Christian could not be true to a proper relationship to the world without real service in the world—without following the command to do good. This service of others was to become the chief business and employment of a Christian life.

In these interpersonal relationships a believer was always to display Christian love. Richard Alleine admonished his readers to "carry yourselves well towards all men" by being true, thereby eliminating even the lying that is usually allowed in trading with one another; being just in both thoughts and actions; being merciful to those in need; being peaceable so as to possess "an unaptness to be provoked"; and being "courteous, sweet, and affable in your carriage towards all."[31] Wesley in his own instructions added to these an admonition to be careful and circumspect in judging others.[32] The Christian was to be separated from the world in such a manner that he or she avoided the degrading influence of those who have no interest beyond worldly gain, but in no sense was one to be separated from interest in and concern for such persons.[33]

Interest in the worldly person also called for proper concern for that person's condition, both material and spiritual. Involved in the Christian's relationship to the world was the correct use of the material possessions and social positions of influence and power. Many of the treatises included by Wesley in the *Library* commented upon this. Sir Matthew Hale's small treatise on stewardship, "The

Great Audit" in his work *Contemplations Moral and Divine*, supplies us with a useful example.[34] Wesley's sermon on "The Good Steward" similarly treats the subject and allows comparison of their teachings. Both men emphasized stewardship not only of material possessions but also of all other abilities and capacities, as well as the privileges of social position, education, and other personal blessings.[35] Wesley's instructions on the true Christian stewardship of one's material possessions were summarized in his well-known axiom "Gain all you can, save all you can and give all you can."[36]

The difficulty of carrying out such high ideals of proper stewardship of possessions and talent was noted by Thomas Manton, commenting on Jesus' familiar "Golden Rule." Manton suggested that even Christians seldom manage to live comfortably by these teachings: **"When your debts are detained, you complain of wrong. Should we not be as *conscionable for* [exact in] the speedy payment of others? To buy with a great measure, and sell with a less, is an abomination of the Lord and to men. We judge things done to us thus and thus, and shall we be careless what we do to them?"**[37] Wesley's sermons on the Sermon on the Mount raised the same issue.[38]

These teachings on dangerous associations, reproof, and the care of one's neighbors called on genuine Christians to take seriously their personal social responsibilities. The Puritans and Wesley clearly understood, however, that all persons were in significant ways affected by the social systems in which they lived. For them Christian responsibilities extended far beyond personal involvement with and care for individual neighbors. Responsibility also included the social conditions in which such neighbors lived. We turn now to the treatment of Christian instruction and action as these relate to the Christian's social context.

Christian Responsibility for Society

The social contexts in which both Puritanism and Methodism arose have been widely investigated.[39] The profound contribution to the vitality and distinctiveness of both movements made by social, political, and economic changes in each century leads to a brief sketch of some elements of these developments.

Social and Economic Changes and Their Consequences

Closure of the monasteries by Henry VIII in the sixteenth century began a series of changes that were to affect the social and economic positions of many in the culture, particularly those of the common people. The sale of monastic lands created new patterns of land proprietorship. One consequence of this redistribution was the loss of property rights and privileges for many who worked the land under the auspices of the church.[40] They were often put off the land or forced to accept the status of laborers for the new landowners. At a later stage of this development the expense of maintaining great manor households led many of the landowners to "break up" estates, again forcing peasants and servants off the land.

Elimination of the abbeys and monasteries had another devastating consequence for many commoners who had been forced into poverty by land redistribution. It meant the loss of a most important traditional source for relief: alms distributed through the monasteries. Responding to the needs created by this development, Henry required parish churches to assume the responsibility of collecting and distributing alms. This pattern was systematized and expanded by the end of the century into a "Poor Law" requiring all parishes to care for their poor through the resources raised by a universally imposed poor tax. Many problems, however, were evident in this new system, including inequitable distribution and inadequate administration.

Changing patterns of cultivating the land also contributed to the disenfranchisement of villagers. An expanding cloth trade demanded a steady supply of sheep. Farming lands traditionally held in common by villagers were fenced or enclosed in the latter years of the sixteenth century. This practice was extended with the development of new and more productive methods of crop production through the seventeenth and eighteenth centuries, even though often criticized and occasionally officially resisted. An ever-rising demand for agricultural land also brought deforestation and draining of marshes, further contributing to the difficulties of the many common people who depended upon these traditionally common holdings for food and sustenance.[41] For the small land holder and the common laborer the results were always the same—the loss of an ability to sustain oneself and one's family. The traditional English class distinctions between nobility, gentry, and commoner were in this process further modified, with the nobility and gentry becoming less responsible for the welfare of their laborers and servants. Again, the negative impact was felt by the commoner. The usual social ills that surround poverty caused by displaced employment and resources were intensified in this changing agrarian context.

On the eve of the seventeenth century (1597) causes of England's poverty were listed by a contemporary as

> (i) excessive luxury expenditure, leading to the racking [increase]

of rents and sale of lands; (ii) excessive consumption of food by the rich, leading to scarcity and high prices; (iii) oppressive landlords; (iv) usury; (v)cornering of corn and holding out for high prices; (vi) wasting of substance at law; (vii) gambling; (viii) breaking up of households, unnecessary dismissals of servants and apprentices; and (ix) failure to execute the poor law.[42]

In addition to these essentially social and economic causes of poverty, England's seventeenth-century political wars further worsened the plight of the nation's poor.

Turning to the eighteenth century to inquire about causes of poverty in Wesley's period, we should not be surprised when we find many of the same social trends and their consequent ills exacerbated by the continuing economic expansion of England both at home and in international markets. Enclosure of common lands continued unabated, aggravating the difficulties of many. The century's flourishing mercantilism called forth the industrial revolution, which brought widespread wage-labor dependency for the common people. Employment, when it could be obtained, was often temporary and held few guarantees. Effective labor laws were still in the future, so low wages, long hours, expanding employment of women and children with minimal compensation, all contributed to a worsening plight for the poor.

In 1773, when supplies of foodstuffs ran low, John Wesley ventured to offer his insights into the reasons for these difficulties in a tract entitled "Thoughts on the Present Scarcity of Provisions." Not surprisingly, he found the causes of poverty to be quite similar to those listed seventy years earlier in the document just quoted. Wesley suggested the central problem was unemployment because there was no "vent for their [the usual employers'] goods." Money was tight because food was so expensive.[43] Bread-corn was expensive because "immense quantities of corn are continually consumed by distilling."[44] The breeding of horses in place of beef and mutton not only raised the price of meat but also the price of oats and other grains.[45] "The land which was some years ago divided between ten and twenty little farmers, and enabled them comfortably to provide for their families, is now generally engrossed by one great farmer."[46] Consolidation of farms meant that pork, poultry, and eggs normally raised by individual farmers were no longer produced, resulting in high prices for the food that was available. In the "kitchens of the great, the nobility and gentry" one might also observe great waste of food.[47] Luxurious living and patronage of the arts contributed to high prices, as these pursuits consumed much of the available capital and cash. Because prices had risen, gentlemen landowners raised rents, forcing farmers to raise prices, an unending circle.[48] Finally, prices were high because of taxes: "I have heard that the national expense, seventy years ago, was, in time of peace, three millions a year. And now the bare interest of the public debt amounts yearly to above four millions! to raise which, with the other expenses of government, those taxes are absolutely necessary."[49] Wesley, in closing his description of the difficulties, summed up the problem, in his usual terse manner, as "distilling, taxes, and luxury."

Luxury, rising rents, monopoly, excessive consumption by the rich, and changing agricultural patterns were common causes of poverty in either century. The usury of the earlier time was in Wesley's period compounded by excessive taxes. The plight of the poor in both centuries remained the same—a constantly changing demand for new skills accompanying sporadic employment, which offered little opportunity for independent economic security. Although the fruits of the industrial revolution improved economic conditions for all classes in the last third of Wesley's century, poverty was still a major threat to many commoners.

Christian Responsibility and Social Ills

Examination of how the Puritans and Methodists responded to the ills of their respective societies, particularly their treatment of poverty, allows us to see how each group attempted to live out the teachings of the gospel among its neighbors. Exploring these patterns, we discover additional similarities between the movements.

Before pursuing these similarities, we need to note a characteristic of Puritanism that ultimately created two clearly distinguishable Puritan social groups. Because the Puritan movement appealed for differing reasons to both gentry and commoners, it is not surprising that attitudes toward the social ills of the time and the possible solutions to these fall into patterns that reflect the two groups' differing social situations.

A distinct Puritan group arose among the merchants, gentry (squire), and artisan classes. Attracted by Calvinistic theological instruction, this group continued the early English Reformers' drive toward purification of the church and, ultimately, the nation. Many Puritan leaders enjoyed the social privileges of the gentry before they took up the Puritan banner of reform. Puritans of the artisan classes, applying the teachings of conscientious, disciplined Christian life to their trades and crafts, experienced a significant rise in economic independence. Acquisition of economic power meant increasing possibilities of participation in the political process and an accompanying change in social status. Each of these changes contributed to their understanding of themselves and their own social position as well as that of others within the society. In this artisan/merchant group hard-fought gains in social position meant acceptance, and defense, of newly achieved social privilege.

A second group of Puritans arose among the poor, those who were often victims of the same changing and expanding economy that aggrandized the merchant and artisan class. Although without social and economic position, many in this group found that the Reformation teachings regarding the Christian gospel gave them hope and assurance not previously accessible in their daily lives. Here were many who, freed to read the scriptures by the religious reforms of the sixteenth century, found in Jesus' teachings invigorating concepts of human dignity, worth, and freedom. Employing these concepts to question economic and political traditions, these poor Puritans threatened, in the words of one of their spokespersons, to "turn the world upside down."[50]

Both groups agreed that gospel teachings, when applied to the problems of English society, demanded nothing less than major cultural change. The focus of each group, however, significantly differed. For the merchant and gentleman Puritan the goal was the transformation of ecclesiastical and political organizations of the nation to reflect their theological understandings. They had little interest in changing the social and economic structures that supported their status even when these aggravated the difficulties of the poor. On the other hand, Puritans drawn from the lower social classes were much more concerned with the alleviation of social, economic, and occasionally political structures that inhibited their religious and economic opportunities.

Social Attitudes of Merchant and Gentlemen Puritans

Puritan leaders drawn from the gentry, merchants, and artisan groups were often well educated, newly wealthy, politically and ecclesiastically well-connected representatives of an established social order. Although their theology and politics led them to seek major change in contemporary political and ecclesiastical systems, they carried with them traditional social perceptions. Their understandings of the place, position, and value of various segments of society, particularly the poor, changed slowly and, apparently, was not greatly modified by their Puritan ideas.

The economic and social changes of the time, however, created both new perceptions and new attitudes among the gentry toward the poor. The poor increasingly found themselves dependent upon the government program of poor relief, through what was, at best, a faulty system subject to the whims and prejudices of local parish and government leaders. With the establishment in the late sixteenth century of taxes to sustain the poor, many of the landed and merchant classes who previously had given alms generously to relieve the plight of the poor no longer saw the necessity of those gifts. Charitable giving was significantly reduced among the gentry. Many Puritans in this group did sustain substantial patterns of giving, but their gifts frequently assumed rather different purposes in this new context.

Many English merchant and gentlemen Puritans also shared Luther's bias against beggars, vagabonds, and the purely lazy. For Luther such persons were classed with monks and friars; they were all idle and unproductive.[51] Gentry Puritans, following Calvin's instructions, insisted that all persons were called by God into gainfully productive vocations. Their participation in the developing capitalism of the time only corroborated this human need for productivity. Persons failing to adapt to differing forms of vocation offered in a changing society, or who were simply lazy, were obviously rejecting the teachings of Christ. William Perkins stated the case succinctly:

> It is a foul disorder in any commonwealth that there should be suffered rogues, beggars, vagabonds; for such kind of persons commonly are of no civil society or corporation, nor of any particular church. . . . To wander up and down from year to year to this end, to seek and procure bodily maintenance, is no calling, but the life of a beast; and consequently a condition or state of life flat against the rule, that every one must have a particular calling. And therefore the Statute made the last Parliament [1597] for the restraining of beggars and rogues is an excellent statute, and being in substance the very law of God, is never to be repealed.[52]

Perkins expressed here the attitude toward the beggar found among the merchant and gentry Puritans—an attitude that failed to consider the latent social reasons for unemployment already noted.[53] To give indiscriminately to such persons or to support them through the poor tax was often equated with sin.

Michael Walzer suggests there were additional reasons for the attitude of gentlemen Puritans toward the working classes. The stringent disciplines of a watchful, charitable Puritan magistracy were necessary, as they established a holy commonwealth seeking to return order, consistency, and security to a world of anxiety, dissolution, and disorder.[54] Revolutionaries themselves against a traditional order that no longer gave security, Puritans saw cultural and political discipline based on religious commitment as a means of restoring order to life, presently and eternally. Combined with their theological understanding of a vocation or call for each person in society, such discipline required that all be subservient to "masters." Those who had been willing to throw off their own political masters were quick to insist upon the necessity of mastery over their workers to ensure social stability. Vagabonds and such, the "masterless men" of the day, were a significant threat to general social discipline and vocation, which, in the eyes of the gentry, provided security. In one sense industrious commitment to vocational productivity illustrated faithfulness to Christ and contributed to one's salvation.

On the other hand, even with their biases against the lazy and seemingly undisciplined poor, gentlemen Puritans often recognized the plight of those unemployed poor who were the victims of economic and agricultural changes, and those persons whose infirmities would not allow them to sustain themselves. We see such concern in the counties that supported Parliament during the civil war providing a more careful administration of the poor law than royalist counties.[55] Merchant and gentry Puritans generally divided the poor into two distinct classes: one that they were willing to help, and one that they were likely to condemn. I will return to a more detailed consideration of their charitable care of the first group.

Social Attitudes among the Puritan Poor

A majority of sixteenth- and seventeenth-century poor were, in one form or another, victims of the changing social and economic patterns within the society. Generally, they were drawn from the servant and laborer classes. If they were able to continue in their traditional vocations during the centuries long enclosure movement that consolidated farm land in the hands of a few, their sources of income were often reduced, and their displacement from the land created new, often very difficult, lifestyles. Walzer points out that one of the first products of the breakdown of traditional social patterns is always a fluid group of "masterless men [and women]."[56]

Christopher Hill describes the large group of "masterless men" among the population preceding and during the Interregnum:

> A masterless man was nobody's servant: this could mean freedom for those who prized independence more than security. . . . Beneath the surface stability of rural England, the vast placid open fields which catch the eye, was the seething mobility of the forest squatters, itinerant craftsmen and building labourers, unemployed and quack doctors, vagabonds, tramps: congregated especially in London and

> the big cities, but also with footholds wherever newly-squatted areas escaped from the machinery of the parish or in old-squatted areas where labour was in demand. It was from this underworld that armies and ship's crew were recruited, that a portion at least of the settlers of Ireland and the New World were found, men willing to run desperate risks.[57]

The disciplines of Christian vocation and social respectability so important to the Puritan merchants and gentry were, at best, only partially effective or respected among this large group of masterless persons.

From the traditional groups of poor laborers and servants and the masterless folk, another form of Puritanism emerged. Representing a broad section of the culture, with a variety of training, background, and interests, those who constituted this underside of society exhibited little cohesion. In these subcultures of society, however, the religious ideas of freedom, equality, and direct spirituality flourished. Embracing gospel teachings made available to them through Reformation teachings and practices, they envisioned greater religious freedom as well as greater economic and social opportunity for themselves and their neighbors.

Among these poor people religious (and political) configurations fractured and multiplied in innumerable patterns—often patterns that frightened the gentry and nobility, including the Puritan gentry. They produced, for example, the "mechanick preacher," the roving evangelist, and the "prophet." Merchant and gentry Puritans could hardly help seeing these developments as a threat to social and religious order.[58]

Of equal importance and potential threat to traditional social patterns were the ideas of equality and personal responsibility these poor people found in their reading of the Scriptures. Combined with the traditional Puritan ideas of a "priesthood of all believers" and its assumption of personal contact with God, Scripture reading among the poor often led to significantly differing understandings of the "leading of the spirit." In this milieu the radical movements of the period, both religious and political, found ready acceptance and therein created a very different pattern of Puritanism.

Among the variety of ideas that arose among these groups, several themes were unmistakable: (1) The "religion of the heart," tempered by congregational testing of its validity, was valid in ways that "academic divinity" could never understand nor control.[59] (2) Anyone, led by God, could preach; therefore, limitations imposed by education, position, or training were understood to be irrelevant. Lay preachers and writers, such as Bunyan, were readily accepted and popular. (3) The gospel taught an equality of humanity that extended to all classes and people, which meant that choice of ministers and other leaders should be determined through "democratic" means rather than the traditional authoritarian episcopal appointments. (4) Religious freedom, assumed in the concept of individual spiritual guidance, demanded toleration for variety in patterns of doctrine and church governance. William Dell, New Model Army chaplain, stated the position clearly: "Unity is Christian, uniformity antichristian," therefore "the variety of forms in the world is the beauty of the world."[60] Another consequence of this freedom was an assumption that voluntary membership within a local congregation required support from the congregation, not from the state. Tithes for a state church were, then, an unnecessary imposition.

Although some aspects of these concepts were shared by merchant and gentry Puritans of an Independent (Congregational) persuasion, they often took a much more radical trajectory among the Puritan poor. The Leveller movement of the 1640s consisted largely of yeomen and craftsmen who asserted that the poor had a right to vote, to decide about the governance under which they would live. They were, as one might expect, critical of both king and Parliament, wanted to open enclosures, elect justices of the peace and sheriffs from the general populace, eliminate the House of Lords, and generally open society for all.[61] Leveller attempts to equalize property rights were often justified on the basis of what they understood were gospel teachings discovered through their reading of Scripture.

Quaker stress upon the leadership of the "Inner Light" eliminated human distinctions and gave the poor personal confidence. Quaker teachings that there were no essential differences between persons before God arose from George Fox's insistence on a personal, direct spiritual experience of God's spirit, which called, like the Levellers' interpretation, for the equality of all. Even though the arguments of the Puritan poor appeared to the gentry as radical understandings of spirit, Scripture, and the church, their arguments sounded very similar to justifications offered by the Puritan gentry when they sought political and ecclesiastical changes in the society.

In 1649 a group of "Diggers" began to dig up commonland and wasteland, claiming the right to the land's productivity for all persons. Digger leader Gerrard Winstanley, rejecting the concepts of property rights, declared: "He that works for another, either for wages or to pay him rent, works unrighteously; . . . but they that are resolved to work and eat together, making the earth a common treasury, doth join hands with Christ to lift up the creation from bondage, and restores all things from the curse."[62] Winstanley and the Digger movement generally saw communal living as the only logical consequence of the gospel.

These few examples from several of the more widely known radical Puritan groups suggest that their solutions to the injustices of society and its religious establishment were many and varied. Central to each was the incorporation of the poor into the governance of their religious and political lives, and genuine responsibility for, and improvement of, their position economically and socially. Obviously, these solutions, offered to right social ills in the community, differed substantially from those proposed and attempted by the merchant and gentry Puritans who dominated the revolution.

As the ruling Puritan gentry gained control of the land, they suppressed these radical groups and slowly restored more traditional patterns of mastery and property.[63] The Puritan poor thereby lost their short-lived freedom to experiment with new and radical concepts of the gospel and with their own social situation.

Among the Puritan communities that survived the restoration of the episcopacy in 1660, Quakers, Baptists, and Independents retained some of the religious patterns attractive to the Puritan poor. However, the Nonconformist churches, which were largely made up of artisan, gentry, and merchant groups, often continued their traditional attitude toward, and treatment of, the poor into the eighteenth century. They successfully ministered to the poor only much later, when they began to modify their concepts that marginalized or depreciated the poor.

Wesley and the Poor

Wesley's delineation of the reasons for poverty in the eighteenth century reminds us that the reality of poverty and its consequent disabilities change little from century to century. By Wesley's time many of the issues of the revolutionary sixteenth century had been settled: Religious freedom was an accepted fact, the average Englishman enjoyed greater opportunity for employment and freedom of vocational choice, a limited monarchy required more cooperative forms of government, and an expansive intellectual and scientific climate provided unanticipated opportunities and possibilities for all.

Nonetheless, relationships between the ruling, monied, and successful merchant gentry, the craftsmen and shopkeepers, and the working poor remained much the same. The broad base of laboring poor who provided the underpinning of society still suffered under numerous barriers to full participation in the community. Disenfranchised because they seldom owned property, they often found employment both sporadic and brutally demanding. Living conditions in the industrializing towns were squalid, making disease a constant threat. Among the gentry, attitudes toward the poor had changed little from earlier days. Although sometimes sympathetic to the plight of the legitimately unemployed, upper class persons often saw the poor as base, lazy, brutal people who cared too little to improve their situation. Apathy and lethargy were common among the poor, as prospects of changing their condition were dismal.

When we compare Wesley's attitudes and activities on behalf of the eighteenth-century poor with what we have learned of Puritan treatment of the sixteenth- and seventeenth-century poor, we find interesting similarities and significant differences. Perhaps the most striking distinction was Wesley's personal attitude toward poverty and the poor. A gentleman by birth, education, and vocation, John Wesley adopted an attitude toward poverty that was exceptional among his peers. From at least the time of the Oxford Holy Club, Wesley and his colleagues endeavored to serve the poor not simply by sharing the gospel but by seeking to understand and relieve their situation. This active participation in the life of the poor became a hallmark of Wesley's Christian faith and of the Methodism that developed from his witness. Early Methodism appealed to the poor because within it they found a message of gospel grace *and* a noncondemnatory, accepting spirit.

Manfred Marquardt suggests that Wesley's own attitude toward the poor and his work among them led to new attitudes "both among the affected poor and the higher strata of English society."[64] This, perhaps, is an overstatement of Wesley's influence, especially among the gentry, but Marquardt's comment correctly denotes the central place of Wesley's attitude toward the poor. Ted Jennings's recent work, along with earlier studies, has convincingly demonstrated Wesley's identification with the poor and his significant work on their behalf.[65]

Clearly, Wesley's identification with the poor was unusual in the eighteenth century. This identification distinguished his approach from the normal attitudes found among the earlier merchant and gentry Puritans. The question may then arise, "Does such a sentiment identify Wesley with the attitudes and patterns of the Puritan poor?" As a Tory, Wesley was a political conservative, which certainly persuaded him to reject many of Puritan poor's radical ideas of freedom and democracy; yet, as Jennings suggests, his empathy for the poor came from his participation in their lives, allowing him to see their condition from their perspective. In his own modifications of worship, use of lay leadership, and insistence on Christian fellowship, he responded positively to many of the Puritan poor's religious innovations. His continual critiques of the rich also sounded much like similar comments raised among the Puritan poor.[66] However, it would be overstating the case to suggest any direct dependence by Wesley on innovations initiated by the Puritan poor. More likely, in his typical pattern, Wesley appropriated those innovations that usefully fulfilled needs within his own movement, without undue attention to where they may have been originated.

Remedies for Social Ills Offered by the Puritans and by Wesley

Wesley's active efforts to relieve or modify the situation of the poor are well-known. In many cases they paralleled programs and patterns established by merchant and gentry Puritans in earlier times. In others Wesley's efforts were uniquely different from Puritan innovations.

Charity

Given the transitions that surrounded charity in the sixteenth and seventeenth centuries, Puritan gentry came to be wary of indiscriminate giving to the poor. Joseph Hall, a bishop of Puritan sympathies, commented: "Thou art very poor: who made thee so? If thine own negligence, laziness, improvidence, unthriftiness, rash engagements, thou hast reason to bear that burden upon thine own shoulders."[67] Acting on such assumptions, Puritans often imposed barriers and tests for those who might receive their alms, attempting to guarantee that such alms would be properly deserved. Therefore, Puritan largesse, though significant, as we will see, had a limited outreach due to somewhat burdensome restrictions.

In addition, Puritan admiration for disciplined personal lives sometimes enticed Puritans to stipulate in their charitable giving some means of imposing their ideas and patterns upon the poor. Sir James Lancaster, Puritan merchant and explorer, provided "thirty pounds for the relief of the poor of Basingstoke who should attend the distinctly Puritan lectures he had founded there."[68] Some Puritan church wardens withheld parish relief from those who failed to attend services.[69] One must wonder how the destitute and hungry poor felt about these measures clearly designed to influence their religious ideas and persuasions.

As these few examples show, while the Puritan gentry

understood they had significant responsibility for the poor, their generosity was often tempered by their desire to convict others.

Compared to these Puritan restrictions, Wesley erected few barriers in his giving, although he occasionally notes giving to the "diligent."[70] Instructions to the societies clearly assumed that charity would be distributed where there was need, "whether they are good or bad, whether they fear God or not . . . never be ashamed to beg for the poor; yea, in this case, be an importunate beggar."[71] Throughout his life Wesley raised alms for the poor and distributed these without significant restrictions. The Oxford Methodists collected for the poor as a part of their charitable work in the 1720s and 1730s. One of Wesley's *Journal* entries in the year of 1785 (when Wesley was eighty-two years old!) illustrates this lifelong pattern:

> At this season we usually distribute coals and bread among the poor of the society. But I now considered, they wanted clothes, as well as food. So on this, and the four following days, I walked through the town, and begged two hundred pounds, in order to clothe them that needed it most. But it was hard work, as most of the streets were filled with melting snow, which often lay ankle deep; so that my feet were steeped in snow-water nearly from morning to evening.[72]

Wesley's active leadership set a lofty example among his followers. Henry Rack notes that, by his later years, Wesley was giving away approximately one thousand pounds per year of his own publication profits—in fact, the majority of his income.[73]

Wesley obviously did not share the widespread Puritan gentry's suspicion of indiscriminate charity. His attitude toward, and identification with, the poor hardly allowed for restrictions on giving, nor would his theology have supported that.

In the poorer Methodist societies Wesley instituted patterns of giving that allowed the poor to help each other. By the simple expedient of asking everyone, no matter how poor, to contribute a penny a week for a charitable fund, Wesley encouraged each member to help others.[74] Charity did not depend upon one's income, nor was one expected to be rich to participate. By this simple pattern Wesley was instilling patterns of personal discipline and charity that the Puritan gentry doubtless would have approved.

Institutions to Train the Poor to Help Themselves

To alleviate the difficulties of the impotent poor, Puritans, along with many others, generously gave vast sums. In the closing days of the sixteenth century and the beginning decades of the seventeenth, England experienced unprecedented economic expansion and accumulation of wealth. Wealthy merchants began to establish endowments with a variety of missions; often they were designed to ameliorate the impact of proverty on laborers and servants. W. K. Jordan, in a detailed study of England's charities, reports that in London 40 percent of charitable gifts during the period from 1600 to 1640 established endowments for the direct household relief of the poor.[75] Many such Puritan endowments were administered through city parish churches, and large sums were committed to support almshouses where the poor could find shelter and relief from life on the streets.[76]

Although direct support to the poor by Puritans was substantial, they were particularly interested in schemes "designed to afford opportunities for the social rehabilitation of poor and ignorant men."[77] Strategies fashioned to provide the poor employment were especially popular. Among these were endowments for the support of apprenticeships and loan funds, including direct loans for emergencies as well as loans to be put out at interest or to be worked off (the latter sometimes being restricted to young men wishing to become tradesmen or merchants).[78] Richard Stock, a successful merchant, stated the widely held Puritan sentiment concerning the necessity of work: "This is the best charity so to relieve the poor as we keep them in labor. It benefits the giver to have them labor, it benefits the commonweal to suffer no drones, nor to nourish any in idleness; it benefits the poor themselves."[79]

Similarly, direct charity to needy poor was only one feature of Wesley's practical efforts to relieve the conditions of poverty. Like the Puritans, Wesley experimented, particularly in London, with a number of self-help programs in an attempt to meet food and housing needs and to offer the poor possibilities for self-improvement. As a part of the total ministry provided at the Foundry, Wesley established work programs when jobs could not be found for the unemployed.[80] Along with this endeavor Wesley founded a "poor house for destitute widows and children" close by the Foundry.[81] In both of these experiments residents learned trades and produced items to sell. In these projects Wesley's care for widows and children, in a society wherein family connection was essential to personal identity, met a social need often overlooked by his contemporaries.

Wesley, early in his public ministries, began to provide interest-free loan funds or, in his words, a "lending stock" for short-term loans.[82] Originally drawn from his own resources, the fund gradually increased through other contributions and was an important resource for the destitute. Similar to other such Puritan funds, the interest-free feature of Wesley's pattern exemplified his identification with their economic situation and his unwillingness to impose "extra" conditions to the help he extended.

For Wesley a central feature of each program was its potential for teaching the poor self-confidence, reliability, and independence. Embedded in the programs were principles exemplifying his innate belief in the worth and possibility of each person, and his conviction that, depending on God's grace, all could improve themselves and their situation. Manfred Marquardt comments that, for Wesley, "Aid should be accompanied by internal and external attitudes of solidarity with the poor, not by condescending charity that helped the poor but at the same time humiliated them."[83] Again, his identification with the poor in these projects contrasted with the experience and attitudes found among some of the Puritan gentry who provided similar programs for the poor but accompanied them with assumptions of superiority.

Prison Relief

In addition to providing charity, Puritan trusts often included endowments designed to help those imprisoned, particularly those in prison for debt and related crimes.[84] Often these had the additional intent of teaching self-respect and self-reliance. Such trusts seldom involved those who established the endowments in direct contact with the persons incarcerated in prison, although many Puritan ministers regularly did carry on ministries within the prisons.

Wesley's concern for prisoners began early in his Oxford ministries and continued throughout his life. Originally based on their evangelical concern for the souls of condemned persons, Methodist prison ministries came to include humanitarian aid for prisoners and their families much like that provided by Puritan trusts. Active work in the prisons produced among Methodists a consciousness of the prisons abject conditions and the inadequacy of the legal system. Wesley's numerous comments on the prisons describing the plight of prisoners may well have contributed to the broad prison reforms begun late in his life.[85]

Medical Help

Hospitals for the care of the poor had been established during the earliest English Reformation and gained substantial support from Puritans during the early seventeenth century.[86] High among the duties of Puritan ministers and laypersons was visitation of the sick. Although instruction given about how to conduct such visits was often evangelical in emphasis, the plight of the ill and sick and the inadequacies of medical attention available to them were genuine concerns.[87]

Comparable to these Puritan efforts, Wesley too was intensely interested in the medical attention available for his society members and for the poor in general. From his Oxford days Wesley regularly visited the sick and later required his preachers to follow his lead by organizing such visits among the societies' members. To implement such a program in London, Wesley divided the city into districts and appointed two society members to each district who were responsible for visitation of the sick.[88] This direct involvement with the ill made Wesley acutely conscious of the dismal medical situation of many, particularly of the poor. Responding to these needs, Wesley occasionally dispensed medicine and treated simple illnesses. Whenever possible he enlisted the aid of pharmacists and occasionally referred more serious cases to doctors.[89] For these continuing needs a dispensary (pharmacy/clinic) was established in 1747.[90]

Perhaps the best known of Wesley's medical endeavors was his *Primitive Physic*, published over many years in multiple editions. This book provided simple medical remedies and aids for his society members and for the general public. Ted Jennings has demonstrated that Wesley's general distrust of physicians may have added to his anxiousness to offer medical help to the uninformed and poor.[91]

Educational Institutions

Puritan appreciation for education contributed to a special interest in schooling as a means of overcoming poverty. Examples of this concern are many: William Jones, a prominent London merchant, left a large endowment in 1616 for the establishment of a grammar school capable of handling one hundred students.[92] Robert Lever, another London merchant, endowed such a school at Bolton-le-Moor, Lancashire.[93] Valerie Pearl, studying Puritan patterns of social experiments, provides an instructive account of an important Interregnum experiment that supplied poor children in London with both employment and education. Under a "Corporation of the Poor" created in 1649, two workhouses were established to educate children and train them for productive trades. Although disbanded at the Restoration, these institutions, while they existed, equipped many of London's poor to care for themselves and to escape their poverty.[94] The Dissenting academies of the post-Revolutionary period, founded in greatly different circumstances and for somewhat different reasons, were antici- pated in these early Puritan school foundations.

Wesley shared the Puritans' conviction that education was a most important avenue to both self-improvement and a full and complete life. Perhaps his most significant and long-term contribution to the betterment of the poor was his provisions for their education. In his endeavors Wesley joined the efforts of charity schools established by the Society for Promoting Christian Knowledge, and some of the Dissenting academies established for those barred from the Anglican-administered public schools and universities.[95] Methodists provided a variety of schools: day schools for boys and girls, orphanages that included educational programs, and schools with a more advanced curriculum, such as the widely known Kingswood School.[96] Day schools usually provided basic instruction, whereas Kingswood was established as a school for the training of itinerant pastors' children and for the preparation of Methodist local pastors. The poor were welcome in all of these schools. Wesley also encouraged Sunday schools when they began to emerge late in his life.[97]

Wesley's enduring and unique educational endeavors arose from his lifelong publishing efforts. These were designed to train and sustain the numerous adults who joined his societies with little or no formal education. Through a vast array of writings, both original and borrowed, Wesley provided his followers instruction in faith and everyday living. He was convinced that all persons, whatever their circumstances, could, through reading, expand not only their knowledge but their faith, and learn thereby to improve their Christian living. Books and pamphlets were provided at the lowest cost possible through a central bookshop in London.[98] Whenever purchase was still not possible, books were provided without charge and circulating libraries were established. In his own day Wesley was providing, in perhaps a more organized program of publication, materials similar to the vast array of Puritan works of instruction examined earlier in this study.

Wesley and the Puritan Gentry

The well-intentioned charity of merchant Puritans no doubt helped many of the poor. The design of much Puritan strategy to improve or eliminate poverty was also helpful; nonetheless, these attempts only partially succeeded. Endowments, generous as they might be, were not sufficient to provide for the increasing numbers of poor. In the midst of these laudable efforts, attitudes prevailed that depreciated the lot of the poor and openly condemned those who did not appropriate the Puritan work ethic. Such attitudes could hardly have ingratiated merchant Puritans among the poor.

In John Wesley's pragmatic efforts to meet needs where he found them, his endeavors on behalf of the poor are certainly similar to those initiated by the merchant and gentry Puritans. Schools, hospitals and medical treatments, loan funds, charitable funds, prison ministries, work programs, and "poor houses" were all familiar patterns of poor relief. In Wesley's case many of the efforts did not attain permanent establishment because he could not maintain each of them personally. Where they could be sustained through local leadership, many succeeded for some years. Several of the schools were built on lasting foundations. Unlike the gentry and merchant Puritans, Methodists, at least through most of Wesley's life, did not have the resources to establish endowments to support such projects. Perhaps the most important Methodist distinction from the Puritan activities in these areas lies in the fact that Wesley's projects were formed among the poor and included the poor in their operation. They were not something done *for* the poor as often as they were done *with* the poor.

Wesley and the Puritan Poor

As we have seen, Wesley's attitude toward the common person corresponded more closely to that of the Puritan poor than it did to that of the Puritan gentry. His willingness to use untrained laypersons in societal leadership, his insistence that members support each other and care for each other, also closely resembled practices among the Puritan poor. His preaching outdoors and allowing vent for powerful religious emotions in worship services certainly paralleled similar preaching and worship services among the poor.

Ted Jennings has investigated Wesley's comments on the New Testament pentecostal church in which Christians held all material goods in common.[99] Wesley was attracted by the concept and held it as an ideal pattern of Christian living. There were even a few experiments that incorporated the practice among Methodists. To that extent Wesley's views on Christian sharing of material assets were similar to those found among the sixteenth-century Diggers. However, his usual political conservatism would not allow him to approve of their more radical attempt to change the country's social and economic fabric through the creation of such communities. Wesley's interest in communal living arose from his preoccupation with how to apply gospel teachings practically. No doubt the Diggers' original motivations were similar; however, their biblical quotations often had the ring of offering a scriptural proof-text for political and economic ideas that actually emanated from other sources.

The Difficulties of Success

Max Weber's well-known work on the rise of capitalism suggests that Wesley's close identification with Puritan emphasis upon conduct, discipline, honesty, and hard work contributed greatly to the rise of modern capitalism. For Weber the stress upon calling and discipline in both movements resulted in a "worldly asceticism" whereby labor became a calling for the common person—and acquisition became the same for the business manager. Such understandings resulted in the accumulation of capital, and therefore wealth, and whetted a capitalistic spirit in England and America.[100] Weber's thesis has certainly been questioned, but he points to an important reality.[101]

The patterns of personal discipline, thrift, work, and calling taught by the Puritans and by Wesley resulted in their movements raising many craftsmen and artisans from poverty into economic independence, and sometimes into wealth. The more responsible merchant and gentry Puritan theologians worked out a "careful casuistry" that allowed them to accept these successes without claiming them as God's favor or as rewards for righteous living.[102] Their extensive charity originated a proper response not only to their blessing of wealth, but to their own salvation as well. The more radical of the Puritan poor questioned this logic, but their experience was very different, and some of them also participated in the rising economy of the post-Revolutionary period.

Wesley's growing anxiety in his later years about the wealth accumulated by diligent Methodists is well known.[103] In spite of his continual warnings about the dangers of riches and his admonitions to give generously of their profits, Methodists appear, like the Puritans before them, to have rationalized their situation. Ted Jennings suggests that Wesley "failed" in his teachings because he provided "Hedges and Qualifications" that allowed Methodists to justify the accumulation of goods and money.[104] When these "hedges" are examined, they turn out to be conventional truths: Wesley recognized that money in itself was not bad; only the misuse of it was to be condemned, so good uses were to be accepted and praised. Riches *are* dangerous; they can indeed lead one into false dependence and selfishness; nevertheless, maintaining oneself and one's family requires responsible use and the retention of some earnings. These are the same truths that gave content to Puritan casuistry; they are true even if they can be, and often were, misunderstood and misused. In the hands of Wesley and more conscientious Puritans, they were carefully guarded and their dangers were clearly noted. It is clear that his instructions related to the use of money correspond to those of many Puritan theologians. His distrust of riches may be more pronounced than that of the Puritans', but the general teachings are similar.

Alongside these similarities with Puritan merchant and gentry teachings, Wesley's substantially different understanding of equality and the gospel imperative that one must bounteously share with others the fruits of diligent labor also closely identifies him with the Puritan poor. An abundant Christian life is one in which human distinctions, whether based on money, position, or education, are irrelevant; sharing is synonymous with living. Although such a description would certainly be affirmed by Puritan merchants and gentry, it was the Puritan poor who more often experimented with such concepts in their attempts to apply these teachings to their lives. These Puritans, seeking to modify the inequalities of the economic system in which they lived, had little use for the distinctions of place and position. They insisted on sharing and tenaciously held to their freedom of conscience. Again, Wesley would not have supported their radical political ideas, but he was certainly sympathetic with many of their perceptions.

Anyone studying Wesley should not be surprised at his endorsement of two contrasting patterns of social responsibility—patterns that produced among Puritans substantially different parties. After all, his theology repeatedly held together many elements in creative tension: faith *and* works, tradition *and* experience, Scripture *and* reason. His eclecticism, clearly evident in his publications, more than once carried him into tension-filled positions. Jennings may be correct in suggesting that Wesley's followers could not sustain the tension inherent in riches and succumbed to the siren song of wealth, but for Wesley this was not the case.[105] He tenaciously taught the disciplines of holiness *expecting* that as holiness grasped the equality of love, it guarded against the inherent dangers that accompany the rewards of a disciplined life. That others could not sustain the tension such a position imposes should not detract from Wesley's experience and vision.

Notes

1. John Flavel, *Husbandry Spiritualized: or, The Heavenly Use of Earthly things* (Elizabeth Town: Printed by Shepard Killock, 1794), 59 [*CL*, 27:166].
2. *Letters*, 7:66.
3. Bolton, *Walking with God*, 73-76 [*CL*, 4:349-50].

4. Stuckley, *Gospel-Glass*, 325 [CL, 19:423]. "What brings destruction on God's people, but their joining with the wicked" (Sibbes, *Christ and His Church*, in *Works of Richard Sibbes*, 2:88 [*CL*, 6:185]).

5. *Works*, 3:146; *MMC*, 158.

6. *Works*, 3:154. Specific instructions are given by Bolton and Wesley as to how one is to handle the delicate problem of visitation among those who are not Christian (*Works*, 3:152; Bolton, *Walking with God*, 86 [*CL*, 4:350-51]).

7. **"It had been better we had gone to the pest-house, and eat and drank with persons infected with the plague,** *even wilst the sore and betch was running on them*, **than to accompany with wicked men; our bodies would have been endangered only by the one; but our souls are by the other"** (Stuckley, *Gospel-Glass*, 327 [*CL*, 19:424]; *Works*, 3:135, 150).

8. *Works*, 3:131; Stuckley, *Gospel-Glass*, 331-32 [*CL*, 19:427].

9. Coomer, "Influence of Puritanism and Dissent" 349-50. Stephen, *History of English Thought in the Eighteenth Century*, 2:433.

10. *Works*, 1:521, 529; Matthew Hale, *Contemplations, Moral and Divine*, 84-85 [*CL*, 17:219-20]; Sibbes, *Christ and His Church*, in *Works of Richard Sibbes*, 2:87 [*CL*, 6:182].

11. [Richard Allestree], *The Whole Duty of Man*, *CL*, 12:106; William Cave, *Primitive Christianity*, *CL*, 19:69.

12. *Works*, 2:514.

13. Kitchin, "How Must We Reprove," in *Morning Exercises*, 1:137 [*CL*, 21:436]; *Works*, 2:514.

14. Kitchin, "How Must We Reprove," in *Morning Exercises*, 1:138-39 [*CL*, 21:437-38].

15. *Works*, 2:513.

16. Baxter, *Saints' Everlasting Rest*, in *The Practical Works of Richard Baxter*, 23:78 [*CL*, 22:181]; Kitchin, "How Must We Reprove," in *Morning Exercises*, 1:141 [*CL*, 21:440]; *Works*, 2:516.

17. **"To tell them of sin, or of heaven, or hell, in a dull, easy, careless language, doth make men think you are not in good** *saddness, nor do mean as you speak* **[earnest]; but** *either you* **scarce think yourselves such things are true,** *or else you take them in such a slight and indifferent manner*" (Baxter, *Saints' Everlasting Rest*, in *Practical Works of Richard Baxter*, 23:81 [*CL*, 22:186]; Kitchin, "How Must We Reprove," in *Morning Exercises*, 1:140 [*CL*, 21:439]).

18. *Works*, 2:517.

19. Baxter, *Saints' Everlasting Rest*, in *Practical Works of Richard Baxter*, 23:84 [*CL*, 22:186-87]; Kitchin, "How Must We Reprove," in *Morning Exercises*, I, 141 [*CL*, XXI, 439-40]; Wesley, *Works*, 2:518.

20. *Works*, 2:519.

21. Baxter, *Saints' Everlasting Rest*, in *Practical Works of Richard Baxter*, 23:85 [*CL*, 22:188]; Kitchin, "How Must We Reprove," in *Morning Exercises*, 1:142 [*CL*, 21:441]; *Works* (Jackson), 6:301.

22. Kitchin, "How Must We Reprove," in *Morning Exercises*, 1:139 [*CL*, 21:439].

23. *Works*, 2:517.

24. Baxter, *Saints' Everlasting Rest*, in *Practical Works of Richard Baxter*,

23:87 [*CL*, 22:189]; Kitchin, "How Must We Reprove," in *Morning Exercises*, 1:37-38 [*CL*, 21:437].

25. *Works*, 2:517.

26. Kitchin, "How Must We Reprove," in *Morning Exercises*, 1:138 [*CL*, 21:437]; Baxter, *Saints' Everlasting Rest*, in *Practical Works of Richard Baxter*, 23:85 [*CL*, 22:195]; *Works*, 2:514-15.

27. *Works*, 2:520.

28. *Works*, 1:522.

29. *Works*, 1:533-34.

30. *Works*, 2:536.

31. Alleine, *Vindiciae Pietatis*, 342-46 [*CL*, 23:202-5].

32. *Works*, 2:650ff.

33. Responsibility for those of the world meant not only responsibility for witnessing to them and seeking to bring them to salvation, but also a real responsibility for their physical well-being as displayed both in their health and their material status. (See Matthew Pool's sermon "On the Visitation of the Sick," in *Morning Exercises,* 1:111ff. [*CL*, 21:478ff.]; Wesley's sermon "On Visiting the Sick," *Works*, 3:385ff.)

34. *CL*, 17:233-63.

35. *Works*, 2:281ff.

36. *Works*, 1:612f.

37. Thomas Manton, "Sermon on Matthew vii.12.," in *The Works of Thomas Manton* (London: James Nisbet, 1871), 2:383 [*CL*, 7:309]. Cf. Stuckley, *Gospel-Glass*, 190-94 [*CL*, 19:350-54].

38. *Works*, 1:566; cf. 1:541ff.

39. Trevelyan, *English Social History*; Hill, *Society and Puritanism*; E. P. Thompson, *The Making of the English Working Class* (New York: Random House, 1964), 46-47; Raymond G. Cowherd, *The Politics of English Dissent* (New York: New York University Press, 1956); Rattenbury, *Wesley's Legacy to the World*; Élie Halévy, *A History of the English People in 1815*, trans. E. I. Watkin and D. A. Barker, 3 vols. (London: T. Fisher Unwin, 1924); Robert F. Wearmouth, *Methodism and the Common People of the Eighteenth Century* (London: Epworth Press, 1945); Maldwyn Edwards, *John Wesley and the Eighteenth Century* (London: Epworth Press, 1955).

40. G. M. Trevelyan suggests that the dissolution of the monasteries and the enclosure movements were perhaps not so immediately devastating to the people of the land as contemporaries and historians have sometimes claimed, yet the changes, even if driven by other economic policies and developments, ultimately brought major agrarian change (*English Social History*, 116-23).

41. Christopher Hill, *The Century of Revolution: 1603-1714* (London: Thomas Nelson & Sons, 1961), 18-20.

42. Christopher Hill, *Society and Puritanism*, 262.

43. *Works* (Jackson), 11:54.

44. *Works* (Jackson), 11:55.

45. *Works* (Jackson), 11:55-56.

46. *Works* (Jackson), 11:56.

47. *Works* (Jackson), 11:56-57.

48. *Works* (Jackson), 11:57.

49. *Works* (Jackson), 11:57.

50. Henry Denne, *Grace, Mercy and Peace* (1645) quoted in Christopher Hill, *The World Turned Upside Down* (New York: Viking Press, 1972), 11.

51. Hill, *Society and Puritanism*, 271-74.

52. William Perkins, *A Treatise of Callings* quoted in Hill, *Society and Puritanism*, 259. The statute Perkins refers to is the comprehensive Poor Law, which sought to control begging while it relieved the working poor who were unable to sustain themselves.

53. See page 215.

54. Michael Walzer, *The Revolution of the Saints: A Study in the Origins of Radical Politics* (Cambridge, Mass.: Harvard University Press, 1965), 310-12. Walzer also offers an interesting critique of Max Weber's suggestions that Calvinism provided the Puritans with a capitalist understanding of "systematic acquisition," 304-6.

55. Hill, *Society and Puritanism*, 278.

56. Walzer, *Revolution of the Saints*, 313.

57. Christopher Hill, *World Turned Upside Down*, 39.

58. Hill, *World Turned Upside Down*, 75.

59. Hill, *World Turned Upside Down*, 76.

60. Dell, *Several Sermons and Discourses*, 264-66; 273-74.

61. Hill, *Century of Revolution*, 129-33.

62. Hill, *Century of Revolution*, 103.

63. Hill, *Century of Revolution*, 132-33.

64. Manfred Marquardt, *John Wesley's Social Ethics*, trans. John Steely and W. Stephen Gunter (Nashville: Abingdon Press, 1992), 29.

65. Theodore W. *Jennings*, Jr., *Good News to the Poor: John Wesley's Evangelical Economics* (Nashville: Abingdon Press, 1990), see especially chap 3.

66. "The Danger of Riches," *Works*, 3:227-46; "On Riches," 3:518-28.

67. Joseph Hall, *The Works of Joseph Hall*, ed. Josiah Pratt (London: Printed for C. Whittingham, 1808), 7:167-8.

68. W. K. Jordan, *The Charities of London, 1480-1660* (London: George Allen and Unwin, 1960), 111.

69. Hill, *Society and Puritanism*, 293.

70. *Works*, 20:10.

71. "On Visiting the Sick," *Works*, 3:387, 390.

72. *Journal*, 4:295; see also 4:451; *Works*, 20:15,18.

73. Henry Rack, *Reasonable Enthusiast: John Wesley and the Rise of Methodism* (Philadelphia: Trinity Press International, 1989), 361. Wesley notes in his "Danger of Riches" that he had "unawares" become rich through the sale of books (*Works*, 3:239).

74. *Works*, 20:10, 15, 159; 19:135-36.

75. Jordan, *The Charities of London,* 88. This study and its companion volumes constitute a detailed study of charity in England. See also *The Charities of Rural England, 1480-1660* (New York: Russell Sage Foundation, 1961), 241, 247-49; *The Forming of the Charitable Institutions of the West of England* (Philadelphia: American Philosophical Society, 1960).

76. Jordan, *Charities of London,* 153, 155.

77. Jordan, *Charities of London,* 167.

78. Jordan, *Charities of London*, 174-75. Thomas White, an early Puritan, provided a complex network of such funds.

79. Hill, *Society and Puritanism*, 277.

80. *Works*, 19:173, 193.

81. *Works*, 9:277.

82. "*A Plain Account of the People Called Methodists*," *Works*, 9:279; 20:19,193; 20:125.

83. Marquardt, *John Wesley's Social Ethics*, 122.

84. Jordan, *Charities of London*, 180-94.

85. *Works*, 19:22; 11:241; *Letters*, 4:84; see also Marquardt, *John Wesley's Social Ethics*, 83-86.

86. Jordan, *Charities of London*, 185-94.

87. Matthew Pool, "On Visitation of the Sick," in *Morning Exercises*, 1:111ff. [*CL*, 21:478ff.].

88. *Works*, 9:275; 19:193.

89. *Works*, 9:274-76; 20:171; *Journal*, 5:513.

90. *Works*, 20:151.

91. Jennings, *Good News for the Poor*, 74-76.

92. Jordan, *Charities of London*, 236.

93. Jordan, *Charities of London*, 244; see also *Charities of Rural England*, 336, 302.

94. Valerie Pearl, "Puritans and Poor Relief: The London Workhouse, 1649-1660," in *Puritans and Revolutionaries*, ed. D. Pennington and K. Thomas (Oxford: Clarendon Press, 1978), 206-32. The Corporation for the Poor was renewed in 1698 and 1700 for orphans and vagrants. After 1720 they became a common feature of the societal program to alleviate poverty.

95. See Marquardt for an extended discussion of the social contribution of Wesley's educational efforts, *John Wesley's Social Ethics*, 49ff.

96. See Rack, *Reasonable Enthusiast*, 354-59; Wesley's *Plain Account of Kingswood School*, *Works* (Jackson), 13:289-300.

97. *Journal*, 7:3, 20,71; *Letters*, 7:364.

98. *Letters*, 6:208; 7:144.

99. Jennings, *Good News for the Poor*, 111-16; 124-26.

100. Max Weber, *The Protestant Ethic and the Spirit of Capitalism*, trans. Talcott Parsons (London: Allen & Unwin, 1930), 139-43, 178-83.

101. Marquardt, *John Wesley's Social Ethics*, 41; Thompson, *Making of the English Working Class*, 365; Walzer, *Revolution of the Saints*, 304-6.

102. Rack, *Reasonable Enthusiast*, 366.

103. Ted Jennings carefully documents this reality and suggestively interprets its meaning. *Good News for the Poor*, chaps. 2, 5, 7.

104. Jennings, *Good News for the Poor*, 159-65.

105. Jennings, *Good News for the Poor*, 177ff.

Conclusion

The obvious similarity between the Puritans and Wesley lies in their respective teachings and practice of an austere, circumspect, holy life, or, in the terminology of their own times, an emphasis on "practical divinity." For Wesley's contemporaries, as well as many of his commentators since, this similarity was sufficient to recognize a significant relationship. We have seen in this study that the similarity rested on other substantial interconnections between the two traditions. The associations relating the two movements permit us to acknowledge the more notable aspects of this connection.

The incidence of Puritan materials in *A Christian Library* and in Wesley's other publications demonstrates that he allowed Puritan expressions of "practical divinity" not only to take a predominant place in his own instruction, but also, in several instances, to become the pattern for that teaching. Wesley's selection was not random; therefore, we may affirm that this preponderance made Puritan teaching a major, though not an exclusive, source of his own instruction concerning Christian life. Remembering that Wesley appropriated materials from a variety of theological traditions, choosing whatever was congenial to his interests, we must nevertheless note that in several incidences of direct dependence on Puritan instruction, he allows these Puritan patterns to help mold the very character of his own movement.

Wesley's distinction between "Nonconformist" (understanding here those Puritan ministers ejected in 1662) and "Dissenters" allowed him to identify with "moderate" Puritans who, like himself, sought to renew the church from within rather than to separate from it. Although he could and did occasionally use materials and instruction from the more radical wing of the Puritan movement, his sympathy clearly lay with the moderates. For example, Richard Baxter's teachings have run like a thread throughout this study. Even though Baxter's guarded Arminian sympathies distinguished him from many Puritans, he was one of their foremost apologists and a leading systematician of their teachings on Christian life. It is not surprising, then, that Wesley continually returned to Baxter, and other moderate Puritans, for support and example. Wesley's willingness to use the insights of the tradition allowed him to disregard the "prejudices" of his education. This willingness also occasionally brought him into conflict with the dominant theology and practice of his contemporaries in the Church of England.

Wesley's appreciation of Puritan insight began as early as his initial readings of their works in 1737-38. His conflicts with antinomianism and later with the Calvinistic Methodists led him to enlist some Puritan formulations to support his own theological arguments. While it would be an overstatement to suggest that Wesley drew his theological understanding of these issues from Puritan expressions, it is clear that, where appropriate, he was willing to go beyond simple use of their instructions to employ the theological underpinnings on which their teachings were grounded. Puritan theology does, then, contribute in limited areas to Wesley's mature theological formulations.

Wesley's willingness to disregard ecclesiastical rules and conventions that he felt limited the proclamation of the gospel identified his movement, in the eyes of the church, with Puritan models. His desire that the church provide a means for continually strengthening the Christian life of the common people led him to embrace in his societal system elements of the "gathered church" principle practiced among many Puritans. When he reluctantly decided to ordain Methodist preachers, his appropriation of Presbyterian patterns for those ordinations further strengthened the identification with Puritan precedents. Each of these practices reinforced Methodist identification with the Puritan ecclesiastical patterns. Combined with his use of extemporaneous prayer, field preaching, and local pastors, these practices contributed, in the eyes of many of his contemporaries, to a de facto separation of the Methodists from the Church of England during Wesley's lifetime. The ultimate break with the church after his death must have been seen as a natural consequence of such practices. These ecclesiastical innovations placed Wesley's followers, albeit reluctantly, in the English "free church" tradition.

The similarity between the spirit, theology, and practice of John Wesley and the Puritans, the substantial relationship evident in theology and teachings, and his dependence upon that tradition for instances of precept and pattern have made it possible for this study to affirm a conscious, distinct, and significant connection between the two movements, one that goes beyond simple correspondence in teachings on "practical divinity." When we add to these connections the affinities evident in his liturgical indebtedness, his educational theory, his biblical concern, as well as the Puritan character of his family background and home training, Wesley's Puritan heritage assumes a place of prominence in his own thought and practice and, to some extent, helps mold some aspects of both thought and practice. Considering the numerous elements in this relationship and their aggregate impact on Wesley, we may affirm with Gordon Wakefield that "the Puritan influence upon him [Wesley] is incalculable."[1]

Once again, however, we need to be warned against overemphasis on this important relationship. Wesley's movement, for all its similarities to the earlier movement, was not a renewed Puritanism, nor was Wesley a Puritan. We must recognize the contribution of the multifarious roots of Wesley's theology and teachings, which, when combined, gave his movement its unique character. Nevertheless, when we do that, Puritanism must appear among those roots and should not be discounted as a significant contributor to the uniqueness of Methodism.

Given the valid and important correlation between Wesley and the Puritans, what elements in their presentations of Christian life and practice proved definitive for their movements? What characteristics became foundational attributes of the churches that grew out of Puritanism and out of Wesley's work?

The discovery that every person—in Wesley's terminology, "I, even I"—has the possibility and promise of a relationship to God is an existential confrontation that lies at the very core of meaningful religious life, be it personal or corporate. For their neighbors Wesley and the Puritans recaptured this essential truth. Out of a personal relationship to God, made possible through grace and appropriated through human faith in Jesus Christ, comes a vibrant awareness of new possibilities for meaningful life. The dynamic energy of this experience demands expression by both precept and example in daily living, so we are not surprised to find Puritans and Methodists urging their followers to express God's love in their daily living. Recapturing such experiential faith and its consequent life as an essential part of Christian commitment continues to challenge every generation of those who succeeded the Puritans and Wesley in the various church groups spawned by their testimony.

The primacy of faith as the ground on which such personal experience rested clearly characterized both the Puritan and the Wesleyan movements. That this faith would be accompanied by "works of love and piety" was no less important to each group even if their understanding of the consequences of such love differed. Their conviction that faith *and* works are essential to Christian life resulted in elaborated instructions for Christian living. Such tutelage and the educational values it incorporated became another characteristic element of the groups formed from Puritan and Methodist roots.

At the heart of the Puritan and Methodist impact on their contemporaries was the changed lives of individuals who committed themselves to Christ through these movements. Presenting a view of the Christian faith that made it meaningful, relevant, and vital to each life, both the Puritans and Wesley were able to convey to their followers an effective and intense appreciation for the disciplined life. Unafraid to proclaim what this meant in specific teachings covering every aspect of daily life, they offered the people a meaningful pattern for living that could be embraced even with all its dangers of legalism and idealism (charges easily, and sometimes appropriately, brought against both movements and their heirs). Puritan casuistry and Wesleyan emphasis on ethical instruction helped fill the void left by the Protestant removal of the earlier elaborate Roman Catholic system of ethical teaching. In doing so, they provided both the rationale and theology for such a life, while pointing to the norms by which Christian living should be judged.

One would not want to defend the extremes to which such teachings were occasionally carried in both movements, particularly their depreciation of the aesthetic. Nevertheless, Wesley and his Puritan mentors must be judged by their intention to speak a relevant and commanding word to their contemporaries who by their choices made "the world," whether consciously or unconsciously, that which gave meaning and purpose to life. They were attempting to restore purposeful modes of discipline in eras when social, moral, and religious complacency at the best, and debauchery at the worst, were stock responses to life. The strength with which both these movements stressed particular patterns of Christian life may have allowed degeneration into pious legalism, but such was not their intent. Their intent was always a "singleness of mind" that sought to experience a relationship to, and glorification of, God in daily life. Historically their heirs have repeatedly slipped from the moorings of this discipline only to embrace its wisdom again when compliancy and identification with social norms have threatened personal religious experience and its social fruits.

Involvement in the social and political life of the community kept the Puritans from the quietest tendencies of seventeenth-century Continental Pietism, to which they were otherwise closely related in emphasis and spirit. Their conviction that God actively works to transform all spheres of life, including "life in the world," with all its ramifications, undergirded their insistence on involvement in the world. Wesley's early asceticism was mitigated by this same conviction. It was his belief that holiness must include involvement in the world, which kept him from embracing the quietistic and separatist tendencies of the Moravian pietists from whom he had learned many lessons about faith. Insistence upon involvement "in the world" is at least a partial explanation of the phenomenal success of Puritanism and Methodism as popular religious movements. Modern churches or religious movements that hope to attract and retain the interest of believers will do well to remember this important lesson of social awareness and involvement so obviously present in Puritanism and Methodism.

This acceptance and affirmation of the world, while recognizing the dangers of corrosion and corruption, also meant both movements not only acknowledged the realities of poverty but actively sought remedies for its consequences. Although the Puritans and the Methodists were perhaps not as cognizant as we might wish of the cultural patterns that repeatedly produce such poverty, they nevertheless worked actively to help their followers overcome its insidious traps through applying the gospel lessons of love, responsibility, and opportunity. The legacy of social concern and particular attention to poverty and its sources led both British and American Methodism to appropriate much of the early-twentieth-century social gospel. Although the social gospel movement's misplaced optimism still needs to be avoided, the basic imperative that Christianity confront the social systems that produce poverty and its debilitating consequences remain essential in every age.

The strength of Puritan and Methodist popular appeal was also substantially dependent on the success of these movements in providing for active fellowship among believers—fellowship patterns that provided interpersonal support for each member's faith through shared experiences of belief, encouragement, and accountability. In such groups members could expect confrontation from their peers when they failed to live out their commitments to the faith, and praise when they kept those commitments. Whether these groups were the family "house churches," the small congregation, or Wesley's system of societies and classes, they provided the constant encounter so necessary to the continuation and development of faith. Historically, the most frequent expression of the communal nature of faith had been in religious communities separated from the world, for example, monastic and pietistic communities. The ability of the Puritans and Wesley to foster an analogous communal fellowship of faith among persons who remained in the world accounts, in part, for their public appeal and for their tenacious ability to weather the storms of controversy that surrounded each movement. The genius of such Christian fellowship groups is even more important today when individualism and privatization have changed the very meaning of community. We will all surely benefit if the significance of such groups within the Christian fellowship is even now being rediscovered.[2]

In at least one area the Puritan and Wesleyan movements and their heirs encountered the same difficulties that their predecessor reform movements had experienced. In organizing their members into lasting ecclesiastical institutions, they discovered that a unified church appealing to many must allow differing ideas and practices among its members and, consequently, a more relaxed pattern of discipline. Such openness often threatens the very emphases—discipline and holiness—that originally distinguished the movement. Achieving a genuine balance between these characteristics, unity and disciplined holiness, has proved to be most difficult throughout Christian history.[3] The heirs of the Puritan and Methodist reforms found it no different—this historical tension between unity and holiness proved to be a persistent problem for both groups.

Puritans of Presbyterian persuasion, and some patterns of Congregationalists, sought to create a theocracy that would embrace both unity and holiness. In doing so, they allowed lay members a limited role in civil and church governance through a synod pattern while insisting on a high degree of disciplined holiness for all. Other Congregationalists, Independents, Baptists, Quakers, and sect groups opted for separation from any state church insisting on local congregational control, for such separation allowed them local responsibility for disciplined holiness. Consequently, no comprehensive ecclesiology combining unity and holiness was achieved among the Puritans.

Wesley's dream that his societies might embrace holiness by becoming "*ecclesiolae in ecclesia*" without the necessity of separation from the Church of England ultimately failed to materialize. By his own refusal to separate from the church or to allow Methodism to do so in his lifetime, he held tenaciously to church unity; yet by stressing disciplined holiness, and by acting, albeit reluctantly, to make separation possible at his death, he embraced a position in dynamic tension with this very unity.

Wesley's followers had already begun to differ over issues of church order before his death. American Methodists established a modified episcopal order supplemented by annual conferences granting all clergy members the right to vote. English Methodism was to debate for decades what elements of church governance

Wesley intended to establish through his ordinations, and to struggle with the nature of authority as it related to the conference.[4]

In Wesley's later years he complained that discipline in the Methodist societies was already weakening, so holiness, though still embraced, was beginning to be subordinated to unity.

The growth of both English and American churches in the nineteenth century added to this trend. In America the expansion of the church across the vast continent meant incorporating persons from a variety of social and ethic backgrounds. This openness to all, following John Wesley's example, meant willingness to be inclusive rather than exclusive—a movement toward unity rather than toward distinctive holiness. By the turn of the twentieth century one of American Methodism's hallmarks was its openness to and inclusion of persons with many opinions regarding the nonessentials of the faith.

In the eyes of many members this inclusive unity came at the expense of holiness. Strong discipline, though affirmed and taught, slowly gave way to the attractions of unity in the American Methodism of the late nineteenth and twentieth centuries. Consequently, generations of American Methodists found themselves able to profess both holiness and unity without clearly understanding the core assertions of either position. They often were also unaware of the historically inherent tensions present between the two ideals.

Responding to the resultant ambivalence present in Methodist ecclesiastical and disciplinary understandings, repeated reform movements have arisen that attempt to reassert an emphasis on disciplined holiness. Smaller Wesleyan churches often lessened the tensions by choosing to separate from the larger bodies. Most often, they reasserted holiness as their defining character.

Willingness to embrace inclusiveness when defining church order and discipline has been part of the uniqueness of Methodism. It is this attribute, however, which markedly contributes to the demand of many current members that church polity and discipline be reformed and clarified.[5] Their contention is that inclusiveness has diluted and modified the original doctrinal and disciplinary teaching of the church. Efforts to obtain, and require of members, definitive doctrinal affirmations and to restore more stringent patterns of discipline inevitably question the requirements and advantages of church unity. Consequently, the historical tension between disciplined holiness and church unity continues to present Methodism with unresolved challenges.

Methodists are not unique in these renewed struggles over church polity, belief, and practice. Many American and European Protestant churches, rooted in the Puritan tradition, also find these same issues of holiness and unity producing current movements for reform and modification of church order and discipline. Just as the Puritans and John Wesley had difficulty holding unity and holiness in dynamic tension, their followers continue the struggle.

Notes

1. Gordon Wakefield, "Puritanism, Its Necessity, Dangers and Future," *Methodist Sacramental Fellowship Bulletin* (Summer 1961): 2.

2. Commentators who contributed to the recovery of such groups in the 1960s include Robert A. Raines, *New Life in the Church* (New York: Harper & Row, 1961); Elton Trueblood, *The Company of the Committed* (Harper & Row, 1961); George Webber, *God's Colony in Man's World* (Nashville: Abingdon Press, 1960). David Watson and others have in recent decades led modern Methodism into rediscovery of the class meeting and its contributions to faith development and discipline (see *Early Methodist Class Meeting*). The development of the "Disciple Bible Study" series by the Methodist Board of Discipleship and introduction of other small group patterns such as those found in the "Walk to Emmaus" movement also point to the recovery of the small group as a most important means of sustaining Christian faith and life. Many mainline Protestant churches have appropriated the small group ministry systems developed by "Stephen Ministries," a system originated by a Lutheran pastor (Stephen Ministries, 8016 Dale, St. Louis, M.). Robert Wuthnow, *"I Come Away Stronger"* (Grand Rapids, Mich.: William B. Eerdmans, 1994), provides case studies and analysis of many such groups in American churches.

3. Max Weber and Ernst Troeltsch early in this century offered useful sociological analysis of the continuing tension between unity and holiness by distinguishing between a "church," understanding unity as primary, and a "sect," emphasizing discipline and holiness. Recent studies by Rodney Stark and William Sims (*The Future of Religion* [Berkeley: University of California Press, 1985]; *A Theory of Religion* [New York: Peter Lang, 1987]), have expanded and modified these theories. A helpful summary of the issue and its larger implications may be found in Robert Monk, Joseph Stamey, et al., *Exploring Religious Meaning* (Upper Saddle River, N.J.: Prentice Hall, 1998), 282-86.

4. Albert Outler provides useful insights into the issues surrounding the Methodists' difficulty with this issue in "Do Methodists Have a Doctrine of the Church?" (in *The Doctrine of the Church,* ed. Dow Kirkpatrick [Nashville: Abingdon Press, 1964]).

5. William Abraham's *Waking from Doctrinal Amnesia* and Thomas Oden's *Doctrinal Standards in the Wesleyan Tradition* are examples of the call for a return to doctrinal clarity. The work and publications of groups such as "The Good News Fellowship" and the "Confessional Movement" often seek doctrinal and disciplinary reforms.

Appendix 1

Authors in *A Christian Library*

The following is a complete list of the authors in the order they appear in the first edition of *A Christian Library*. The authors are categorized for easier identification.

The initials used in this appendix indicate bibliographies of the period and the author list given to Wesley by Phillip Doddridge. Wesley's list of authors is compared to these works to ascertain the general usage of the works included in the *Library* and to discover how closely Wesley followed book lists that emphasized Puritan materials.

Doddridge's "Letter to Mr. Wesley" is indicated by the initial (D). As shown here, Wesley included some of Doddridge's suggestions as to authors from both the Puritan and Established Church traditions. However, Doddridge had also suggested many of his own contemporaries whom Wesley chose not to include in the *Library*; he used practically no literature of his own period. Wesley obviously depended upon Doddridge's list for guidance but went beyond it for his authors; only eight of Wesley's thirty-one Puritan authors are found in Doddridge's list.

Comparison is also made with the bibliographies of John Wilkins and Richard Baxter, indicated by the initials (W) and (B). Like Bishop Hall, Wilkins (1614-72), Bishop of Chester, had Puritan sympathies. His work *Ecclesiastes, or, A Discourse Concerning the Gift of Preaching*, republished in 1651, contained a systematic catalog of English religious literature, including most of the important Puritan writings of the period.[1] In all, a third of the Puritan writings Wesley used are recommended in this early list. Baxter's bibliography, included in *A Christian Directory*, may also have served Wesley as a source list, for it contains recommendations of more than a third of the Established Church authors and more than half of the Puritans used by Wesley.[2] These comparisons show that Wesley, to a large extent, used well-recognized writers who had been authoritative and reliable spokesmen of the tradition.

Several of the treatises included by Wesley in the *Library* bear no indication of their authorship in either the first or the second edition. Wesley may have considered some of them so well-known that indication of an author was unnecessary; for example, *The Whole Duty of Man*, usually credited to Richard Allestree (d. 1681), enjoyed from its first printing in 1658 at least twenty printings or editions by 1700.[3] For the majority of the anonymous material, however, it is more likely that Wesley did not know the authors. These tracts were presumably published works current during his own lifetime but without indication of authorship. Many authors of such tracts have since been identified.[4] Where identification has been possible, the tracts are listed by author and bracketed. Where available, identifying information is included in the endnotes.

Ancient Fathers

- Clement of Rome (B) (W)
- Polycarp (W)
- Ignatius (B) (W)
- Macarius

Foreign Authors

- John Arndt (German)
- Blaise Pascal (French)
- Anthoniette Bourignon (French)
- Don Juan D'Avila (Spanish)
- Miguel de Molinos (Spanish)
- (Devotional tracts translated from the French)

Anonymous Materials

- Devotional tracts translated from the French
- *A Collection of Prayers for Families*
- *A Country Parson's Advice to His Parishioners*

Church of England Authors

- Jeremy Taylor (1613-67) (B) (W)
- Ralph Cudworth (1617-88)
- Nathanael Culverwell (d. 1651)[5]
- John Smith (1618-52)
- [Richard Allestree (1619-81), *An Extract from the Whole Duty of Man*][6] (B)
- Robert Sanderson (1587-1663) (B) (W)

[James Garden (n.d.), *A Discourse Concerning Comparative Religion*][7]
John Worthington (1618-71)
Seth Ward (1617-89) (B)
Thomas Ken (1637-1711)
[Nicholas Horsman (d. 1683), *The Spiritual Bee*][8]
Anthony Horneck (1641-97) (D)
William Cave (1637-1713) (W)
Simon Patrick (1626-1717)
Abraham Cowley (n.d.)
John Goodman (1640-75)
Robert Leighton (1611-84)
Isaac Barrow (1630-1677) (D) (B) (W)
Henry More (1614-87) (B)
Richard Lucas (1648-1715) (D)
Edward Reynolds (1599-1676) (W)
[Susannah Hopton, *Devotions for Every Day of the Week*][9]
Robert South (1634-1716)
Benjamin Calamy (1642-86)[10]
Henry Scougal (1650-78) (D)
John Tillotson (1630-94) (D) (B)
Edward Young (1643-1705) (B) (W)
Charles Howe (1661-1742)
William Beveridge (1637-1708)

Puritan Authors
John Fox (1516-87) (B) (W)
Extracts from the Acts and Monuments of the Christian Martyrs
Samuel Clarke (1599-1683) (B) (W)
Supplement of Mr. Fox's *Acts and Monuments*
Extracted from Mr. Samuel Clarke's General Martyrology
The Lives of Various Eminent Persons
Joseph Hall (1574-1656) (D) (B) (W)
Meditations and Vows, Divine and Moral
Heaven upon Earth, or Of True Peace of Mind
Letters on Several Occasions
A Passion Sermon, Preached on Good Friday, *1609*
Holy Observations
Solomon's Song Paraphrased
Robert Bolton (1572-1631)[11] (D) (B) (W)
A Discourse on True Happiness
General Directions for a Comfortable Walking with God

Instructions for Comforting Afflicted Consciences
A Treatise Concerning the Word of God
A Treatise on Self-Examination
A Treatise on Fasting

John Preston (1587-1628) (B) (W)
The Breast Plate of Faith and Love
The New Covenant, or The Saint's Portion

Richard Sibbes (1577-1635) (D) (B) (W)
A Fountain Opened; or The Mystery of Godliness Revealed
The Nativity of Christ Celebrated by Angels
A Discovery of the Near Union and Communion betwixt Christ and the Church

Thomas Goodwin (1600-80) (D) (W)
A Child of Light Walking in Darkness
Christ the Object and Support of Faith
The Heart of Christ in Heaven towards Sinners on Earth
The Return of Prayers
The Trial of a Christian's Growth

Sir Matthew Hale (1609-76)
Contemplations, Moral and Divine

Richard Alleine (1611-81) (B)
Vindiciae Pietatis; or, A Vindication of Godliness
A Rebuke to Backsliders, and a Spur for Loiterers
The Nature and Necessity of Godly Fear

John Bunyan (1628-88)
A Relation of the Holy War

[Lewis Stuckley (1622-87)
A Gospel-Glass: or, A Call from Heaven, to Sinners and Saints by Repentance and Reformation, to Prepare to Meet God][12]

John Brown (1610-79)
Christ the Way, the Truth, and the Life

Samuel Annesley (1620?-96)
How We May be Universally and Exactly Conscientious[13]
God's Sovereignty Our Support in All Worldly Distractions
The Hindrance and Helps to a Good Memory of Spiritual Things
The Adherent Vanity of Every Condition Is Most Effectually Abated by Serious Godliness

John Kitchin (d. 1662?)
How Must We Reprove, That We May Not Partake of Other Men's Sins
Matthew Pool (1624-79)
How Ministers or Christian Friends May and Ought to Apply Themselves to Sick Persons, for Their Good, and the Discharge of Their Own Conscience
Richard Baxter (1615-91) (D) (W)
The Saints' Everlasting Rest
[Thomas Crane (1631-1714)
A Prospect of Divine Providence][14]
Stephen Charnock (1628-1680)
Of the Knowledge of God
Of the Knowledge of God in Christ
John Flavel (1630-91)(D)
Husbandry Spiritualized: or, the Heavenly Use of Earthly Things
Navigation Spiritualized: or A New Compass for Seamen
The Causes and Cures of Mental Error
John Howe (1630-1705) (D) (B)
The Living Temple
William Bell (d. 1664)
Christ's Spirit, a Christian's Strength
The Building, Beauty, Teaching, and Establishment of the Truly Christian Church
The Stumbling-Stone
Thomas Manton (1620-77) (B)
Sermons on Several Subjects
Isaac Ambrose (1604-63)
The Doctrine of Regeneration
The Practice of Sanctification: Exemplified in the Believer's Privileges and Duties
Looking unto Jesus: or, the Soul's Eying of Jesus, as Carrying on the Great Work of Man's Salvation
Francis Rous (1579-1659)
Academia Coelestis: The Heavenly University
John Owen (1616-83) (D) (B) (W)
The Mortification of Sin in Believers, the Necessity, Nature, and Means of It
The Nature, Power, Deceit, and Prevalency of the Remainders of Indwelling Sin in Believers
Of Temptation, the Nature and Power of It

ΧΡΙΣΤΟΛΟΓΙΆ, *or A Declaration of the Glorious Mystery of the Person of Christ, God, and Man*
Of Communion with God the Father, Son, and Holy Ghost

Herbert Palmer (1601-47) (B)
Memorials of Godliness and Christianity
Of Making Religion One's Business
An Appendix, Applied to the Calling of a Minister

William Whateley (1583-1639) (B) (W)
Directions for Married Persons

Joseph Alleine (1634-68) (B)
An Alarm to Unconverted Sinners
A Counsel for Personal and Family Godliness
Two Practical Cases of Conscience Resolved

Samuel Shaw (1635-96) (B)
Immanuel: or, A Discourse of True Religion
Communion with God
An Extract from the Assembly's Shorter Catechism; with the Proofs thereof out of the Scriptures (B)

Samuel Rutherford (1600-61) (B) (W)
Extracts from the Letters of Mr. Samuel Rutherford

Hugh Binning (1627-53)
Fellowship with God: or, Sermons on the First Epistle of St. John

Notes

1. John Wilkins, *Ecclesiastes, or, A Discourse Concerning the Gift of Preaching* (London: Printed by T. R. and E. M. for Samuel Gellibrand, 1651), ii; *DNB*, 61:266.

2. Baxter, *Christian Directory*, 917-29.

3. For a summary of the question of authorship of this work and a discussion of its influence on Wesley, see G. Thompson Blake, "The Whole Duty of Man," *LQHR* 183 (1958): 293-97.

4. Later scholarship has made identification possible through extremely helpful bibliographical studies such as *The Dictionary of Anonymous and Pseudonymous English Literature*, ed. James Kennedy, 8 vols. (London: Oliver & Boyd, 1926); Donald Wing, *Short Title Catalogue of Books Printed in England, Scotland, Ireland and Wales*, 3 vols. (New York: For Index Society of Columbia University Press, 1945); Douglas Bush, *English Literature in the Earlier Seventeenth Century: 1600—1660*; and others.

5. Nathanael Culverwell is listed by John Newton, *Methodism and the Puritans,* 8, as a Puritan. However, because Culverwell was one of the Cambridge Platonists and conformed to the Established Church in 1662, he is considered in this study a Church of England author (*DNB*, 13:288).

6. Also included in the *Library* is another work credited to Allestree, *Private Devotions for Several Occasions*. Both are works of the 1660 period and, though published anonymously, are now generally attributed to Allestree, who served as a confidant of Charles II during his exile (Bush, *English Literature in the Earlier Seventeenth Century*, 295; Donald Wing, *Short Title Catalogue*, 1:29; *DNB*, 1:324-25).

7. This tract bears the exact title of a university discourse published anonymously by James Garden in both English and Latin. Garden was deposed from his professorship at Aberdeen for refusing to sign the Westminister Confession of Faith *(Dictionary of Anonymous and Pseudonymous English Literature*, 1:387; Donald Wing, *Short Title Catalogue*, 2:96; *DNB*, 20:409).

8. This work is now credited to Horsman, a fellow of Corpus Christi College, Oxford, who was a supporter of the Church of England throughout his life (*Dictionary of Anonymous and Pseudonymous English Literature*, 5:347; *DNB*, 27:388).

9. This title covers a work commonly known as *Hickes's Reformed Devotions*. Originally written by the Roman Catholic John Austin around 1668, it was "reformed" under the pen of Mrs. Susannah Hopton for use in the Church of England and issued anonymously with a preface by Dr. George Hickes, from which it drew its popular name (Green, *Bibliography*, 93; *Dictionary of Anonymous and Pseudonymous English Literature*, 2:49.)

10. Wesley abridged three sermons, noting them as those of "Dr. Calamy": "On Christian Benevolence," "On the Wickedness of the Heart," and "On the Resurrection" [*CL*, 23:271-323] In the first edition of this study these were identified as being the works of Edmund Calamy (1600-66) a Puritan leader. I am indebted to Lawrence McIntosh for pointing out that these sermons were actually the work of Benjamin Calamy (1642-86), the son of Edmund. Benjamin was a well-known and respected High Church Anglican minister whose theological and ecclesiastical differences did not separate him from his brother Edmund (1635-85) and his nephew Edmund (1671-1732), both of whom were Puritan in sympathy. As noted above on Chapter 1 this correction changes the numbers of Anglican and Puritan authors included in *A Christian Library*. For comments on Benjamin see Edmund Calamy (the Younger), *An Historical Account of My Own Life* (London: Colburn & Bentley, 1829), 1:57-63.

11. Along with the treatises, Wesley included brief biographies of several of the authors: Robert Bolton, John Preston, Richard Sibbes, Thomas Goodwin, Matthew Hale, John Howe, Isaac Ambrose, John Owen, Joseph Alleine, Hugh Binning, and Samuel Shaw.

12. Stuckley's work was a popular Puritan treatise. Stuckley was ejected from his position as a preacher in Exeter Cathedral in 1662, where he had gathered a Congregational church that met alongside the dominant Presbyterian congregation (Wing, *Short Title Catalogue*, 3:310; *Journal*, 4:189 n; Matthews, *Calamy Revised*, 469).

13. The first edition of *A Christian Library* includes six sermons credited to Samuel Annesley, which purport to have been preached by him at Cripplegate during his pastorate there. In editing the second edition, however, Thomas Jackson credits one of these, "How Must We Reprove, That We May Not Partake of Other Men's Sins," to the Rev. Mr. John Kitchin (d. 1662?). Two others, "The Visitation of the Sick" and "How We May be Universally and Exactly Conscientious," he credits to the Rev. Matthew Pool (d. 1679). The discrepancy occurs because these three sermons were published in the first volume of a series of four volumes of sermons by eminent Puritans, edited by Samuel Annesley between 1661 and 1690. Annesley wrote a prefatory letter and the first sermon of each of these volumes. The first edition of the first volume, entitled *The Morning Exercises at Cripplegate* (London: Printed for J. Kirton and N. Webb, 1661), designated no authors for the various sermons, but the fourth edition (London: Printed by A. Maxwell and R. Roberts for Tho. Cockerill, 1677) does give the authors of each sermon. Because this edition appeared in Annesley's own lifetime, it is assumed that the author listings are reliable. According to the list in the fourth edition, Jackson was correct in designating Pool as the author of the sermon on visitation and Kitchin as the author of the sermon on reproving. He is incorrect, however, in crediting "How We May Be Universally and Exactly Conscientious" to Pool. This is Annesley's work. It is so designated in the fourth edition, and it is the first sermon in the volume, Annesley's pattern of including one of his own sermons as the first in each volume is being carried out in this volume. Wesley most likely was working from an early edition in his preparation of *A Christian Library* and did not have the designation of authors before him. Pool and Kitchin were ejected in 1662 (Matthews, *Calamy Revised*, 310, 394).

14. Thomas Crane, author of this tract, had been given a church and its living by Cromwell and was ejected upon the restoration (*Dictionary of Anonymous and Pseudonymous English Literature*, 4:748; Wing, *Short Title Catalogue*, 1:393; *DNB*, 13:12).

Appendix 2

Exemplary Christian Lives in *A Christian Library*

The following is a complete list of the men whose lives are recounted in *A Christian Library* as examples of Christian faith and piety. Those Puritan lives that are noted in appendix 1, note 11, are not listed here. The Puritan bibliographies to which Wesley's list of authors is compared are indicated as: (B) Baxter, *A Christian Directory*; (W) Wilkins, *Ecclesiastes, or a Discourse Concerning the Gift of Preaching*.

Foreign Leaders		
Philip Melanchthon	(B)	(W)
John Calvin	(B)	(W)
Galeacius Caracciolus		
Philip de Mornay	(B)	(W)
Henry Atling		
Frederick Spanheim		
Gregory Lopez		
Peter Martyr	(B)	(W)

Church of England Leaders		
Bernard Gilpin (1517-83)		
Richard Hooker (1554-1600)	(B)	(W)
Henry Wotton (1568-1639)	(B)	
John Donne (1573-1631)		(W)
George Herbert (1593-1633)		
William Bedell (1571-1642)		
Henry Ussher (1550?-1613)	(B)	(W)
Henry Hammond (1605-60)	(B)	(W)

Puritan Leaders

- William Whitaker (1548-95) (B) (W)
- John Bruen (1560-1625)
- Richard Blackerby (1574-1648)
- Philip Sidney (1619-98)
- Richard Mather (1596-1669) (W)
- John Rowe (1588-1662)
- Joseph Woodward (?-1660)
- Nicholas Leverton (1600-62)
- Nathanael Barnardiston (1588-1653)
- Samuel Fairclough (1594-1677)
- James Fraser (1639-99)
- Thomas Tregoss (?-1671)
- Samuel Winter (1603-66)
- Scottish Divines (Hugh Kennedy, Patrick Simpson, Andrew Steward, Mr. Davidson, Robert Bruce, Robert Blair, John Welsh)
- Thomas Cawton (1605-59)
- Philip Henry (1631-96)
- George Trosse (1631-1713)
- Thomas Wilson (1601-53) (W)
- John Eliot (1604-90)

Select Bibliography

Primary Sources

John Wesley Publications

Wesley, John. *A Christian Library: Consisting of Extracts from and Abridgments of the Choicest Pieces of Practical Divinity Which Have Been Published in the English Tongue*. 2d ed. 30 vols. London: Printed by T. Cordeux, for T. Blanshard, 1819-26.

———. *A Concise Ecclesiastical History*. 4 vols. London: J. Paramore, 1781.

———. *A Concise History of England*. 4 vols. London: R. Hawes, 1776.

———. *Directions for Renewing Our Covenant with God*. London: Printed by J. Paramore, 1780.

———. *Explanatory Notes upon the New Testament*. London: Epworth Press, 1958.

———. *Explanatory Notes upon the Old Testament*. 3 vols. Bristol: Printed by William Pine, 1765.

———. *An Extract of The Rev. Mr. Baxter's Aphorisms of Justification*. 4th ed. London: Printed for G. Whitfield, 1797.

———. *The Journal of the Rev. John Wesley, A.M.* Edited by Nehemiah Curnock. 8 vols. London: Epworth Press, 1909.

———. *The Letters of the Rev. John Wesley, A.M.* Edited by John Telford. 8 vols. London: Epworth Press, 1931.

———. *The Sunday Service of the Methodists in North America with Other Occasional Services*. London: 1784.

———. *Wesley's Standard Sermons*. Edited by Edward H. Sugden. 2 vols. London: Epworth Press, 1921.

———. *The Bicentennial Edition of the Works of John Wesley*. Edited by Frank Baker and Richard Heitzenrater. Nashville: Abingdon Press, 1984— (Volumes 7, 11, 25, and 26 originally appeared as the *Oxford Edition of the Works of John Wesley*. Oxford: Clarendon, 1975-83.).

———. *The Works of the Reverend John Wesley*. Edited by Thomas Jackson. 3rd ed. 14 vols. London: Wesleyan Conference Office, 1872.

John Wesley Abridgments

Wesley, John. *An Alarm to Unconverted Sinners*, by Joseph Alleine. Abridged by John Wesley. 2d ed. Dublin: Printed by Robert Napper, 1794.
———. *A Call to the Unconverted*, by Richard Baxter. Abridged by John Wesley. 2d ed. Dublin: Printed by Robert Napper, 1795.
———. *Christian Letters*, by Joseph Alleine. Abridged by John Wesley. 2d ed. Bristol: Printed by William Pine, 1767.

Puritan Publications

Alleine, Joseph. *An Alarm to Unconverted Sinners*. London: Printed by Nevil Simmons, 1672.
———. *Christian Letters*. London: Printed by J. Darby for Nevil Simmons, 1672.
———. *Divers Practical Cases of Conscience Satisfactorily Resolved*. London: Printed for Nevil Simmons, 1672.
Alleine, Richard. *Vindiciae Pietatis: or, A Vindication of Godliness*. London: 1664.
Ambrose, Isaac. *The Works of Isaac Ambrose*. 1 vol. London: Printed by Henry Fisher, n.d.
Ames, William. *The Marrow of Sacred Divinity*. London: Edward Griffin, 1642.
Annesley, Samuel, ed. *The Morning Exercises at Cripplegate or, Several Cases of Conscience Practically Resolved, by Sundry Ministers, September 1661*. London: Printed for Joshua Kirton and Nathaniel Webb, 1661.
———, ed. *The Morning Exercises at Cripplegate, St. Giles in the Fields, and in Southwark*. Edited by James Nichols. 6 vols. London: Printed for Thomas Tegg, 1844.
Baxter, Richard. *Aphorisms on Justification*. London: Printed for Francis Tyton, 1644.
———. *A Call to the Unconverted to Turn and Live and Accept the Mercy While Mercy May Be Had, as Ever They Would Find Mercy in the Day of Their Extremity*. London: Printed by R. W. for N. Simmons, 1669.
———. *A Christian Directory: or, A Summ of Practical Theologie, and Cases of Conscience*. London: By Robert White for Nevil Simmons, 1673.
———. *Gildas Salvianus: The Reformed Pastor*. Vol. 14 of *The Practical Works of Richard Baxter*.
———. *The Practical Works of Richard Baxter. Introduction and Life by William Orme*. 23 vols. London: James Duncan, 1830.
———. *Reliquiae Baxterianae, or Mr. Richard Baxter's Narrative of His Life and Times*. Published from his own manuscript by Matthew Sylvester. London: 1696.
———. *Richard Baxter's Confession of His Faith, Especially Concerning the Interest of Repentance and Sincere Obedience to Christ, in Our Justification and Sanctification*. London: Printed by R. W. for Tho. Underhil, 1655.
———. *The Saints' Everlasting Rest*. Vols. 22 and 23 of *The Practical Works of Richard Baxter*.

Binning, Hugh. *The Works of Hugh Binning*. London: A. Fullarton, 1851.
Bolton, Robert. *A Discourse about the State of True Happiness*. London: Printed by Felix Kyngston for Thomas Weaver, 1631.
———. *General Directions for a Comfortable Walking with God*. London: 1641.
———. *Instructions for a Right Comforting of Afflicted Consciences*. London: Printed by Felix Kyngston for Thomas Weaver, 1631.
———. *The Saints' Selfe-enriching Examination*. London: Printed by Anne Griffin for Rapha Harford, 1634.
Burnett, Gilbert. *The Life and Death of Sir Matthew Hale*. London: Printed for William Shrowsbury, 1682.
Calamy, Edmund. *An Abridgement of Mr. Baxter's History of His Life and Times with an Account of the Ministers, etc. Who Were Ejected after the Restoration of King Charles II and Their History to the Year 1691*. London: Printed for John Lawrence, 1713.
———. *An Account of the Ministers, Lecturers, Masters and Fellows of Colleges and Schoolmasters Who Were Ejected or Silenced after the Restoration in 1660 by the Act of Uniformity*. London: Printed for John Lawrence, 1713.
———. *A Continuation of the Account of the Ministers, Lecturers, Masters and Fellows of Colleges and Schoolmasters Who Were Ejected or Silenced after the Restoration in 1660 by the Act of Uniformity*. 2 vols. London: Printed for John Lawrence, 1713.
———. *The Nonconformist's Memorial*. Edited by Samuel Palmer. 2 vols. London: Printed for W. Harris, 1775.
Clarke, Samuel. *A General Martyrology Containing a Collection of All the Greatest Persecutions Which Have Befalled the Church of Christ from the Creation to Our Present Times; Where is Given Exact an Account of the Protestant Sufferings in Queen Mary's Reign. Together, with a Large Collection of Lives of Great Persons, Eminient Divines, and Singular Christians, Famous in Their Generations for Learning and Piety; and Most of Them Sufferers for the Cause of Christ*. Glasgow: J. Galbraith, 1770.
The Confession of Faith of the Assembly of Divines at Westminster, from the Original Manuscript Written by Cornelius Burges. Edited by S. W. Carruthers. London: Presbyterian Church of England, 1946.
Dell, William. *Several Sermons and Discourses*. London: Printed by J. Sowle, 1709.
Doddridge, Philip. "Letter to Mr. Wesley: A Scheme of Study for a Clergyman," *The Arminian Magazine*, 1 (1778): 419-25.
Flavel, John. *Husbandry Spiritualized: or, The Heavenly Use of Earthly Things*. Elizabeth Town: Printed by Shepard Killock, 1794.
———. *Navigation Spiritualized or, A New Compass for Seamen*. London: Printed by J.C. for Thomas Fabian, 1682.
The Form of Presbyterial Church Government and of Ordination of Ministers Agreed upon by the Assembly of Divines at Westminster. Edinburgh: Printed by E. Robertson, 1766.
Foxe, John. *Acts and Monuments of the Christian Martyrs, and Matters Ecclesiasticall Passed in the Church of Christ, from the Primitive Beginning to These Our Daies*. 4 vols. London: Printed for the Company of Stationers, 1641.

Goodwin, John. *Imputatio Fidei, or a Treatise on Justification*. London: Printed by P. O. and G.D., 1642.

Goodwin, Thomas. *A Child of Light Walking in Darkness: or A Treatise Shewing the Causes, by Which, the Cases, wherein, and the Ends, for Which God Leaves His Children to Distresses of Conscience. Together with Directions How to Walk, so as to Come Forth of Such Condition*. London: Printed by F. G. for R. Dawlman, 1659.

———. *The Tryall of a Christian's Growth*. London: Printed for R. Dawlman, 1643.

Hale, Sir Matthew. *Contemplations, Moral and Divine*. London: Printed by William Godbid for William Shrowsbury, 1676.

Hall, Joseph. *The Works of Joseph Hall*. Edited by Josiah Pratt. 10 vols. London: Printed by C. Whittingham, 1808.

Henry, Matthew. *An Account of the Life and Death of Mr. Philip Henry*. 3d ed. London: Printed for J. Lawrence, J. Nicholson, J. and B. Sprint, N. Cliffe, and D. Jackson, 1712.

Kitchin, John. "How Must We Reprove That We May Not Partake of Other Men's Sins," In *The Morning Exercises at Cripplegate, St. Giles in the Fields, and in Southwark*. Edited by James Nichols. 6 vols. London: Printed for Thomas Tegg, 1844.

Manton, Thomas. *Twenty Sermons*. Vol. 2 of *The Works of Thomas Manton*. London: James Nisbet, 1871.

Owen, John. *The Works of John Owen*. Edited by Thomas Russell. 28 vols. London: Printed for Richard Baynes, 1826.

———. *Concerning the Holy Spirit*. Vols. 2 and 3 of *The Works of John Owen*.

———. *The Doctrine of Justification by Faith through the Imputation of the Righteousness of Christ Explained, Confirmed, and Vindicated*. London: Printed for R. Boulter, 1677.

———. *On Communion with God the Father, Son, and Holy Spirit*. Vol. 10 of *The Works of John Owen*.

Palmer, Herbert. *Memorials of Godliness and Christianity in a Discourse of Making Religion Ones Business*. London: Printed for Samuel Crouch, 1681.

Perkins, William. *The Works of William Perkins*. 3 vols. London: John Legatt, 1616.

Pool, Matthew. "How Ministers or Christian Friends May and Ought to apply Themselves to Sick Persons, for Their Good, and the Discharge of Their Own Conscience," In *The Morning Exercises at Cripplegate, St. Giles in the Fields, and Southwark*. Edited by James Nichols. 6 vols. London: Printed for Thomas Tegg, 1844.

Preston, John. *The Breast Plate of Faith and Love*. London: Printed by W. I. for Nicholas Bourne, 1630.

———. *The New Covenant, or The Saints' Portion. A Treatise Unfolding the All-Sufficiencie of God, Man's Uprightness, and the Covenant of Grace, Delivered in Fourteen Sermons upon Gen. 17:1.2*. London: Printed by I. D. for Nicholas Bourne, 1630.

Shaw, Samuel. *Communion with God*. Glasgow: Printed by R. Urio, 1749; Glasgow: For William Collins, 1894.

———. *Immanuel: or a Discovery of True Religion; as it Imports* a *Living Principle in the Minds of Men*. Glasgow: Printed by R. Urio, 1749.

The Shorter Catechism of the Westminster Divines: Being a Facsimile of the First Edition "with the Proofs thereof out of the Scriptures;" *Which Was Ordered to Be Printed by the House of Commons, 14th April 1648*. Edited by J. H. Cotton and J. C. Pears, Jr. Nashville: Printed for Presbyterian Theological Seminary, Chicago, 1943.

Sibbes, Richard. *The Works of Richard Sibbes*. Edited by A. B. Grossart. 7 vols. Edinburgh: James Nichol, 1862.

———. *Bowels Opened: or A Discovery of the Neere and Deere Love. Union and Communion betwixt Christ and the Church*. Vol. 2 of *The Works of Richard Sibbes*.

———. *A Description of Christ*. In vol. 1 of *The Works* of *Richard Sibbes*.

———. *A Fountain Opened*. In vol. 5 of *The Works of Richard Sibbes*.

———. *A Fountain Sealed: or the Duty of the Sealed to the Spirit, and the Worke of the Spirit in Sealing*. London: Printed by T. Harper for L. Chapman, 1637.

———. *Light from Heaven*. London: E. Purstow, 1638.

———. *The Nativity of Christ*. In vol. 5 of *The Works of Richard Sibbes*.

———. *Salvation Applied*. In vol. 5 of *The Works of Richard Sibbes*.

Stuckley, Lewis. *A Gospel-Glass: Representing the Miscarriages of English Professors or, A Call from Heaven to Sinners and Saints, by Repentance and Reformation to Prepare to Meet God*. London: Printed by R. Edwards, 1809.

Whateley, William. *A Bride-Bush: or, A Direction for Married Persons*. London: Printed by Bernard Alsop for Beniamin Fisher, 1623.

Wilkins, John. *Ecclesiastes, or, A Discourse Concerning the Gift of Preaching*. 3d ed. London: Printed by T. R. and E. M. for Samuel Gellibrand, 1651.

Other Seventeenth-Century and Eighteenth-Century Publications

Church, Stephen. "Letter to the Rev. Mr. Wesley," *The London Magazine*, 29 (1760): 587-90.

The Country Parson's Advice to His Parishioners. London: For Benjamin Tooke, 1680.

Fletcher, John. *Checks to Antinomianism*. 4 vols. New York: J. Soule and T. Mason, 1820.

———. *Works of John Fletcher*. 4 vols. New York: Carlton and Lanahan, n.d.

Fuller, Thomas. *The History of the Worthies of England*. London: By J. G., W.L. and W.G., 1662.

Hill, Richard. *A Review of All the Doctrines Taught by the Rev. Mr. John* Wesley; *Containing, a Full and Particular Answer to a Book Entitled, "A Second Check to Antinomianism." In Six Letters of the Rev. Mr. F----r. Wherein the Doctrines of a Twofold Justification, Free Will, Man's Merit, Sinless Perfection, Finished Salvation, and Real Antinomianism, Are Particularly Discussed: and the Puritan Divines and Protestant Churches*

Vindicated from the Charges Brought against Them of Holding Mr. Wesley's Doctrines. To Which Are Added a Farrago; and Some Remarks on the "Third Check to Antinomianism." London: E. and C. Dilly, 1772.

Neal, Daniel. *History of the Puritans, or Protestant Non-Conformists from the Reformation to the Toleration Act of King William and Queen Mary*. 4 vols. Dublin: Printed for Brice Edmond, 1755.

Owen, T. E. *Methodism Unmasked; or the Progress of Puritanism from the Sixteenth to the Nineteenth Century*. London: Printed for J. Hatchard, 1802.

Walton, Isaac. *The Lives of Donne, Wotton, Hooker, Herbert, and Sanderson*. Cambridge: Brown, Shattuck, 1832.

Secondary Sources

Articles and Periodicals

Baker, Frank. "The Beginnings of the Methodist Covenant Service," *LQHR* 180 (1955): 215-20.

———. "John Wesley and Practical Divinity," *Wesleyan Theological Journal* 22 (1987): 7-15.

———. "John Wesley's Churchmanship," *LQHR* 185 (1960): 210-15, 269-74.

———. "A Study of John Wesley's Readings," *LQHR* 168 (1943): 140-45.

———. "Unfolding John Wesley: A Survey of Twenty Years' Studies in Wesley's Thought," *Quarterly Review* 1 (1980): 44-58.

———. "Wesley's Ordinations," *WHSP* 24 (1944): 76-80, 101-3.

———. "Wesley's Puritan Ancestry," *LQHR* 187 (1962): 180-86.

Betz, Ernst. "Pietist and Puritan Sources of Early Protestant World Missions," *Church History* 20 (1951): 28-51.

"A Bibliographical Catalogue of Books Mentioned in John Wesley's Journals," *WHSP* 4 (1903-4): 17-19, 47-51, 74-81, 107-111, 134-40, 173-76, 203-10, 232-38.

Blake, G. Thompson. "The Whole Duty of Man," *LQHR* 183 (1958): 293-97.

Blankenship, Paul R. "The Significance of John Wesley's Abridgement of the Thirty-Nine Articles as Seen from His Deletions," *Methodist History* (1989): 35-47.

Bowmer, John C. "Wesley's Revision of the Communion Service in *the Sunday Service of the Methodists*," *LQHR* 176 (1951): 230-37.

Brauer, Jerald C. "Reflections on the Nature of English Puritanism," *Church History* 23 (1954): 99-108.

Brown, W. Adams. "Covenant Theology." in *Encyclopedia of Religion and Ethics*, vol. 4, edited by James Hastings. Edinburgh: T. & T. Clark, 1912.

Butterworth, R. "Wesley and the Dissenters," *WHSP* 8 (1911-12): 25-29.

Cameron, Richard M. "John Wesley's Aldersgate Street Experience," *The Drew Gateway* 25 (1955): 210-19.

Campbell, Ted. "The 'Wesleyan Quadrilateral': The Story of a Modern Methodist Myth," *Methodist History* 29 (1991): 87-95.

Cannon, William R. "John Wesley's Doctrine of Sanctification and Perfection," *The Mennonite Quarterly Review* 35 (1961): 91-95.

Chiles, Robert E. "Methodist Apostasy: From Free Grace to Free Will," *Religion in Life* 27 (1957): 438-49.

Church, Leslie. "The Pastor in the Eighteenth Century," *LQHR* 181 (1956): 19-23.

Clapper, Gregory. "'True Religion' and the Affections: A Study of John Wesley's Abridgement of Jonathan Edwards' *Treatise on Religious Affections*," *Wesleyan Theological Journal* 19 (1984): 77-89.

Cooke, Richard J. "Our Methodist Episcopacy," *Methodist Review* 114 (March 1931): 206-14.

Coomer, Duncan. "The Influence of Puritanism and Dissent on Methodism," *LQHR* 175 (1950): 346-50.

Cushman, Robert E. "Theological Landmarks in the Revival under Wesley," *Religion in Life* 27 (1957): 105-18.

Davies, Horton. "Epworth's Debt to Geneva--A Field for Research," *The Livingstonian* (1960): 5-6.

["Didymus"]. "Mr. Wesley's *Christian Library*," *The Wesleyan-Methodist Magazine* 6 (1827): 310-16.

Dreyer, Frederick. "Faith and Experience in the Thought of John Wesley," *American Historical Review* 88 (1983): 12-30.

English, John C. "The Cambridge Platonists in Wesley's 'Christian Library,'" *WHSP* 25 (1968): 161-68.

Field, Clive D. "Bibliography: John Wesley-Theology." In *A History of the Methodist Church in Great Britain*, vol. 4, edited by Rupert Davies et al. London: Epworth Press, 1988.

Fortney, Edward L. "The Literature of the History of Methodism," *Religion in Life* 24 (1955): 443-51.

Halévy, Élie. "La Naissance du Methodisme en Angleterre," *La Revue de Paris* 4 (1906): 519-40, 841-67.

Harrison, A. W. "Fifty Years of Studies in Methodist History," *WHSP* 24 (1943-44): 17-26.

[H.R.O.]. "Tract Societies," *The Wesleyan Methodist Magazine* 70 (1847): 269-70.

Hunter, Frederick. "The Origins of Wesley's Covenant Service," *LQHR* 164 (1939): 78-87. Also found in *WHSP* 22 (1940): 126-30.

———. "Sources of Wesley's Revision of the Prayer Book in 1784-88," *WHSP* 23 (1941-42): 123-33.

Jackson, George. "John Wesley as a Bookman," *LQHR* 160 (1935): 294-305.

Joy, James R. "Wesley: Man of a Thousand Books and a Book," *Religion in Life* 8 (1939): 71-84.

Lindström, Harald. "The Message of John Wesley and the Modern Man," *The Drew Gateway* 25 (1955): 186-95.

Lloyd, A. Kingsley. "Charles Wesley's Debt to Matthew Henry," *LQHR* 171 (1946): 330-37.

Martin, E. "The Christian Library," *WHSP* 2 (1899-1900): 190-92.

Matthews, Rex. "'With the Eyes of Faith': Spiritual Experience and the Knowledge of God in the Theology of John Wesley." In *Wesleyan Theology Today*, edited by T. Runyon. Nashville, TN: Kingswood Books, 1985.

McIntosh, Lawrence D. "The Place of John Wesley in the Christian Tradition." In *The Place of John Wesley in the Christian Tradition*, edited by Kenneth E. Rowe. Metuchen, N.J.: Scarecrow Press, 1976.
Melton, J. Gordon. "An Annotated Bibliography of Publications about the Life and Work of John Wesley," *Methodist History* 7 (1969): 61-66.
Mumford, Norman W. "The Organization of the Methodist Church in the Time of John Wesley," *LQHR* 171 (1946): 35-40, 128-35.
Newton, John. "Letter from Susanna Wesley to Her Son John," *Wesley Chapel Magazine* (January 1965): 8-12.
———. "Perfection and Spirituality in the Methodist Tradition," *Church Quarterly* 3 (1970): 95-103.
Noll, Mark A. "John Wesley and the Doctrine of Assurance." *Bibliotheca Sacra* 132 (1988): 161-77.
Norwood, Frederick A. "Methodist Historical Studies, 1930-1959," *Church History* 28 (1959): 391-417; 29 (1960): 74-88.
———. "Wesleyan and Methodist Historical Studies, 1960-1970, a Bibliograhpical Article," *Church History* 40 (June 1971): 182-99.
Outler, Albert. "Do Methodists Have a Doctrine of the Church?" In *The Doctrine of the Church,* edited by Dow Kirkpatrick. Nashville: Abingdon Press, 1964.
———. "John Wesley: Folk-Theologian," *Theology Today* 34 (1977-78): 150-60.
———. "Towards a Re-Appraisal of John Wesley as a Theologian," *The Perkins School of Theology Journal* 14 (1961): 5-14.
———. "The Wesleyan Quadrilateral—in John Wesley," *Wesleyan Theological Journal* 20 (1985).
Pearl, Valerie. "Puritans and Poor Relief: The London Workhouse, 1649-1660." In *Puritans and Revolutionaries,* edited by D. Pennington and K. Thomas. Oxford: Clarendon Press, 1978.
Platt, Frederic. "Wesley's 'Ordinations'—A Retrospect," *LQHR* 160 (1935): 63-73.
Rattenbury, J. Ernest. "Note on Article on 'Sources of Wesley's Revision of the Prayer Book of 1784-88,'" *WHSP* 23 (1941-42): 173-75.
"Review of the Christian Library," *The Methodist Magazine* 1 (1821): 306-8.
Rivers, Isabel. "Dissenting and Methodist Books of Practical Divinity." In *Books and Their Readers in 18th Century England*. New York: St. Martin's Press, 1982.
Rogers, Charles. "John Wesley and Jonathan Edwards," *Duke Divinity School Review* 31 (1966): 20-38.
Runyon, Theodore. "The Importance of Experience for Faith." In *Aldersgate Reconsidered*, edited by Randy Maddox. Nashville: Kingswood Books, 1990.
Rupp, E. Gordon. "Some Reflections on the Origin and Development of the English Methodist Tradition," *LQHR* 179 (1953): 166-75.
Sanders, Paul S. "What God Hath Joined Together," *Religion in Life* 29 (1960): 491-500.
Shipley, David C. "Wesley and Some Calvinistic Controversies," *The Drew Gateway* 25 (1955): 195-210.
Swift, Wesley. "Methodism and the Prayer Book," *WHSP* 27(1949-50):33-41.

———. "The Sunday Service of the Methodists," *WHSP* 29 (1953-54): 12-20.
Thompson, Edgar. "Episcopacy: John Wesley's View," *LQHR* 181 (1956): 113-18.
Trinterud, Leonard J. "The Origins of Puritanism," *Church History* 20 (1951): 37-57.
von Rohr, John. "Covenant and Assurance in Early English Puritanism," *Church History* 34 (1965): 195-202.
Wakefield, Gordon. "Puritanism, Its Necessity, Dangers, and Future," *Methodist Sacramental Fellowship Bulletin* (Summer 1961): 2-5.
Wilkinson, John T. "The Mind of the Puritan," *LQHR* 187 (1962): 35-38.

Books

Abraham, William J. *Waking from Doctrinal Amnesia: The Healing of Doctrine in the United Methodist Church.* Nashville: Abingdon Press, 1995.
Ainslie, James L. *The Doctrines of Ministerial Order in the Reformed Churches of the 16th and 17th Centuries.* Edinburgh: T. & T. Clark, 1940.
Allison, C. FitzSimons. *The Rise of Moralism.* New York: Seabury Press, 1966.
Baines-Griffiths, David. *Wesley the Anglican.* London: Macmillan, 1919.
Baker, Eric. *The Faith of a Methodist.* Nashville: Abingdon Press, 1958.
Baker, Frank. *John Wesley and the Church of England.* Nashville: Abingdon Press, 1970.
———. *John Wesley: London Publisher, 1733-1791.* London: Friends of Wesley's Chapel, 1984.
———. *Representative Verse of Charles Wesley.* Nashville: Abingdon Press, 1962.
———. *A Union Catalogue of the Publications of John and Charles Wesley,* Revised Edition. Stone Mountain, Ga: George Zimmerman, 1991.
Beal, William. *The Fathers of the Wesley Family.* London: T. Mason, 1833.
Bett, Henry. *The Spirit of Methodism.* London: Epworth Press, 1943.
Bishop, John. *Methodist Worship: In Relation to Free Church Worship.* London: Epworth Press, 1950.
Body, Alfred H. *John Wesley and Education.* London: Epworth Press, 1936.
Bready, J. Wesley. *England before and after Wesley.* New York: Harper & Brothers, 1938.
Brook, Benjamin. *The Lives of the Puritans.* 3 vols. London: Printed for James Black, 1813.
Burtner, Robert W., and Robert E. Chiles, eds. *A Compend of Wesley's Theology.* Nashville: Abingdon Press, 1954.
Bush, Douglas. *English Literature in the Earlier Seventeenth Century: 1600-1660.* Oxford: Clarendon Press, 1945.
Campbell, Ted A. *John Wesley and Christian Antiquity: Religious Vision and Cultural Change.* Nashville: Kingswood Books, 1991.
Cannon, William R. *The Theology of John Wesley.* Nashville: Abingdon Press, 1945.
Carter, Henry. *The Methodist Heritage.* Nashville: Abingdon Press, 1951.

Cell, George Croft. *The Rediscovery of John Wesley*. New York: Henry Holt, 1935.

Chiles, Robert. *Theological Transition in American Methodism*. Nashville: Abingdon Press, 1965.

Church, Leslie. *The Early Methodist People*. London: Epworth Press, 1948.

———. *More About the Early Methodist People*. London: Epworth Press, 1949.

Clapper, Gregory S. *John Wesley on Religious Affections: His Views on Experience and Emotion and Their Role in the Christian Life*. Metuchen, N.J.: Scarecrow Press, 1989.

Clarke, Adam. *Memoirs of the Wesley Family*. London: Printed by J. and T. Clarke, 1823.

Cobb, John B. *Grace and Responsibility: A Wesleyan Theology for Today*. Nashville: Abingdon Press, 1995.

Coke, Thomas, and Henry Moore. *Life of the Reverend John Wesley Including an Account of the Great Revival of Religion in Europe and America of which He Was the First and Chief Instrument*. London: G. Paramore, 1792.

Collins, Kenneth. *A Faithful Witness: John Wesley's Homilectical Theology*. Wilmore, Ky: Wesley Heritage Press, 1993.

———. *The Scriptural Way of Salvation*. Nashville: Abingdon Press, 1997.

Cowherd, Raymond G. *The Politics of English Dissent*. New York: University Press, 1956.

Crowther, Jonathan. *The History of the Wesleyan Methodists*. 2nd ed. London: Richard Edwards, 1815.

Davies, Horton. *The English Free Churches*. London: Oxford University Press, 1952.

———. *Worship and Theology in England: From Watts and Wesley to Maurice, 1690-1850*. Princeton: Princeton University Press, 1961.

———. *The Worship of the English Puritans*. London: Dacre Press, 1948.

Deschner, John. *Wesley's Christology*. Dallas: Southern Methodist University Press, 1960.

The Dictionary of Anonymous and Pseudonymous English Literature, ed. by James Kennedy. 8 vols. London: Oliver & Boyd, 1926.

Dictionary of National Biography, ed. Leslie Stephen. 59 vols. London: Smith, Elder, 1885.

Edwards, Maldwyn. *Family Circle: A Study of the Epworth Household in Relation to John and Charles Wesley*. London: Epworth Press, 1949.

———. *John Wesley and the Eighteenth Century*. London: Epworth Press, 1955.

———. *Methodism and England*. London: Epworth Press, 1943.

Emory, John. *History of the Discipline of the Methodist Episcopal Church*. New York: Lane & Scott, 1851.

Flew, R. Newton. *The Idea of Perfection in Christian Theology*. London: Oxford University Press, 1934.

Green, Richard. *John Wesley: Evangelist*. London: The Religious Tract Society, 1905.

———. *The Works of John and Charles Wesley: A Bibliography*. London: Methodist Publishing House, 1906.

Green, V. H. H. *The Young Mr. Wesley*. New York: St. Martin's Press, 1961.
Gunter, W. Stephen. *The Limits of 'Love Divine.'* Nashville: Abingdon Press, 1989.
———, et al. *Wesley and the Quadrilateral: Renewing the Conversation.* Nashville: Abingdon Press, 1997.
Halévy, Élie. *A History of the English People in 1815*. Translated by E. I. Watkin and D. A. Barker. 3 vols. London: T. Fisher Unwin, 1924.
Haller, William. *The Rise of Puritanism*. New York: Harper & Row, 1957.
Harmon, Nolan B. *The Rites and Rituals of Episcopal Methodism*. Nashville: Publishing House of the M. E. Church, South, 1926.
Harper, J. Steven. *John Wesley's Message for Today.* Grand Rapids, Mich.: Zondervan, 1983.
Heitzenrater, Richard P. *The Elusive Mr. Wesley.* 2 vols. Nashville: Abingdon Press, 1984.
———. "John Wesley and the Oxford Methodists." Ph.D. thesis, Duke University, 1972.
———. *Mirror and Memory: Reflections on Early Methodism.* Nashville: Kingswood Books, 1989.
———. *Wesley and the People Called Methodists.* Nashville: Abingdon Press, 1995.
Herbert, Thomas W. *John Wesley as Editor and Author*. Princeton: Princeton University Press, 1940.
Hilderbrandt, Franz. *Christianity According to the Wesleys*. London: Epworth Press, 1956.
Hill, Christopher. *The Century of Revolution: 1603-1714*. London: Thomas Nelson & Son, 1961.
———. *Society and Puritanism in Pre-Revolutionary England.* New York: Schocken Books, 1964.
———. *The World Turned Upside Down*. New York: Viking Press, 1972.
Huehns, Gertrude. *Antinomianism in English History*. London: Cresset Press, 1951.
Hunt, John. *Religious Thought in England from the Reformation to the End of Last Century*. 3 vols. London: Strahan, 1870-73.
Ives, A. G. *Kingswood School in Wesley's Day and Since.* London: Epworth Press, 1970.
Jarboe, Betty. *John and Charles Wesley: A Bibliography.* Metuchen N.J.: Scarecrow Press, 1987.
Jennings, Theodore W. *Good News for the Poor: John Wesley's Evangelical Economics*. Nashville: Abingdon Press, 1990.
Jordan, W. K. *The Charities of London, 1480-1660*. London: George Allen & Urwin, 1960.
———. *The Charities of Rural England, 1480-1660*. New York: Russell Sage Foundation, 1960.
Langford, Thomas. *Practical Divinity: Theology in the Wesleyan Tradition.* Nashville: Abingdon Press, 1983.
———. ed. *Doctrine and Theology in the United Methodist Church.* Nashville: Kingswood Books, 1991.
Lawson, John. *Notes on Wesley's Forty-Four Sermons*. London: Epworth Press, 1952.

Lee, Umphrey. *John Wesley and Modern Religion*. Nashville: Cokesbury Press, 1936.

Legg, J. Wickham. *English Church Life: From the Restoration to the Tractarian Movement*. London: Longmans, Green, 1914.

Lindström, Harald. *Wesley and Sanctification*. London: Epworth Press, 1950.

MacDonald, James A. *Wesley's Revision of the Shorter Catechism Showing* the *Connection of Methodist Doctrine with That of the Reformed Church, the Ancient Faith, and the Word of God*. Edinburgh: George A. Morton, 1906.

Maclaren, Alexander, ed. *The Ejectment of 1662 and the Free Church*. London: National Council of Evangelical Free Churches, n.d.

Macphail, Andrew. *Essays in Puritanism*. London: T. Fisher Unwin, 1905.

Maddox, Randy. *Aldersgate Reconsidered*. Nashville: Kingswood Books, 1990.

———. *Responsible Grace*. Nashville: Kingswood Books, 1994.

Marquardt, Manfred. *John Wesley's Social Ethics*. Transated by John Steely and W. Stephen Gunter. Nashville: Abingdon Press, 1992.

Matthews, A. G. *Calamy Revised: Being a Revision of Edmund Calamy's Account of the Ministers and Others Ejected and Silenced, 1660-1662*. Oxford: Clarendon Press, 1934.

Matthews, Rex. "Religion and Reason Joined: A Study in the Theology of John Wesley." Th.D. thesis, Harvard University, 1986.

McConnell, Francis J. *John Wesley*. Nashville: Abingdon Press, 1939.

Meeks, M. Douglas, ed. *The Portion of the Poor*. Nashville: Kingswood Books, 1994.

Miller, Perry. *The New England Mind: The Seventeenth Century*. New York: Macmillan, 1939.

Minutes of the Methodist Conferences, 1744-1798. London: John Mason, 1862.

Neely, T. B. *Doctrinal Standards of Methodism*. New York: Fleming H. Revell, 1918.

Newton, John. *Methodism and the Puritans*. London: Dr. William's Trust, 1964.

———. *Susanna Wesley and the Puritan Tradition in Methodism*. London: Epworth Press, 1968.

Nichols, James H. *History of Christianity: 1650-1950*. New York: Ronald Press, 1956.

Nuttall, Geoffrey F. *The Holy Spirit in Puritan Faith and Experience*. Oxford: Basil Blackwell, 1947.

———. *Visible Saints: The Congregational Way 1640-1660*. Oxford: Basil Blackwell, 1957.

Outler, Albert. *Evangelism in the Wesleyan Spirit*. Nashville: Discipleship Resources, 1971.

———. ed. *John Wesley*. New York: Oxford University Press, 1964.

———. *Theology in the Wesleyan Spirit*. Nashville: Discipleship Resources, 1975.

———. *The Wesleyan Theological Heritage: Essays of Albert D. Outler*. Edited by Thomas C. Oden and Leichester R. Longden. Grand Rapids, Mich.: Zondervan, 1991.

Overton, J. H. *The Evangelical Revival in the Eighteenth Century*. London: Longmans, Green, 1886.

Peters, John L. *Christian Perfection and American Methodism*. Nashville: Abingdon Press, 1956.

Phillips, James M. "Between Conscience and the Law: The Ethics of Richard Baxter (1615-1691)." Ph.D. thesis, Princeton University, 1959.

Piette, Maximin. *John Wesley in the Evolution of Protestantism*, Transated by J. B. Howard. New York: Sheed & Ward, 1937.

Pritchard, F. C. *Methodist Secondary Education*. London: Epworth Press, 1949.

Rack, Henry. *Reasonable Enthusiast: John Wesley and the Rise of Methodism*. Philadelphia: Trinity Press International, 1989.

Rattenbury, J. Ernest. *The Eucharistic Hymns of John and Charles Wesley*. London: Epworth Press, 1948.

———. *Wesley's Legacy to the World*. London: Epworth Press, 1928.

Rees, Thomas. *The Holy Spirit in Thought and Experience*. New York: Charles Scribner's Sons, 1915.

Rogers, Charles A. "The Concept of Prevenient Grace in the Theology of John Fletcher." Ph.D. thesis, Duke University, 1967.

Rowe, Kenneth E., ed. *The Place of Wesley in the Christian Tradition*. Metuchen, N.J.: Scarecrow Press, 1976.

Runyon, Theodore H. *The New Creation: John Wesley's Theology Today*. Nashville: Abingdon Press, 1998.

———, ed. *Sanctification and Liberation*. Nashville: Abingdon Press, 1981.

———, ed. *Wesleyan Theology Today*. Nashville: Kingswood Books, 1983.

Rupp, E. Gordon. *Religion in England, 1688-1791*. Oxford: Clarendon Press, 1986.

———. *Six Makers of English Religion, 1500-1700*. London: Hodder & Stoughton, 1957.

Schaff, Philip, ed. *The Creeds of Christendom*. 6th ed. 3 vols. New York: Harper & Brothers, 1931.

Schmidt, Martin. *John Wesley, A Theological Biography*. 3 vols. New York: Abingdon Press, 1962-73.

Shilling, S. Paul. *Methodism and Society in Theological Perspective*. Nashville: Abingdon Press, 1960.

Shipley, David C. "Methodist Arminianism in the Theology of John Fletcher." Ph.D. thesis, Yale University, 1942.

Simon, John S. *John Wesley and Advance of Methodism*. London: Epworth Press, 1925.

———. *John Wesley and the Methodist Societies*. London: Epworth Press, 1923.

———. *John Wesley and the Religious Societies*. London: Epworth Press, 1921.

———. *John Wesley, the Last Phase*. London: Epworth Press, 1934.

———. *John Wesley, the Master Builder*. London: Epworth Press, 1927.

Smith, George. *History of Wesleyan Methodism*. 3 vols. London: Longman, Green, Longman, & Roberts, 1863.

Southey, Robert. *The Life of Wesley and the Rise and Progress of Methodism*. New York: Wm. B. Gilley, 1820.

Stacey, John, ed. *John Wesley: Contemporary Perspectives*. London: Epworth Press, 1988.

Starkey, Lycurgus M., Jr. *The Work of the Holy Spirit*. Nashville: Abingdon Press, 1962.

Steele, Richard B. *"Gracious Affections" and "True Virtue" according to Jonathan Edwards and John Wesley*. Metuchen, N.J.: Scarecrow Press, 1994.

Stephen, Leslie. *History of English Thought in the Eighteenth Century*. 2 vols. London: Smith, Elder, 1881.

Stevenson, George J. *Memorials of the Wesley Family*. London: S. W. Partridge, 1876.

Sykes, Norman. *Church and State in England in the Eighteenth Century*. Cambridge: University Press, 1934.

———. *Old Priest and New Presbyter*. Cambridge: University Press, 1956.

Thompson, E. P. *The Making of the English Working Class*. New York: Random House, 1964.

Towlson, Clifford W. *Moravian and Methodist*. London: Epworth Press, 1957.

Trevelyan, G. M. *English Social History*. London: Longmans, Green, 1958.

Tyerman, Luke. *The Life and Times of the Rev. John Wesley, A.M.* 3 vols. New York: Harper & Brothers, 1872.

———. *The Life and Times of the Rev. Samuel Wesley, A.M., Rector of Epworth*. London: Simpkin, Marshall, 1866.

Wakefield, Gordon Stevens. *Puritan Devotion: Its Place in the Development of Christian Piety*. London: Epworth Press, 1957.

Walzer, Michael. *The Evolution of the Saints: A Study in the Origins of Radical Politics*. Cambridge, Mass.: Harvard University Press, 1965.

Watkin-Jones, Howard. *The Holy Spirit from Arminius to Wesley*. London: Epworth Press, 1929.

Watson, David Lowes. *The Early Methodist Class Meeting.* Nashville: Discipleship Resources, 1987.

Watt, Robert. *Bibliotheca Britannica*. 4 vols. Edinburgh: Archibald Constable, 1824.

Wearmouth, Robert F. *Methodism and the Common People of the Eighteenth Century*. London: Epworth Press, 1945.

Webber, F. R. *A History of Preaching in Britain and America*. 3 vols. Milwaukee: Northwest Publishing House, 1952.

Whitefield, George. *Journals*. London: Banner of Truth Trust, 1960.

Whitehead, John. *The Life of the Rev. John Wesley*. 2 vols. London: Printed by Stephen Couchman, 1793.

Willey, Basil. *The Eighteenth Century Background*. London: Chatto & Windus, 1940.

Williams, Colin W. *John Wesley's Theology Today*. Nashville: Abingdon Press, 1960.

Wing, Donald. *Short Title Catalogue of Books Printed in England, Scotland, Ireland and Wales, 1640-1700*. 3 vols. New York: For Index Society by Columbia University Press, 1945.

Yates, Arthur. *The Doctrine of Assurance*. London: Epworth Press, 1952.

Index of Selected Names

Index of Selected Subjects

About the Author

Robert C. Monk is emeritus professor of religion at McMurry University in Abilene, Texas, where he taught from 1964 to 1995. As a participant in the quinquennial Oxford Institutes on Methodist Studies and the Wesley Study Group of the American Academy of Religion, he continues his interests and work in Wesley and Methodist Studies. While his broader study has centered in seventeenth- and eighteenth-century English church history, his recent studies have included work in American Methodism, particularly investigation into Methodist campus and student ministries. Previous publications include two introduction to religion textbooks, articles on teaching religion, and articles relating to American Methodism. Service as an regional officer and a member of the national board of directors in the American Academy of Religion and a member of the General Commission on Archives and History of the United Methodist Church significantly contributed to his historical and theological study.